INSIDERS' GUIDE® TO
BIRMINGHAM

FIRST EDITION

TODD KEITH

INSIDERS' GUIDE

GUILFORD, CONNECTICUT
AN IMPRINT OF GLOBE PEQUOT PRESS

All the information in this guidebook is subject to change. We recommend that you call ahead to obtain current information before traveling.

INSIDERS' GUIDE ®

Editor: Kevin Sirois
Project Editor: Heather Santiago
Layout: Maggie Peterson
Text Design: Sheryl Kober
Maps: Sue Murray © Morris Book Publishing, LLC

ISBN 978-0-7627-6467-9

Printed in the United States of America
10 9 8 7 6 5 4 3 2 1

CONTENTS

CONTENTS

Directory of Maps

ABOUT THE AUTHOR

A native of Alabama, writer/editor Todd Keith has written *The Rivers of Alabama,* and *Cahaba: A Gift for Generations,* two books of essays focusing on the rivers of his native state, as well as Old Cahawba, a history of Alabama's first state capital. His most recent book, *Birmingham Then and Now,* a look at the architectural history of his hometown, was published in 2009. After completing an MA in English and teaching freshman literature in the early 1990s, Todd taught English as a second language in Czechoslovakia, which led to an interest in travel writing—as well as tmave pivo and slivovice. He has produced articles for national magazines such as *Coastal Living, Robb Report, National Geographic Traveler, Southern Living* and others, as well as edited *SweetTea Journal,* a lifestyle magazine about Northwest Florida produced by Southern Progress in Birmingham. He has covered diverse destinations such as Iceland, Grenada, Sweden, Argentina, South Africa, Switzerland, Mongolia, and Andalusia. He has lived in exotic foreign climes like Des Moines, Iowa. He has been a partner and senior editor at *PORTICO* and *Thicket,* two lifestyle magazines about his hometown and state, respectively. Todd lives in Birmingham—more specifically, in the Edgewood neighborhood of Homewood—with his wife, Julie, and their two soccer-loving sons, Collins and Fletcher. They enjoy their old bungalow and walking to everything nearby from parks and schools to restaurants and neighbors' houses. He mourns the loss of Birmingham's extensive electric streetcar system that used to run in front of his house until the 1950s. Birmingham's public transit system reached an all-time peak of 93 million passengers in 1948. But that's for another book.

ACKNOWLEDGMENTS

A special thanks to two wonderful, industrious interns Riley Barnacastle (from Samford University, Homewood) and Shan Sheikh (from the University of Alabama in Birmingham, downtown) for their contributions. Riley, a native of Cahaba Heights—now incorporated into Vestavia Hills—and Shan, a native of Vestavia Hills, offered great input into this project, keeping it fresh and new always with an eye to the city's offerings that might appeal to a younger generation (translation: they aren't as jaded as me, nor are they as relatively old). Their writing and researching skills were a tremendous asset. Thanks, guys.

Thanks to my wonderful neighbor, Greg, who in addition to cutting our grass just for the heck of it sometimes, is also an incredibly competent fisherman and contributed his vast knowledge to the fishing section. To my father-in-law for his golfing expertise. To Richard Banks, fellow writer and friend for his Memphis expertise and love of The Red Lion. To my rock-climbing friend David for his input. And to Tom Maxwell, Senior Environmental Planner at Regional Planning Commission of Greater Birmingham, for his aid with the Greenways chapter. For anyone wanting a complete index of attractions, restaurants, shopping, nightlife, and more, download *Birmingham Magazine*'s City Guide on iTunes for use as a reference. I certainly did when working on this book (a disclaimer: My wife and her editorial team created the app along with Appsolute Genius).

For anyone interested in Birmingham's past (or writing a guidebook), the excellent historians, preservationists, and writers with the Birmingham Historical Society produce a wide range of quality publications about the city's history and culture (www.bhistorical.org). The BHS is the required first stop for those wanting to learn about the city's history.

A gracious thanks to my wife, Julie, for her editorial skills, encyclopedic knowledge of Birmingham, and general support during the project. Her editing skills are only exceeded by her generous nature. Finally, to my wonderful two young boys, Collins and Fletcher: Grow up and make Birmingham even better.

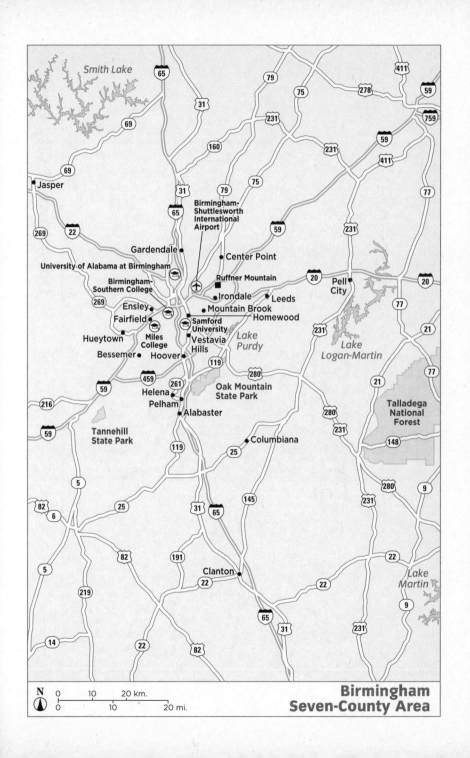

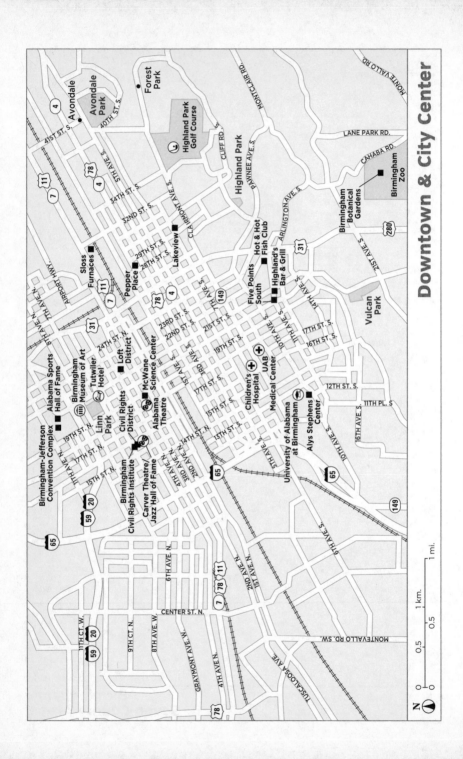

Downtown & City Center

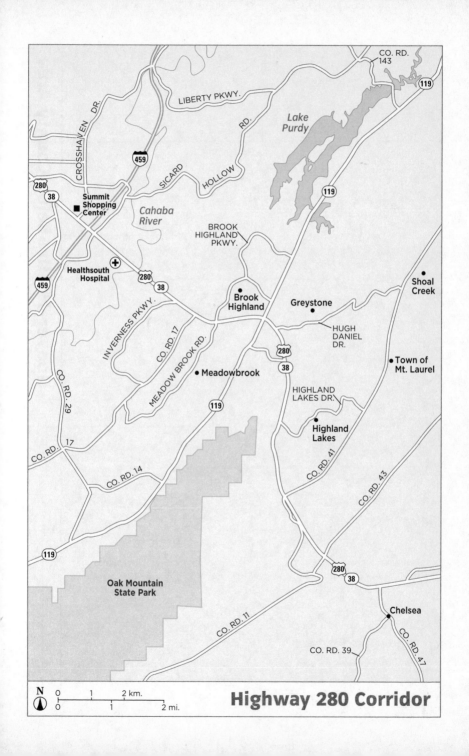

Highway 280 Corridor

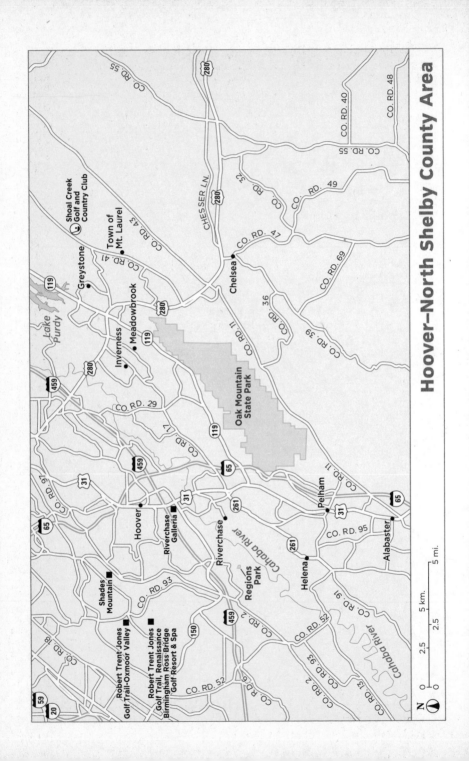

Hoover–North Shelby County Area

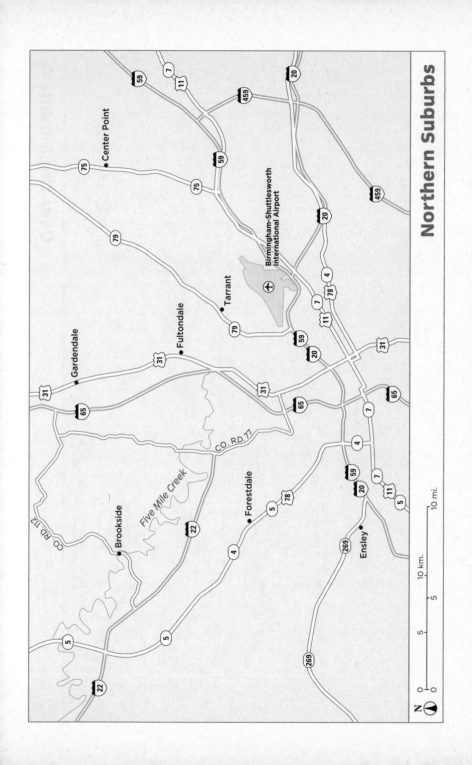

Northern Suburbs

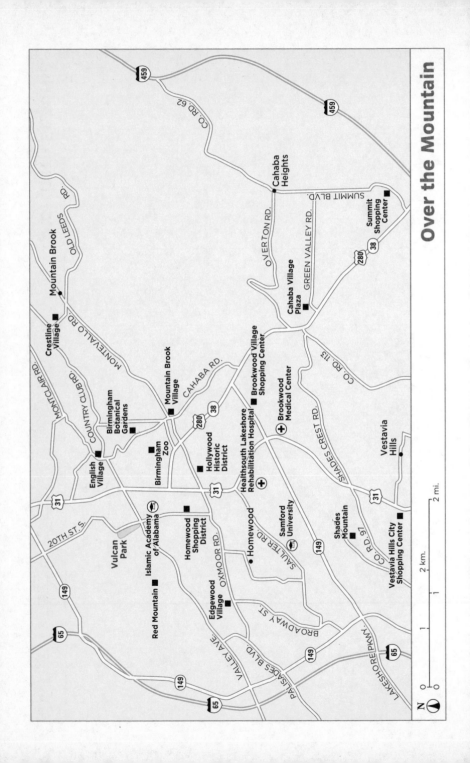

Over the Mountain

INTRODUCTION

Moving back to Birmingham in 2002 was the best thing my wife, Julie, and I could have done for our growing family. We were entering our 30s. We had a fussy 9-month old boy. We missed our family and our home. While we made plenty of new friends in Iowa, but boy, did that cold weather get old fast. Some good friends were launching a new, upscale city magazine, *PORTICO,* and they wanted Julie to help with the editorial and me to be one of the primary writers on the project. Birmingham was overdue in this department. Other than a chamber of commerce title, at the turn of the millennium, there were few lifestyle magazines of note covering the people and places that make up Birmingham.

Before the move back home, we spent nearly five years on the "oil rigs," as we called it, in Des Moines, Iowa. Julie worked for the Crafts Group of Meredith Corporation, publisher of *Better Homes & Gardens, Ladies Home Journal,* and other national titles. I was doing freelance writing, primarily finishing up a book about Alabama's Cahaba River that flows through the heart of the state and skirts the city of Birmingham just a few miles to the south. I'd also been doing web work for *Better Homes & Gardens* and other sites at Meredith, playing soccer with a couple fun teams, and was active in B.O.M.S., the Benevolent Order of Misplaced Southerners, a zany group of ex-pat Southern writers, designers, and editors stranded in the Midwest missing gumbo, barbecue, Marti Gras, and our native accents. The time had come to go "Backin' to Birmingham" as Lester Flatt's old bluegrass song goes.

The first pressing—and difficult—question was "Where to live?" Growing up in Vestavia Hills in an "Over the Mountain" community, I knew the southern suburbs of Mountain Brook, Hoover, Homewood, and of course, Vestavia, quite well. They are affluent, well-educated cities bunched together just over Red Mountain in a series of ridge and valleys before Oak Mountain several miles to the south. Ranging from cute 1920s bungalows and elegant English Tudor gems to more modern ranches and 1960s and '70s split levels, the architectural styles of 20th century United States can be seen in these communities and their migration patterns.

My wife was raised just north of Birmingham in Gardendale. A small town in a sea of British-sounding towns like Forestdale, New Castle, and Cardiff. Gardendale maintained its own unique identity, seldom conforming to contemporary trends or the generic pattern of suburban development: At the time there were no movie theaters, few chain restaurants, all in a small, homogenous conservative town with good schools, great sports teams, and little crime. An Alabama Mayberry RFD? Maybe.

While we were courting, that 46-mile nightly round-trip along I-65 seemed so far (but completely worth it) for me to drive, but all told, it's a revealing perspective on what growing up in the new suburbs was like for me in the '70s and '80s. We largely stayed and played in our own Over the Mountain realm, seldom venturing to downtown Birmingham proper except to hang out in Southside or Lakeview where all the cool bars and restaurants were at the time. It was against our parents' wishes. Urban Birmingham seemed edgy and even a little bit dangerous in high school, even during the early days of college.

But Birmingham changed in the 1990s, nearly all of it for the better. New festivals cropped up, new restaurants, and an exciting downtown revitalization picked up pace. The University of Alabama in Birmingham's medical center came into its own. Southern Progress in Homewood was the home to excellent magazines like *Southern Living, Cooking Light, Health,* and *Coastal Living,* as well as to the creative types who write, photograph, and produce the publications. Health care, banking, insurance, and other service industries made Birmingham into one of the most important business centers in the Southeast while a new Birmingham Civil Rights Institute at Kelly Ingram Park provided a positive coda to a difficult part of the city's history.

Still, it is the people that make Birmingham such a great place to live. Visitors from larger cities are often surprised at just how friendly folks can be here: Don't make eye contact walking downtown unless you're prepared to offer back a friendly nod or "Hello" after a perfect stranger greets you or says, "Good morning." Birmingham is not a place to get lost in a crowd; you go there to mingle with and become part of the group. "I had no idea it was so great here," is a phrase long-time residents are more than accustomed to hearing from their out-of-town guests.

So, when did we know we were moving back to Birmingham from Iowa? If I am completely honest, it was as soon as we had our first child. He might have been born someplace else, but he was certainly going to be raised in Birmingham among family, friends, and a familiar culture all our own. As we returned home for Thanksgiving, Christmas, and other holidays, we kept returning to our favorite restaurants and neighborhoods. We kept meeting with friends and seeing old acquaintances. We missed all the trees, hills, weather, and festivals, even the quirks of this city. Birmingham has a distinctive *terroir:* It may not suit everyone's palette, but once you come to recognize that sense of place, it stays with you. It got to be that we were so busy packing in so much during those few days when we visited, we realized just what we were missing. And so we returned home.

And finally, yes, the song doesn't lie: The sky *really* is so blue here.

HOW TO USE THIS BOOK

If you've never been to Birmingham, well, you're in for a treat. To familiarize yourself with the greater metropolitan area, start with the Area Overview for broad brushstrokes on city's urban core and surrounding communities that make up the greater metropolitan area. Next, see the Getting Around chapter for the ins and outs and other practical matters. After this, you can pretty much pick and choose where you go depending on your needs, interests, or curiosities about Birmingham.

Birmingham and its suburbs cover a huge geographical area. Across the seven-county region, there are a host of small towns and municipalities. County and city lines are often blurry. Users will notice that for the sake of convenience, this book breaks the Greater Birmingham–Hoover Metropolitan Area into five categories: **City Center** (or Downtown), **Over the Mountain** (primarily the communities of Homewood, Mountain Brook, and Vestavia Hills), **Highway 280 Corridor, North Shelby County,** and **Regional** (a catch-all for the peripheries beyond the central areas). These categories ensure that those new to town can readily differentiate between the various neighborhoods and areas.

In practice, however, residents will typically name an individual town or community when giving directions, so this book adheres to those names for practical reasons, listing "Downtown," "Hoover," or "Homewood" and so on next to most entries for clarity. It also allows for more specificity: for example, Edgar's Bakery, a popular spot for coffee and a roll, is in the Inverness area but officially within the city of Hoover, which itself began in Jefferson County but soon dramatically spilled over and into Shelby County to the south. In fact, the distinction "North Shelby," which brands everything from library systems and fire districts to animal control and school districts, emerged to account for Hoover's spectacular growth during the past 20 years. Inverness, a neighborhood that is mostly in Hoover, also extends into unincorporated Shelby County. How's that for confusing? That's why folks just say, "Inverness."

It's no surprise that the chapter on food is the longest in the book—a remarkable fact since there was no way to include all the great restaurants in town: It could have been longer. In Restaurants, you'll find the range of culinary options to be far broader and of more quality than most visitors expect: Birmingham is a town for foodies, no doubt about it. The secret is out, and it only becomes more true as time goes by and the more well-known chefs have begun to see their protégées spin off with their own new restaurants and bistros, further reinforcing the image of Birmingham as a restaurant destination.

When you find a moment waiting for your food at some delicious eatery, look through the History chapter to gain a bit of insight about what made Birmingham tick, why it ticked in that particular manner, and what remains ticking today. How did the same geography that shaped the city in the late 19th century contribute to the turbulence of the late 20th century? And how might geography be shaping the equation in a positive manner today? "May you live in interesting times," is the much-cited Chinese proverb that comes to mind when considering Birmingham's turbulent and dramatic history. Birmingham may be only 140 years old, but those have certainly been some interesting years.

After your meal, if you're looking for somewhere to go for an after-dinner drink or a show, try the Nightlife and Performing Arts chapters. If you're around for longer, the Annual Events chapter is full to the brim with festivals, art shows, races, and special events to enjoy. The fall in particular, as the city's warm weather begins to mitigate, remains the time to stay in town and enjoy the city's best offerings.

You'll also find listings accompanied by the symbol ✳—these are our top picks for attractions, restaurants, accommodations, and everything in between that you shouldn't miss while you're in the area. You want the best this region has to offer? Go with our Insiders' Choice.

Moving to the Birmingham area or already live here? Be sure to check out the blue-tabbed pages at the back of the book, where you will find the **Living Here** appendix that offers sections on relocation, child care, education, health care, retirement, and media.

More of a visual learner? The maps at the beginning of the book are for you. Hopefully they provide a handy reference when you're getting orientated or driving about town looking for that perfect English Tudor home, cute bungalow, or hip downtown loft. Welcome to town.

Finally, while compiling the *Insiders' Guide to Birmingham,* the idea was to offer as much information as possible in an up-to-date fashion. Still, things change. And they often change quickly, so just in case, please call or visit the websites before heading out for a night on the town.

AREA OVERVIEW

The Birmingham Metropolitan Area, sometimes referred to as the Birmingham-Hoover Metropolitan Area, is made up of seven counties in the central part of the state. With 1.2 million residents, that's about one-fourth of Alabama's population centered around one city. The city of Birmingham itself only holds around 230,000 persons, and it gets a bit confusing after that when considering neighboring cities and suburbs, counties, and neighborhoods.

Since Birmingham wasn't founded until 1871, unlike most of its Southern neighbors, it is a purely post-industrial city founded at the height of mechanization and modernization that followed the Civil War in the South. In lieu of a graceful river cutting through Birmingham's urban core like Nashville's Cumberland, we have the 19th-century equivalent: the railroad. Consequently, the downtown streets are split into a north-south division on either side of the railroad tracks with the north side being the commercial core while the slopes of Red Mountain to the south were initially the early residential area. Not unlike many cities, most of those older homes have been demolished or altered beyond recognition as the city grew and the commercial area expanded. But today, many of those houses still stand at the foot of the mountain in the older residential districts like Highland Avenue, Glen Iris, Redmont, and to a lesser degree, Five Points South.

Still, as many observant visitors to downtown Birmingham notice, the city's core holds a remarkable number of architectural gems. After historic treasures like the Terminal Station, Tutwiler Hotel, and the old city hall were demolished, a groundswell of anger served to motivate residents concerned about preserving the city's architectural heritage. Today, a glance at nearby Nashville or Atlanta confirms that Birmingham has survived with a large portion of its historical character intact. But that preservation, ironically, is also one of the perverse benefits of the white flight and urban decay of the 1960s and 1970s.

Linked by I-65 to the west and Highway 280 to the east—as well as the relatively newer I-459 that marks the southern beltway, metro Birmingham's communities are all convenient to downtown yet self-contained. Highway 31 runs through Hoover, Vestavia, and Homewood and is the commercial and transportation artery that links the three communities. I-59 and I-20 lead northeast and west to Chattanooga, Tennessee, and Atlanta, Georgia, respectively. On the west side of Birmingham, I-20 and I-59 merge, leading to New Orleans, Louisiana, while the newer I-22 leads to Memphis, Tennessee, to the northwest.

OVERVIEW

Birmingham is a pleasant place to live. The climate is mild. The sun shines bright. It rarely freezes. And though the summers are warm and humid, the region is a place for year-round outdoors recreation. On sultry August weekends, throw a rock in any direction and you're bound to hit someone heading to his or her lake house or driving to the Gulf for a beach getaway. Affordable housing, excellent schools, comparatively light traffic (other than Highway 280 and to a lesser extent, I-65 during rush hours), friendly neighbors, and an active arts-and-culture community are just more reasons why those who visit too often are likely to make a new home here. The people that live here are generous, too. In fact, the city is the most generous city in the United States according to two independent studies by the Tijeras Foundation and the United Way: Area residents donate 3.6 percent of their income to charity, the highest figure in the nation.

The seven-county region covered in this book includes **Bibb, Blount, Chilton, Jefferson, St. Clair, Shelby,** and **Walker** counties. Within that region, you'll notice the book divides this huge area into smaller regions for simplicity's sake (as previously noted in How to Use This Book): **City Center, Over the Mountain, Highway 280 Corridor, North Shelby County,** and **Regional.**

Thus, when someone says they are from "Birmingham," chances are they are not from the city of Birmingham proper, but rather from one of the dozens of suburbs surrounding the central city. "I have to explain to people that I live in Cahaba Heights, which is now an annexed part of Vestavia Hills, which is in metro Birmingham," jokes Riley Barnacastle, an intern helping with this guidebook. It's an apt description for the intriguing geographic fragmentation that is Birmingham.

CITY CENTER/DOWNTOWN

Avondale

Incorporated into Birmingham in the early 20th century, Avondale grew up in the mid-1800s around a natural spring at which stagecoach passengers stopped at the junction of the Huntsville and Georgia roads. Today, the stream is paved over, but the 40 acres surrounding the spring form Avondale Park, one of Birmingham's earliest recreational spaces. As the railroad developed, industrial businesses such as Avondale Mills and the Smith Gin Company sprang up. After some years of neglect, the neighborhood has seen new commercial resurgence, an influx of artists, and performance venues like Bottletree Cafe and Old Car Heaven. Many of the turn-of-the century homes have been renovated and restored.

Crestwood

Crestwood, an adjacent neighborhood divided by Crestwood Boulevard/US 78, is made up of a mix of older homes dating back to the early 1920s as well as newer ones from the 1940s. A section of Crestwood North was included in the National Register of Historic Places in 2005 as gentrification has meant that many older historic homes are being purchased and renovated.

Forest Park

Forest Park, a more exclusive area of fine homes, hip boutiques and restaurants, was part of businessman and developer Robert Jemison's earlier planned 1906 community,

Mountain Terrace. Set on the north slope of Red Mountain, Forest Park was the city's most prestigious address. The neighborhood was the first subdivision to have concrete sidewalks, curbs and gutter, sewers, landscaping—a tremendous amount of planning and design. It has been on the National Register of Historic Places since 1980, and includes much of Clairmont Avenue and Highland Park Golf Course. Again, gentrification in the 1980s and 1990s utterly transformed this area. Forest Park is once again one of the city's most desirable neighborhoods.

> **i** **Birmingham is the fourth-largest banking center in the country, after New York, Charlotte, and Chicago.**

Downtown Birmingham

Downtown Birmingham, the city's central business district, has seen its ups and downs through the years. No longer are the department stores located here. Tragically, the extensive streetcar lines have all been removed. But in the past decade, a revival is going on as a surge of new development has drawn young professionals, artists, hipsters, and even families to live in the loft district and other emerging residential areas. There are nearly 4,000 people living in city center lofts, and the occupancy rate is 94 percent with only around 80 condominiums available for sale. The revival has been transformative. Even a few years ago, to see people walking the streets on a Friday or Saturday night would be relatively remarkable. Today, restaurants are staying open at night, galleries host showings, and the level of activity is astonishing to many natives who recall the downtown ghost-town days of the 1980s.

Accordingly, civic and city leaders are exploring ways to improve the city center by creating new connective threads that link disparate areas of downtown and encourage growth and new development. The new Birmingham City Center Master Plan calls for a green corridor extending from beyond I-65 to Sloss Furnaces to 32nd Street to be linked by an open space or greenway. This "green corridor" is a key organizing element in the Master Plan that will create a system of "green streets" in and around the city center that are connected to a regional system of greenways first proposed in the 1924 Olmstead Plan. The greenway links key elements between the Railroad Park to the west and Sloss Furnaces National Historic Landmark and the proposed Sloss Business District on the east.

> **i** **People in this city are generous. Birmingham ranks as the most generous city in the United States according to a recent study by the Tijeras Foundation. Measuring 60 metropolitan areas in percentage of household income given to charity, area residents donate 3.6 percent of their income to charity. The United Way calculates giving to charitable community organizations as a percentage of estimated buying income, and Birmingham ranks first in the country in that category as well.**

The Downtown Improvement Association (renamed the Operation New Birmingham in 1963) has been working to improve the downtown business district since 1957 when suburban expansion first challenged downtown as the city's prime commercial area. In the past few decades, Operation

New Birmingham has been pivotal in rescuing and finding uses for the many vacant downtown buildings by serving as a go-between for investors, developers, and individuals looking to purchase historic buildings in the city center. Consequently, law and architectural firms, galleries, retail shops, restaurants, and other businesses have located downtown, creating a dramatically more dynamic downtown scene. Numerous historical gems like the 27-story City Federal Building (1913) have been converted to residential lofts, creating the first influx of middle class residents to the city center in more than 40 years.

Property values in the city center have increased by 67 percent since 1998. There has been a solid decline in the number of vacant buildings found here, too, dropping from a high of 245 in 1995 to less than 70 by the start of 2011.

i With 80,000 employees, the city center holds the largest concentration of jobs in the state of Alabama. It occupies only 2 percent of the city's area, but contributes 35 percent of the tax revenues received by the city of Birmingham and the Board of Education.

City Action Partnership

City Action Partnership (CAP), a team of dedicated professionals who patrol on bicycles and in vehicles with rotating green lights, work with law enforcement and downtown businesses to keep downtown safe—as well as friendly. When CAP was founded in 1995, downtown was already fairly safe. Since then, however, crime has decreased by 67 percent in the 90-block CAP District, making it one of the safest places in the entire metro area. The chance of someone in Over the Mountain suburbs like Vestavia and Mountain Brook—as well as someone in the CAP District—being a victim of serious crime is about 1 in 100, while the risk of being a victim of violent crime is less than 1 percent of that, or 1 in 1,000.

Glen Iris

Robert Jemison Sr. developed Glen Iris, another early planned community, in 1898. Set on 30 acres about a mile from the center of downtown on the north side of Red Mountain, it is essentially a long central driveway terminating in a circle with 20 lots, a private subdivision for Jemison and many of his friends. While the neighborhood suffered during the 1970s, several of the large, elegant homes have been restored.

Norwood

At the northern tip of Birmingham's original grid lies Norwood, developed in the early 1890s by the Elyton Land Company. The community centers around Norwood Boulevard, a mile-long, 200-foot wide parkway of grand old homes. White flight and newer suburbs hit this area particularly hard, and the construction of I-20/59 right through the area further severed the community. Recently a new set of homebuyers have begun eyeing Norwood as the next big opportunity to own a Greek Revival mansion, Prairie farm house, or Craftsman bungalow for an affordable price. It's a modest renaissance, but it's a renaissance nonetheless.

i **The Birmingham Museum of Art's Ireland Sculpture Garden was named one of "10 Great Public Spaces" for 2010 as part of the Great Places in America program of the American Planning Association. This is the first time an Alabama location has earned such a designation.**

Southside

Southside, an area of the city center south of the Railroad Reservation, is the city's midtown (though few use that terminology) between downtown proper and the residences on the slopes of Red Mountain. It includes the Five Points South entertainment district, home to some of the city's best restaurants, as well as the University of Alabama at Birmingham campus, surrounding neighborhoods, and Glen Iris.

Redmont Park

Redmont Park, while not downtown, is certainly not fully Over the Mountain, either. Zoned as the City of Birmingham, Redmont is a 1920s development along the crest of Red Mountain built in a series of subdivisions winding along the ridge overlooking the city below. It is home to many of the city's finest mansions from the early days of Birmingham, built by the city's iron and steel barons.

HIGHWAY 280 CORRIDOR

Highway 280, once a sleepy two-lane road taking Birmingham residents to Lake Martin for the weekend or to Auburn for a college football game is now a six-lane corridor overflowing with traffic passing through a densely packed commercial and residential area. In many ways, the Highway 280 Corridor is a self-sufficient neighborhood unto itself with retail shopping, restaurants, and numerous national chain stores. That's a good thing, since during most of the day, the traffic congestion is considerable. A new study on the most congested areas in the state for traffic listed several stretches of Highway 280 among the top ten worst. The Regional Planning Commission of Greater Birmingham and the Alabama Department of Transportation have done transit studies and a plan for elevated toll roads has been circulated. Area residents formed groups such as Rethink280 and Citizens to Save 280 to propose their own alternate plans. But beyond the traffic, there are numerous pleasant communities surrounding this booming traffic artery that the average passerby would never notice.

i **In addition to a fine mountaintop view of the valley below, the grand homes built along Red Mountain's crest allowed the wealthy better air quality. Anecdotes from those living in Redmont Park during the early 20th century recall how white tablecloths and clothes hung up to dry would turn black or grey with soot from Birmingham's steel furnaces.**

Brook Highland

Brook Highland, a large development of more than 800 homes with a variety of residential options surrounding a retail core, connects with Highway 280 and Highway 119 about 3 miles past I-459. Its location is convenient for residents commuting east to Leeds or Irondale. Brook Highland

Racquet Club—with 23 tennis courts, an Olympic-size swimming pool, and an extensive exercise center—is also a big attraction for potential residents.

African American–Owned Businesses

According to the US Census Bureau, the Birmingham-Hoover Metropolitan Area experienced a 50-percent increase in the number of African American–owned businesses in the 1990s. Indeed, Black Enterprise magazine ranked Birmingham among the top ten metropolitan areas to work, live, and play, and the Birmingham region is among the major US centers of African-American population and business development. That trend continues today as census data shows black-owned firms constitute nearly 10 percent of all Alabama firms compared with only 5 percent nationwide.

Chelsea

Chelsea, once just a small rural community outside of Birmingham, has in recent years become more connected and developed. Today it is the fastest-growing city in Shelby County, itself the fastest-growing county in Alabama. There are still farms sharing land with big new developments like Chelsea Park, and the medical and retail services at The Narrows, a commercial complex along Highway 280, have transformed the community.

Inverness

One of the first developments along 280, Inverness is a neighborhood mostly in Hoover but still has parts in unincorporated Shelby County. It stretches from Highway 280 to I-65 and is 15 minutes from downtown—during optimal traffic. Surrounding the man-made Lake Heather, the community enjoys retail complexes like Inverness Plaza and Inverness Corners as well as a private country club. With curving roads, large wooded lots, and many charming neighborhoods, it is a popular home for families.

Meadowbrook

Meadowbrook, an unincorporated community of 5,000 located across from Brook Highland along 280, is another early development. It offers a variety of apartments, condominiums, and homes. Valleydale Road gives residents a convenient route east and west. Many major retailers and boutiques are located here.

Greystone

Greystone, an exclusive gated community developed in the 1990s and known for stunning large homes, is located just south of the Highway 119 junction of Highway 280. Many will also recognize the name from the many top PGA Tour events held at Greystone Golf & Country Club and the newer Greystone Legacy golf course.

Mt. Laurel

Just over Double Oak Mountain, the New Urbanist Town of Mt. Laurel is a deliberate throwback to the city's small-town past—and perhaps a reaction to Highway 280's unchecked growth. Organized around a town center, the traditional neighborhood features Craftsman and English-village-style homes boasting high energy efficiency. All homes are within a short walk of the commercial center so that cars are not necessary. It features an organic farm and market, dog park, swimming and fishing lake, and Hilltop Montessori School, Alabama's first LEED-certified "green" school. Mt. Laurel was designed by Duany Plater-Zyberk & Company, the renowned town planners and creators of Seaside, Florida, the community that began the New Urbanism movement in 1981.

Birmingham's Hispanic/Latino Population

New US Census Bureau data shows Alabama's 2009 Hispanic or Latino population was 152,516 or about 3.2 percent of the total state population. Jefferson County's Hispanic population was estimated to be more than 23,600 out of 665,027 total residents, making Hispanics around 3.6 percent of the county's total population. By contrast, in 1990 Hispanics represented only 2,745 of Jefferson County's 651,525 residents or .42 percent, reflecting the tremendous growth and changes in Birmingham's demographics.

Over the Mountain

Why the significance of the Over the Mountain designation? Back in the heyday of the iron and steel industry in Birmingham, environmental laws were not exactly stringent about the particulate waste that was thrown up into the atmosphere. Traditionally, the term signified the areas south of Red Mountain that were largely protected from both the smoke and rougher elements of the downtown area. Today, the term largely denotes the more affluent suburbs with excellent school systems nestled close to the city around Shades Valley and Shades Mountain.

Homewood

Though you might not guess it from looking at the city, Homewood is Alabama's most densely populated city, with nearly 25,000 residents. Incorporated in the 1920s when Edgewood, Rosedale, Grove Park, and Hollywood combined, the city was linked by early streetcar lines that miraculously made it over Red Mountain along 20th Street. Hemmed in by Red Mountain to the north and Shades Mountain to the south, this early streetcar community's appealing 1920s and 1930s architecture (primarily bungalows, Tudor, classic cottage, and Spanish revival) keeps the property values among Birmingham's most expensive when measured per square foot. It is also one of the few OTM communities with a relatively mixed ethnic demographic with substantial Hispanic and African-American populations. It is home to Samford University, the Islamic Academy of Alabama, and Our Lady of Sorrows Catholic School. The downtown retail district is among the entire region's most vibrant. It is (largely) bounded by I-65 to the west and Highway 280 to the east.

Mountain Brook

Mountain Brook, one of Birmingham's most beautiful neighborhoods, began as Mountain Brook Estates in 1929, the vision of developer Robert Jemison. The planned community was among the first in the nation to include a village shopping center. From Georgian and Tudor revival to bungalows and the most modern designs, the architectural landscape of Mountain Brook is remarkable. Similar design and planning has meant that pedestrian sidewalks and parks now accentuate the original horse trails and greenways established by Jemison in the 1920s. Today, "the Villages" or shopping districts Jemison incorporated—Mountain Brook Village, English Village, and Crestline Village—are among Birmingham's most exclusive and upscale shopping areas. A 2009 survey of America's wealth concentrations conducted by American City Business Journals identified Mountain Brook as the United States' 8th wealthiest city. Other studies consistently place Mountain Brook among the highest educational attainment in the nation. Indeed, in SAT and ACT scores, Mountain Brook High School regularly ranks in the top 15 to 20 public high schools in the country.

i | If someone says they live "Over the Mountain" it typically means they are from Mountain Brook—but don't want to say it. If someone says they are from Homewood or Vestavia, it means they are from Homewood or Vestavia. Understandably, some Mountain Brook residents want to be judged by who they are rather than where they are from.

Higley 1,000

A fascinating website run by Stephen R. Higley, Professor of Urban Geography at the University of Montevallo, tracks the 1,000 wealthiest neighborhoods in the country: http://higley1000.com. There are 9 Higley 1,000 neighborhoods in Birmingham. Two are in the city, three are in Mountain Brook, and four are gated suburban enclaves: Forest Park, Redmont Park, Mountain Brook Estates-Canterbury, The Country Club of Birmingham, The Mountain Brook Club-Shook Hill, Greystone, Liberty Park, Highland Lakes, and Shoal Creek.

Vestavia Hills

Vestavia Hills, incorporated in 1950, is just what it sounds like: hilly. Set atop Shades Mountain some 5 miles from downtown Birmingham, this community of 31,000 is in many ways emblematic of post-war suburban development. Linked by I-65 to the east and southeast, I-459 to the south, and Highway 280 to the west, the city grew up around Highway 31, which runs north and south through the heart of the community. The oldest portions of the city are on the slopes of Shades Mountain and as you go south farther from Birmingham, you'll reach the newer residential and commercial areas. The school system is excellent—the high school math team finished 3rd in a national competition as recently as 2010. This is nothing new. The school system's standardized test scores consistently are among the

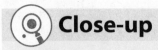

Close-up

The Elephant in Any Alabama Room

Let's be honest: Most people with only a passing awareness of Birmingham or Alabama tend to fall back to the early 1960s and the Civil Rights Movement when forming an opinion of the city. People often overlook the simple fact that Rosa Parks, John Lewis, Ralph Abernathy, Coretta Scott King, and Fred L. Shuttlesworth, and other heroes of the Civil Rights struggles were all Alabamians, but that's a different story. An actual visit to Birmingham nearly always reverses those old stereotypes, but that's not to say that Birmingham is perfect. We have inherited similar challenges to those of any other metropolitan area. The city vs. suburbs issues that much of the country faces still applies here—just as it does in most Southern or Northern cities. White flight in the 1960s and 1970s sent Birmingham city schools, politics, and neighborhoods into turmoil.

Today the divide is largely economic and there is a kind of voluntary racial separation that compares to what one sees in Atlanta, Nashville, or Des Moines, Iowa, for that matter. It's what some experts call "hypersegregation," where facilities, opportunities, and services are grouped along racial lines. This parlance that explains how Detroit, Michigan's population is 80 percent black and Dearborn's is 1 percent. The City of Birmingham itself is 73 percent black and 24 percent white, a far less striking example of this modern kind of racial separation.

In the 1960s and 1970s, Over the Mountain communities created school systems that consistently rank among the top schools in the state (and in many cases, nation) while Birmingham city schools drop off dramatically in national averages. The cities of Mountain Brook and Vestavia Hills are overwhelmingly white, 99 percent and 95 percent, respectively. They are wonderful communities with strong civic participation from wonderful people, but there's no other way to put it when speaking in terms of race. Of the Over the Mountain communities, only Homewood (and Hoover if you consider it OTM) are relatively mixed at all with Homewood being 80 percent white and 15 percent black.

top three in the state, and the graduating classes average an astonishing $9 million in scholarships annually. Recent annexations of two non-contiguous areas, Liberty Park, a master planned community off I-459, and Cahaba Heights, a community on the east side of Highway 280, enlarged Vestavia Hills considerably.

North Shelby County

One of the country's fastest growing areas, the city of Hoover and much of northern Shelby County are a foil to the city of Birmingham itself. There's a reason why the area is called the Birmingham-Hoover Metropolitan Statistical Area. Indeed, at the rate of growth, return in 50 years and it may be called the Hoover-Birmingham MSA.

Alabaster

Alabaster, a city of close to 30,000 located 17 miles south of Birmingham, continues to experience explosive growth, expanding some 60 percent from 2000 to 2100. It made *Money Magazine*'s "100 Best Places to Live" in the 2009 list. After incorporating in the 1950s, the town thrived based on its location along Highway 31, the main route from Birmingham to Montgomery until the advent of I-65. Today, it's still largely a highway town, stretching north-south along the travel artery. It is home to the county's only hospital, Shelby Baptist Medical Center. The latest new development, The Colonial Promenade, is a large retail center with shops, movie theaters, and restaurants along Highway 31 at I-65.

Wealth Distribution in Alabama

Of Alabama's 20 wealthiest cities, 14 are Birmingham suburbs, according to the most recent census data. At the same time, the City of Birmingham and Bessemer are among the poorest cities in the Alabama. Another interesting if slightly contrary fact: The City of Birmingham has almost as many families earning more than $100,000 per year as wealthy Mountain Brook. Of course the city of Birmingham contains a far larger overall population.

Helena

Helena, located 5 miles north of Alabaster, while experiencing growth, has managed to retain much of its small-town charm in the process. Part of the reason is smart-growth policies instituted by the city, as well as its location a short distance from Highway 31. It also certainly helps that a few buildings from the late 1800s remain, adding great character. Old Town Helena, the area's most popular shopping district, offers a host of dining and shopping spots. *Business Week* named Helena the 13th "Best Place to Raise Your Kids" recently, and it can claim the eighth-lowest crime rate per population in the United States. Buck Creek, a feeder stream to the Cahaba River, cuts through the old downtown, providing a scenic anchor to the town.

Hoover

Hoover, incorporated in 1967, is a city of more than 70,000, and offers all the amenities a community needs to be self-sufficient. As Highway 31 widened in the 1950s, the city grew accordingly. It annexed Riverchase in the 1980s and then Inverness and Greystone in the early 1990s. Hoover contains everything from shopping at the Riverchase Galleria—one of the largest malls in the Southeast—to the Birmingham Barons baseball team. The schools are almost uniformly excellent, and the facilities, many of them new (such as Spain Park High School in Hoover), are among the region's most modern buildings—many will recognize Hoover High School for the popular MTV reality show, *Two-A-Days*, chronicling the school's football team. Blue Cross/Blue Shield, Regions Bank, AT&T, and other corporate giants all have large facilities in the city. Since 2004 Hoover has been a leader in the use of ethanol and biodiesel in its municipal vehicles—something around 80 percent of the fuel used by its fleet is alternative fuel. It was also a leader in 2009 when it became the first city in the United States to power its police cars with fuel from the city's collected wood waste. The International Awards for Livable

Communities in London, England, recognized the city for its environmentally sensitive practices in 2007. Hoover also is home to a sizable Latino population, particularly around the Lorna Road area, making it one of the city's most diverse populations.

> **i** Hoover operates a fleet of nearly 200 flex fuel vehicles on 85 percent ethanol and close to the same number of vehicles and equipment on B-20 biodiesel. Hoover's municipal fleet also collects used cooking oil from area restaurants and converts it to bio-diesel fuel, both saving money and running city vehicles on cleaner fuel.

Pelham

Pelham, a city of 21,000 just south of Hoover, lies at the foothills of Oak Mountain and enjoys a mix of recreation, shopping, and business opportunities along with natural green space that makes the community unique in the area. Like the other communities of North Shelby, Pelham and other smaller entities like Helena, Alabaster, Riverchase, and Greystone, are part bedroom community, part suburb to the city of Birmingham.

REGIONAL

The massive land area contained in the Birmingham-Hoover Metropolitan Area—some 1.2 million people contained in seven counties in the heart of the state—makes for a particular unwieldy organizational premise for anyone attempting a guidebook about Birmingham. With the exceptions of Jefferson County, with its county seat of Birmingham, the counties of Bibb, Blount, Chilton,

St. Clair, Shelby, and Walker are clustered around Birmingham proper. While some people living in the following suburbs, when asked what city they are from, will reply, "Birmingham" for simplicity's sake, many residents in cities like Jasper, Pell City, and Gardendale lie farther outside the orbit of this principal city and have a strong local identity all their own. Their local identity owes more to the city where they reside. Still, it's common for many regional residents to drive into or near Birmingham for work, shopping, or entertainment.

Bessemer

Founded by iron and steel magnate Henry Fairfield DeBardeleben in 1886, Bessemer was a booming industrial town and middle class stronghold during its early years and up until the 1960s when the steel industry began to decline. After diversifying its economy in the 1990s, the city of 29,000 has begun a clear comeback with first-time homebuyers eyeing the city's admirable architecture—a sure sign that things are changing for the better. It is home to Alabama Adventure theme park, The Bright Star restaurant, and Watermark Place outlet mall.

Center Point

Center Point in Jefferson County's northeastern area only incorporated in 2002. With a population of more than 60,000 in the 1970s, the area was the nation's most populated unincorporated area at the time. The population has fallen dramatically since then, but this community found just north of I-65 along Center Point Parkway is still bustling.

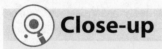 **Close-up**

You're So Birmingham If . . .

An amalgam of Facebook and e-mail chains, Tweets, and input from friends, here's a quick look at the curious, silly, and just plain funny things that make Birmingham, Birmingham.

- You say something "tumped" over instead of spilled.
- You say "Vulcan" and not "The Vulcan."
- You call a garden hose a "hose pipe."
- You only season your steak with Dale's Seasoning. And your second choice is Mr. P's.
- You see as many of your neighbors at the beach as you do in Birmingham.
- You refuse to attend Bruno's, the Crawfish Boil, or City Stages (when it was around) without free tickets AND VIP passes.
- You miss Ollie's barbecue.
- You're wary of Harpersville police speed traps.
- The Bass Pro Shops store is a destination unto itself.
- You graduated from a local high school, attended a state or local university, and now work or hope to work for *Southern Living*.
- One of the first things you find out about someone is who they pull for: Alabama or Auburn.
- The second thing you do is ask where they go to church.
- You don't tell your customers whom you pull for in the Iron Bowl because you don't want them to hold this against you.
- You remember when Dreamland Bar-B-Que only offered ribs, white bread, and sauce.
- You not only know who Cousin Cliff was . . . you were on his television show.
- You think driving 15 minutes is way out of your way.
- You can name Auburn and Alabama coaches but not Birmingham's mayor.
- Grapico and Buffalo Rock Ginger Ale are your sodas of choice.
- You can describe where you live as "over the mountain," "the village," or "diaper row" and others understand.
- You've dressed up as a former Jefferson County Commissioner for Halloween.
- You can't go grocery shopping without wearing lipstick.
- You remember Vulcan's lights glowing red when there was a fatality from a car accident.
- You know someone who knows someone who knows Courtney Cox.
- You know someone who knows someone who dated/went to school with/is best friends with Taylor Hicks (and convinced him to audition for *American Idol*).

Columbiana

Located on the other side of Birmingham, the sleepy hamlet of Columbiana is the county seat of Shelby County. Dating back to 1832, the city of 3,300 is 25 miles south of Birmingham. The city's Main Street underwent a revitalization a few years ago, and local attractions like the old County Courthouse, Shelby County Historical Museum, and George Washington Museum offer a unique perspective.

Biofuel Birmingham

One national effort passing through Birmingham is America's first biofuel corridor, established in 2008 along I-65. The corridor starts in Mobile, Alabama, and runs through Tennessee, Kentucky, and ends in Indiana, allowing drivers to go from the Gulf of Mexico to the Great Lakes on ethanol or biodiesel. Gas stations in Athens, Prattville, Vestavia Hills, Flomaton, Warrior, Evergreen, Montgomery, and Mobile offer clean burning alternative fuels such as E-85 Ethanol and B20 Biodiesel at the pumps. And with nearly 200 vehicles in the state motor pool on E-85, Alabama is one of the most progressive in this respect. Alabama is third in the nation in terms of E-85 and biodiesel usage.

Ensley

Founded in 1886, Ensley is one of the area's original steel towns with a historical pedigree nearly unmatched in the story of Birmingham. Located a few miles west of downtown Birmingham along I-20, Ensley's blast furnaces and massive Tennessee Coal, Iron and Railroad Company (TCI) operations kept the town growing until the Great Depression. It was also known for lively spots like Tuxedo Junction, a dance and jazz club that local musician Erskine Hawkins and Glenn Miller made famous in their 1939 song of the same name. When TCI consolidated its manufacturing in nearby Fairfield in the 1980s, hard times fell on Ensley. Today, Ensley's appealing downtown and surrounding homes are in real need of a revival.

Fairfield

Neighboring Fairfield has fared better than Ensley in the past decades. Planned by TCI as a model city with worker housing, today the city has its own school system separate from Jefferson County. US Steel's Fairfield Works produces sheet and tubular metal products and has helped keep the small city going. It is the only US Steel facility still in production in the Birmingham area. Western Hills Mall is the city's major retail center.

According to a joint study of the Environmental Quality Institute at UNC, Rutgers University and the National Defense Institute, Birmingham's water quality received an "A" ranking (only 13 of 101 cities nationwide were as highly ranked). No cities were ranked higher.

Gardendale

Gardendale, found north of Birmingham along I-65 and Highway 31, is a prosperous

Birmingham Vital Statistics

Important dates in history: Birmingham founded at the crossing of two rail lines near a concentration of iron ore, coal, and limestone, 1871; Truman H. Aldrich, J. W. Sloss, and Henry F. DeBardeleben, owners of the Pratt Coal and Coke Company, open the Pratt mines and jumpstart the city's growth, 1878; Tennessee Coal and Iron Company purchased by US Steel, 1907; Elyton and several other surrounding towns incorporated, giving rise to the nickname "The Magic City" for its rapid growth, 1911; A city-wide plan for a system of parks by the Olmstead Brothers, 1925; The Birmingham Campaign leads to the Civil Rights Act the following year, 1963; University of Alabama at Birmingham established, 1969; Dr. Richard Arrington Jr. elected as Birmingham's first African-American mayor, 1979; Birmingham Civil Rights Institute opens, 1993; McWane Science Center opens downtown, 1998; A renovated Vulcan Park opens, 2004; Birmingham Mayor Larry Langford convicted on all 60 counts in federal corruption trial, 2009; *Southern Accents* and *Cottage Living* magazines close, 2008 and 2009; Railroad Park, a 19-acre green space in downtown, opens, 2010.

Alcohol:

Drinking age: 21

DUI: .08 percent or more for those 21 and older; .04 percent limit for commercial drivers; .02 percent for those operating a school bus or day care van or under 21.

Sunday sales: No alcoholic beverage sales are allowed between 2 a.m. and noon on Sun.

Dry counties: Bibb, Blount, Chilton, Walker

Open container law: It is illegal for people to drive with an open container in the passenger compartment of a vehicle.

Bar sales: end daily at 2 a.m. Mon through Sat.

Sales locations: Government-run ABC stores sell liquor. Private shops sell wine and beer. Local ordinances govern availability. Allowable alcohol by volume (ABV) in beer increased from 6 percent to 13.9 percent in 2009.

Capital of Alabama: Montgomery

Major metropolitan cities (in order of size): Birmingham, Montgomery, Mobile, Huntsville, Tuscaloosa, Hoover, Dothan, Decatur, Auburn

Outlining counties and their county seats: Bibb (Centreville), Blount (Oneonta), Chilton (Clanton), St. Clair (Pell City and Ashville), Shelby (Columbiana), Walker (Jasper)

Population:

City of Birmingham: 229,800

Metro area: 1.2 million

State of Alabama: 4.6 million

Climate: Average summer high temperature 91°; average winter low 29°; average annual 61.8°

Leading employers: University of Alabama at Birmingham, AT&T, Regions Bank, Birmingham Board of Education, City of Birmingham, Jefferson County Board of Education, Children's Health System, Wells Fargo (formerly Wachovia), Alabama Power Company, Blue Cross-Blue Shield of Alabama.

Birmingham colleges and universities: University of Alabama at Birmingham, Samford University, Jefferson State Community College, Virginia College–Birmingham, Birmingham–Southern College, Lawson State Community College, Herzing University, ITT Technical Institute, Southeastern Bible College.

Birmingham health care: Princeton Baptist Medical Center, Trinity Medical Center, Brookwood Medical Center, Callahan Eye Foundation Hospital, Children's Hospital of Alabama, Cooper Green Hospital, HealthSouth Lakeshore Rehabilitation Hospital, Hill Crest Behavioral Health Services, St. Vincent's Hospital, St. Vincent's East, University of Alabama at Birmingham Health System, VA Hospital, Shelby Baptist Medical Center, Walker Baptist Medical Center.

Jefferson County average home price: $194,994 (estimated median home price in Birmingham is $230,031)

Birmingham's famous sons and daughters: Mother Mary Angelica of the Annunciation, Eternal World Television Network founder and host; Hugo Black, Supreme Court Justice; Courtney Cox, actress; A.G. Gaston, African-American businessman; Emmylou Harris, singer; Lionel Hampton, bandleader; Odetta Holmes, folk singer and human rights activist; Diane McWhorter, Pulitzer Prize–winning author; Walker Percy, author, Howell Raines, former New York Times editor; Condoleezza Rice, former US Secretary of State; Ruben Studdard, singer and *American Idol* winner; E.O. Wilson, entomologist and author.

Famous Birmingham sports figures: Charles Barkley, basketball player; Bobby Bowden, football coach; Bo Jackson, multi-sport athlete; Carl Lewis, Olympic gold-medalist and world champion in track and field; Willie Mays, baseball player; Satchel Paige, baseball player; Neil Bonnett, NASCAR driver.

State holidays: New Year's Day, Martin Luther King Jr./Robert E. Lee Birthday, George Washington, Mardi Gras Day (Baldwin & Mobile counties only), Confederate Memorial Day, National Memorial Day, Jefferson Davis' Birthday, Independence Day, Labor Day, Columbus Day and American Indian Heritage Day, Veterans' Day, Thanksgiving, Christmas.

Major airports: Birmingham-Shuttlesworth International Airport

Major interstates: I-20, I-22, I-59, I-65, I-459

Driving laws:

Car seats: required for children under 6 years old.

Right turn on red: after a complete stop, unless otherwise posted.

Seat belts: required for all passengers over 6 years old.

Headlights: required when operating windshield wipers during inclement weather.

community of 14,000 with deep local roots and pride. The past few years has seen this somewhat isolated city expand, welcoming large shopping centers and new national chain restaurants. Most business development in the past decade has been along Fieldstown Road. Since the 1980s, the city has annexed large surrounding areas, signaling the city's desire to grow and expand.

Hueytown

Located west of Birmingham, Hueytown is known by many as home to the legendary Alabama Gang of NASCAR drivers: Bobby, Davey, and Donnie Allison; Neil and David Bonnett; and Red Farmer. With an industrial past similar to Ensley and Fairfield, Hueytown's coal-mining industry underlined the city's success into the 1950s when the mines closed. The city's hub is located a few miles west of I-20/59.

Irondale

Found to Birmingham's east, the city of Irondale was made famous by native author Fannie Flagg, whose book and subsequent film, *Fried Green Tomatoes at the Whistle Stop Cafe*, popularized the community and the landmark Irondale Cafe. Today, the city's annual Whistle-Stop Festival attracts thousands for a fun mix of food, arts and crafts, and music. The town has 10,000 people and over 500 businesses and got its start as a mining and railroad community.

Leeds

The city of Leeds on the far eastern end of Jefferson County prides itself on offering country living with all the advantages of the big city. Just 17 miles from downtown along I-20, Leeds has developed rapidly in the last decade with the addition of the Barber Vintage Motorsports Museum and Racetrack, the nation's second largest Bass Pro Shops Outlet, and The Shops at Grand River retail center, which opened in 2010.

Pell City

Pell City, one of two county seats of St. Clair County, is a city of 16,000 located less than an hour away from Birmingham on I-20. Its proximity to Logan Martin Lake makes it a popular recreation destination, and it has hosted the B.A.S.S. Masters Classic fishing tournament several times.

Trussville

Trussville, another satellite town surrounding Birmingham, was until the 1960s a self-contained small community. Today, its population has grown to more than 20,000 after a series of annexations of surrounding areas in the 1980s, when it had only 3,500 residents. Appealing older neighborhoods like the Cahaba Project are now complemented by newer ones like Trussville Springs, a New Urbanist development on a rehabilitated former industrial site along the Cahaba River. Protecting its major natural asset, the Cahaba River, has been a priority for the town, which funded a $2.2 million Greenways Project along the river. Trussville was recently ranked 56 out of 100 in *Money Magazine*'s Best Places to Live.

Visitor Information Centers

**GREATER BIRMINGHAM CONVENTION
  & VISITORS BUREAU**
2200 9th Ave. North, Birmingham
(800) 458-8085
www.birminghamal.org

**GREATER BIRMINGHAM CONVENTION
  & VISITORS BUREAU: AIRPORT**
5900 Messer Airport Hwy., Birmingham
(205) 458-8002

**GREATER BIRMINGHAM CONVENTION
  AND VISITORS BUREAU:
  VULCAN PARK**
1701 Valley View Dr., Birmingham
(205) 558-2005
www.visitvulcan.com

FOURTH AVENUE VISITOR CENTER
319 17th Street North, Birmingham
(205) 328-1850

GETTING HERE, GETTING AROUND

Like many American cities, if you're visiting Birmingham for a few days, you're going to need a car. The City of Birmingham—not including suburbs—covers more than 150 square miles, and while there is limited bus service within the city and to some suburbs, the only real way to get around with any efficiency is by automobile. A well-developed system of federal and state highways makes this an easily navigable town for anyone behind the wheel.

For those wishing to try the bus to get to places in and around the city, you are brave souls: Birmingham has been in need of adequate public transport since the city ripped up its extensive streetcar lines in the early 1950s, and it may take intrepid, dedicated public transport advocates to deliver better service for the general public. The MAX (Metro Area Express) does run during work hours downtown, providing those working in the city with convenient, clean-burning natural gas trolleys available along three routes in the city center. The transit authority also offers fixed-route service in Birmingham and some neighboring suburbs. The truth is, the Greater Birmingham area is quite spread out, making the automobile the most practical means of transport for the area. For those commuting in and out of downtown on I-65 as well as those navigating Highway 280, Alabama's second-busiest roadway, collective frustration will at some point surely boil over in the form of light rail or some type of public transport. There are around 100,000 good reasons for this daily going to and from work along the route.

With more and more loft dwellers downtown, though, there are the increasing few who walk or bike to work, and biking organizations like the Bici Cooperative (www.bicicoop.org) have made a valiant effort to encourage residents to bike to work. Granted, the hilly environment, as well as hot and humid temperatures, provide a few obstacles, as do the lack of many dedicated bike lanes in and around the city. As more restaurants, shops, and businesses continue to open in the city center, this is improving steadily. If you're visiting though, think of Birmingham as a series of small neighborhoods to explore on foot. Park your car, walk about, and get to know the city.

ROADWAYS

One of Birmingham's big selling points for businesses and residents is the relative accessibility the areas extensive road networks provide. The north/south orientation of **I-65** moves goods and people from the Gulf Coast to the heart of the country while **I-20** leads east to Atlanta, Georgia, and the Eastern Seaboard. The new **I-22** points to Memphis, Tennessee, and beyond while **I-20/59** leads to New Orleans, Louisiana.

Highway 280, which begins in Birmingham, continues southeasterly to Columbus, Georgia. **I-459,** Birmingham's 32-mile long southern bypass provides an alternate route for those wishing to avoid downtown during high traffic hours. Conversely, the proposed northern bypass that will theoretically connect I-59, I-65, and I-20 is still on the drawing board. Unlike neighboring Atlanta where the bypass has long since developed to the point where the quickest route through the city is found by going through the city on I-20, I-459 is (except for high traffic hours) still a bypass.

Compared to many cities of its size, travel though the city center is a fairly simple prospect: If you are coming from the north or the south on the interstate, you are on I-65. If you are traveling from the east or northeast on the interstate, you will take I-59/20 and either continue past I-65 or merge with it, depending on where you're going. The Red Mountain Expressway, a dramatic cut through Red Mountain made in the 1970s, connects I-59/20 with Highway 280 going southeast from the city center.

For travelers and commuters living south of the city, I-65 and Highway 280 are the primary routes (some would argue "only") into the city center. Since the overwhelming bulk of the suburban growth is along both corridors, there is a self-fulfilling element to the high amount of congestion during rush hours on both arteries. **Highway 31,** which parallels much of I-65, historically was the north/south route through Birmingham. Today, it is still a vibrant, important highway for residents, but for commuting purposes, it is largely used on a local basis or as an alternate route in case of catastrophic congestion on I-65. Another alternate route is **Green Springs Highway,** which parallels

I-65 as both enter Homewood from downtown. Green Springs Highway follows SR 149 until it reaches Columbiana Road passing through Vestavia Hills and then on to Hoover as is one of the few options to I-65 going in and out of the city on the south side.

North of Birmingham, the communities of Gardendale and Fultondale have grown in recent years, and I-65 has been widened to accommodate that growth. The Fieldstown Road exit in Gardendale in particular keeps expanding, and during high-volume times, expect some slowdowns at this point. To the east, dramatic growth in Leeds and Trussville along the I-20 and I-59 corridors, respectively, means that these formerly sleepy towns are now part and parcel of Birmingham's commuter system.

Highway 280, known by some old timers as the "Old Florida Short Route" (an irony I won't comment on) is just about the only game in town for those living south of town along Highway 280 in neighborhoods such as Chelsea, Shoal Creek, Mt. Laurel, and Meadow Brook. Locals have their favorite short cuts along Caldwell Mill Road, Valleydale Road, Cahaba Valley Road/Highway 119, and others when the traffic is particularly bothersome. If you don't know these winding roads, don't bother trying: Your best bet is probably to take your chances on Highway 280.

i Dangerous by design? Researchers at Surface Transportation Policy Partnership ranked the 52 most dangerous metro areas (over one million) for pedestrians and Birmingham-Hoover is eighth. The list correlates to a lack of spending on smart infrastructure investments to make roads safer for everyone.

AROUND BIRMINGHAM

Living in a valley means drivers are going to have to deal with the reality of **Red Mountain.** Running southwest-northeast and dividing Jones Valley from Shades Valley in the Appalachian Mountains, Red Mountain is only a measly 1,025 feet but the consequence is that Birmingham's grid pattern follows the ridge's southwest-northeast orientation. What this has also meant is that before the Red Mountain Expressway was cut through the mountain in the 1970s to connect the city with its southern suburbs, Highways 31 and 280 bottlenecked at the small two-lane 21st Street South and crept over the ridge.

The **Railroad Reservation** divides downtown Birmingham. Any address with a North designation is north of the railroad. Any address with a South designation lies south of the railroad. The bulk of the downtown is bounded by I-65 to the west, I-59/20 to the north, and Highway 31/Red Mountain Expressway to the east. Red Mountain itself is essentially the southern border. The closer one gets to Red Mountain, the more the roads begin to lose their right angles and twist and turn according to the hilly landscape. It's a bit part of the attraction of the Highland Park, Altamont Park, and Forest Park sections.

i DART (Downtown Area Runabout Transit) Trolleys are a cheap and easy way to navigate the city center and the clean-burning natural gas that fuels the DARTs is a welcome relief to Birmingham's pollution plagued skies.

AIRPORTS

BIRMINGHAM-SHUTTLESWORTH INTERNATIONAL AIRPORT

Located a convenient 5 miles from downtown Birmingham, the **Birmingham-Shuttlesworth International Airport (BHM)** serves 3 million passengers a year and is the busiest in the state. Nearly 140 daily flights to more than 56 cities in the United States are carried out on six different airlines including American Airlines, Continental Airlines, Delta Air Lines, Southwest Airlines, United Express, and US Airways/America West. BHM offers one-stop flights to Atlanta, Chicago, Dallas, Houston, Las Vegas, Memphis, Miami, Minneapolis, New Orleans, New York, St. Louis, Tampa, and other cities. Real-time tracking of arrivals, departures, and in-air traffic is available at **www.bhamintlairport.com.**

Navigating the small airport couldn't be simpler. The airport is separated into a lower and upper level. The upper level is for passenger drop-off, and contains ticket desks, security, business center, and food courts. The ground level is for baggage claim, taxi service, and pickup. Though there's no curbside parking allowed, a parking deck across the street is a short distance from the terminal and curbside shuttle service area. The deck offers 5,600 spaces for hourly parking and daily parking. The airport remote lot has 900 parking spaces. A complimentary shuttle is available from the remote lot. Hourly parking in the deck is $1 per hour or $24 per day and daily parking is $1 per hour or $12 per day. Remote parking is $1 per hour or $10 per day. Both **AirMed International,** (800) 356-2161, www.airmed.com, and **MedJet Assistance,** (800) 963-3538, www.medjetassistance.com, are found at the airport and provide emergency medical air transportation.

Amenities

All food and gift shops are on the upper level. Between Concourse B and C (before security checkpoint) passengers and visitors can shop or dine at Golden Rule Barbeque, Charley's Steakery, Pizza Hut Express, TCBY, and Terminal Station. On Concourse C (past security checkpoint), ticketed passengers can dine or shop at Birmingham Varsity Grill, Hudson News/Gift Shop, The Magic City (Rotunda), and Wall Street Deli. On Concourse B (past security checkpoint), ticketed passengers have access to the Birmingham Raceway Cafe and Hudson News. Free wireless Internet is accessible anywhere inside the airport terminal free of charge. The self-service business center is between Concourse B and C and open Mon through Fri 5 a.m. to 9:30 p.m. and on weekends 5 a.m. to 7 p.m. ATM machines are found on the upper level between Concourses B and C. Skycap service is offered on the upper level at curbside to assist passengers by checking their bags.

Transportation from the Airport

Limousine and shuttle service is available at the airport, but generally run by reservation only so make arrangements prior to arrival. They are **Airport Express (Atlanta Airport Shuttle),** (205) 591-7770; **Birmingham Door to Door,** (205) 591-5550; **eShuttle,** (205) 702-4566; **Meteors Shuttle,** (205) 980-1083; and **Alabama Limousine,** (bus charter) (800) 633-0223. Taxis are also available on the ground level outside the baggage claim area. The following companies serve the airport: **American Cab, Award Cab Company, Birmingham Cab Company, Hill Cab Company,** and **Yellow Cab.** It is roughly 5 miles by interstate to the city center.

The rental car counters are located at ground level of the terminal near the baggage claim area and Concourse B. They are: **Avis,** (205) 592-8901; **Budget,** (205) 322-3596; **Dollar Thrifty,** (205) 510-0026; **Enterprise,** (205) 591-1927; and **Hertz,** (205) 591-6090.

BUSES

Greyhound serves Birmingham through its downtown station at 618 North 19th St. roughly between Linn and Kelly Ingram parks. Call (205) 252-7190. It is within walking distance of many downtown sites.

The **Birmingham-Jefferson County Transit Authority's (BJCTA) Central Station** is located on 1735 Morris Ave. and represents the first phase of a facility that will house and provide connections to multiple forms of ground transport such as airport shuttle service. BJCTA serves the municipalities of Birmingham, Bessemer, Fairfield, Homewood, Mountain Brook, Hoover, and Vestavia Hills. Exact cash of $1.25 or a BJCTA pass is required for local trips. An adult transfer is $0.25. A 5-day pass is $14. Most routes are run hourly Mon through Sat from 5 a.m. to 10 p.m. Unless you are familiar with the route and schedule, passengers should visit the BJCTA website to familiarize themselves with stops along their route. For assistance, call (205) 521-0101 Mon through Fri from 6 a.m. to 9 p.m. or on weekends and holidays from 8 a.m. to 9 p.m. See **www.bjcta.org** for further fare pricing, maps, and schedules.

The **DART** or **Downtown Area Runabout Transit** uses vintage trolleys for downtown residents and workers to navigate the business and entertainment districts. Each ride costs $0.25. There are two routes in the central business district and one in the UAB area. DART trolleys run on a more frequent schedule than buses and begin service at 10 or 11 a.m. with extended evening hours on Fri and Sat and limited Sun service. See www.bjcta.org for maps and schedules.

i BJCTA is in the process of replacing its entire fleet with Compressed Natural Gas vehicles for the benefit of its riders and to help improve Birmingham's air quality and pollution control efforts.

TAXIS

While taxi service has improved in the past few years, for the most part, taxis in Birmingham are transporting visitors to and from the airport. If you need a taxi, in general, you'll need to call to arrange a pickup. There are also a number of shuttle services operating in the city, which require reservations. Most service generally ends at 12 a.m. but some offer 24-hour service.

AMERICAN CAB COMPANY
(205) 322-2222
Primarily serves Birmingham-Shuttlesworth International Airport. Limited 24-hour service on weekends.

AWARD CAB COMPANY
(205) 243-5552
Serves Birmingham-Shuttlesworth International Airport only.

BIRMINGHAM DOOR-TO-DOOR SHUTTLE SERVICE
(205) 591-5550
www.birminghamdoortodoor.com
Provides van service from the Birmingham-Shuttlesworth International Airport to any point within the state of Alabama. Reservations required.

E-SHUTTLE SERVICE
(205) 702-4566
www.eshuttle.net
Provides car and van service from the Birmingham-Shuttlesworth International Airport to all points within a 900-mile radius. Reservations required.

YELLOW CAB OF GREATER BIRMINGHAM
(205) 328-4444
Radio dispatch service covering metropolitan Birmingham area 24 hours a day, 7 days a week. Provides package delivery.

TRAINS

Amtrak stops at Birmingham's station at 1819 Morris Ave. downtown on its **Crescent route** offering daily trips between New York City and New Orleans. The next major stops are in Atlanta, Charlotte, Washington, D.C., and Philadelphia. The Crescent route also includes stops in Anniston, Alabama, and Tuscaloosa, Alabama. The station fronts the railroad reservation and has a small waiting room. Across the tracks is the new **Railroad Park,** a much more pleasant spot to wait for a train than the station itself.

HISTORY

efore coal and iron ore transformed Jones Valley in the 19th century, the area was home to several Native American tribes. When the first Paleo-Indians came to the fertile lands in this area some 20,000 years ago, the forests and rivers gave them all of the natural resources they needed to survive. During the Mississippians' time (AD 1050–1540) when the temperatures warmed, the people built large permanent towns and villages, planted their crops, and built many large earth mounds. When this agrarian culture was at its height, it established a major religious and commercial center at Moundville, Alabama, a short 70 miles southwest from present-day Birmingham. Other mound builders left several cone-shaped mounds along Village Creek and in the southwestern portion of the valley near Jonesboro.

Hundreds of years later, when the Europeans arrived in greater numbers in what would one day be called "Alabama," around half of the historic Native American tribes were either Creek or from smaller groups within the Creek confederacy who occupied central and eastern Alabama, including the Birmingham area. The Chickasaws lived in the northwest, and the Choctaws occupied the southwest. The Cherokee inhabited northeastern Alabama. It is hard to imagine that just a scant 200 years ago, at the start of the 19th century, this was the scene. Paths that Native Americans had followed for centuries ran along the summit of Red Mountain and most likely along the valley floor as well. Beyond what is today's Birmingham, trails ran from Big Spring in Huntsville to Tuscaloosa, from Talladega to the Warrior River and beyond. Native Americans created permanent towns at Old Town on the Warrior River and Mud Town along the Cahaba River. Within less than a century—from 1800 to 1898 when Birmingham was one of the world's largest producers of pig iron—the area of Jones Valley would transform dramatically from a sylvan landscape populated by Creeks and Cherokee tribes wielding bows and arrows to a mighty powerhouse of the Industrial Age: Birmingham.

EARLY HISTORY

The first European to pass through the interior of Alabama was Spanish explorer Hernando de Soto and his forces in 1540 in what was one of the most important events in 16th century North America. He was hoping to discover gold, but what de Soto and other European explorers left were diseases such as smallpox and measles that devastated native populations. Later, Tristán de Luna y Arellano sailed into Mobile Bay in 1559, and over the next century Spanish forces would explore the southern portion of the state in their eagerness to prevent the French from establishing colonies in the region. But by the late 1600s, the rising power along the Cahaba, Black Warrior, and Alabama Rivers was French and British traders offering rum, cloth, and weapons for deerskin and Native American Indian labor.

After 200 years of contact with Europeans, about half of the southeastern Indian's population had died from the diseases they contracted from them. Entire tribes began to fall apart and disappear because so many of them were sick. It wasn't until the mid-1700s that most tribes reorganized into four larger nations—Creek, Choctaw, Chickasaw, and Cherokee. During this time the Cahaba River served as the Choctaw's eastern border with the Creeks, and Jones Valley was something of a disputed neutral zone between the lands of the Creek, Cherokee, Choctaw, and Chickasaw peoples. Over the next century, the French from Mobile, the British from Charleston, and the Spanish from Mobile would claim the area. By the middle of the 18th century, the British military and explorers, surveyors, and trappers began making extended forays into the region. Finally, in 1795, the land was ceded to the United States.

It wasn't until the American expansionist period from the 1780s to 1819 and the inevitable conflict with the Creeks and other Native Americans that the area around Jones Valley saw a real influx of settlers. Some of the early settlers to Alabama were the soldiers of Andrew Jackson, who fought in the Creek War of 1813–14 and returned to make a home in the center portion of Alabama (then known as the Mississippi Territory). While the Choctaws were forced off their lands through a series of treaties between 1814 and 1830, the Creek Nation was utterly defeated at the Battle of Horseshoe Bend in 1814. What the Creeks then ceded to the upstart Americans would become the center of the state of Alabama.

EARLY STATEHOOD

By the time the area became a territory in 1817, "Alabama Fever" was running rampant among those in Virginia, the Carolinas, and Georgia seeking a better life. Returning soldiers described the region as a paradise. Planters in nearby states lived in what they considered a farmed-out area, so when the Alabama Territory opened after the Creek Indian War, they saw the chance to settle this inexpensive fertile land as an opportunity. Squatters and settlers both poured into the area in numbers and built homes, cleared fields, and planted. On December 14, 1819, Alabama became the 22nd state.

John Jones was one of the first settlers in the area in 1815 and accordingly, Jones Valley takes its name from him and his brother Jeremiah. By the following year there were 140 people from Georgia, South Carolina, and Virginia living in the valley. Davy Crockett and a few companions even passed through on an extended hunting expedition that same year. Many place names still in use today come from the first families that arrived in the area: Acton, Overton, McAdory, Tarrant, Jonesboro, Hewitt, Elyton, and others. In 1848 professor Michael Tuomey, the state's first geologist, identified two large coal reserves, the Warrior and Cahaba coalfields, in the area. Along with an abundance of iron ore and limestone, all the ingredients for making iron were on hand just below the rocky soil that these settlers were using to scrape out a farming existence. As the early pioneer days of what had been designated Jefferson County passed, it became apparent that those in Jones Valley stood on a divide between the great wealth of the aristocratic cotton plantations of the Black Belt to the south and the small farmers of the hill country to the north. By the 1860 census, Jefferson County held 9,078 whites and 2,649 slaves owned by only 284 families. That same year the county raised 586,785 bushels of corn and a measly 4,940 bales of cotton. This was not the Cotton Kingdom.

By the beginning of the Civil War, the region's abundant mineral wealth was being increasingly used to make iron for the war effort. Before the war, the entire region of north Alabama had some 17 forges, 9 primitive furnaces, and 1 rolling mill producing iron. This effort would soon be intensified. Streams and rivers powered these early iron works, and by 1865, the blast furnaces surrounding Jones Valley, such as Tannehill, Oxmoor, Brierfield, and Irondale were producing nearly 70 percent of the South's iron supply. Those same ironworks were also the targets of Union General James Wilson, who led 13,500 cavalrymen, "Wilson's Raiders," on an extended sortie through Alabama destroying the primitive furnaces. Wilson established his headquarters in Elyton at Arlington, the home of Judge William Mudd. Not long after the war when the first coke was used to smelt iron at the Oxmoor furnace in 1876, the foundation for the steel industry that would make Birmingham boom was set. A new industrial city began to rise near the valley's head that would help carry the state into the Industrial Age.

i Like many of the place names, rivers, and physical features of Alabama, the state's name has Native American origins as well. "Alabama" is derived from the Choctaw *alba* meaning "plants" and *amo* "to cut" or "to gather," that is "those who clear the land" or "thicket clearers."

INDUSTRIAL BIRMINGHAM

Birmingham didn't start with a port or a river landing. There wasn't even much of a rural crossroads in and around Jones Valley, though one of the early stagecoach and Pony Express lines intersected at the hamlet of Elyton in the valley's western portion. Soon Elyton or Ely's Town (located in West End today) had grown to approximately 1,000 residents. Founded in 1871 at the crossing of the Alabama & Chattanooga and South & North Alabama railroads, the rival town of Birmingham was situated to the east of Elyton in the middle of Alabama's mineral district, one of the world's richest deposits of coal, red and brown iron ore, and limestone: everything necessary to make iron. That was good news because this relatively poor hill country had no navigable river, and with the September Panic of 1873 that drained capital investments and the devastating cholera epidemic of the same year, the city certainly needed a break.

It received it when the Warrior coalfield opened in 1874, and the first production of coke pig iron occurred in 1876. Two years later owners of the Pratt Coal and Coke Company—Truman H. Aldrich, James W. Sloss, and Henry F. DeBardeleben—opened the Pratt mines. In 1881 Sloss founded the Sloss Furnace Company, realizing the enormous potential the area possessed as an iron-making center. The Tennessee Coal, Iron and Railroad Company arrived in 1886, an essential element as the minerals and pig iron could be moved to market in increasing volume. The first steel was produced in Birmingham in 1888. By 1890, more than 20,000 people worked at the mines, furnaces, mills, and foundries dotting the county. By 1898 Birmingham was the world's third largest exporter of pig iron. Entire communities rapidly organized around the industry, and

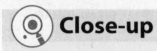

Close-up

"Heaviest Corner on Earth"

At the turn of the previous century, the young city of Birmingham was in fierce competition with nearby cities like Atlanta and Chattanooga. Civic boosters, business leaders, and investors actively promoted positive monikers like "the Magic City" or "Pittsburgh of the South" for obvious reasons as they attempted to attract new businesses, residents, and investments. When several notable tall buildings were completed at the intersection of 1st Avenue North and 20th Street, it was an opportunity. The term **"Heaviest Corner on Earth"** entered the local vocabulary when four of the taller buildings in the region—the 10-story **Woodward Building** (1902), 16-story **Brown Marx Building** (1906), 16-story **Empire Building** (1909), and the 21-story **American Trust and Savings Bank Building** (1912, and at 284 feet, the tallest building in Alabama until the RSA tower was built in Mobile four years ago)—were built on this corner. It marked a turning point in Birmingham's history that put the young upstart city on more of a level playing ground with other cities in the South. And Birmingham was going to play that card as far as it would take the civic interests. In 1911 *Jemison Magazine* asserted "Birmingham to Have the Heaviest Corner in the South." That should have been enough, but before long, the Birmingham PR corps turned the volume up to silly levels and the term "Heaviest Corner on Earth" was established. In 1985 the Birmingham Historical Society and Operation New Birmingham placed a marker on the sidewalk outside of the Empire Building. A few months later that same year, the "Heaviest Corner on Earth" was added to the National Register of Historic Places. So it must be true.

the city grew at an astounding rate, thus the nickname, "The Magic City." The city was more Wild West than Southern Belle. When US Steel purchased Tennessee Coal and Iron, massive financial resources and investments ensured the city's industrial and commercial success.

Until the Great Depression, northern capital combined with European immigrant and African-American labor (often coerced) caused Birmingham to boom. It is an aside, but increasingly scholars, researchers, and museum curators are examining the practice of forced labor—in effect, an age of neo-slavery—in the coal mines, farms, corporations, and steel industries in the South in a form of industrial slavery. See *Wall Street Journal* writer Douglas A. Blackmon's *Slavery by Another Name: The Re-Enslavement of Blacks from the Civil War to World War II* for more on this practice. Iron flowed in the Magic City's veins, but it was often the sweat and blood of the disenfranchised that sounded the city's pulse.

POST-DEPRESSION 20TH CENTURY

Of course, from the early part of the previous century, the city recognized, albeit fitfully and episodically, the value of Birmingham's natural environment. On the wooded slopes of Red Mountain, the natural breezes brought some relief to the area's humid summers. Additionally, in a town where iron and steel are produced, the air quality was fairly terrible, thus those higher elevations had the obvious benefit of cleaner air—as well as excellent views of the valley below. Warren Mannings completed one of the first city plans in 1919. Then in 1924 the nation's foremost park-planning architectural firm, the Olmsted Brothers, developed a park system for the city that suggested a network of parks, greenways, and blueways throughout the booming young city—though the city's poor finances, limited private support, and controversy over the library at Linn Park slowed implementation.

i Though not as well known among most of today's residents, Birmingham's early days were a bit more like the Wild West than anything else. A sign on the old Chamber of Commerce building at the corner of 1st Avenue and 19th Street downtown perhaps unintentionally echoed this reality in its bold claim: "Everything to Make Steel—Iron Ore, Coal and Limestone—Are All Within Gunshot of This Building."

When the Great Depression hit, it struck Birmingham especially hard. President Hoover's administration famously called Birmingham "the hardest hit city in the nation." Entire mills shut down for the best part of a decade. It was not until World War II, when the need arose to build the nation's arsenal, that the city recovered, but by then, Birmingham had learned a hard, hard lesson: diversification. From the University of Alabama in Birmingham's rapid expansion to new industries like chemicals and manufacturing as well as finance, the city was growing at a rapid clip again. In 1950 Atlanta's metro population was 550,000 while Birmingham's was 320,000. Yet when Atlanta's mayor cleverly described his city "too busy to hate,"

Birmingham increasingly appeared to have the opposite plan in mind. As the civil rights movement picked up steam in the 1950s and 1960s, all too often Birmingham and Alabama became the battlefield and bore the brunt of the nation's struggle for true equality.

CIVIL RIGHTS & BEYOND

By the turn of the century, African Americans represented more than half of Birmingham's industrial workers—its backbone and its strength—yet their living and working conditions were miserable due to the system of segregation and the Jim Crow Laws largely enshrined in Alabama's ruinous constitution of 1901. The US Supreme Court's ruling against segregated schools in *Brown v. Board of Education* in 1954 and the following year's Montgomery Bus Boycott effectively signaled the beginning of the end of state-sponsored segregation in Alabama and beyond. But it was just the start of the struggle. See the Civil Rights chapter for more details and sites to visit in Birmingham.

In the 1963 the "Birmingham Campaign," led by Birmingham's Reverend Fred Shuttlesworth and Dr. Martin Luther King Jr., the proponents of the city's system of segregation, clashed against massive protests that captured the nation's attention. After the police dogs, the water hoses, the bombings, and the recalcitrance of Police Commissioner Eugene "Bull" Connor, the city's image and reputation were in shambles. The passage of the Civil Rights Act of 1964 was due in a large part to the success of civil rights leaders in Birmingham. By 1979 Birmingham had elected its first black mayor, Richard Arrington Jr.

Not unlike many urban areas, Birmingham consistently grew in size until the late 1960s then began a steady decline—the city lost roughly 70,000 people from 1970 to the present. The closing of Sloss Furnaces in 1971 signaled further changes in the city's landscape. Yet Birmingham managed to adapt once again, becoming a center of bioscience, technology, steel making, manufacturing, and publishing as well as home to some of the nation's top construction and engineering firms. Birmingham is also one of the nation's largest banking centers. As the city shifted its focus from heavy industry to other commerce, in 1983 Sloss Furnace reopened to the public as a National Historic Landmark and monumental reminder of the city's founding industry. Today, the old industrial grounds still ring out with activity with jazz and rock concerts, folk festivals, and special events interpreting Birmingham's industrial history and heritage. By telling the story of Birmingham, Sloss is educating and entertaining a whole new generation of visitors to the Steel City.

LOOKING FORWARD

Today, Birmingham's urban center is in the process of (re)transforming into the urban attraction it was during the first half of the 20th century. While four decades of steady population losses are not going to be reversed anytime soon, the steady trickle of new businesses and residents returning downtown seems to have crossed a threshold. This development parallels Birmingham's transformation from an industrial base to a more diversified economy. While many businesses vacated downtown Birmingham for the suburbs—Trinity Medical Center, Red Diamond, and Southern Natural Gas Corporation, for instance—several such as Renasant Bank and Harbert Management Corporation, as well as smaller firms like Integrated Medical Systems, Frost Cummings Tidwell Group, Sheppard, Harris & Associates, and others have moved downtown.

The Birmingham City Council recently voted to increase and extend the city's lodging tax to fund a downtown luxury hotel and entertainment district at the BJCC and has given initial funding approval for a downtown baseball stadium. Studies suggest that a baseball park near Railroad Park could have a $500-million economic impact on downtown. Art galleries, white linen restaurants, stylish bars, and focal points like Urban Standard coffee house are specifically choosing downtown rather than the suburbs. Following the historic Alabama Theatre's renovation and revitalization in the late 1980s and 1990s, the Lyric Theatre—located across 3rd Avenue North—is now the focus of a fundraising campaign to return this 1914 gem to its former glory. It is the only surviving vaudeville theatre in the city, and combined with the magnificent Alabama Theatre, could transform the area into a burgeoning theatre and performing arts district once again. Just around the corner from the Lyric, the old Pizitz Building, built in 1923 and once the premier department store in the region, used to be the largest vacant building downtown. The 211,000-square-foot building is currently part of a $57-million redevelopment to hold offices, retail businesses, and restaurants, as well as a 6,000-square-foot gourmet grocery store run by local merchant, V. Richards Market.

Birmingham is also a part of the new green movement. There's been unofficial talk of calling the city "The Gateway to Nature," and local civic promoters might do well to latch onto that moniker and make it their own. Admittedly, as in many large cities, nature has at times taken a backseat to industrial progress, but it was in Birmingham that Pat Mitchell, better known as "Auntie Litter," launched her campaign to teach environmental awareness to young people. And there are good reasons to be inspired

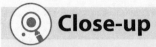 **Close-up**

The Recent Unpleasantness

There's no ignoring the facts: A spate of public corruption in Birmingham has made for national headlines and local hand wringing and disgust. Bribery, municipal bankruptcy, and incompetence . . . the list is long and ugly, stemming from when Jefferson County was ordered to rebuild its sewer system in 1996 following an environmental lawsuit. It stinks, quite literally. The county has about $3.9 billion in debt from its sewer project. And, not surprisingly, it cannot afford to pay the high interest rates. Chapter 9 still looms as a possibility, which would be the largest municipal bankruptcy in US history. Exactly the time Birmingham needed good civic leadership to solve the mess, right? Yet in 2010 former Birmingham Mayor Larry Langford was sentenced to 15 years in prison for accepting bribes while serving as president of the Jefferson County Commission. A federal jury convicted him on all 60 counts, including bribery, fraud, and money laundering. But that's not all: Between 2002 and 2008, 96 public corruption cases were brought to trial in Birmingham and Jefferson County.

by Birmingham's environmental advantages. Whitewater kayaking, bouldering, expanding greenways, trails, and an assortment of rivers, lakes, and streams surround the city. From Birmingham Botanical Gardens to the new Red Mountain Park, Birmingham is number one in the amount of green space per capita, leading the nation with 17.9 acres of public green space per 1,000 residents. In fact, Ruffner Mountain, with 1,000 acres and more than 11 miles of hiking trails and paths, is larger than New York City's Central Park. If Birmingham chooses to capitalize on this advantage, there's no stopping the city.

All that nature may be one of the reasons the farm-to-table movement has taken off in Birmingham. Following the successes of Jones Valley Urban Farm, the Pepper Place Market, and other early pioneers, the organic produce market and urban farming movement are having a positive impact not just on the restaurants smart enough to source locally, but also on outlying communities

through innovative programs aimed at the young. With the extended months of warm weather, if you can't grow your own garden in Birmingham, you might as well give up now. Consequently, new co-ops, urban farmers' markets, organic options, local sourcing in restaurants, and the occasional urban chicken coop (shhhhh . . . don't tell: many of Birmingham's ordinances are behind the time when it comes to chicken keeping) are popping up all over the city. Slow Food Movement? Well, frankly, that's just how many Alabama grandmothers and great aunts used to cook. It's good to see this generation catch on to what our older relatives know already.

Birmingham is an odd bird—it's true. It is Southern, yes, but not of the Old South. A post–Civil War enterprise, the city was not created because of any convenient proximity to a navigable river or natural crossroads. It grew from the very ground, lifted and dug by wealthy northern industrialists and their financiers. Consequently, some argue that what social segregation remains in the city today owes less to the inherent racism of the Old South than it does to the Boston Brahmins or capitalist class of New York. The challenges that remain for Birmingham are often the self-inflicted wounds that can still be traced to our past. But the opportunity for urban renewal and regional participation in this growing entity that is Birmingham promise a future that is brighter for all.

i There's no consensus on just what exactly you call a native-born person from Birmingham. Birminghamian? That's probably the most common, if a bit awkward. Birminghamite? Never heard that in practice, only jest. Brummie? No, that's for our sister city of the same name in England. Birminghamer? Again, you'll never hear that said in practice. The truth is, we probably don't have a good way to name a native son or daughter of Birmingham.

THE TORNADOS OF APRIL 27, 2011

A historic series of tornadoes cut a swath across the northern half of the state on April 27, 2011, killing nearly 250 people in the state of Alabama alone, injuring thousands and destroying homes and entire communities. One EF-4 tornado with winds of 165 miles an hour left a path of destruction 80 miles long and 1.5 miles wide stretching through Tuscaloosa, Birmingham and beyond, killing at least 65 people and injuring more than 1,000. All told, the storms killed around 350 people in 7 southern states in what many are calling one of most destructive single days of tornados in the nation's history.

Many in Birmingham watched the dramatic live TV footage as the tornado that was taking Tuscaloosa apart grew stronger, and held their breath as it made a beeline straight for their beloved city. Though the path of the storm ultimately veered just north of the downtown area, nearly every resident of Birmingham—and indeed, the seven-county region—has found pieces of plywood, tatters of insulation and shreds of asphalt roofing material in their yards, parks and playgrounds, much of it from the destroyed homes and businesses of Tuscaloosa 50 miles away. (Our neighbors found a legal document blown from a Tuscaloosa medical psychiatric facility in my family's front yard the day after the storm. It's a sobering reality to consider.)

Although only a few of the sites mentioned in this book were affected, the larger Central Alabama region has suffered tremendously. In Birmingham, most of the damage was in the Vestavia Hills/Cahaba Heights area along Highway 280 and the Pleasant Grove/Pratt City areas north of I-59/I-20. Regions Bank, headquartered in downtown Birmingham, quickly took action and contributed $1 million to help those in communities affected by the disaster. BBVA Compass followed with $500,000 and Protective Life contributed $250,000. The Newhouse Foundation also made a $1 million donation on behalf of Advance Alabama Publications, which includes the *Birmingham News, Huntsville Times,* and *Press-Register* in Mobile. Many others followed suit.

Just as the vast scale of the damage was almost beyond comprehension, so too was the overwhelming response and generosity of Birmingham–area citizens, businesses, faith-based groups, and volunteers that mobilized to help the survivors and start the long, painful process of recovery and rebuilding. It will certainly require ongoing efforts beyond just the immediate.

ACCOMMODATIONS

Just as the city has grown in the past decade, so too have the number and variety of places to stay in and around Birmingham. If you're looking at cost and convenience, there are a number of chain motels found in the suburbs and on the city's peripheries. If you're looking for a romantic getaway or a place to relax in luxury, you won't be disappointed. If you want a hip city escape for a girls' night out or to entertain out-of-town guests, you'll find options that will delight your friends and be pleasing to your budget. While in the past business travelers might have bemoaned the lack of quality downtown accommodations, that's no longer the case.

Hotels in Birmingham cluster in four main areas. Although there are many attractions within walking distance, you should expect that no matter where your hotel is located, you might have to do some driving to reach some of Birmingham's most attractive destinations. Downtown hotels are among the city's most refined and expensive hotels. Staying in the Southside section of downtown means you're probably within walking distance of Five Points South, the center of much of Birmingham's nightlife scene. Another area of consolidated lodging is along the Highway 280 corridor in Inverness. These hotels are mostly upscale business-class hotels with excellent amenities and higher pricing than the average chain hotel. Though the traffic on Highway 280 can be dispiriting during rush hour, the density of shops and restaurants on there means you can always find a 24-hour grocery store or big-box super store just around the corner. The third area is the dense conglomeration of lodging in the Homewood just a few miles from the city center. Homewood contains the largest amount of modestly priced lodging choices in the entire metropolitan area, as well as a few high-end hotels. Most are located just off I-65, which passes along the western side of Birmingham, making them easily accessible if you're unfamiliar with the area. If you get off I-65 at either of the Oxmoor Road exits (265A or 265B) or the Lakeshore Drive exit (266), you're sure to find a hotel. Some annual weekend events like the Magic City Classic or NASCAR races at Talladega can cause the Homewood hotels to fill up, so plan in advance. Farther south on I-65, the city of Hoover has a selection of hotels that make up a fourth area of lodging. Most of these hotels are chain hotels that offer decent prices and comfortable rooms.

OVERVIEW

Most of the hotels listed here have wheelchair-accessible rooms. Unfortunately, many of the listings only have a few rooms designed to be completely accessible. If a location offers either above-average or below-average wheelchair accessibility, the description will

ACCOMMODATIONS

indicate this. Modern hotels are becoming increasingly accommodating to pet lovers. Still, most hotels don't allow pets, so if an entry doesn't include information on pets then the location is pet-free. Following the current national trend, the majority of Birmingham's hotels are smoke-free facilities. All the listings in this chapter accept at least two major credit cards as payment.

Price Code

The prices listed represent the average rate for prime season, double-occupancy accommodations. Prices for suites will be greater. Prices do not include occupancy taxes.

$................. **Less than $60**
$$ .... **$60 to $110**
$$$ .... **$110 to $160**
$$$$ .... **More than $160**

Quick Index by Cost

$$$$

Hyatt Place Birmingham/ Downtown, Birmingham, 36

Hyatt Place Birmingham/ Inverness, Inverness, 39

Renaissance Birmingham Ross Bridge Golf Resort & Spa, Hoover, 42

Sheraton Hotel Birmingham, Birmingham, 37

$$$–$$$$

Aloft Birmingham Soho Square, Homewood, 41

Marriott Hotel Birmingham, Birmingham, 39

Residence Inn by Marriott Inverness, Inverness, 39

Residence Inn Birmingham Downtown at UAB, Birmingham, 37

The Wynfrey Hotel, Hoover, 42

$$$

Cobb Lane Bed & Breakfast Inn, Birmingham, 35

Courtyard Birmingham Downtown at UAB, Birmingham, 35

Doubletree Hotel Birmingham, Birmingham, 35

Embassy Suites Birmingham, Birmingham, 36

Hampton Inn & Suites Hoover Galleria, Hoover, 41

Homewood Suites by Hilton Birmingham–South/ Inverness, Inverness, 40

Hilton Birmingham Perimeter Park, Birmingham, 38

The Tutwiler Hotel, Birmingham, 38

$$–$$$

Courtyard by Marriott Hoover, Hoover, 40

Hotel Highland at Five Points, Birmingham, 36

The Redmont Hotel, Birmingham, 37

$$

Comfort Inn Homewood, Homewood, 40

Medical Center Inn, Birmingham, 36

Microtel Inn & Suites Hoover, Hoover, 41

$–$$

Candlewood Suites, Homewood, 39

Quality Inn, Vestavia Hills, 41

$

Super 8 Motel Homewood, Homewood, 40

BED-AND-BREAKFASTS

Downtown

Perhaps at no time since the city center's heyday in the 1940s and 1950s have there been so many good lodging options in Birmingham. From new boutique hotels to renovated older gems, there are a broad range of styles and locations to choose from for visitors.

✳COBB LANE BED & BREAKFAST
INN $$$
1309 19th St. South
(205) 918-9090
www.cobblanebandb.com

The only bed and breakfast in Birmingham is also one of the most sumptuous lodging choices in town. Originally a private residence built in 1898, the building has seen a number of different uses over the past century but is now a Victorian-styled bed and breakfast. Owners Ira and Sheila Chaffin have lovingly restored and updated the building in an effort to preserve as much of the original design. Their work has won preservation awards, and the building is now on the National Historic Registry. The furnishings and appointments in the hotel match the period, inviting you to relax in Victorian comfort and style. The seven unique guest rooms each have their own personality—two of the rooms are luxurious suites with plush parlors for entertaining. A full breakfast is served in their formal dining room. Conveniences like in-room cable television, and wireless Internet help prevent guests from missing any modern amenities.

HOTELS & MOTELS

Downtown

COURTYARD BIRMINGHAM
DOWNTOWN AT UAB $$$
1820 5th Ave. South
(205) 254-0004
www.marriott.com

Located in the midst of UAB's medical sprawl, the Courtyard at UAB is the perfect place to stay for anyone wanting incredibly convenient access to UAB. From the hotel, you can literally walk through most of UAB's world-class hospital. For outpatients and relatives, a stay in this hotel relieves the stress of traveling into the city and searching for parking. The new rooms are filled with the latest conveniences, including mini-refrigerators and high-speed wired and wireless Internet. Wheelchair-accessible rooms are available with roll-in showers, grab bars, and other options. Suites feature expanded sitting rooms separated from the bedroom. The hotel restaurant, The Bistro, serves a delicious breakfast and dinner in addition to cocktails at night. For guests with business downtown or in the hospital, the Courtyard offers a variety of services including on-site copy and fax service, package delivery and pickup, and a full-service business center. The hotel also features 7 meeting rooms with seating from 10 to 108, making it an easy choice for hospital-related events. The Five Points South entertainment district is located less than a mile from the hotel.

DOUBLETREE HOTEL
BIRMINGHAM $$$
808 20th St. South
(205) 933-9000
www.doubletree.com

The Doubletree in Birmingham sits in a prime location of downtown that's perfect for a stay in the city. The UAB university campus and hospital are within walking distance, and the hotel is two blocks away from the Five Points South entertainment district. For business in the city center, it's only a short drive to city hall and the many corporations headquartered on downtown's northern side. The contemporary business facilities include a banquet hall, business center, 11 meeting rooms with seating from 5 to 900, and the infrastructure to support a wide variety of occasions.

✳EMBASSY SUITES
BIRMINGHAM $$$
2300 Woodcrest Place
(205) 870-4523
www.embassysuites1.hilton.com

A full-service all-suite hotel located on the southern slopes of Red Mountain, Embassy Suites has for years been one of the city's foremost upscale hotels. Poised minutes from downtown and minutes from the shopping and dining of Homewood and Mountain Brook, the three-diamond AAA Hotel offers two-room suites with separate bedrooms and roomy living areas. Satisfaction is found in the details: 2 flat-screen televisions, 250-thread-count Sleep Essentials™ bedding, furnished living room, 2 telephones, a mini-fridge, wet bar, microwave, and more. Guests receive a free cooked-to-order breakfast, and many choose to visit the on-site restaurant, Ruth's Chris Steak House, arguably the city's top steak house. In-suite dining is provided for guests. The 24-hour business center and fitness center and gym are complimentary.

HOTEL HIGHLAND
AT FIVE POINTS $$–$$$
1023 20th St. South
(205) 271-5800
www.thehotelhighland.com

One of only a few boutique hotels in Birmingham, the Hotel Highland offers gorgeously appointed accommodations conveniently located right in the middle of Five Points South, making it perfect for a glamorous night in the city. The rooms and suites are adorned in Brazilian furnishings and fine linens, and the decor throughout the building maintains a sophisticated modern style. The martini bar in the hotel's lobby is a new Five Points favorite that provides guests a sophisticated spot for a drink or casual meeting. The location is also perfect for guests attending events on the UAB campus or hospital. Pets weighing 15 pounds and under are allowed with a $35 non-refundable fee, and pets must remain crated while in the hotel.

HYATT PLACE BIRMINGHAM/
DOWNTOWN $$$$
2024 4th Ave. South
(205) 322-8600
www.birminghamdowntown.place
.hyatt.com

One block away from UAB's celebrated Kirklin Clinic, the Hyatt Place is an innovative hotel in a newly designed setting. Everything about the hotel is new and exquisite. The lobby and cafe areas are filled with contemporary furnishing and styling that make some other chains appear mundane. The kitchen runs 24 hours a day, and a refrigerated self-serve area offers pre-made selections for guests on the run. The Hyatt is one of a few new upscale hotels downtown, and guests have been consistently pleased by the hotel's flawless design and excellent service. Business and event options include up to 1,700 square feet of meeting space as well as the services of the hotel's on-site Hyatt Place Meeting Host, a full-time sales associate ready to support any function. Complimentary Wi-Fi is available throughout the hotel.

MEDICAL CENTER INN $$
800 11th St. South
(205) 933-1900
www.medicalcenter-inn.com

The Medical Center Inn is an affordable hotel located on the western edge of the UAB campus. Just minutes from the UAB hospital and Five Points South, the hotel's low prices and prime location make it a thrifty choice for visitors needing easy access to the downtown area. The on-site Waffle House is a trusted choice for simple Southern diner food without the frills. At its core, the Medical Center Inn is simply a hotel with a Waffle House, but sometimes that's all one needs.

THE REDMONT HOTEL $$–$$$
2101 5th Ave. North
(205) 324-2101
www.theredmont.com

After years of decline the historic Redmont Hotel is once again a showpiece on the downtown scene. After recent improvements—including newly renovated deluxe guest rooms—the hotel's convenient location, modern amenities, and 114 rooms and suites make this boutique hotel an attractive draw for visitors staying downtown. Its proximity to the Loft District and 2nd Avenue's burgeoning entertainment scene puts the hotel squarely in the action. Its popular rooftop bar, Above, formerly the hotel's penthouse, draws downtown professionals and guests alike with its superior views of the city. Look for weekly rooftop jazz concerts in the summer. Opened in 1925 with 250 rooms, The Redmont remains the oldest hotel in Birmingham still in use today.

RESIDENCE INN BIRMINGHAM
DOWNTOWN AT UAB $$$–$$$$
821 20th St. South
(205) 731-9595
www.marriott.com

Whether you're staying in the city for a night or a week, the Residence Inn at UAB is a trusty stop for quality lodging that's made to feel like home. The one- and two-bedroom suites have a full kitchen that comes stocked with everything you need to prepare meals in your room. As the name states, the Residence Inn at UAB is located in the heart of the hospital area and is a few blocks away from both the UAB campus and the Five Points South entertainment district. The majority of UAB's hospital facilities are within 2 blocks of the hotel. Families with loved ones in the hospital for long-term care often choose the Residence Inn at UAB as a home away from home. Pets allowed with a $100 non-refundable fee.

✴SHERATON HOTEL
BIRMINGHAM $$$$
2101 Richard Arrington Jr. Blvd.
(205) 324-5000
www.sheraton.com/birmingham

Situated in the midst of the skyscrapers that make up downtown Birmingham's resurgent financial district, the Sheraton has blossomed as many financial institutions have relocated to downtown Birmingham. The Sheraton has always been a solid bet for events at the Birmingham Jefferson Civic Center (BJCC) and Boutwell Auditorium, but the abandonment of Birmingham's downtown area in the 1980s and 1990s left it without a steady market to serve. With the ongoing revitalization of the city center, the Sheraton has completed a $21-million renovation to attract executives and business leaders staying in town. The result is that the Sheraton is the premiere modern hotel in Birmingham, offering rooms and facilities unmatched by most of the city's lodgings. The design of the hotel is grand in scale and presentation, starting with the atrium lobby's vertical view that reaches the height of the building. The Sheraton has over 350,000 square feet of meeting rooms and exhibition halls as well as a 25,000-square-foot ballroom—the largest in the state. Guests with business at the BJCC will also enjoy the convenient skyway that connects the two buildings. A variety of room and suite options are available including the presidential suite, a group of rooms whose only competitor for quality is the presidential suite at The Wynfrey. The Sheraton allows pets up to 80 pounds with a deposit that is waived on any subsequent stays if you have a credit card on file with the hotel.

✳ THE TUTWILER HOTEL $$$
2021 Park Place North
(205) 322-2100
www.thetutwilerhotel.com
Opened in 1914 by Robert Jemison, The Tutwiler was a Birmingham landmark, a grand dame with a lavish lobby and a ballroom that could hold 1,200 people. But the 1960s and 1970s were tough years and the hotel was eventually demolished in 1974. Just over a decade later and a block away, The Ridgely Apartment building, owned by the Tutwiler family and built the same year as the hotel, was renovated and became the new Tutwiler Hotel. A $9-million transformation of the building in 2007 returned this historic hotel to the forefront of Birmingham lodgings. The "new" hotel essentially preserved the building's historic shell while outfitting an almost all-new interior hotel. The 149 rooms are completely restored, as are the original windows. Amenities such as Wi-Fi, a fitness room, and cafe with city views have been added. The Tutwiler is full service with valet parking, doormen, bell service, a concierge, 24-hour room service, and all one would expect from one of downtown's premier hotels. Historic photos of Birmingham are displayed throughout the marbled lobby,

rooms, and public spaces, reminding guests that if the Tutwiler didn't exist, the city would surely have to invent it.

Highway 280 Corridor

Once a quiet two-lane road leading to Auburn, Alabama, Highway 280 from Rocky Ridge Road south has seen massive growth and development, providing a concentration of hotels, restaurants, and big-box chain stores. It's proximity to the Summit Shopping Center, Colonnade Shopping Center, and other national retailers, as well as office parks makes this corridor a convenient location in which to choose a hotel for many visitors.

HILTON BIRMINGHAM
PERIMETER PARK $$$
8 Perimeter Park South
(205) 967-2700
www.hilton.com
As part of the Perimeter Park area on Highway 280, the Perimeter Park Hilton brings upscale lodgings to what is now one of the most bustling areas in the city. The Hilton is centered in the middle of hundreds of businesses concentrated in the cluster of office parks surrounding the hotel. The Hilton's function facilities are suitable for more than just business events with a grand ballroom suitable for any large occasion. For events a full catering menu is available, as well as the services of the hotel's own event manager. Standard rooms and two levels of suites are available. Specially designed wheelchair accessible rooms are also offered. Pets 75 pounds and under are allowed with a $50 non-refundable fee.

HYATT PLACE BIRMINGHAM/ INVERNESS $$$$
4686 Hwy. 280 East
(205) 995-9242
www.birminghaminverness.place
.hyatt.com

A smaller version of the downtown Hyatt Place, the Inverness location of this upscale brand features the same modern amenities as the downtown location in a lesser scale. Just because this Hyatt is smaller than the one in the city doesn't mean the quality of the hotel is diminished in any way. The Inverness Hyatt has ample meeting facilities with a full-time sales staff available to assist in the organization of any event.

MARRIOTT HOTEL BIRMINGHAM $$$–$$$$
3590 Grandview Pkwy.
(205) 968-3775
www.marriott.com

Located just south of the I-459 interchange near the Colonnade Shopping Center, the Marriott is one of the first choices for hotels for guests and business executives looking for a convenient place to stay along the Highway 280 Corridor. It is next to the Grandview Corporate Park and HealthSouth. The 8-floor hotel has 291 rooms and 4 suites. With 2 concierge levels, 15 meeting rooms in nearly 15,000 square feet of meeting space, it is a popular location for seminars, meetings, weddings, and gatherings of all types.

RESIDENCE INN BY MARRIOTT INVERNESS $$$–$$$$
3 Greenhill Pkwy.
(205) 991-8686
www.marriott.com

Nestled in the tree-lined suburb of Inverness just off the eastern end of Highway 280's path out of Birmingham, this hotel offers apartment-type living with amenities and services not available in most extended-stay lodgings. Enjoy the natural beauty of one of Birmingham's quiet suburbs in a hotel that stops at nothing to accommodate its guests. The standard suites are large and sleep up to four, but if you're with a group of up to five, the Penthouse Suite is an incredible indulgence at an incredible price. The two-level suite has a loft master bedroom and an incredible amount of living space, giving guests the ability to spread out and forget about cramped conventional rooms. A major road links the hotel to the Hoover area, making this hotel an excellent selection for any guest needing access to the Highway 280 or Hoover areas. Don't forget to bring your golf clubs because the Eagle Point Golf Course (see the golf section in Recreation) is located only 1.5 miles away from the hotel, allowing even short-term guests the ability to squeeze in a few rounds after the day is done. Pets allowed with a $100 non-refundable fee.

Homewood

Homewood holds one of the greatest concentrations of the city's affordable mid-priced lodging, particularly the areas surrounding I-65 at the Lakeshore Drive (exit 255) and Oxmoor Road (exit 256) exchanges, where many visitors tend to stay when they are looking for moderate prices for brief stays in Birmingham. For those looking to shop downtown Homewood's distinctive boutiques, the hip Aloft hotel is an excellent option.

CANDLEWOOD SUITES $–$$
400 Commons Dr., Homewood
(205) 769-9777
www.candlewoodsuites.com

One of three Candlewood Suites in the Birmingham area, this location offers 81 guest rooms with fully equipped kitchen, large recliner, and free movie library to make any stay more enjoyable. For business travelers, an executive desk, speakerphone, and free high speed Internet make conference calls and in-suite work a breeze. The location is home to many chain restaurant options and convenient to I-65.

COMFORT INN HOMEWOOD $$
226 Summit Pkwy., Homewood
(205) 916-0464
www.comfortinn.com

Conveniently located near I-65, this 115-room hotel is typical of the many lodging offerings in the vicinity. Free continental breakfast, public computer with Internet access, in-room desks, on-site meeting facilities, access to copy and fax services, as well as guest laundry are some of the amenities. Non-smoking rooms are available and rooms have free coffee, hair dryers, and wireless Internet access.

HOMEWOOD SUITES BY HILTON BIRMINGHAM–SOUTH/ INVERNESS $$$
215 Inverness Center Dr.
(205) 995-9843
www.hilton.com

One of the nicer offerings in the area, the Homewood Suites by Hilton is a 95-room hotel and a popular destination for those desiring temporary housing in Birmingham. Each suite contains complimentary wired and wireless Internet access, 2 televisions with DVD players, 2 telephones with data ports, separate kitchen with full-size refrigerator, and a coffeemaker and microwave. The rooms also have custom-designed alarm

clock/radio with back-up alarm system, a nice touch. A free hot breakfast buffet each morning is complemented with a reception in the evening, Mon through Thurs, with drinks and light snacks for guests.

SUPER 8 MOTEL HOMEWOOD $
140 Vulcan Rd., Homewood
(205) 945-9888
www.super8.com

A destination for those looking for familiarity and basic comfort for a competitive price, Super 8 Homewood offers just what one would expect. A business center provides the essentials while a free continental breakfast, high speed Internet and gym complete the picture. Pets are allowed. The location is close to a number of chain and local restaurants. Of the 95 total rooms, 5 are suites.

Vestavia Hills & Hoover

Comprising a large geographic area, Vestavia Hills and Hoover offer many disparate south-of-town hotel offerings ranging from the familiar moderately priced chains to higher-end distinctive lodgings such as The Wynfrey Hotel at the Galleria Shopping Mall and the Renaissance Birmingham Ross Bridge Golf Resort & Spa, part of the Robert Trent Jones Golf Trail at Oxmoor Valley.

COURTYARD BY MARRIOTT HOOVER $$–$$$
1824 Montgomery Hwy., Hoover
(205) 988-5000
www.marriott.com

Located south of Birmingham just off I-65 and I-459, the recently renovated Courtyard by Marriot is close to a number of attractions like Riverchase Galleria Mall, Hoover Met Stadium, and other dining and shopping destinations. The 4-floor structure has 140 rooms (13 suites), 2 meeting rooms, and 1,274 square feet of total meeting space. The hotel is smoke free, does not allow pets, and offers wireless Internet in public areas.

HAMPTON INN & SUITES HOOVER GALLERIA $$$
4520 Galleria Blvd., Hoover
(205) 380-3300
www.hamptoninn.com
A popular spot for those coming to town to shop, the Hampton Inn & Suites Hoover Galleria is close to the Riverchase Galleria, one of the largest shopping centers in the Southeast. The 102-room hotel offers a complimentary beverage area as well as free breakfast. Laundry and valet service are provided. All rooms have coffeemakers, hair dryers, irons, and a free in-room movie channel. Pets are not allowed.

MICROTEL INN & SUITES HOOVER $$
500 Jackson Dr., Hoover
(205) 444-3033
www.microtellinn.com
Found just off Highway 150, a busy commercial artery connecting to Highway 31 in Hoover, this Microtel location is in the thick of shops, restaurants, and a host of entertainment options. The hotel provides free local and long distance calls within the continental United States, as well as free high-speed wireless Internet access in rooms. Advance online check-in and checkout is another Microtel convenience. Guest can enjoy HD flat-panel TVs and complimentary continental breakfast.

QUALITY INN $-$$
1485 Montgomery Hwy., Vestavia Hills
(205) 823-4300
www.qualityinn.com

With easy access to I-65 and I-459, location is a perk with this 159-room Quality Inn in Vestavia Hills. Amenities include free deluxe continental breakfast, free coffee in the lobby, free local calls, and a free weekday newspaper. Guests can enjoy an outdoor pool in nice weather. Data-port telephones and access to fax and copy services are on tap for business travelers, and for events, more than 3,200 square feet of banquet and meeting space can hold up to 250 people. Non-smoking rooms are available.

Unique Hotel Experiences

While most Birmingham area hotels are simply that—lodgings, or a place to spend the night out of necessity for travel or business—there are a few destination hotels that are a draw unto themselves for the entertainment options they provide. **Aloft** in SoHo Square offers a hip new getaway popular for local girls'-night-out events that, well, last an entire night. **Ross Bridge** is a lovely new resort, suitable for large weddings and events but also where residents go to get away for a romantic weekend of fine dining, spa treatments, and golf. **The Wynfrey Hotel,** abutting the Riverchase Galleria shopping mall in Hoover, is a few decades old now but still serves as an upscale destination for honeymooners and business executives as well as those from out of town who want a hotel amenable to a serious shopping spree in the sprawling mall.

ALOFT BIRMINGHAM SOHO SQUARE $$$-$$$$
1903 29th Ave. South, Homewood
(205) 874-8455
www.alofthotels.com/birmingham
One of the more intriguing new hotels on the scene, Aloft, a 111-room boutique hotel

in the SoHo Square development in down-town Homewood, appeals to those enjoying modern architecture and a great proximity to some of the city's best shopping. Trendy boutiques, delicious eateries, and a host of unique shops are just beyond the hotel's front doors. The clean lines, hip furnishing, and funky stylings of Aloft set it apart from other area hotels. The rooms range from 285 to 335 square feet and offer 9-foot ceilings, large windows, free Wi-Fi, and 42-inch LCD televisions. Bath amenities were created by Bliss® Spa just for Aloft. Michael's Steak & Sea-food Restaurant, (205-871-9525, www.eat atmichaels.com), one of the city's premier steakhouses, is located on the premises serv-ing certified Hereford beef. The posh WXYZ Bar is a popular meeting spot for before or after dinner drinks.

✳RENAISSANCE BIRMINGHAM ROSS BRIDGE GOLF RESORT & SPA $$$$
4000 Grand Ave., Hoover
(205) 916-7677
www.rossbridgeresort.com

Located on the city's western edge, Ross Bridge Golf Resort & Spa is surrounded by lakes, woods, and rolling hills, setting the stage for an elegant resort experience. From the exterior the hotel's architecture is designed to evoke Old World associations of grand European retreats. The 259-rooom resort offers private balconies so that guests can enjoy the views while the rooms contain amenities like oversize bathrooms with gran-ite counters, tiled bathtubs, and separate showers. It is one of only three hotels in the state to earn a four-diamond rating from AAA. *Travel + Leisure* named it one of the world's top 500 hotels. The 12,000-square-foot spa draws many local residents who want a plush retreat from their everyday

cares. Located on the newest Robert Trent Jones Golf Trail (see Recreation chapter for details), the hotel is a popular spot for golfers intent on playing some serious golf along the trail. At 8,191 yards the course is the third longest golf course in the world.

THE WYNFREY HOTEL $$$–$$$$
1000 Riverchase Galleria, Hoover
(205) 987-1600
www.wynfrey.com

There's a good reason why so many newly-weds in Birmingham head off to The Wynfrey Hotel in Hoover for that special first night before the honeymoon: French chandeliers, Italian marble, 329 well-appointed guest rooms, complimentary shuttle service to the airport, and of course, Spa Japonika, an Aveda spa, for the required pamper-ing after a long busy day. Walking in the hotel, the high ceilings and grand open space create an immediate impression. The rooms are warm and comfortable, deco-rated in a traditional style with warm wood tones and orate, formal touches. For those who want a view, the Presidential Suite, an 1,800-square-foot penthouse suite complete with a Chippendale dining room table, large living room, connecting guest room, and, up the staircase, a spacious bedroom with adjoining sitting area. The suite's rooftop balcony offers panoramic views of the area. Connected to one of Alabama's top tourist destinations, Riverchase Galleria, all guests can walk out of the hotel into more stores such as Macy's, Belk, and more than 200 specialty stores such as the LEGO Store. Many visit the hotel just to dine at Shula's Steak House, one of the Alabama's top steak houses, for custom center cuts of premium Black Angus beef—there are private dining options for hotel guests.

RESTAURANTS

The dining scene in Birmingham constantly catches first-time visitors off guard. It's not just the meat 'n' three style endemic to the South that catches peoples' attention or the surprisingly pervasive Greek influence found in local fare—from hot dog and hamburger joints to barbecue and white-linen establishments. It's more the scope and variety of locally owned restaurants that seems to receive steady media attention in magazines such as *Bon Apetit, Food & Wine, Esquire, The New York Times,* and of course, locally produced *Southern Living.* In fact, I worked for years at a local magazine that primarily focused on the higher-end Over the Mountain audience and don't recall us ever needing to cover anything other than independent restaurants for that monthly column. In a city of Birmingham's moderate size, that's remarkable.

As many residents—and many in the food-writing business in New York or at *Southern Living* here in town—will attest, chef and restaurateur Frank Stitt, has been the figure who has most shaped the city's dining habits. No less than *The New York Times* has credited the third-generation Alabamian with turning Birmingham into a "sophisticated, easygoing showplace of enticing, southern-accented cooking." Having trained with Alice Waters of the renowned Chez Panisse back in the 1970s, Stitt opened the near legendary Highland's Bar & Grill in 1982 to meld French technique and approach with local seasonal Southern flavors. Stitt has gone on to win numerous local and national gastronomic awards. Owner of Highland's Bar & Grill and Bottega, as well as his newest restaurant, Chez FonFon, a casual French bistro, Stitt was using local ingredients before local was cool.

By taking the kind of humble ingredients most Alabamians took for granted when their grandparents cooked, Stitt and others such as Chris Hastings of Hot & Hot Seafood and Chris Dupont of Cafe Dupont have helped secure Birmingham's reputation as the little restaurant town that could. Accordingly, folks from nearby cities often make culinary pilgrimages to town just to visit their favorite chef and perhaps try a new dish. And the local scene has blossomed with new restaurants, urban farms, local purveyors, and new farmers' markets like the Pepper Place Saturday Market (www.pepperplace market.com) springing up all over the city. It's encouraging news for the farm-to-table movement and for those looking for some delicious organic tomatoes!

OVERVIEW

A quick word about the way people in Birmingham (and the state, in general) tend to think about eating. We grow veggies in our suburban back yards. We expect a variety of good produce choices, at home and dining out. It's a contrast to what many modern

Americans are used to. My wife and I, both Birmingham natives, spent a few years in the Midwest, and at one memorable dinner served a vegetarian shepherd's pie to a good friend from the area. He seemed to enjoy it and inquired about the ingredients. "Eggplant, mashed potatoes, mushrooms, garlic, onion, celery, bell pepper, English peas . . . " we said before he interrupted. "English peas, what are those?" he asked. We explained they were the little green peas you dreaded facing back in your elementary school cafeteria. "Oh, well, why don't you just call them *peas*?" he asked incredulously. "Well, let's see, there are English peas, black-eyed peas, field peas, butter peas, crowder peas, purple hulls, snow peas, snap peas, and so on," we rattled off. You have to differentiate somehow!

Finally, detailing every restaurant in the area worth of inclusion would turn this chapter into the start of a new book of its own (and produce its own chapter on barbecue!); therefore this section aims to provide an overview of many of Birmingham's most notable independent restaurants. It's an overview of the region's diversity, both in styles of restaurants and geographic location, though the best concentration of dining options is largely found near the center core and Over the Mountain areas. Restaurants are divided by genres and listed within that by geography. Birmingham is a medium-size town spread out over a wide geographic area, but don't worry: The restaurants listed here are well worth the drive. For fun, see Alabama Tourism's "100 Dishes to Eat in Alabama Before You Die" for a wide assortment of fine and casual dining ideas (www.800alabama.com/yof/topDishes).

Price Code

All the restaurants listed take credit cards and are wheelchair-accessible unless otherwise noted. The price code includes the average price of two dinner entrees. Lunch and breakfast are generally less expensive.

$. . . . . Less than $15
$$ . . . . $15 to $30
$$$ . . . . $30 to $60
$$$$ . . . . More than $60

Chez Fonfon, Birmingham, French, $$, 63

Cocina Superior, Homewood, Mexican, $$, 72

Continental Bakery, Mountain Brook, Bakeries, $, 50

Cosmo's, Birmingham, Pizza, $$, 76

Courtyard 280 Oyster Bar and Grill, Hoover, Grills, Pubs & Sandwiches, $$, 64

Crape Myrtle's Cafe, Homewood, Breakfast & Brunch, $$, 56

Crestwood Coffee Company, Birmingham, Coffee Shops, $, 58

Culinard Cafe, Birmingham, Bakeries, $, 51

Daniel George, Mountain Brook, Contemporary American, $$$, 47

Dave's Pizza, Homewood, Pizza, $$, 76

Demetri's BBQ, Homewood, Barbecue, $$, 53

DeVinci's of Homewood, Homewood, Pizza, $$, 76

Diplomat Deli and Spirits, Vestavia Hills, Grills, Pubs & Sandwiches, $$, 65

Dodiyo's, Homewood, Mediterranean, $$$, 70

Dreamcakes, Homewood, Bakeries, $, 51

Dreamland Bar-B-Que Ribs, Birmingham, Barbecue, $$, 53

Dyron's Lowcountry, Mountain Brook, Seafood, $$$, 77

Edgar's Bakery, Hoover, Bakeries, $, 51

Famous Doodles Cajun Cuisine, Fultondale, Cajun & Creole, $, 57

Fire, Mountain Brook, Cajun & Creole, $$$, 57

Fish Market, Birmingham, Seafood, $$, 78

Flip Burger Boutique, Vestavia, Hamburgers, $$, 66

Fox Valley, Helena, Contemporary American, $$$, 48

Full Moon Bar-B-Que, Birmingham, Barbecue, $$, 53

The Garage Cafe, Birmingham, Grills, Pubs & Sandwiches, $$, 65

Gianmarco's, Homewood, Italian, $$$, 69

Golden Rule Bar-B-Q, Irondale, Barbecue, $$, 54

Golden Temple Cafe, Birmingham, Organic & Vegetarian, $, 75

Green Valley Drugs, Hoover, Grills, Pubs & Sandwiches, $, 65

Hamburger Heaven, Multiple locations, Hamburgers, $, 66

Highlands Bar and Grill, Birmingham, French, $$$, 64

Hot & Hot Fish Club, Birmingham, Seafood, $$$, 78

Jackson's Bar & Bistro, Homewood, Breakfast & Brunch, $$, 57

Jim Davenport's Pizza Palace, Mountain Brook, Pizza, $$, 76

Jim 'n Nick's Bar B Q, Multiple locations, Barbecue, $$, 55

Jinsei Sushi Bar & Lounge, Homewood, Japanese & Sushi, $$$, 69

John's City Diner, Birmingham, Meat 'n' Three, $$, 60

Johnny Ray's Bar-B-Que, Multiple locations, Barbecue, $, 55

Klingler's European Bakery & Cafe, Vestavia, Bakeries, $, 52

La Paz, Mountain Brook, Mexican, $$, 73

Little Savannah, Birmingham, Contemporary American, $$$, 48

Lloyd's Restaurant, Hoover, Meat 'n' Three, $, 60

Lucy's Coffee and Tea, Birmingham, Coffee Shops, $, 58

Maki Fresh, Mountain Brook, Japanese & Sushi, $$, 69

Mandarin House, Hoover, Asian, $$, 49

Milo's Hamburgers, Multiple locations, Hamburgers, $, 67

Miss Myra's Pit Bar-B-Q, Vestavia, Barbecue, $$, 55

Mountain Brook Creamery/ Edgewood Creamery, Mountain Brook, Desserts & Ice Cream, $, 61

Mr. Chen's Authentic Chinese Cooking, Hoover, Asian, $$, 48

Mr. P's Deli, Bluff Park, Grills, Pubs & Sandwiches, $, 65

Nabeel's Cafe and Market, Homewood, Mediterranean, $$, 71

New Orleans Food & Spirits, Vestavia Hills, Cajun & Creole, $$, 58

New York Pizza, Homewood, Pizza, $$, 77

Nikki's West, Birmingham, Meat 'n' Three, $$, 61

O'Carr's Restaurant, Homewood, Grills, Pubs & Sandwiches, $, 66

Ocean, Birmingham, Seafood, $$$, 79

O'Henry's Coffees, Homewood, Coffee Shops, $, 59

Organic Harvest Market & Cafe, Hoover, Organic & Vegetarian, $, 75

Oscar's at the Museum, Birmingham, Breakfast & Brunch, $$$, 57

OT's, Birmingham, Meat 'n' Three, $, 61

Pastry Art Bake Shoppe, Homewood, Bakeries, $, 52

Pho Que Huong, Homewood, Asian, $$, 49

Pita Stop, Birmingham, Middle Eastern, $$, 74

Primavera Coffee Roasters, Vestavia Hills, Coffee Shops, $$, 59

Purple Onion, Hoover, Middle Eastern, $, 74

The Red Cat, Birmingham, Coffee Shops, $, 74

Red Pearl, Homewood, Asian, $$, 59

Rojo, Birmingham, Mexican, $$, 73

Salvatore's Pizza and Pasta, Hoover, Pizza, $$, 77

Sam's Deli and Grill, Homewood, Middle Eastern, $, 74

Savage's Bakery and Deli, Homewood, Bakeries, $, 52

Saw's BBQ, Homewood, Barbecue, $$, 55

Sekisui, Birmingham, Japanese & Sushi, $$, 70

Serendipity Sweets, Vestavia, Desserts & Ice Cream, $, 62

Soho Sweets, Homewood, Desserts & Ice Cream, $, 62

Sol Y Luna, Birmingham, Mexican, $$$, 73

Surin West, Birmingham, Asian, $$, 50

Taj India, Birmingham, Indian, $$, 68

Taziki's Mediterranean Cafe, Multiple locations, Mediterranean, $$, 72

Ted's, Birmingham, Meat 'n' Three, $, 61

Top Hat Barbecue, Blount Springs, Barbecue, $, 56

Trattoria Centrale, Birmingham, Italian, $$, 69

Urban Cookhouse, Homewood, Contemporary American, $$, 48

Urban Standard, Birmingham, Coffee Shops, $, 60

Veranda on Highland, Birmingham, Cajun & Creole, $$$, 58

Yogurt Mountain, Mountain Brook, Desserts & Ice Cream, $$, 63

Zoës Kitchen, Multiple locations, Mediterranean, $$, 72

CONTEMPORARY AMERICAN

AVO RESTAURANT AND DRAM WHISKEY BAR $$$
2721 Cahaba Rd., Mountain Brook
(205) 871-8212
www.avorestaurant.com

A relatively new entry in the Mountain Brook Village dining scene, Avo's posh, upscale restaurant is set in a new brick building and located upstairs from the more casual Dram Whiskey Bar (both owned by Chef Ben Kirk). Influenced by California-style approach ("Avo" being California shorthand for avocado), the restaurant makes use of fresh local ingredients and regional seafood for what it calls a "Cal-abama cuisine" combination. The modern decor is open with large windows, and there's a popular covered terrace outside for fresh-air dining. Meanwhile, Dram, a Scottish term for a pour of whiskey, holds what may be the city's best collection of bourbon and Scotch. It's a full restaurant, too, serving Tennessee and Kentucky cuisine. Try the bacon-infused bourbon for a novel thrill.

BAUMHOWER'S WINGS
RESTAURANT $$
Hoover
www.baumhowers.com

It says something about your product when you're the one everybody compares others to. In Birmingham, and in much of the state, Baumhower's Wings Restaurant is the go-to comparison that comes to mind for fans of the chicken wing. Bob Baumhower, an All-American from the University of Alabama and six-time All-Pro for the Miami Dolphins, opened his first modest wings shop in 1981. Today, the sports-themed restaurants are in seven locations from Mobile to Huntsville. With two locations in Hoover—1001 Doug Baker Blvd. #112, (205) 995-5151 and 4445 Creekside Ave., (205) 403-7474—Baumhower's is a great spot to get your fingers greasy and satisfy your hunger while catching a game. Don't go for the 2-pound basket of wings unless you are a professional.

✳BRICK & TIN $
214 20th St. North, Birmingham
(205) 297-8636
www.brickandtin.com

Quick . . . it's 11:47 a.m. Do you know where your food comes from? At Brick & Tin, you will. Their good pedigree shows: chef/owner Mauricio Papapietro, the former Highlands Bar & Grill Chef de Cuisine, elevates Southern-style ingredients to their proper place. Field pea salads, roasted pork shoulder and country ham Cuban sandwiches on freshly baked bread, Vidalia onion soup with corn and basil—you can't go wrong. The original brick walls and tin tile ceiling give the historic downtown establishment its name while reclaimed wood provides a warm, earthy appeal. After opening in 2010, word quickly spread, transforming the space into one of downtowns hottest lunch spots. Try the deviled eggs. Your grandmamma will forgive you for loving them more than hers.

> **i** Go to Brick & Tin's website prior to dining in order to download their Source Guide, a listing of what quality local food purveyors supply them their food. From grits and veggies to humanely raised beef and hormone/antibiotic free pork, it'll make you feel good about eating there.

DANIEL GEORGE $$$
2837 Culver Rd., Mountain Brook
(205) 871-3266
www.danielgeorgerestaurant.com

Chefs Daniel Briggs and George McMillan are longtime Mountain Brook favorites for their casual contemporary American cuisine that caters to an audience who appreciates the gulf coast seafood, game, and quality local produce. Located in the quaint Mountain Brook Village, the interior is open and elegant, a fitting setting for this white-linen establishment that is widely regarded as one of Birmingham's premier restaurants. The menu changes daily but expect items like red snapper, sautéed scallops, and grilled filet of Angus beef to make routine appearance. It has a reputation for boldly flavored food such as grilled meats and wild game. The wine list is extensive.

FOX VALLEY $$$
6745 Hwy. 17, Helena
(205) 664-8341
www.birminghammenus.com/foxvalley

One of the few established white-linen restaurants that folks in town will drive to dine (Helena is 20 miles south of downtown), Fox Valley quietly goes about its business of offering some of the best out-of-town dining around. Loyal patrons continue to drive from Birmingham, Montgomery and Tuscaloosa to dine at the upscale yet unpretentious restaurant. Don't let the humble, strip mall setting fool you: Fox Valley has won *Wine Spectator Magazine*'s Award of Excellence for years now. The menu changes daily but expect the crowd-pleasing combo of their famous filet mignon and crab cake with brown garlic butter to always be available. Don't leave without trying the Key lime pie.

> **i** When cooking Indian or simply in want of a spread for a humble ham sandwich, Alecia's Tomato Chutney hits the spot. There's nothing to it but tomatoes, sugar, vinegar, ginger, raisins, garlic, red pepper, and salt. Made in Leeds, it's available in many local grocery stores. Foodie John T. Edge, director of the Southern Foodways Alliance, is a fan: That should be reason enough for anyone.

*LITTLE SAVANNAH $$$
3811 Clairmont Ave., Birmingham
(205) 591-1119
www.littlesavannah.com

This Southern bistro nestled in the historic Forest Park neighborhood offers innovative programs like a Community Farm Table and fun cooking classes with owners Maureen and Chef Clif Holt. It makes for fresh ways to experience Little Savannah's distinctive take on food. Known for their wine list and specialty martinis (start with a bee's knees or the spicy peach margarita), the restaurant and bar are also among the city's best for taking familiar regional foods and elevating them to a higher culinary level: Alabama red ranger chicken breast on gumbo risotto with Alecia's tomato chutney aioli, anyone? When you don't know where to go on the weekend, you couldn't do much better than Little Savannah's Sunday brunch. Open for dinner only.

URBAN COOKHOUSE $$
2846 18th St. South, Homewood
(205) 879-0883
www.urbancookhouse.com

Focusing on local ingredients, sustainable practices, and fresh salad and sandwich options, Urban Cookhouse in the center of downtown Homewood practices what it preaches. Before opening the restaurant in 2010, the owners started a small farmers' market in Homewood on Saturdays just across the street from their shop. "Buy local, eat urban" is the password for husband and wife David and Andrea Snyder's new venture: but the password is no secret. The word is out and they quickly adjusted to serving dinner as well as lunch to accommodate the crowds. Local produce fills the salads, wraps, and healthy kid options, as well as great sides like the delicious broccoli salad with grapes, bacon, and sunflower seeds. Try the chipotle braised pork or the grilled pineapple ham sandwich on yeast rolls with hot mustard for a treat. And no French fries to be found!

ASIAN

✳MR. CHEN'S AUTHENTIC
CHINESE COOKING $$
1917 Hoover Court, Hoover
(205) 824-8283
www.mrchenschinesecooking.com
For authentic Taiwanese and regional Chinese dishes, Mr. Chen's is your top choice in Hoover. Indeed, Mr. Chen and his wife used to run Red Pearl, and many fans of his cooking there will certainly recognize much on the menu of his new restaurant. And he's developed quite a new following, as well. A few typical Chinese dishes are scattered about a menu that offers more diverse fare such as cold plates of braised beef shanks and pig ears, steamed buns, garlic spiced bacon, tofu dishes, and whole fish in a hot soy paste. For newcomers, it's a place to experiment and share dishes (so you can try more!). For old hands familiar to Mr. Chen's, it's a chance to enjoy some of the best Chinese in the state. In 2009 the restaurant won Best Chinese Meal in *Birmingham Magazine*. Located in an old strip mall, Mr. Chen's has made real effort to create a welcoming atmosphere.

MANDARIN HOUSE $$
1550 Montgomery Hwy., Hoover
(205) 822-1761
Need a quick Chinese fix for lunch or take-out? Mandarin House, found in your run-of-the-mill strip mall, has been serving up the fried rice for more than 30 years. And while the management has changed, many of the old standbys are just as good as ever. The sizzling rice soup is always a treat for children as

the rice sizzles and pops as the server slides it into the soup, but for many it is the sweet and sour soup that is the main attraction. Tangy and with a zip, it's the ideal start to any dinner. Sesame chicken and Mongolian beef, both sticky and sweet, are delicious.

PHO QUE HUONG $$
430 Green Springs Hwy., Homewood
(205) 942-5400
Where do you go to get your pho? In Birmingham the go-to for traditional Vietnamese cuisine has been Pho Que Huong. Steaming bowls of noodles with various shrimp, pork, or beef options with mounds of bean sprouts, jalapeños, basil, and lime are the big attraction, obviously. Cucumber and shrimp salad, banh mi sandwiches, or a plate of fried tilapia with a cilantro and tomato sauce are just some of the other options. If they've still some left—it's a popular dish and they tend to run out—try the bún riêu (#22A on the menu). It's a tomato broth soup with shrimp and crabmeat balls along with tofu. Delicious! A iced cup of Vietnamese coffee and condensed milk polishes off the palate just right. A recent sprucing up of the interior makes for a nicer dining experience, though it's still a bit short on atmosphere. Nearby in the same strip mall you'll find a Korean restaurant and a Middle Eastern market.

✳RED PEARL $$
243 West Valley Ave., Homewood
(205) 945-9558
www.superorientalmarket.com
Don't let the fact that the best Chinese food in the state is in a supremely modest setting stop you from going inside. You'd miss the city's (and probably the state's) largest market as well as some of the most authentic ethnic dishes in town—there's a reason why

half the clientele or more are typically Asian American. Looking for live tilapia, a wide variety of Chinese and Japanese foods, and the most affordable live lobster in town? This is the place for you. Try the sautéed greens as a side (sweet pea leaves, Chinese broccoli, bok choy, Chinese okra, and more). And don't miss the salted crispy shrimp— you can order them peeled, but for the real thing, order the whole shrimp and eat it, shells and all. The chef prepares each dish to order, so on crowded Friday or Saturday nights it might take a bit longer than usual to get your food—don't worry, it's worth it. A recent shuffling around of the restaurant, seafood market, and grocery inside is a welcome addition.

i Red Pearl's website, www.super orientalmarket.com, incorporates photos of the many Chinese and Japanese dishes they prepare. It's a handy way for those of an experimental bent to see an exotic new dish before ordering it.

SURIN WEST $$
1918 11th Ave. South, Birmingham
(205) 324-1928
www.surinwest.com
After getting his start in Atlanta, Georgia, Surin Techarukpong moved to Birmingham after opening what is now a Five Points South dining landmark, Surin West. Continuously expanded, the original Southside restaurant Surin West is the destination for most residents when they think of Thai food. With three large dining areas, plus the bar, seating is amble, and unless you arrive right at noon, there is not typically much of a wait. Spicy garlic scallops, chicken masaman with avocado, spicy beef salad, and of

course, Thai noodle (pad Thai) are among the favorite dishes. A full sushi bar adds to the offerings: Try the Super Crunch for a delicious treat of smoked salmon, tempura, masago, and special sauce. Menus vary from location to location but expect most of the popular dishes to remain similar to the original Surin West location. Additional locations include: **Surin of Thailand,** 64 Church St., Mountain Brook (205-871-4531); **Surin 280,** 16 Perimeter Park South, Inverness, (205-968-8161); and **Surin Thai Bowl,** 2100 3rd Ave. North, #100, Birmingham (205-297-0996).

BAKERIES

✳CONTINENTAL BAKERY $
1909 Cahaba Rd, Mountain Brook
(205) 870-5584
www.chezlulu.us
Author James Baldwin has a great line from *The Fire Next Time:* "It will be a great day for America, incidentally, when we begin to eat bread again, instead of the blasphemous and tasteless foam rubber that we have substituted for it. And I am not being frivolous now, either." What does this have to do with Continental Bakery? When Carole Griffin, owner/baker/chef, opened the bakery some two decades ago, the stark contrast between the artisanal breads she introduced to Birmingham and the tasteless foam rubber most people ate was striking. After learning the trade in France, Griffin returned to her hometown and begun crafting handmade breads daily from scratch.

Today, Continental Bakery is a Birmingham institution, known for its crusty baguettes, olive boules, flaky croissants, Irish soda bread, and muffins. Located in the quaint English Village, the round English Tudor tower in front provides a charming setting for the distinctive bakery. Try the French feta and kalamata olive baguette or the hand-rolled, kettle-boiled bagels. But certainly, certainly, buy a loaf of the wild yeast sourdough. Leavened with a natural, 20-year-old starter that Griffin patiently developed for more than a year, this is perhaps the single greatest loaf of bread one can taste. A wide assortment of cheeses, delicious desserts, gift hampers, and quick lunch options are available as well. By the way, they serve what many patrons think is the city's best cup of coffee.

i Check the day-old stand to the right of the bagel and croissant case at Continental Bakery. But go first thing in the morning if you want to be picky: The half-price, still-tasty items go fast!

CULINARD CAFE $
1500 1st Ave. North, Birmingham
(205) 314-3456
www.culinardcafe.com
An offshoot of the Culinard Culinary Arts Institute, Culinard Cafe at Innovation Depot is a welcome addition to the downtown dining scene. Located in the Innovation Depot, a business incubation facility in the swankily refurbished old Sears store near the new Railroad Park, the cafe's mod architectural stylings, the use of wood and metal, and the floor-to-ceiling windows make for an open, pleasant vibe. The fact that their breads, pastries, breakfast, and lunchtime offerings are fresh and delicious isn't so bad, either. Try their many flavors of gelato.

Baking fresh breads daily, the cafe's is known for its honey wheat (typically sells out), jalapeño cheddar, raisin walnut, and the goat cheese and tomato herb focaccia—many of which are available Saturday mornings at the popular Pepper Place Saturday Market. Try the pulled chicken salad on croissant or the salmon and brie salad, two customer favorites. The cafe offers complete wedding and birthday cake services as well. Though a solid staff of professional chefs run the cafe—many of whom are Culinard graduates—the cafe is also a learning environment for culinary and pastry arts students doing their internships. It's a win-win for the student and the patrons.

*DREAMCAKES $
960 Oxmoor Rd., Homewood
(205) 871-9377
www.dreamcakes-bakery.com
When dreamcakes (lowercase) settled in to the historic Edgewood shopping area of Homewood, local residents couldn't wait to sample the cupcake creations of owner Jan Moon. Kids and parents salivated impatiently, staring through the glass storefront, waiting for the interior refurbishing to be completed. An alum of the test kitchens of *Southern Living* and *Cooking Light* magazines before opening her first dreamcakes in Cahaba Heights, Moon has been creating wedding cakes in Birmingham for more than two decades. The menu changes by season, but special favorites are nearly always available. Coconut cream, Mississippi mud, caramel sea salt mocha, and simply strawberry should be on everyone's list. The red brick walls, elegant cake displays, and hand-written menu on a large chalkboard on the wall make for an elegant, appealing little shop that sweet tooths both young and old alike love to peruse. Inventive, creative birthday and special occasion cakes are made to order.

EDGAR'S BAKERY $
Four locations, Hoover
(205) 987-0790
www.edgarsbakery.com

Started in 1998 in Inverness, Edgar's soon opened three more locations of their popular bakery in Pelham, Patton Creek, and Greystone, consolidating their position as the go-to bakery for those living in the Hoover area. Known for their cakes, the bakery also offers a wide range of sweets from brownies and cookies to petit fours and various pastries—as well as breads, of course. With their deli menu, Edgar's is a popular spot for lunch and a great cup of coffee. Edgar's offers wholesale orders and their bread and desserts are found in many area restaurants. It's also a good spot to shop for sweet presents, gift items, and assorted food-related goodies as each store offers an eclectic market.

KLINGLER'S EUROPEAN
BAKERY & CAFE $
621 Montgomery Hwy., Vestavia
(205) 823-4560
www.klinglers.com

There's a great old world vibe to Klingler's, a Vestavia hotspot and gathering place for two decades. Serving breakfast, lunch, and Sunday brunch, Klingler's is the place in town for German food, be it strudel, bratwurst, or schnitzel. But it's the bakery that draws most fans. The bakery is known for its Black Forest cheesecake, German chocolate cake, and other German specialties, but they offer a host of desserts and special occasion cakes. Pastries such as apple dumplings, klingle, and plum tarts keep customers coming back for more. Try the fresh-baked Bavarian farmer's rye bread. And be sure to check out their online gift shop full of unique items like antique beer steins, cuckoo clocks, and kitchen products.

PASTRY ART BAKE SHOPPE $
1927 29th Ave. South, Homewood
(205) 877-3852
www.pastryartcakes.com

Maybe it is the perfectly styled cakes and their elaborate designs. Or perhaps the cute little baby bites of caramel, strawberry, turtle, and carrot flavors for sale when you just want a taste rather than a whole cake. Other flavors include marble, chocolate, or vanilla cake covered with chocolate icing and vanilla drizzle. Regardless, women in particular seem to swoon over the baby bites, which could explain why they often sell out of choice flavors the same morning—they literally draw people off the street. Many customers in the store have pre-ordered a cake or baby bites for bridesmaids' luncheons, receptions, weddings, and other events. And then once they're in line for pickup inside the store, they inevitably buy more baby bites. You can't stare at the enticing display case without eventually giving in.

SAVAGE'S BAKERY AND DELI $
2916 18th St. South, Homewood
(205) 871-4901
www.birminghammenus.com/savages/

Founded in 1939 Savage's is one of the last great mid-century Birmingham bakeries still creating on-site from-scratch treats daily. Relocated to downtown Homewood in the 1950s, it has a pedigree that few can match in the city. The deli offers a host of sandwiches, box lunches, salad plates, and delicious sides. The bread is fresh baked, of course. Don't leave without trying a meltaway, a yeast sweet dough rolled in a cinnamon streusel crumble and stuffed with apple, apricot, cream cheese (these sell out!), raspberry, and other delicious fillings. Kids love the gingerbread men, cupcakes, and decorated sugar cookies. Try the cheese straws!

i The day-old shelf often offers great choices, particularly if you get there early enough. And for kids: Download a coloring page from Savage's website, and bring it into the bakery for a free cookie.

BARBECUE

BOB SYKES BARBECUE $
1724 9th Ave. North, Bessemer
(205) 426-1400
www.bobsykes.com

Run by Van Sykes, whose parents opened the first location in 1957, Bob Sykes Barbecue and its distinctive yellow sign is a Bessemer landmark. If you're hungry enough, order the combination plate to sample Sykes' offerings. The sauce, which is sweet and a tad sour, certainly has its admirers: If you find you are one, you can buy it online or in the store. Check the website for a solid bibliography of recommended books about barbecue and southern cooking—a handy guide for those interested in knowing their 'cue better. Bob Sykes, a great personality, was a slow foods proponent before slow food was cool. Rumor has it Bob Sykes opened one of the first drive-through windows in the country, and was one of the first to try to franchise barbecue in the state—a case of too early, too soon, perhaps.

DEMETRI'S BBQ $$
1901 28th Ave. South, Homewood
(205) 871-1581
www.demetrisbbq.com

Open for breakfast, lunch, and dinner, Demetri's is a firm favorite eatery in Homewood since the early 1970s where its location near Highway 31 and Main Street in Homewood made it the dominant barbecue joint south of downtown for years. The Birmingham-Greece food connection continues with Demetri Nakos' son, Sam, still running the family restaurant. As is customary, the sauce is an old family recipe. And like his dad did, Sam only uses a Greek pit master to watch over the pit and its 100-percent hickory smoke. There always seems to be a breakfast crowd at Demetri's, especially on Saturday. The French toast on Texas-style bread is a favorite, as is the tender, moist ham.

DREAMLAND BAR-B-QUE RIBS $$
1427 14th Ave. South, Birmingham
(205) 933-2133
www.dreamlandbbq.com

It's a rare thing for an outsider barbecue outfit to make it in Birmingham, but Dreamland broke the rules and succeeded. The treasured barbecue joint started in Tuscaloosa, Alabama, in 1958 (the same year as Coach Paul "Bear" Bryant started coaching at the university), and since has opened franchises in Birmingham and other cities. Originally serving just ribs and white loaf bread slices, the Dreamland of today is radically different from the simple one "Big Daddy" opened all those years back, but you'll still see Dreamland referenced as one of the top 10 barbecue joints in the country by *USA Today*. In fact, if there's a barbecue establishment in Alabama (or the South, for that matter) that is known around the globe, Dreamland is it. Go with the ribs: Thousands upon thousands of satisfied people have before.

Close-up

B'ham BBQ

There's no way to fully discuss barbecue and what it means to most residents of Birmingham. Suffice it to say, in Birmingham, barbecue is primarily pork (you can, of course, still get chicken and beef). Barbecue is a noun. Proper barbecue is cooked over wood. Slowly. It is not frilly. It is about tradition: When you find the way to do a thing right, you keep doing it that way. That goes for sauces, cuts of meat, and the trust one has in a cook's abilities. Barbecue is something to talk about, to argue its merits, to engage in diatribe, to bond over, but finally, it is something to eat and enjoy. To give an idea of how pervasive the 'cue is to Birmingham culinary culture, since 1920, more than 500 barbecue restaurants have opened in town.

Yes, in Birmingham, one's affinity for barbecue is like the clan system of Scotland: You are born into it and the only way out is through personal revolt or by way of a mixed marriage (your spouse's family devotedly attends another BBQ establishment, meaning you have the option to stray from the 'cue of your upbringing if you so choose). When people say the cult of barbecue is something akin to religion in Alabama, they are only slightly exaggerating. Personally, I was raised Golden Rule Bar-B-Q, flirted with Jim 'N Nicks Bar-B-Q as an adult, and now frequent Saw's BBQ due to a combination of belief and convenience (it's 2 blocks away). But I confess to a secret barbecue agnosticism: Certain claims about the existence or non-existence of a supreme Birmingham barbecue establishment are ultimately unknowable. Consequently, when a plate of hot barbecue with a side of beans and turnip greens is presented to me, I take a sip of my sanctified sweet tea and dig in.

To witness this first hand, try Stokin' the Fire BBQ & Music Festival, a two-day celebration and world-class barbecue competition sanctioned by the prestigious Kansas City Barbeque Society, at Sloss Furnaces National Historic Landmark every August, www.slossfurnaces.com. Hallelujah.

FULL MOON BAR-B-QUE $$
337 Valley Ave., Birmingham
(205) 945-9997
www.fullmoonbbq.com
A relative newcomer, Full Moon was founded by former University of Alabama football assistant coach, Pat James in 1981—though the Maluff brothers now run it. Branching out from just the traditional barbecue staples, Full Moon offers Black Angus beef brisket, hickory smoked turkey, fried catfish, and other items. They are known for their chow-chow, a spicy/sweet relish, as well as their chocolate-dipped "half moon" cookies. Full Moon was recently recognized by Gayot.com as one of the Top 10 BBQ restaurants in the country. There are six locations in the Birmingham-Hoover area. After you're finished and you're trying to digest all the food you've just eaten, take a look at some of the extensive Alabama-related sports memorabilia covering the walls.

GOLDEN RULE BAR-B-Q $$
2504 Crestwood Blvd., Irondale
(205) 956-2678
www.goldenrulebbq.com

Founded in 1891 in Irondale, Golden Rule is one of the oldest barbecue joints in the city, and for more than 40 years was operated by the Stone family. Michael Matsos took over in 1969, and has expanded throughout Alabama (with some 14 locations in the Birmingham-Hoover area). Techniques and styles vary from location to location but the sweet-sour vinegar-base slaw and custom-made barbecue sandwich are two signature items: Request inside or outside meat, depending on your preference. The sauce is tomato-based, like many in the area. Many also think that Golden Rule serves a great hamburger. Golden Rule makes their own pies, and lemon icebox is one of the biggest sellers, though it's hard to beat their fried peach pie. A rarity these days: Irondale, Pinson, and a few other Golden Rule locations still stock the 6-ounce Coca-Cola glass bottles, a tribute to days gone by. Some say Irondale's ribs are the best in town.

✳JIM 'N NICK'S BAR-B-Q $$
Multiple locations
www.jimnnicks.com

Birmingham's most successful expansionist barbecue restaurant (with locations in seven states), Jim 'N Nick's opened in 1985 when Jim Pihakis and son Nick started the restaurant. Focusing on made-from-scratch sides and barbecue authenticity in a culture of fierce barbecue regionalism, Jim 'N Nick's has managed to keep the locals happy—wherever the locals reside. The chain has earned praise from *Saveur* magazine as the "tastiest Birmingham export since Emmylou Harris." With catfish, pulled pork and chicken sandwiches, ribs, addictive cheese muffins, and more, Jim 'N Nick's offers plenty of options for those not inclined toward barbecue. Unusual for a barbecue restaurant, Jim 'N

Nick's has shown a serious commitment to local and sustainable food sourcing. A good corporate citizen, Jim 'N Nick's is highly visible and involved in supporting the efforts of those looking to better the Birmingham community. There are seven locations in the Birmingham-Hoover area.

JOHNNY RAY'S BAR-B-QUE $
Multiple locations
www.johnnyraysbbq.com

Started in 1954 by none other than Johnny Ray, this old-school Birmingham barbecue joint has four locations in the Birmingham-Hoover area. Ask most people about Johnny Ray's and the first thing they'll mention are the delicious pies made from recipes developed by Johnny's wife, Honey. Banana, lemon, chocolate, and coconut cream, the pies keep people coming back for more and are a popular pickup item for holidays and parties.

MISS MYRA'S PIT BAR-B-Q $$
3278 Cahaba Heights Rd., Vestavia
(205) 967-6004
www.missmyrasbbq.com

As far as barbecue loyalty goes, one would be hard pressed to find more solid devotees than those of Myra Grissom Harper's. Run by Myra and family, this Cahaba Heights stalwart has been drawing in the faithful since 1985. In the beginning, it was just a convenience store serving barbecue until the word spread. Eventually barbecue took over the whole operation, and Miss Myra's ribs, beef, pork, chicken, and sausage gained more notoriety. Though the ambience is decidedly down-home, the sides are fresh, the signature white sauce is a draw, and many feel the ribs are among the best in town. Universally, Miss Myra's seems to do so much of every type of barbecue right.

*SAW'S BBQ $$
1008 Oxmoor Rd., Homewood
(205) 879-1937
www.sawsbbq.com

It's rare for folks to switch barbecue allegiances lightly. However, allegiances were abandoned at the drop of a hat when Mike Wilson, a trained chef and former employee of *Cooking Light* magazine, opened Saw's in 2009 in the historic Edgewood neighborhood of Homewood. The menu is simple, and the food is served in plastic baskets with wax paper, largely due to the size limitations of the small space it occupies. But Saw's secret is that everything there—from the smoked chicken with white barbecue sauce to the ribs—is almost universally excellent. The sides vary by season, though the signature three-cheese mac and cheese is nearly always available. The turnip greens are just right, requiring no additional pepper sauce to flavor. End with the homemade banana pudding. Ask Mike where he got the acronym S.A.W. for his restaurant and signature sauce—a thin tangy, vinegary delight that is perhaps more North Carolina than Alabama.

TOP HAT BARBECUE $
8725 Hwy. 31, Blount Springs
(256) 352-9919

Located 30 miles north of downtown, Top Hat has been a barbecue destination since 1952, drawing from Blount Springs and well beyond. Run by the Pettit family since the late 1960s, the customers come, drawn by the lasting reputation and the knowledge that the barbecue is cooked over hickory the way it always has been. Top Hat prospered along the busy highway, yet even today after I-65 bypassed the restaurant, devotees continue to frequent the establishment. The distinctive dark interior has a comfortable

quality to it, the way an old barbecue joint should. Interestingly, the original tomato-based sauce comes from the Waldorf-Astoria Hotel in New York—though the family has changed it slightly over the years. In addition to the pork sandwich, try the catfish fillets.

BREAKFAST & BRUNCH

BOGUE'S RESTAURANT $
3028 Clairmont Ave. South, Birmingham
(205) 254-9780

A Lakeview neighborhood staple since the 1940s, Bogue's is a reassuring throwback to the diners of yesteryear with its orange vinyl booths and Spartan interior. The breakfast is simple and without pretensions. You know what you're getting: eggs, grits, and the usual. Try the sweet roll. For lunch, the vegetable plates are the way to go. Bogue's is open Sunday but does not serve dinner. A proposal before the city to raze Bogue's, the adjacent service station, and Birmingham Fire Station No. 22 to build a Walgreen's is on the table. Here's hoping it doesn't happen.

> **i** There are many other great restaurants in town that offer brunch, including Avo (www.avorestaurant.com), Chez Lulu (www.chezlulu.us), Little Savannah (www.littlesavannah.com), Original Pancake House (www.originalpancakehouse.com), and Veranda on Highland (www.verandaonhighland.com).

CRAPE MYRTLE'S CAFE $$
2721 18th St. South, Homewood
(205) 879-7891
www.cmycafe.com

A breath of breakfast fresh air a few years back when it opened, Crape Myrtle's Cafe is the type of quality breakfast and brunch restaurant Homewood had been missing. Set inside the Little Professor Bookstore, there are plenty of book and magazine browsing options to indulge while waiting to be served. Crape Myrtle's serves lunch and dinner, as well. As always, it's the little details that make for a positive dining experience. Sweet potato gratin, white cheddar grits, pepper bacon, country ham, chicken apple sausage, and other gourmet touches make breakfast a joy. Similarly, the brunch menu features delicious items like oatmeal brulée, smoked trout, house benedict, and other tasty options. Granola with yogurt and fruit and fresh juices are healthy options.

JACKSON'S BAR & BISTRO $$
1831 28th Ave. South, Homewood
(205) 870-9669
www.jacksonsbarandbistro.com
Located in SOHO Square, Jackson's modern, roomy interior and bold colors are a contrast to many of the breakfast and brunch destinations in town. That's largely because the bar and bistro is seen as more of a hip lunch and dinner destination. But on Saturday and Sunday, Jackson's brunches out, serving a host of breakfast items sure to please any palate. Omelets to order, corned beef hash, salad Lyonnaise, and even a brunch pizza with scrambled eggs, are just some of the items available. A good selection of teas and alcoholic beverages like kir royale and peach mimosas add a dash of fun.

✳OSCAR'S AT THE MUSEUM $$$
Birmingham Museum of Art
2000 Rev. Abraham Woods Jr. Blvd.,
Birmingham
(205) 254-2775
www.oscarsatthemuseum.com

If location matters it's certainly an advantage to have the Birmingham Museum of Art as your restaurant's backdrop. Under the management of A Social Affair and headed by chef Lorrin Rames, Oscar's focuses on fresh, sourcing as many foods as possible from local purveyors like the Jones Valley Urban Farm just a few blocks away. Lunch is the main draw, but every other Sunday, brunch is an event. Field peas with okra, Gulf shrimp with tomato gravy and grits, fried chicken, and redeye gravy are just a few typical items served at brunch.

i Museum members get 10 percent off Oscar's brunch. But be sure to make reservations by phone or email. Tables will only be held 15 minutes past the reserved time, after which they will be released.

CAJUN & CREOLE

FAMOUS DOODLES CAJUN CUISINE $
1415 Decatur Hwy., Fultondale
(205) 849-4444
www.officialdoodles.com
Set just north of town in Fultondale, Doodles has made a name for itself serving Cajun specialties such as etouffee, muffuletta, gumbo, po boys, and boudin. Doodles also has their own line of spices and mixes such as red beans and rice, dirty rice, shrimp Creole, jambalaya, and more available for order online. For those not crazy about Cajun, there are plenty of conventional options like chicken tenders, chili, hot dogs, and hamburgers. Don't miss their 10-percent off promotion on Tuesday.

FIRE $$$
212 Country Club Rd., Mountain Brook
(205) 802-1410
www.firebirmingham.com

Starters include turtle soup, truffle fries, and crab claws. There's a fancy Creole/Cajun theme to many of the items such as the po boys, fried oysters, and muffaletta. Entrees like filet mignon, crab cakes and lamb shank are often accompanied by distinctive sauces such as crawfish butter, charred tomato vinaigrette, or in the case of Fire's delicious shrimp and grits, a buerre blanc drizzle. It's one of the few places in Mountain Brook where you can sit outside and enjoy your meal. Owner and executive chef Steve Luther has fashioned a casual, neighborhood environment serving the kinds of Southern food that Alabamians recognize—yet with a haute twist. They serve a great Bloody Mary.

NEW ORLEANS FOOD & SPIRITS $$
1919 Kentucky Ave., Suite 101,
Vestavia Hills
(205) 822-7655
www.wix.com/jonrobert/nofsvestavia

With sister restaurants in New Orleans, New Orleans Food & Spirits provides an authentic take on the Creole recipes so many love. Crawfish corn soup, Creole gumbo, shrimp and grits, catfish Loosianne and the de rigor red beans and rice are just some of the delicious fare available. There's also a large selection of salad for those wanting a lighter option. End the night with some beignets. An outdoor covered patio with black wrought iron railing goes a long way to creating the right New Orleans atmosphere, but one wonders how this cornerstone restaurant in the Vestavia Hills City Center would do in a better location.

✳VERANDA ON HIGHLAND $$$
2220 Highland Ave. South, Birmingham
(205) 939-5551
www.verandaonhighland.com

Set in one of Birmingham's grand old homes on Highland Avenue, those appreciating historical character will enjoy their visit to Veranda on Highland. Warm wood tones contrast pleasantly with white linen tablecloths while turn-of-the-century details run throughout. Surrounded by redwood cabinets in a private wine room, the chef's table is just one of several spots that are perfect for an intimate dinner party or gathering. In addition to a long main dining room with bar, there's a small sunroom, the private Hemingway Room and board room, and an outdoor patio. Keep in mind the seasonal nature of Veranda's menu, but one could do worse than start with Louisiana softshell crawfish with mirliton avocado slaw and smoked jalapeño butter. Entrees like the New Orleans–style barbecued jumbo shrimp and pork porterhouse with Lyonnaise new potatoes, braised cabbage, and Jack Daniel's Creole mustard honey show the French and Creole influences of executive chef Tom Robey, who spent nearly two decades at the celebrated Commander's Palace in the Crescent City.

COFFEE SHOPS

CRESTWOOD COFFEE COMPANY $
5512 Crestwood Blvd., Birmingham
(205) 595-0300

A small, charming coffee enclave in a nondescript shopping center, Crestwood Coffee fills a caffeine void for the Crestwood/Avondale crowd. There are a wide variety of espresso drinks, breakfast options, and pastries. The owner and baristas do a fine job of making regulars and drop-ins alike feel welcome. Wi-Fi is free. Expect the usual suspects of ex-pats huddled together watching Dutch or English soccer matches in HD. They serve

Higher Ground Coffee, a local roaster of fine organic fair trade coffee.

✳LUCY'S COFFEE AND TEA $
2007 University Blvd., Birmingham
(205) 328-2007
www.lucyscoffeeandtea.com

When you think coffee downtown, it's hard not to think of Lucy's with a smile. A longtime downtown fixture, Lucy's began selling coffee from a cart across the street before opening the cozy little shop a couple years later. With the warm colors, and comfy couches and chairs, Lucy's is the perfect coffee nook. She's still there today, selling espresso drinks, specialty teas, soups, and sandwiches Mon through Fri. "The Board," a chalkboard behind the register keeps track with customers' tabs on an honor system—as well as tracks the occasional walk-in who forgot their wallet. A testament to how loyal Lucy's customers are? The Starbucks that opened around the corner on 20th Street is now out of business. There's free Wi-Fi, of course.

O'HENRY'S COFFEES $
2831 18th St. South, Homewood
(205) 870-1198
www.ohenryscoffees.com

The oldest pedigree of the city's coffee houses, O'Henry's Coffees opened in 1993 in the historic downtown Homewood commercial district. Popular with moms-on-the-go, downtown merchants, and Bible study groups, the shop also has a small retail space selling coffee products. A sister company roasts the coffee house's beans as well as acts as a wholesale roasting endeavor for various markets, restaurants, and bakeries, making O'Henry's a great spot to purchase fresh roasted coffee by the pound. O'Henry's has several retail locations, in Brookwood

(205-870-1148), Regions/Harbert Tower (205-323-1198), Samford University, and St. Vincent's East Hospital (205-838-3420).

PRIMAVERA COFFEE ROASTERS $$
4133 White Oak Dr., Vestavia Hills
(205) 969-1177
www.primaveracoffee.com

For the serious coffee and espresso aficionados, this little Cahaba Heights specialty coffee roaster has almost single-handedly turned the coffee world around in Birmingham when the store opened in 2006. Generally recognized as the city's premier roaster of beans, many of the cities finest restaurants and cafes serve Primavera coffee. The shop itself, hidden away on a side street near Miss Myra's Pit Bar-B-Q, is fairly non-descript from the outside. Inside, warm orange walls, hardwood floors, and spare modern furnishings all serve notice that it is the gas-fired coffee roaster and large mounds of bagged coffee beans that are the focal point of this establishment. Well, that and the espresso-based drinks the barista on duty makes for those fortunate enough to live or work near the shop. Primavera uses organic ingredients when possible, and the quality of the beans they roast mean drinks are slightly more than other coffeehouses, as are the beans: a 12-ounce bag of espresso is $11, and coffee can go as high as $14. But it is so worth it.

THE RED CAT $
2901 2nd Ave. South, Birmingham
(205) 616-8450
www.theredcatcoffeehouse.com

Located in a large industrial space in the charming Martin Biscuit Building in Lakeview, The Red Cat enjoys a surfeit of charm and atmosphere as great natural light bathes the space. Besides espresso drinks and several signature lattes, the coffeehouse offers panini, deli sandwiches, wraps, and salads. Their beans are primarily fair-trade and are roasted in-house, and the coffee brewed by extraction, a mix of both the drip brew and French press process. On weekends, The Red Cat frequently hosts live acoustic singer/songwriters in concert.

✳URBAN STANDARD $
2320 2nd Ave. North, Birmingham
(205) 250-8200

A great, inviting European atmosphere in a historic old storefront, Urban Standard quickly became the hot spot to grab a quick breakfast or cup of coffee after it opened in 2007. Proprietor Tomek Wrzesien, an artist and native of Poland, filled it with charming artwork, antiques, and curiosities flanked by the exposed brick and plaster walls. A draw for creatives, professionals, hipsters, curious suburbanites, and loft dwellers from the surrounding district, "Urban," as it is often affectionately called, manages to be a bit of everything to everyone. It doesn't hurt that the coffee from local roaster Primavera is excellent. Try the homemade cupcakes.

MEAT 'N' THREE

For those not familiar with the term, "meat 'n' three" is basically the down-home, old-fashioned cooking that many Southerners grew up enjoying at home. It's what Grandma used to make whenever you visited for Sunday dinner. Some will call it a "blue plate" (don't try that in Birmingham unless you want a vacant stare) and still others "Southern comfort food" or even "soul food" in some instances. But really, the venerable meat 'n' three combination transcends race or economic divisions. It obliterates the importance of educational attainment. It comes down to a simple choice of one meat (beef, fish, chicken, pork) and loads upon loads of vegetables. That's something everyone loves, and everyone can agree upon.

BLUFF PARK DINER $
591 Shades Crest Rd., Hoover
(205) 824-4320

What you see is what you get at the Bluff Park Diner (formerly Bert's on the Bluff). The cafeteria-style meat 'n' three offers homestyle cooking such as fried chicken, turnip greens, black-eyed peas, meat loaf, country-fried steak, catfish, fried okra, mac and cheese, and the usual suspects. An added attraction, the view from atop Shades Mountain offers a wonderful panorama of the Oxmoor Valley below.

JOHN'S CITY DINER $$
112 21st St. North, Birmingham
(205) 322-6014
www.johnscitydiner.com

A longtime downtown favorite, John's City Diner received a much-needed facelift and, indeed, culinary transformation a few years back, bringing the landmark back into relevance. With a strong emphasis on Southern cuisine and ingredients, the diner now adds Asian, Mexican, and Creole touches to one of the more inventive and fun menus in town. Try the fried green tomato stack or the kung fu shrimp with sweet chili glaze and honey-soy drizzle on ginger slaw with sesame seeds. For dinner, prime rib, meat loaf with red wine mushroom gravy, or blackened Atlantic salmon vie for your attention. And there's a host of fresh vegetable sides, burgers, and blue plate offerings. Watch for half-price bottles of wine on Thursdays.

LLOYD'S RESTAURANT $
5301 Hwy. 280, Hoover
(205) 991-5530

As long-time residents know, Lloyd's is the original Highway 280 landmark, dating back to the days when the busy thoroughfare was just a curvy two-lane road heading over Double Oak Mountain and on to Lake Martin and Auburn beyond. Back then, sighting the comfort food restaurant meant you were in the country; today, in its modern location some 5 miles south of I-459, it's right in the middle of everything. But not to worry, the fried onion rings, fried chicken, chili, barbecue, and massive plastic glasses of iced tea are still the same. Plain Southern family fare in plum-colored booths, as expected.

i Don't you dare use your cell phone while ordering in Nikki's cafeteria line. Especially if it's your first visit, you'll need all your faculties to choose between the many vegetable choices, and you will receive no pity from the regulars not accustomed to waiting while you try to make up your mind and ask questions. Better yet, go with someone who knows the ropes. It's an experience unto itself.

✴NIKKI'S WEST $$
233 Finley Ave. West, Birmingham
(205) 252-5751
www.nikiswest.com

Bankers, construction workers, lawyers, day laborers, politicians, African Americans, Whites, and Latinos all merge at Nikki's West, the quintessential Birmingham meat 'n' three. Nikki's great Southern food trumps race, educational background, and profession. Owners Teddy and Pete Hontzas took over the business after their father, Gus Hontzas,

passed away, and the quality and staggeringly extensive menu of vegetables, meats, and desserts is legendary. From greens and rutabagas to black-eyed peas and fried green tomatoes, you could visit five times a week and try something new each time. Be sure to get a cornbread and yeast roll: They come with your meal.

OT'S $
720 29th St. South, Birmingham
(205) 323-6727
www.birminghammenus.com/ots

Not being solely a country-cooking establishment is no reason to short a mention of the great meat 'n' three offerings of Ot's Neighborhood Sports Grill in the Lakeview District. Specials change daily, and all the usual suspects are there: chopped steak, baked chicken, collards, okra and tomatoes, boiled cabbage, and snapper fingers, as well as some pleasant departures like crawfish pie, dirty rice, and salmon croquettes. Get there early in nice weather to secure a seat outside on the concrete tables.

TED'S $
328 12th St. South, Birmingham
(205) 324-2911
www.tedsbirmingham.com

With its distinctive sign out front, Ted's has been a downtown standby since the 1970s. About a decade ago, the new owners added to the meat 'n' three an infusion of Greek dishes like souvlaki and salads that, along with interior renovations, freshened up the menu without compromising the diner's character. Inside, the simple booths, Formica top tables, and cafeteria-style arrangement seem the perfect fit for an establishment with a loyal clientele who know what they want, and get it at Ted's.

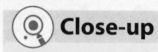

Close-up

Sweet Tea

Throughout Alabama and most of the South, if you order iced tea, you're likely to get sugar-sweetened iced tea where the sugar is added while the beverage is still warm. This especially applies in more traditional diners and meat 'n' three joints. It will be served cold in an ice-filled glass (or Styrofoam, depending the size of the establishment). When you ask for "tea," this is what you get, and it is deliberately so sweet that diabetics should take warning. In more contemporary restaurants, this tradition is fading, sadly—of course, in 2006 McDonald's began offering sweet tea in thousands of locations in the South, an ironic nod to tradition coming from a fast food giant.

Why always cold? Well, because it is often hot in the South, and cold water or ice was historically something of a luxury of the rich—as was tea itself. Truvy Jones, a character from *Steel Magnolias,* calls sweet tea the "house wine of the South." It's an apt description for a drink that is commonly found on many dinner tables year-round in Alabama. It is difficult to imagine a formal dinner without a pitcher of sweet tea "sweating" on the table. And since many conservative Christians frown on wine and beer (really, any alcoholic drink), sweet tea certainly fills the void even today. An interesting side note: Prior to World War II, most sweet tea in the South was brewed from green tea—as an Allied nation, our supplies to green tea were cut off and the United States began importing black tea from British India—today it is primarily made from black tea.

DESSERTS & ICE CREAM

MOUNTAIN BROOK CREAMERY/ EDGEWOOD CREAMERY $
2715 Cahaba Rd., Mountain Brook
(205) 870-0092

Offering handmade shakes, sundaes, ice cream cakes and Only 8 frozen yogurt (8 calories per ounce and no fat or artificial ingredients), Mountain Brook and Edgewood Creameries are neighborhood favorites for kids and adults of all ages. Situated in Mountain Brook Village and Edgewood (936 Oxmoor Rd., 205-874-1999), respectively, both locations enjoy a historic setting that provides a great deal of charm. Expect lots of walk-in traffic from nearby neighborhoods, especially after school lets out.

SERENDIPITY SWEETS $
2518 Rocky Ridge Lane, Vestavia
(205) 834-8263

Since opening in 2008, this neighborhood favorite has become known as a hangout on Rocky Ridge for those sweet tooths looking to indulge in ice cream and treats. There are frozen coffee drinks, Mexican ice pops, sundaes, shakes, ice cream cakes, SnoBiz, and more. On the candy side, gummy bears, sour candies, truffles, hand-dipped pretzels, and other items offer just about anything you need to spoil your dinner or complement a full stomach. Serendipity Sweets also hosts birthday parties and makes custom cakes. Call for reservations.

SOHO SWEETS $
1830 29th Ave. South, Suite 110, Homewood
(205) 871-4420
www.sohosquare.info/sweets.php
Prepare for sugar overload. With something like 100 sweets for purchase by the pound, SoHo Sweets is the modern incarnation of the corner sweets shop from days gone by. Colorful candies, chocolates, homemade cookies, cheesecakes, and other treats line the small store. Expect to see kids lined up at the soda bar enjoying fountain drinks, floats, shakes, and icees. Located in the SOHO Square development downtown Homewood, the shop stays open later on the weekends, attracting an older crowd looking for that special sweet bite to top off their meal.

YOGURT MOUNTAIN $$
3000 Cahaba Village Plaza, Suite 120, Mountain Brook
(205) 970-7778
www.yogurtmountain.com
With 16 rotating flavors of frozen yogurt paired with 50 toppings, Yogurt Mountain may be overwhelming for adults but to children, it is heaven. A relatively new concept, the idea is cafeteria-style self-serve setup with a pay-by-the-ounce scheme that can add up if you're not too careful. There is fruit, sauces, candy, nuts and a host of great toppings to choose from. Fat free and no sugar or low fat options abound. A second store is located in Tuscaloosa, 1800 McFarland Blvd. East, Suite 605.

FRENCH

*CAFE DUPONT $$$
113 20th St. North, Birmingham
(205) 322-1282
www.cafedupont.net

One of the most esteemed chefs in town, Chris Dupont's restaurant is reminiscent of the typical Parisian bistro. Nestled in an 1870s storefront downtown, the brick walls and original floors provide an elegant background fitting the excellent cuisine. Natural light pours in the windows during lunch, illuminating the wonderful pains taken to preserve the character of the historic space.

A longtime proponent of local growers, Dupont's lunch and dinner menu reflects the best of what area purveyors offer by way of fresh fruit, vegetables, and organic offerings. Look carefully at the selections each day, and you'll spy a tell-tale sign of Dupont's New Orleans background and culinary heritage. Signature items include buttermilk fried chicken with lemon basil sauce, fried oysters in cayenne butter sauce and horseradish crème fraîche, seared scallops with goat cheese soufflé, and black sesame-crusted tuna. End your meal with coffee and Dupont's beignets buried in mounds of powdered sugar. The expanded bar makes for a great downtown meeting place or spot to prolong the anticipation before your meal.

*CHEZ FONFON $$
2007 11th Ave. South, Birmingham
(205) 939-3221
Birmingham cannot get enough of Frank Stitt. And rightly so, considering his newest culinary adventure. Chez Fonfon, the corner bistro at Five Points on Southside, is a neighborhood destination and hangout for locals out for an evening on the town. Call it cultivated French casual. The old wooden French bistro tables from 1930s, marked-up floor, antique light fixtures, and long bar make for a relaxed atmosphere. That they have no tablecloth speaks volumes for Chez Fonfon. Reservations are not taken.

Specials change daily, and the weather and season influences the lightness or fullness of the food. But standards such as the hamburger Fonfon, the charcuterie platter, the shrimp and avocado salad with sauce remolded, griddled ham and cheese, and others remain year-round. The trout with brown butter, capers, lemon, and haricots vert comes in a golden crispy crust and has a healthy, light feel to it. And it doesn't get more bistro than steak frites: simply cooked meat with a pile of fries. Bon appétit!

✳HIGHLANDS BAR AND GRILL   **$$$**
2011 11th Ave. South, Birmingham
(205) 939-1400
www.highlandsbarandgrill.com
No doubt, far more has been written about Highlands and Chef Frank Stitt than any other restaurant or chef in the state. What's left to say but to second all the press, the awards, and the acclaim heaped upon the Cullman, Alabama, native? Most recently the James Beard Foundation nominated Highlands Bar and Grill for 2009's Most Outstanding Restaurant. Stitt received the James Beard Award for Best Chef/Southeast in 2001, and was nominated in 2008 for Outstanding Chef. The atmosphere of the Five Points neighborhood setting adds a cultured, historical appeal to the experience of dining at Highlands.

Is it a classic "French" restaurant? No, not exactly, but the daily menu is informed by classic French techniques while relying on the native foods of Alabama. Fresh seafood from the Gulf of Mexico, locally sourced fruits and vegetables, and stone-ground grits are typical of the changing menu, but so is roast quail stuffed with foie gras—and bourbon. Call it Deep South meets South of France. Highlands is distinctively American, but hums inside with the busy glow of the best French bistros. The staff is phenomenally knowledgeable and educated daily on the latest wine offerings or that evening's specials. Does Highlands deserve its laudable ranking of fifth on *Gourmet* magazine's list of the top 50 best restaurants in the United States? You better believe it.

i   A fan of Frank Stitt's approach to food? Then try out his two enormously popular cookbooks, *Frank Stitt's Southern Table* and *Frank Stitt's Bottega Favorita: A Southern Chef's Love Affair with Italian Food.*

GRILLS, PUBS & SANDWICHES

BILLY'S BAR AND GRILL   **$$**
2012 Cahaba Rd, Mountain Brook
(205) 879-2238
www.billysbarandgrill.com
Nestled in the charming English Village, Billy's has been a popular lunchtime and after-work spot since the late 1970s. The corner bar and grill benefits from the appealing Tudor stylings of the 1920s village development. The food is unassuming pub fare, offering a good grilled chicken sandwich, hamburger, club, and Rueben as well as a choice of salads and wraps. A new location at 4520 Overton Rd., Birmingham (205-956-2323) continues the tradition.

COURTYARD 280 OYSTER BAR
   AND GRILL   **$$**
4618 Hwy. 280, Hoover
(205) 980-9891
One of the south-of-town hotspots, Courtyard 280 serves American-style food with an emphasis on seafood. And good times. Live music can usually be found seven nights a

week, but happy hour is the time to go for fun and people-watching—and for enjoying the free buffet and drink specials. You'll find weekly events like pool or poker tournaments, Wii games, and plenty of flat-screen televisions to enjoy your favorite sports team.

DIPLOMAT DELI AND SPIRITS $$
1425 Montgomery Hwy., Suite 101, Vestavia Hills
(205) 979-1515
www.diplomatdeli.com

For nearly 30 years Diplomat Deli has been serving food and spirits in Vestavia Hills. Rubens, muffalettas, Long Island subs, BLTs, bagels, and a host of specialty hot and cold sandwiches made to order make the deli a popular lunchtime spot. With a large selection of wine—and over 200 beers in stock, including high-gravity—Diplomat Deli also serves as an impromptu package store for the neighborhood.

*THE GARAGE CAFE $$
2304 10th Terrace South, Birmingham
(205) 322-3211
www.garagecafe.us

If it's atmosphere and street credibility you're looking for with your beer and sandwich, the Garage is what you're after. Cited by *GQ* magazine as the number-three bar in "The World's Best Places to Fly To," there's an undiluted sense of originality to the place. Winding wisteria, cement sculpture, loads of dusty antiques, and old iron gates greet you in the courtyard area outside the bar itself. The space used to be where the city's elite stored their cars in the 1920s. Today, the locked stalls replete with antiques of all sorts and sizes looks like a massive estate sale gone awry. In the warmer months you'll often find live music. For sandwiches, just choose your

meat, bread, and toppings—and choose a beer buried under all the ice. Bring cash; that's all they take.

i Fritz, owner of The Garage Cafe, might sell you an item from this overflowing, permanent estate sale. Or he might not. You never know. Ask an employee when might be a good time to meet him for an appointment.

GREEN VALLEY DRUGS $
1915 Hoover Court, Hoover
(205) 822-1151

A drugstore and soda fountain since Hoover was just a tiny blip on Highway 31, Green Valley Drugs is like a trip back in time for many long-time area residents. With vinyl upholstery and round steel stools, the lunch counter looks like it hasn't changed since the early 1960s when it was one of the main dining options in the area. Though Hoover has radically grown since that time, Green Valley Drugs' lunch counter keeps doing what it has always done best. Try the burger or BLT. Be sure to enjoy a thick chocolate milkshake made in the dented tin canister just like it has been for decades. There's no reason to change something when you've got it down just right.

MR. P'S DELI $
813 Shades Crest Rd., Bluff Park
(205) 823-6136
www.mrpdeli.com

A great old Bluff Park institution, Mr. P's has the down-home, comfortable feel of an establishment that knows its customers and what they want: fresh deli and breakfast sandwiches. Everything else is a bonus. A good source for food gift boxes, tailgating items during football season, and of course, a great cut of steak or pork, Mr. P's is also known for their Pilleteri's Liquid Marinade. That and other Birmingham products like Ollie's World's Best Bar-B-Q sauce, Sneaky Pete's Hot Dog Sauce, John's Dressing, and others are available at www.pilleteri.com.

O'CARR'S RESTAURANT $
2909 18th St. South, Homewood
(205) 879-2196
www.ocarrs.com
When the same old sandwich or burger just doesn't cut it, O'Carr's is where many Over the Mountain denizens head for a healthy alternative to the usual lunch fare. Best chicken salad in Birmingham? Many people think so. From fruit and cheese plates to poached pear salad and various sandwiches, there's always something fun and different to try. With the brightly colored chairs, white table clothes, and framed pictures and curiosities on every inch of wall space, there's also a funky atmosphere to the tiny original restaurant in downtown Homewood. It's not your grandmother's tearoom. Additional locations are at 150 Cahaba Heights Village Rd., Cahaba Heights (205-967-4173), and 300 Richard Arrington Jr. Blvd., Birmingham (205-777-4002).

HAMBURGERS

BAHA BURGER $
4745 Chace Circle, Hoover
(205) 682-6980
Surfboards, grass skirts, and other surfer-dude accoutrement provide a fun theme to this serious burger joint. Choose from Angus, chicken, salmon, pork, lamb, or turkey—as well as veggie—for your burger. Or build your own with numerous cheese, tops, and buns to choose from on the menu. Even the

sides freshen up the typical French fry option with offerings like fruit and sweet potato fries. But it's the details that make the difference: Try the grilled pork loin burger with ginger lime aioli, provolone, and romaine or a lamb burger with roasted red peppers, feta, and tzatziki sauce. A second location is at 3439 Colonnade Pkwy., Vestavia (205-969-7998).

FLIP BURGER BOUTIQUE $$
220 Summit Blvd., Vestavia
(205) 968-2000
www.flipburgerboutique.com
Flip Burger Boutique is not your Daddy's hamburger, no matter how good your Daddy's hamburger is. And that's the point of this posh, design-conscious chain with one location in both Birmingham and Atlanta, Georgia. *Food and Wine Magazine* and even the *Wall Street Journal* have taken notice. The brainchild of creative director and chef, Richard Blais, Flip brings his creativity and molecular gastronomy to the humble burger in Birmingham in the upscale environs of the Summit. Steak tartare with garlic and capers, country fried beef with pimento cheese, spicy Thai chicken with smoked mayo and pickled carrots—the range of burgers and the creative possibilities are a delight. Try the Krispy Kreme–flavored milkshake.

> **i** It's not a hamburger joint by any stretch, but *Birmingham Magazine* gave a nod to V. Richards Market and Cafe's James Beard Burger (along with Jinsei, VJ's on the Runway, Blackwell's, Rogue Tavern, Velma's Place, Chicago Mike's, and Dram Whiskey Bar, among others) as the best hamburgers in town in a 2010 issue. www.vrichards.net.

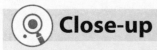

Close-up

Hot Dogs, the Greek Way

Birmingham's culinary outlook is of a decidedly sauce-based culture, be it hot dogs or barbecue. Here, hot dogs are arguably as much an all-American as they are an all-Greek food. And that's a good thing. A few things first: In Birmingham, hot dogs are typically grilled rather than boiled as they commonly are in other regions. Condiments like slaw, chili, and beef are common toppings. In lieu of ketchup they are often served with a tangy-sweet peppery sauce.

From Gus' and Pete's Famous to Sneaky Pete's and the odd stand about town, the city is dominated by Greek-run or -founded hot dog stands. Gus Alexander opened **Gus' Hot Dogs** (205-251-4540) in the 1940s, developing his own special sauce that is still served there today, with some modifications (it is reputed to be less spicy than before). Go to the 1915 4th Ave. North location (there are three in Birmingham) for the real deal—the line is often out the door right at the lunch hour and the owner, George Nasiakos, a native of Greece, is great.

Pete's Famous Hot Dogs (205-252-2905), with its glowing, triangular neon sign above the door, seems more auspicious from the outside. Once inside, the small nook of a restaurant holds no more than six customers at a time, as well as the familiar figure of owner Gus Koutroulakis behind the counter. Gus, who has been serving hot dogs here since 1948, is a legend. As for a dog "all the way" for one with mustard, special sauce, and sauerkraut: It's a Birmingham classic, like Gus. Pete's Famous is at 1925 2nd Ave. North.

Sneaky Pete's Hot Dog, founded by Pete Graphos in 1966, is the relative newcomer to the Greek hot dog scene, but "relative" is the operative word. Ask for their signature dog: mustard, kraut, onions, and sauce. The most visible of hot dog restaurants in town, Sneaky Pete's has more than 20 locations in the Birmingham area. **Sneaky Pete's Hot Dog Sauce** is available in many local grocery stores.

Sam Graphos, Pete's brother, opened a Homewood store in 1970 that is still run by Sam and was renamed **Sam's Super Samwhiches** (yes, the spelling is correct). Like other hot dog eateries in Birmingham, Sam's is a melting pot of high school students getting a snack after school, business men and women grabbing a quick dog and Grapico soft drink, and shoppers succumbing to hot dog temptation. Sam's dry personality is a big draw, too. Sam's is at 2812 18th St. South, (205) 871-0046.

HAMBURGER HEAVEN　　　　　$
Multiple locations
www.hamburgerheavenrestaurant.com
Started in the early 1980s by Jack Caddell—who also founded the Jack's fast-food chain—Hamburger Heaven has earned its place in the hamburger stratosphere in Birmingham. The menu focuses on just what you'd expect, but Hamburger Heaven also offers some deli sandwiches and salad options. There are five locations. A curious side note, Hamburger Heaven was named "#1 Hamburger" by *USA Today* in 1992.

MILO'S HAMBURGERS　　　　　$
Multiple locations
www.miloshamburgers.com

Proving that simplicity works with regards to hamburgers, Birmingham's most well-known hamburger chain has been making hamburgers and cheeseburgers for more than 60 years. Special touches such as grilled buns, a sprinkling of spices on the fries, and their famous sweet (very sweet!) tea are a fast-food staple. The distinctive smoky sauce on every burger sets Milo's apart from other hamburgers, as do the only toppings: pickles and onions. Like the food, the decor is simple and functional. Chicken fingers are a recent addition to the menu.

i Want something to go with your hot dog or hamburger? Try Grapico, a delicious, caffeine-free soft drink with roots in Birmingham since 1917. Crisp and refreshing, Grapico is bottled by Buffalo Rock, which is based in town.

INDIAN

TAJ INDIA $$
2226 Highland Ave. South, Birmingham
(205) 939-3805
www.tajindia.net
A Southside favorite, Taj India is the comfort food when the weather turns cold and spicy Indian food comes to mind. Located in an older strip mall, the charming restaurant looks the part inside with the many intricately carved wooden screens and artwork. It is open for lunch and dinner, but it's the excellent lunch buffet that is always popular—if you're lucky that day, they've prepared sag paneer, a delicious cooked spinach dish with homemade cheese. It's a great way to sample many of Taj's best menu items such as chicken korma, chana masala, raita, and tandoori chicken.

ITALIAN

*BETTOLA $$
2901 2nd Ave. South, Birmingham
(205) 731-6497
Pizza made in the Neapolitan style is the distinguishing feature of Bettola, which is located in the quaint Pepper Place in Lakeside District. The modern wood-fired oven creates a pizza crust delightfully crispy on the outside yet deliciously soft on the inside. Rather than a long-simmered pizza sauce, Bettola is known for pulping tomatoes fresh and spreading the fresh-tasting sauce on the bread. Try the create-your-own antipasti, a fun way to start any meal by choosing from meats, cheeses, and condiments like roasted eggplants or fresh marinated olives. On a nice day, arrive early to secure one of the tables on the patio, a great spot to people-watch while enjoying your meal.

*BOTTEGA RESTAURANT AND CAFE $$$
2242 Highland Ave. South, Birmingham
(205) 933-2001
www.bottegarestaurant.com
Another of renowned chef and restaurateur Frank Stitt's creations, Bottega offers Mediterranean fare that is inspired by regional Italian cuisine. Located in the historic Bottega Favorita Building, the restaurant's setting is inspired with heavy black iron gates at the entrance and a warm wood-paneled interior that manages to effect a casual elegance. The cafe side serves pizza, pasta, sandwiches, and roast meats from the wood-burning oven, and does not accept reservations, making for an impromptu atmosphere. The main dining room area is more formal, accepts reservations, and holds a more elaborate seasonal menu with favorites such as beef carpaccio with parmigiano cheese, oven-roasted figs, campania

seafood salad, tagliatelle, pan-roasted lamb, and homemade ravioli. For those interested in the social scene, Bottega remains arguably *the* place to be seen in the city. Fortunately, it also remains one of the city's best dining spots.

*GIANMARCO'S $$$
721 Broadway St., Homewood
(205) 871-9622

Gianmarco's is the neighborhood restaurant every neighborhood should be fortunate enough to have. Located at the residential end of Broadway Street where the old street-car line used to run, Gianmarco's is typically overflowing with customers, including many walk-ins from the neighborhood. It's white tablecloth but somehow the intimate setting feels more casual. Veal piccata, chicken Francese, pan-roasted grouper, and an assortment of delicious pasta dishes make for a difficult choice when it comes time to order. Wine is available by the glass, carafe, or bottle. Daily specials focus on fish and game meat, as well as seasonal favorites. Forget to make a reservation? Pull up a chair at the tiny bar as you wait and enjoy a cocktail while catching up with the local gossip.

*TRATTORIA CENTRALE $$
207 20th St. North, Birmingham
(205) 202-5612
www.trattoriacentrale.com

Just the kind of quick, delicious eatery downtown needed, Trattoria Centrale (formerly Za Za Trattoria) became a firm favorite immediately after opening. And there are no signs of slowing. Maybe it's the open setup where patrons can watch their food preparation as they order, but there's a matter-of-fact authenticity about Trattoria Centrale that is undeniably appealing. Indeed the pizza, pasta, and salad eatery can partially be credited with

making this stretch of 20th a culinary hub (along with Cafe Dupont). Typically there are four types of pizza on house-made dough available by the slice, and the fresh seasonal salad makes for an idea complement. Pasta dishes change daily, and the breakfast menu has expanded as the establishment gains in popularity. Take a hint from the shining 3-foot-tall copper Victoria Arduino espresso machine: Order an espresso.

JAPANESE & SUSHI

*JINSEI SUSHI BAR & LOUNGE $$$
1830 29th Ave. South, Homewood
(205) 802-1440

When people in Birmingham think sushi, Jinsei is the pinnacle. Easily the most inventive and exciting sushi in the state, Jinsei brings an elevated approach to a Japanese cuisine that by now has become omnipresent in town. The sophisticated setting with its lime-green-and-black contrasting tones create a warm, polished setting in Homewood's SoHo Square. Premium sake and champagne are suggested complements to your sushi, which includes delightfully unexpected ingredients such as cilantro, Serrano peppers, mango, asparagus, Kobe beef, and lemon sprouts. Sitting outside on the small patio makes for a nice evening, but then you face the dilemma of missing the cultured atmosphere inside. Jinsei sets the standard.

MAKI FRESH $$
2800 Cahaba Village Plaza,
Mountain Brook
(205) 970-3242
www.makifresh.com

Set in a new strip mall near Whole Foods, Maki Fresh is as close as it comes to fast-food sushi, but that's intended as no slight. The interior is no-nonsense with industrial steel and green and brown shades that provide a pleasant background. A Japanese grill and sushi bar, Maki Fresh has the presentation down, be it rolls, sashimi, salads, or bowls. Grilled chicken, burgers, salmon, and steak offer a bit wider range than some other sushi establishments. Watch for the specials. Maki Fresh also caters meetings and events.

SEKISUI $$

1025 20th St. South, Birmingham

(205) 933-1025

www.sekisuiusa.com

With two locations in town, Sekisui offers casual dining and some of the most affordable sushi and Japanese cuisine around. Tempura, teriyaki, and donburi options vie with soba, udon, and buckwheat noodle dishes while appetizers like sautéed shitake mushrooms, gyoza dumplings, and fried soft-shell crab fill out the menu. Try the Cajun tuna roll with crawfish and seared tuna with fajita seasonings for something different. The Vestavia Hills location (700 Montgomery Hwy., Suite 178, 205-978-7775) has covered patio seating. Watch for the early-bird specials. Reservations may be made online.

i For coupon offers at Sekisui and other Birmingham-area restaurants, visit www.restaurant.com. A $25 gift certificate is available for $15, a $50 gift certificate sells for $18, and so on.

MEDITERRANEAN

✳THE BRIGHT STAR $$$

304 19th St. North, Bessemer

(205) 426-1861

www.thebrightstar.com

A "Greek" restaurant? Not exactly, but the much-loved Bright Star represents the best fusion of Southern ingredients and cuisine with a Greek culinary touch. Many people will object and consider The Bright Star a meat 'n' three. Regardless, the Bright Star is the oldest continually operating restaurant in Alabama, having started by Tom Bonduris as a 35-seat cafe in the booming town of Bessemer in 1907. Expanded upon several times, the heart of the place remains the central dining room with its romantic murals painted by an itinerant European artist. In 2010 the James Beard Foundation recognized it as an American Classic Restaurant.

Today, Jim and Nick Kiokos run the 330-seat white-tablecloth establishment known for its seafood such as the Greek-style broiled snapper, crab cakes, and seafood gumbo, as well as broiled chicken and fresh vegetables. Their fried red snapper throats, house-cut from whole fish from the Gulf of Mexico, are a must-try. Many a meal has descended into tasty chaos arguing over what dessert to share: lemon icebox, coconut cream, pineapple cheese, or peanut butter pie. Go with the lemon icebox, then settle the argument with the pineapple cheese. And a cup of their great coffee.

DODIYO'S $$$

1831 28th Ave. South, #110, Homewood

(205) 453-9300

www.dodiyos.com

With food from every country touching the Mediterranean Sea—as well as handmade textiles, antiques, and other collectibles—Dodiyós combines the flavors and the culture of this region in a way that manages to remain authentic and distinctive. And delicious. Yes, that is an actual Roman keystone you see on the wall. The food is seasonal, with an emphasis on lamb and fish as well as locally sourced produce. The 45-seat curved

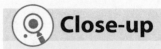 **Close-up**

Greek Restaurateurs

"When a Greek meets a Greek, they open a restaurant," or so the saying goes. Looking at Birmingham's culinary history over the past 130 years, the saying rings true. For almost as long as Birmingham has been here, so have the first Greek immigrants. The city's first Greek immigrant, George Cassimus, arrived in 1884, and after saving a little money, he opened a short-order cafe. By the turn of the century, Birmingham had one of the largest Greek communities in the South, and the *Birmingham Age-Herald* reported that Greeks had cornered the market on the city's fruit stands—a first step toward the restaurant business.

In Birmingham—unlike in many northern cities—Greek immigrants settled throughout the city in places like Ensley, Southside, and Norwood, spreading this fusion of Southern and Mediterranean cooking styles. As more Greeks arrived, they brought others into the business, and the cycle perpetuated itself. When they earned enough money, the men then brought their wife, children, and other family members to settle in Birmingham.

Why the food industry? Some have suggested that Greek men living together without wives took turns cooking for each other, which eventually turned competitive. Others posit that since many immigrants were shepherds, living alone for days or weeks at a time meant these men quickly developed their cooking skills. From barbecue and hot dog stands to meat 'n' threes and seafood establishments, Greek restaurateurs have left a permanent and positive imprint on Birmingham gastronomy. How many barbecue or hot dog joints in America serve baklava as a dessert? How often does a meat 'n' three offer souvlaki or Greek Chicken and rice as an entree? Want Greek-style potatoes with a Greek salad to accompany your Greek-style red snapper? Why not throw in some mint-flavored iced tea while you're at it.

By combining a Mediterranean flair with the rich panoply of Southern foods, Greeks have not only brought a bit of the old country to Birmingham, they're created an entirely new hybrid: The phrase "down-home Greek-Southern cooking" doesn't exactly roll off the tongue, but it sure does taste good going down.

tapas bar, the undisguised centerpiece to the restaurant, lets patrons order off a separate menu with items like keflograviera cheese flambé, char-grilled octopus, and various tapenades and Greek spreads. They can also watch while these small-plate foods are prepared before them.

NABEEL'S CAFE & MARKET $$
1706 Oxmoor Rd., Homewood
(205) 879-9292
www.nabeels.com

Some may recall that Nabeel's started in the early 1970s as a small corner ethnic grocery, a place where those adventurous souls wanting to escape the monotony of the era's diet of meat loaf, fast food, and mushroom soup–based casseroles went for fresh pita, Greek coffee, and "exotic" specialties. The market and cafe occupying the location today has long been a favorite spot for Greek and Mediterranean food. Inside it's reminiscent of a little Greek bistro with the dried peppers and garlic hanging from the ceiling. Dishes like moussaka, Greek and Italian salads, sou-vlaki, gyro, and bifteki, are just a few favorites from their broad menu. Many items from the menu such as taramosalata dip and homos are available in bulk from the market, which also includes a great selection of olives, cheeses, salami, nuts, imported jams, spices, candies, Russian food items, and more.

TAZIKI'S MEDITERRANEAN CAFE $$
Multiple locations
www.tazikiscafe.com

A newcomer to the Mediterranean food scene in Birmingham, Taziki's offers a modern synthesis of the region's food with a dash of American thrown in. And judging by their ever-expanding number of restaurants, they are doing something right. Greek salads, grilled chicken, lamb, gyro, and more traditional dishes share the menu with smoked turkey gyro, roasted pork loin, spicy pimento cheese sandwiches, and other fare. Look for the daily special, as well as the take-out feast for families of four.

ZÖES KITCHEN $$
Multiple locations
www.zoeskitchen.com

Zoës Kitchen, a homegrown restaurant started by Marcus and Zoë Cassimus in the mid-1990s, has been polished and expanded by the couple's son, John, and grown to include numerous locations in Alabama and several states beyond. Such is the success of the appealing design and menu that the operation hardly feels like a chain at all. Typical Greek dishes like Greek salad and grilled chicken with rice pilaf are prepared next to items like chicken salad and the popular grueben, a grilled turkey, Swiss cheese, and slaw sandwich on rye. There is an assortment of heart-healthy dishes to choose from, and

the several take-home tubs and pre-made dinners are a family-pleasing surprise when Mom or Dad walks in the door at 5:30 p.m. with a delicious dinner in hand.

MEXICAN

*CANTINA $$
2901 2nd Ave. South, Suite 110, Birmingham
(205) 323-6980
www.cantinabirmingham.com

Opened by the same great restaurateur who brought Birmingham Sol Y Luna, Cantina is a delightful place to enjoy Mexican cooking done right. It's not pretentious. The menu is deceptively simple, but make no mistake, Cantina offers some of the freshest, most delicious Mexican cuisine in the city. Try the tilapia fish burger or molletes, refried beans on a bolillo roll with melted Chihuahua cheese and pico de gallo. Mix and match their taco choices (fish, chicken, pork, tenderloin, vegetarian) with delicious sides like saffron rice and beans, spicy slaw, or sweet potato fries. Entrees include grilled shrimp quesadillas, churrasco steak, cilantro chicken, and daily specials. Set in the dynamic Pepper Place, with a full bar, key lime and prickly pear margaritas with premium tequila, expect a jovial after work or post-soccer match crowd to be on-hand. There is plenty of atmospheric indoor seating as well as umbrella-covered outdoor seating during nice weather. Cantina, a casual spot with room for restless children to stretch their legs, is a great for destination for families.

COCINA SUPERIOR $$
587 Brookwood Village, Homewood
(205) 259-1980
www.thecocinasuperior.com

Set in its stylish digs in Brookwood Village Shopping Center, Cocina Superior offers a modern take on Tex Mex that attracts those wanting to be seen as well as those wanting fresh food at a fair price. The white stucco and mod glass exterior, along with the interior's leather booths, thoughtfully designed lighting, and mahogany bar make a statement. With its proximity to the mall, Cocina enjoys a solid lunchtime crowd, but at night, especially on weekends, you'll want to make reservations. Despite the large heated outdoor patio, side lounge, and ample seating inside, the space fills up quickly. Their oysters, chargrilled on the half shell and topped with garlic butter and cheese make for an excellent start to any meal. Fun, inventive specialty drinks like the Mexican Mai Tai and pomegranate margarita add spice to any outing at Cocina.

LA PAZ $$
99 Euclid Ave., Mountain Brook
(205) 879-2225
www.lapaz.com
A popular Crestline neighborhood hangout, La Paz may be a chain with five restaurants in five Southern states, but don't tell the Birmingham restaurant's patrons that: They've completely adopted the spot as their very own. For the healthy set an assortment of salads like mango chicken, honey-glazed salmon, or tamarind barbecue chicken provide lighter options. Dinner selections include burritos, enchiladas, street tacos, and more. Try the grilled Black Angus sirloin enchilada, blackened salmon on a bed of fresh spinach and calabacitas, or the tamarind citrus–marinated chicken with mango and sliced avocados.

ROJO $$
2921 Highland Ave. South, Birmingham
(205) 328-4733
www.rojo.birminghammenus.com
A Highland Avenue hub, especially when the weather's nice, Rojo is a fun neighborhood eatery that provides Latin and American food sure to please most any palate. The two-sided menu offers Latin dishes like quesadillas, paella, and blackened-tilapia tacos, as well as plenty of vegetarian options such as spinach burritos. Flip the menu, and it's more traditional American fare like grilled mahi mahi salad, Philly cheesesteak, cheeseburgers, and organic New York strip. There's a reason Rojo is always on the "best of" lists for its warm ambience, great outdoor patio, and quality, affordable dining. Owners Laney DeJonge and Clark Lopez are frequently on-site, adding their personal touch. Watch for trivia nights, games, films on weeknights, and most importantly, European soccer matches on Rojo's big screen in their side room. Look for their weekend brunch from 11 a.m. to 3 p.m.

✳SOL Y LUNA $$$
2811 7th Ave. South
(205) 322-1186
www.birminghammenus.com/solyluna
Sol Y Luna stands out as the finest Mexican restaurant in Birmingham. Serving a comprehensive Nuevo Mexican tapas menu glittering with perfect portions of refined traditional cuisine, Sol Y Luna is the destination for Mexican fine dining. The salsas and chile sauces are handmade and accompany delights like the cochnita pibil, a banana leaf stuffed with steamed pork and rice, the chile relleno, covered in a unique pomegranate and goat cheese sauce, and the beef flautas with creme fresca. The chicken tortilla soup

will make you forget all the approximations you've previously tasted of this classic dish. Be sure to make reservations on Tuesday for their famous paella. Sol Y Luna matches its culinary excellence with an extensive tequila menu that features over 60 different brands of tequilas, most of which are available nowhere else in the city.

ℹ️ **Not sure where to start? Reposado or añejo? Tell your helpful waiter you're a novice and would like to begin with a "flag," a flight of tequila with both a sangrita (red) and a lime-based (green) chaser. Together with blanco tequila, they make the colors of the Mexican flag.**

MIDDLE EASTERN

ALI BABA PERSIAN RESTAURANT $$$
1694 Montgomery Hwy., Suite 110, Hoover
(205) 823-2222
www.alibabagrillkabob.com

As the only Persian restaurant in town, Ali Baba has its devoted following. Located in a strip mall, the exterior of the restaurant is predictably nondescript. Inside, however, the decor certainly sets an exotic scene with white Corinthian columns, mirrors, and traditional textile tablecloths. Assorted kabobs, fresh bread, lamb stew, and Cornish hens marinated in lemon and pepper are just some favorites. For more options—or for first-timers—try the Sunday buffet with some 20 items to see the wealth of Persian food that Ali Baba offers. Children will love the belly dancers performing live every Thursday night.

PITA STOP $$
12th St. South, Birmingham
(205) 328-2749
www.thepitastop.com

Another long-time landmark, the Pita Stop near the University of Alabama has been a downtown favorite for more than 30 years. With its striking Venetian style and glazed polychrome terra cotta, this small retail block is a great example of the architectural style of commercial buildings built in Birmingham during the late 1920s. Though the interior looks about the same as it did 30 years ago, don't let that scare you. From kabobs to grilled kafta, falafel to a range of omelets, the food is the reason to keep coming to Pita Stop.

PURPLE ONION $
1550 Montgomery Hwy., Suite P, Hoover
(205) 822-7322
www.purpleonionofhoover.com

A well-loved local hybrid of American and Middle Eastern–style food, Purple Onion offers breakfast omelets, wings, burgers, and sub sandwiches, as well as kabobs, gyros, pastries, and other ethnic options. While the atmosphere is basic, the food is served quickly and makes for a great lunchtime dining or convenient take-home option. Without going into the complicated history of the Purple Onion, there are three locations in Birmingham, but the Hoover location and downtown location (1717 10th Ave. South, Birmingham, 205-933-2424) are under the same ownership. An additional Purple Onion is in Homewood at 479 Green Springs Hwy. (205-941-9979).

SAM'S DELI AND GRILL $
932 Oxmoor Rd., Homewood
(205) 871-0383
www.birminghamrestaurant.us/270335

An Edgewood neighborhood destination, Sam's is always full of families, middle-school kids hanging out, local police officers, and the like—it's a cross section of Homewood if ever there was one. While many enjoy the baba ghanoush, gyros, falafel, and tabouli salad, it's a well-known secret that Sam's makes one of the best cheeseburgers in town. Try the salmon or tilapia plate special. Another positive note: You can rely on Sam to have SEC football and English Premier League soccer on all the time on one of his three televisions. If you are also a Manchester United fan, you'll get along famously with Sam, the owner.

ORGANIC & VEGETARIAN

*BOTTLETREE CAFE $
3719 3rd Ave. South, Birmingham
(205) 533-6288
www.thebottletree.com
A culinary breath of fresh air—and the best spot to catch an indie band in town—Bottletree is one of those little treats that make your quality of living index rise, appreciatively. A cafe, bar, and venue, look for vegetarian food, fresh homemade soups (some great chili!), healthy salads, tacos, and if you want, chicken and the occasional pork item. The decor shows a sense of humor, liberally commented on by patrons, as is the custom. Their Sunday brunch is one of the few in the Avondale neighborhood. You will see groovy hipsters and 50-somethings at shows and lunch, giving the local cafe its own unique style. Shows are typically quite affordable, starting around $5 and up—look for all ages and 18+ shows, too. Rumor has it the combination of quality fare, cool accommodations in a renovated old trailer, and just downright good hosts make Bottletree one

of the hottest venues in the United States. Everybody wants to play Bottletree.

i Catch "We Have Signal," a very cool, live music program that runs on Alabama Public Television, to get a feel for the great acts that grace the stage. It's on Bottletree's site, as well as its own Vimeo channel.

GOLDEN TEMPLE CAFE $
1901 11th Ave. South, Birmingham
(205) 933-8933
www.goldentemplehealthfoods.com
If Birmingham didn't have Golden Temple Cafe, the city would be all the poorer for it. Open since 1973 on the Southside, the market offers nutritional supplements, natural groceries, herbs, natural fiber clothing, incense, crystals, and the like. But the Five Points South location also serves vegetarian breakfast, lunch, and dinner Mon through Fri and breakfast and lunch on Sat. Veggie burgers, guacamole and hummus sandwiches, veggie chicken, as well as an organic juice bar and smoothies are just some of the fresh, healthy items to choose from. While you're waiting on your meal, browse the adjacent shop. An additional location is at 3309 Lorna Rd., Hoover (205-823-7002). Parking in Five Points South can be problematic at lunchtime, but Golden Temple customers can park to the left of the store in a lot watched by an attendant. Just tell him where you're going, and it's free.

ORGANIC HARVEST
   MARKET & CAFE $
1580 Montgomery Hwy., Suite 12, Hoover
(205) 978-0318
www.orgharvest.com

Organic produce, nutritional supplements, beauty products, and organic wines are all available at this general-purpose health food store, but it is the cafe that draws the customers, especially at lunchtime. Try the wraps, sandwiches, vegetable juices, and smoothies. A great range of gluten-free and dairy-free salads are prepared daily in the deli, such as bean salad, roasted butternut squash salad, broccoli salad with toasted almonds, and chicken and tuna salad.

PIZZA

COSMO'S $$
2012 Magnolia Ave., Birmingham
(205) 930-9971
www.birminghammenus.com/cosmos
One of the early gourmet pizza joints, Cosmo's remains the creative alternative to the usual pizza in a box. With white or whole-wheat crust, plus novel toppings such as alligator sausage, fontina cheese, pine nuts, prosciutto, roasted eggplant, smoked gouda, and tasso ham, a smoked peppery cut from the shoulder butt, Cosmo's provides plenty of options to stoke the curiosity of the most jaded pizza fan. Give their weekend brunch with its create-your-own Bloody Mary a try.

DAVE'S PIZZA $$
1819 29th Ave. South, Homewood
(205) 871-3283
www.davesontheweb.com
Somehow, Homewood became the city's pizza hub, and for many, Dave's Pizza is the place to go for fun toppings and the great open-air atmosphere. Located across the street from SoHo, Dave's is a popular lunch destination. Toppings like broccoli, sun-dried tomato, pesto, blue cheese, mesquite grilled chicken, spinach, and zucchini keep the pizza options fresh (there are, of course, all the standard toppings, as well). Get crazy with a specialty pizza like the Double Cheeseburger—marinara, beef sausage, bell peppers, onion, olives, mozzarella cheese— or Sweet Tang for pie with mesquite chicken, bacon, red onion, sharp cheddar cheese, and a sweet and tangy sauce. Additional offerings like calzones, gourmet classic pizzas, as well as sandwiches, wraps, and salads keep just about anyone happy at Dave's. Ask about the Velvet Elvis Painting Saga . . . the story never gets old.

DEVINCI'S OF HOMEWOOD $$
2707 18th St. South, Homewood
(205) 879-1455
www.devincispizza.com
It's not pretentious or showy. In fact, it is what it is: a family-style Italian trattoria that's been serving the Homewood community since the 1960s. You don't go there for the decor, but rather for the atmosphere. The Mona Lisa, topped with four meats and four vegetables, is a signature dish, as is the fettuccini DeVinci. But it's more than just pizza: Try the stromboli steak sandwich, gnocchi, and a host of pasta options. And after the recent addition of some modest outdoor seating and a daily breakfast menu, DeVinci's seems even more popular than ever. Kids eat free on Tues. Check the website for coupons.

*JIM DAVENPORT'S PIZZA
PALACE $$
2837 Cahaba Rd., Mountain Brook
(205) 879-8603
www.davenportspizza.com
Love it or leave it, that's how many feel about Jim Davenport's pizza. If you are expecting the usual banal slice of pizza, Davenport's delivers something refreshingly different and

delicious. Their thin-crust style, sliced into squares, is not for everyone, though judging how packed the restaurant is most evenings, Davenport's enjoys no lack of customers. Arrive before 5:30 p.m. or expect a wait. With its wrought iron decor and red vinyl seats and booths, the interior is refreshingly dated and has not changed since the 1970s. Children love lining up at the counter to peer through the glass to watch the cooks roll out, toss, and top the pizza—it's endless fascination. Vintage video games like Donkey Kong and Pac Man complete the portrait. Go with the classic ham and green olives for the right mix of salt and vinegar—some customers indulge in the bizarre ritual of squeezing a few drops of lemon on the slices for added tartness. Not for everyone, but worth a try.

NEW YORK PIZZA $$
1010 Oxmoor Rd., Homewood
(205) 871-4000
www.thenewyorkpizza.com
An anchor pizzeria at the center of Edgewood, the venerable New York Pizza has been pleasing baseball teams, church groups, couples, and neighborhood families for years. This Homewood landmark is known for the calzones, such as the Broadway stuffed with spinach, sun-dried tomatoes, mushrooms, mozzarella, and feta. The tomato sauce is thick with spicy undertones. There are assorted pasta dishes and sandwiches to choose from but let's be honest, everyone goes there for pizza. The Little Italy, a pizza topped with olive oil, fresh tomatoes, roasted garlic, basil and Parmesan cheese is especially delicious. A caveat: When ordering wine, know that it is served in plastic glasses—kid-friendly, perhaps, but certainly disappointing for some adults who prefer a glass of wine. Free delivery is offered in Homewood.

i If you come to New York Pizza with children, be prepared. Bring quarters: The packed game room is a chaotic frenzy of kids playing pinball and video games while the quarter-less jockey around for the best vantage point while their buddies are gaming. It is not for the faint hearted.

SALVATORE'S PIZZA AND PASTA $$
1594 Montgomery Hwy., Hoover
(205) 823-7206
www.salvatorespizzeria.com
For the south-of-town crowd, Salvatore's is the go-to pizza joint. Salvatore learned his trade with his father, a first-generation immigrant from Naples, Italy, who worked as a chef and restaurateur in Manhattan. The tradition continues today. Ingredients are homemade, prepared fresh everyday—and it shows. There's New York–style thin-crust pizza as well as Sicilian deep dish, and you can buy by the slice or personal 10-inch pizzas. Calzones, salads, subs, and vegetarian, seafood, pork, chicken, and beef entrees round out the menu. Salvatore's provides a kids' menu with linguini and ziti in several combinations (marinara, meat sauce, meatball, alfredo, butter). An additional location is at 4673 Hwy. 280, Inverness (205-991-2881).

SEAFOOD

DYRON'S LOWCOUNTRY $$$
121 Oak St., Mountain Brook
(205) 834-8257
www.dyronslowcountry.com
Located in Crestline Village in Mountain Brook, Dyrons's Lowcountry offers the regional cuisine of coastal South Carolina and Georgia that is influenced by a proximity to water. But really, there are plenty of

nods to Alabama and even New Orleans cuisine, too. Crabs, shrimp, oysters, and fish are predominant, as are the rice and grits that fans of this style of cooking love. Start with the East Indies salad with fresh Alabama jumbo lump crap and scallions or cornmeal-crusted oysters over a black-eyed pea salad with remoulade. Crab cakes, crawfish tails in étoufée, or Duroc pork over grits are fantastic. Other mouth-watering options include braised duck pasta, pan-fried Georgia mountain trout, wood-grilled quail, and Gullah étoufée. Owners Dyron and Sonya Powell have created that rare place where customers can close their eyes and point to an item on the menu, and without going wrong—everything is good. Look for daily specials, a raw bar, and now, a Sunday brunch.

i After a visit to Dyron's Lowcountry, stop by the Oak Street Garden Shop next door for fresh local produce, gourmet food, local honey, plants, herbs, and gifts. Better yet, stop by before eating at Dyron's: Otherwise you'll be too full!

✳FISH MARKET   **$$**
612 22nd St. South, Birmingham
(205) 322-3330
www.birminghammenus.com/
thefishmarket

One of the places locals love to take out-of-town friends, George Sarris' Fish Market is a Birmingham culinary institution. Fresh fish market, grocery, wine seller, and import market, as well as the source for some of the freshest fish in town, Fish Market is consistently reliable. Sarris, a 30-year veteran of the restaurant business in Birmingham, is perhaps the epitome of the Greek-Southern connection and what that's meant for the city's rich culinary heritage. And, with a recent move into a huge renovated warehouse, Sarris finally has the perfect location to complement the food. High ceilings, exposed interior brick, separate dining areas, an oyster bar, and a fresh-air patio for year-round outdoor dining provide plenty of options and plenty of space. (Unlike his previous, restrictive space on 21st Street South, Fish Market now has room for all its loyal patrons!)

Ordering is a snap: Grab a menu by the trout tank when you walk in, and take your time since it is one of the most extensive menus in town. Check the daily specials on the chalkboard. Follow the line to the register, place your order, take the buzzer, and then go find a table until your meal is ready in a few minutes. Greek salads, crawfish tails, an oyster bar, and a fresh seafood gumbo with a dark roux that's prepared daily are just a few ways to start your meal. Several new items such as Royal red shrimp, grilled redfish, jambalaya, alligator, and other specialties are a great option. Or go with the standards: Greek islands shrimp, Greek snapper, baked snapper Creole, oyster stew, Gulf grouper, or artichoke hearts with shrimp and scallops. Yes, there are land-lover options but why would anyone do that? Bring your appetite.

i A Birmingham original, the spicy, carbonated Buffalo Rock Ginger Ale has been produced in town since 1901. Poured on top of ice cream floats or to relieve an upset stomach, Buffalo Rock is a staple for many long-time residents. Try and drink the last swallow from a can without a gasp from the strong ginger bite at the end!

✳HOT & HOT FISH CLUB $$$
2180 11th Court South, Birmingham
(205) 933-5474
www.hotandhotfishclub.com

There's an ongoing debate among many in Birmingham: Hot & Hot or Highland's Bar and Grill? In a way it does a disservice to both restaurants. They stand on their own among the city's best dining destinations. Any city in the country—the world, in fact—would be fortunate to have them. Hot & Hot Fish Club owners Chef Chris and Idie Hastings focus on keeping things simple and serving foods that are close to their source. Ironically, this requires an enormous amount of behind-the-scenes work cultivating relationships with local and regional farmers, artisans, and purveyors. See their website for a complete listing of their local purveyors.

The distinctive building, though small, is full of charm and was a burger joint in the 1950s and then the popular Upside-Down Plaza pool hall until the 1980s. Elegant and modern inside, customers can choose from the arched limestone chef's counter and its view of the kitchen, the main dining room, or the more secluded Harvest Room. When the weather is nice, the outdoor patio makes for a perfect, romantic spot for couples. Well-known local potter, Tena Payne of Earthborn Pottery in Leeds, created the restaurant's line of dinner plates, bowls, and espresso cups.

Start with one of Hot & Hot's signature drinks (updated seasonally), like the Pimm's Cup or the Hot & Hot Martini, with pepper-infused Stolichnaya vodka muddled and with a pepper garnish. Be sure to sample the homemade pickled okra and boiled peanuts.

The menu changes daily, but items like the charcuterie plate, okra basket with chive aioli, and grilled quail are always a delight. If they are in season, the Hastings' heirloom tomato salad is a must. Entrees like duck breast and Fudge Farms pork are always reliable, as are most any seafood dishes such as red snapper or flounder. If you've the room, the Hot & Hot doughnuts with apple butter and cinnamon sugar, pecan pie, and chocolate persimmon cream are sure to please.

OCEAN $$$
1218 20th St. South, Birmingham
(205) 933-0999
www.oceanbirmingham.com

Another strong Birmingham restaurant, Ocean is somewhat new on the scene, less than a decade old, but a firm favorite for those wanting fresh seafood in a stylish, modern setting with swanky lighting and an eye-catching water wall. It's a change of pace for the typical seafood restaurant, which is probably why Ocean immediately became a dining destination. Winner of a 2007 AAA Four Diamond Award, fresh seafood from around the globe is the theme of this South-side hotspot. From fresh sushi to Greek, Thai, Southern, and contemporary American styles of preparation, there's a cosmopolitan feel for the way Ocean approaches seafood. For an energetic, eclectic pairing, try the Ocean's sister restaurant, the adjacent 26 (www.twentysix26.com). You'll find similarly excellent seafood along with rib eyes, pork, and burgers, all with the same quality attention to detail as Ocean.

NIGHTLIFE

While the nightlife may not be hopping seven days a week in Birmingham, there are certainly plenty of nighttime hotspots and diversions in the Magic City to keep your energy level up late into the night. Options range from swanky bars to neighborhood watering holes, from the comforting dives we all love to the more edgy Five Points South destinations. In addition to heading to Southside or Lakeview downtown, Over the Mountain communities have plenty of entertainment options that allow parents a few hours of escape together while the babysitter watches their kids at home. Whether you are 18 or 80 years old, there are a broad variety of ways to pass the time in Birmingham.

There are two main entertainment districts that offer a dense cluster of nightlife, though nightlife venues can be found in most any area of town. The most prominent district is the Five Points South area centered at the intersection of 11th Avenue South and 20th Street South. These and the surrounding streets feature a mix of some of the best nightlife entertainment options in Birmingham. Residents call the area "Five Points," and you can be sure that you'll find something of interest. The best way to explore is to simply park your car and walk. Parking on the street is free after 6 p.m. and usually doesn't fill up until late at night. Pay lots with attendants and valets are available and can take the hassle out of a crowded night. After parking take your time and investigate all the white line restaurants, dive bars, dance halls, sushi joints, pool halls, tattoo parlors, and clubs that line the streets.

The Lakeview district is a smaller entertainment district centered at the intersection of 7th Avenue South and 29th Street South. Although it doesn't contain as many choices as Five Points, the nighttime crowd here is usually a little older and the locations here are all one-of-a-kind. Lakeview has free parking on the street, so if the weather is nice, be sure to walk around and take a look at all the area has to offer.

There is an open container law in effect in Alabama, so be aware. It is illegal to drive with a blood alcohol concentration of .08 percent or greater—designate a driver or call a taxi if you plan to go over the limit.

COMEDY

COMEDY CLUB STARDOME
1818 Data Dr., Hoover
(205) 444-0008
www.stardome.com

The Comedy Club Stardome is without a doubt the reason stand-up comedy exists in Birmingham. Formerly known as The Comedy Club, this institution single-handedly created Birmingham's stand-up comedy scene in the 1980s and continues to serve the comedy needs of the city. Founder Bruce Ayers presents an entertaining night that draws top comedy acts as well as dinner theater, hypnotists, and other variety acts typical in much larger cities. Entertainers and those seeking to be entertained know that for the best in comedy, the Stardome is the only choice in town. Features include a full drink menu including a variety of frozen cocktails, food options ranging from burgers and chicken sandwiches to rib-eye steaks and seafood, and a selection of snacks and appetizers. The Stardome Theatre is available for booking to support a variety of events including banquets, receptions, and corporate events. Tickets cost $10 to $40 while dinner runs from $10 to $25. There is a $5 minimum food and drink per person.

DANCE CLUBS

CLUB 1120
1036 20th St. South, Birmingham
(205) 324-1120
Dance clubs in the Five Points South area come and go, but the operators of Club 1120 seem to have what it takes to cause locals to wait in line on weekend nights for admission into the club. Dance parties on the huge dance floor upstairs last until the early morning. The VIP area overlooks Five Points and provides a dramatic view of the surroundings. The three bars on the upstairs floor and the bar in the lounge downstairs have quick service even during the busiest times, that won't keep you from the dance floor for long. $10 valet parking is available. A cover of around $5 is usually required. The main club area (and the huge dance party) opens Thurs, Fri, and Sat at 10 p.m. The lounge opens at 10 p.m. 7 days a week. Patrons must

be 18 to enter and 21 to drink. The dress code is strict and enforced, so leave your street clothes and sneakers at home.

THE QUEST CLUB
416 24th St. South, Birmingham
(205) 251-4313
www.the-quest-club.com
As other Lesbian, Gay, Bisexual, and Transgender clubs have come and gone in Birmingham, The Quest remains the one club in town that offers a safe, welcome place for people of all persuasions to enjoy the nightlife. The Quest hosts a number of popular drag shows as well as frequent pool and dart tournaments. DJs and occasional touring acts keep the dance floor packed most nights. Cover for those 21 and older is $5. Adults aged 19 and 20 are allowed to party in the club Wed through Sun with a cover that ranges from $10 to $15.

> **i** The Quest is Alabama's only club open 24/7/365, making it the only spot in Birmingham where 24-hour party people can dance the night and day away. Bottom line: If you love to dance, you'll love The Quest.

LIVE MUSIC

*BOTTLETREE CAFE
3719 3rd Ave. South, Birmingham
(205) 533-6288
www.thebottletree.com
When Bottletree opened a few years back, the cafe/bar/nightclub was enthusiastically welcomed with open arms by a local indie community desperate for a music venue more indicative of their tastes. Located in Avondale just east of downtown, the club is a cultural sign of life surrounded by

industrial warehouses. Owned by siblings Brad and Merrilee Challiss and partner Brian Teasley, the club is a mix of Southern folk sensibilities and European neighborhood cafe with a hint of independent rock-n-roll thrown in for fun. The venue is enjoyed for its innovative music, ability to attract nationally known bands (Band of Horses, Vampire Weekend, Animal Collective, Nada Surf) and local favorites (Through the Sparks, 13 Ghosts, Vulture Whale), film series, and special events. In 2010 it was named one of the 10 Greatest New Music Venues of the 21st century by Flavorwire. Alabama Public Television's Emmy-winning live music program, *We Have Signal*, www.aptv.org/WHS, is filmed at Bottletree.

THE NICK
2514 10th Ave. South, Birmingham
(205) 252-3831
www.thenickrocks.com
Rolling Stone calls The Nick "the CBGB of the South" for good reason—this rock-n-roll dive serves up cold beer and live music in a dark, smoky hall that looks like a trailer from the outside. Hell, it kind of looks like a trailer on the inside. Pool tables end up as coasters during larger shows and the bathrooms make a truck stop toilet look appealing, but locals continue to flock to The Nick for some of the best music in the Southeast. It may not be pretty, but if you're looking for local rockers, this is it. Many acts are rock or metal, but The Nick does offer a variety of performances ranging from country and bluegrass to emo and pop. True to form, most shows don't begin until 10 p.m. or later and often run well into the night (and morning). If you're looking to rock all night and sleep all day, The Nick will not disappoint.

ONA'S MUSIC ROOM
Pepper Place, Birmingham
www.onasmusicroom.com
After nearly 15 years, Ona's Music Room closed its Southside location near UAB, announcing plans to relocate in the popular Pepper Place in the Lakeview District. Owner and singer Ona Watson created a favorite spot for locals to enjoy the best in jazz and R&B. *American Idol* winner Taylor Hicks sang for years at Ona's before catapulting to fame after his victory on the show. Ona's is a critical part of Birmingham's unique music scene, providing a way for quality up-and-coming acts and local musicians to gain exposure in a top-class environment. As of yet, the new location has not opened.

SPRING STREET FIREHOUSE
412 41st St. South, Birmingham
www.myspace.com/springstreet
firehouse
For the past 10 years, Birmingham has hosted a thriving "DIY" scene, a music scene dedicated to safe-for-all-ages shows in no-frills venues that usually have little or no services besides a stage and a bathroom. Locals remember Cave 9 as the place that crystallized the movement in Birmingham, and after that club's unfortunate closing, the Spring Street Firehouse has picked up the torch and blazed a new trail of sonic excellence. Located in a former Birmingham firehouse and locally known as "the Firehouse," shows are staged in the old fire engine bay at the bottom of the building. The simple, appealing setup keeps the shows cheap and the bands coming. The Firehouse books some of the nation's best underground music in a variety of genres.

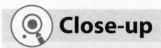

Close-up

Entertainment Districts

Despite the presence of Birmingham-Southern College, Samford University, and the University of Alabama at Birmingham, Birmingham lacks a core area of college bars, clubs, and eateries. The entertainment districts are more like separate neighborhoods, each with their own style and patrons. The **Southside/Five Points South Area** runs the gamut from white-linen restaurants to tattoo parlors, from late-night bars to dance clubs. It's the place your parents told you not to go during your high school days 25 years ago. It is still that place. You might see someone busking or panhandling. There's certainly an exciting edge to the area, but at the same time, it's home to **Highland Bar & Grill,** a nationally known restaurant of unrivaled pedigree in Alabama. That's the attraction of Five Points.

The **Lakeview District** around 7th Avenue South and 29th Street serves as the city's second-largest entertainment areas. It has college-age pubs, dance clubs, restaurants, and live music, as well as some upscale restaurants. The **Barking Kudu** and **Innisfree Irish Pub** cater to the younger set while reliable standbys like **Lou's Pub** serve an older clientele. **Joe's on Seventh,** with female impersonators, serves an entirely different set of customers. **Lakeview Oyster House** and **Sol Y Luna** offer fine dining for those looking to have a meal to accompany their good times. If you're in the mood for tequila, Sol Y Luna is the Birmingham destination for fans of the agave liquor.

Other good nightlife districts include the emerging **Loft District** around 2nd Avenue North. With **Rogue Tavern, Pale Eddie's Pour House, The Metro Bar & Music, Wine Loft,** and other spots, 2nd Avenue is becoming its own destination. And now the popular **Urban Standard** is expanding their weekend hours, too. For foodies, **20th Street North** between 2nd and 3rd Avenues is quickly turning into an evening destination with delicious eateries like **Brick & Tin,** owned by former Highlands Bar and Grill Chef de Cuisine Mauricio Papapietro, **Trattoria Centrale, Brannon's Public House,** and the long-established **Cafe Dupont.** As the area gains popularity, there are signs that more establishments are opening for business during the evenings on weekends. It's a positive trend.

✳**WORKPLAY**
500 23rd St. South, Birmingham
(205) 879-4773
www.workplay.com
When you first see Workplay, you know you're in for something special. The brainchild of native son and original MTV VJ Alan Hunter, Workplay is an upscale multipurpose venue specializing in live music. The building is an original construction that stands out among the surrounding architecture. Boasting both a large soundstage for traditional musical performances as well as an intimate theater, Workplay is one of Birmingham's best venues for a wide range of live music. Workplay also hosts a variety of non-musical shows ranging from improvisational comedy to theater. Even if you aren't attending a show at Workplay, the clean, modern stylings of the bar area have a big-city ambience that feels more like Manhattan than midtown Birmingham. On

the night of a popular musical performance, twentysomethings mingle with white-collar professionals and city socialites. In addition to its nightlife options, Workplay also offers full event support including catering, audio-visual support, live music, and office space.

ZYDECO
2001 15th St. South, Birmingham
(205) 933-1032
www.zydecobirmingham.com
Zydeco is yet another one of Birmingham's fine venues for live music. With two stages, multiple bars, and a roomy patio, Zydeco is a great spot to catch a show or just drinks at the bar. There's a definite "just out of college" feel to the crowds at Zydeco, but all types are welcome at this longtime hotspot. Located just up the hill from Five Points South, Zydeco regularly features drink specials as well as a Battle of the Bands that brings out some of Birmingham's best groups. Most bands that play here tend to be rock or rock-oriented with the occasional acoustic, punk rock, bluegrass, or jam band performance. Most shows range from $5 to $15 with more expensive prices for the occasional national act that plays at Zydeco.

PUBS & BARS

THE BARKING KUDU
2929 7th Ave. South, Birmingham
(205) 328-1748
www.barkingkudu.com
Named after an African antelope, The Barking Kudu is an award-winning young bar that immediately became a local favorite upon its opening in the Lakeview district. Along with Innisfree, The Barking Kudu is responsible for revitalizing the nightlife in Lakeview for a younger demographic.

Like most Birmingham bars, The Barking Kudu often has live music, especially Thurs through Sat. On Mon nights The Barking Kudu offers open mic comedy, popularly known as "Comic-kaze." It opens at 11 p.m. and serves a deli-style lunch menu together with late night Tex-Mex selections. You can depend on The Barking Kudu as an easy choice for drinks in Lakeview. The bar's soccer team isn't that bad, either.

DAVE'S PUB
1128 20th St. South, Birmingham
(205) 933-4030
www.davespubsouthside.com
This award-winning bar has become a Five Points South favorite with a patio that gives a perfect opportunity to see and be seen in this popular entertainment district. If you're looking to grab a quick beer with a friend in Southside after work, Dave's Pub is the place. A full bar includes gourmet and high-gravity beers. Dave's also features an excellent cigar menu for those wishing to enjoy a smoke and a drink in the night air. Those who wish to stay inside are offered conversation, live sports on multiple televisions, and live music on the weekends. There is no cover charge.

*DRAM WHISKEY BAR
2721 Cahaba Rd., Mountain Brook
(205) 871-8055
www.dramwhiskeybar.com
Don't be fooled by the name. Besides having one of the most extensive bourbon and whiskey menus in the area, Dram also features a full line of draft and bottled beer as well as an extensive wine list. Located in upscale Mountain Brook Village, Dram offers patrons posh surroundings and a refined drinks menu to enjoy with friends after work. A limited but inventive dinner menu

is complemented by a smaller late-night menu as well as Sunday brunch. As far as whiskey goes, this is a required stop for those who appreciate the fiery amber liquid. Dram offers traditional whiskies normally found in most bars in addition to a strong selection of rare Kentucky bourbons and single malt Scotch. It's a place to be seen.

✳THE GARAGE CAFE
2304 10th Terrace South, Birmingham
(205) 322-3211
www.garagecafe.us

On one of those perfect nights when the Birmingham weather makes you forget about the sweltering summer, head down to what locals refer to as the "Garage" and enjoy a drink in the unforgettable outdoor area behind the bar. What was once a pile of random sculpture and antiques is now an award-winning bar with an atmospheric grotto filled with nooks and tables perfect for couples and groups alike. See the entry in the Restaurant chapter for information about their scrumptious sandwiches. The Garage is a Birmingham original.

THE IRON HORSE CAFE
1694 Montgomery Hwy., #184, Hoover
(205) 978-5599
www.ironhorsecafe.net

Even if you don't own a motorcycle, the Iron Horse Cafe is one of Hoover's best choices for a night on the town. With live music every day of the week and a full dinner menu, Iron Horse has something for everyone. Enjoy live band karaoke on Sunday nights and see the bikes on Thursday bike night. If you appreciate motorcycles or want to show off your own chopper, this is the place to watch the hogs.

INNISFREE IRISH PUB
710 29th St. South, Birmingham
(205) 252-4252
www.facebook.com/innisfreebham

As one of the bars that helped revitalize the flagging Lakeview district, Innisfree is an Irish pub that continues to dominate the bar scene in Birmingham. Innisfree often hosts live music and has a trivia night for those who like to exercise their brains while they hang out at the pub. In the fall and winter enjoy football games on their multiple televisions. Whatever the season, Innisfree is a top choice for those who enjoy the comfort of an Irish pub. As the night wears on, the lively Innisfree becomes a top destination for Birmingham's night owls.

JOE'S ON SEVENTH
2627 7th Ave. South, Birmingham
(205) 321-2812
www.joesonseventh.com

Recently opened, Joe's on Seventh offers Birmingham's LGBT community a place to unwind and enjoy a cold drink in the open and friendly confines of a smoke-free environment. In the early hours of the night, Joe's serves primarily as a neighborhood bar, but as the night wears on, it turns into a dance club. Joe's is an 18-and-up club with an $8 cover for those ages 18 to 20 and a $5 cover for those 21 and over. On Thurs nights, the "Drag Queens Drink Free" theme keeps things fun while Fri and Sat nights mean shows, cabaret, and other entertainment.

✳THE J. CLYDE
1312 Cobb Lane, Birmingham
(205) 939-1312
www.jclyde.com

When Alabama's alcohol limit for beer was raised in 2009 and it became legal to sell the newly available gourmet beers, The J. Clyde was ready. It was one of the first bars in Birmingham to offer a variety of the new "high-gravity" beers on tap and by the bottle. In a short time, The J. Clyde became a local favorite for its vast selection of craft beers and its surprisingly refined dinner menu. The main area inside has a cozy bar with a dining area for patrons to enjoy their food while another bar in the back serves the ample patio area in the rear of the building. Ask the bartenders to describe some of the exclusive gourmet beers available nowhere else but The J. Clyde.

✳LOU'S PUB & PACKAGE STORE
726 29th St. South, Birmingham
(205) 322-7005
www.louspub.com
Birmingham will miss the lovely, crass namesake of Lou's Pub, late founder Lou Zaden, but the quaint Lakeview mainstay continues to attract locals who depend on Lou's as a simple watering hole unadorned by the distractions of food and live music. The fusion of bar and package store includes a wide selection of all types of spirits in a casual atmosphere that often lures people who stop in for a bottle to settle down for a drink. It's one of only three package stores with bar services in the state grandfathered into Alabama's licensing law. Featured in *Esquire* magazine's Best Bars in America, Lou's Pub is a uniquely Birmingham entity and something to see for yourself.

MARTY'S
1813 10th Court South, Birmingham
(205) 939-0045
www.martysbar.com
When other clubs and bars are closing, things at Marty's are usually just picking up. Open from 4 p.m. to 6 a.m., 365 days a year,

Marty's is often the last stop before heading home for many locals enjoying the nightlife in the Southside/Five Points South area. The bar and patio area are unassuming and often packed on the weekends. Marty's serves a limited grill and sandwich menu centered around their legendary burger. Once you've had a 2 a.m. cheeseburger at Marty's, you'll agree that they put the convoluted gourmet burgers at many fancy restaurants to shame. The kitchen opens at 11 p.m. Most nights feature live music, and there is usually a $3 to $5 cover on weekend nights. As Marty's is often literally one of the only places open late at night, the crowd is one of the most diverse in town. If you're out on the town and you hear "last call" and you're not ready to call it a night, stop by Marty's and see why locals continue to flock here for late, late night fun. Marty's does not accept credit cards but does accept checks with proper ID and offers an ATM on-site.

i If you need something to take your mind off of the bathroom line at Marty's at 3 a.m. on a jam-packed Sunday morning, grab a book off the wall. Yes, that's a small library. If you find something you like, borrow it. Just don't forget to bring it back.

OAK HILL BAR AND GRILL
2835 18th St. South, Homewood
(205) 870-8277
www.myspace.com/oakhillbar
For years Oak Hill was one of the few neighborhood bars for those living in the Homewood area. Located "on the curve" in Homewood on 18th Street, Oak Hill, is the community's default joint for an after-work beer with friends. Inside it's warm and casual, and the lunch and dinner fare attracts its

own crowd. Now that 18th Street and the neighboring SoHo development are offering more nightlife options, Oak Hill remains a solid favorite for those looking to have a good time or meet someone new.

OTEY'S TAVERN
224 Country Club Rd., Mountain Brook
(205) 871-8435
www.oteystavern.com

A long-time favorite for the Crestline Village crowd, Otey's is the after-work spot to grab a cheeseburger or cold brew. Inside, the atmosphere is friendly and neighborly as many of the patrons have known each other for years. The after-work crowd is moms, dads, kids, and some of the world's saltiest (kids love them) chicken fingers. Open for lunch, Otey's serves dinner until 8 p.m., then the tavern converts into a place for live music. New picnic tables and extra seating on the patio make for a more pleasant experience, as do the flat-screen TVs. It celebrated its 20th anniversary in 2009. Rodney, the cook, has been there for most of those years. It is a Mountain Brook institution, and yes, Otey is a real person, though he doesn't own the watering hole anymore.

RED LION LOUNGE
1926 29th Ave. South, Homewood
(205) 871-8552

If you are surprised that the Red Lion doesn't have a website, this probably isn't the place for you. A true Homewood original, the Red Lion is a lounge in the true sense of the word. Stepping down into the cave-like interior, it is about as local as a dive can get. Caricatures of the regular patrons hang on the walls, and on some nights you'll find a potluck dinner with casseroles and other homemade dishes on the side table. Dig

in. Oddly, there's a Wii game console in the back. Cigarette smoke is par for the course. Go more than twice, and you'll likely start to recognize folks at the bar. The fact that it's hard to find is part of the Red Lion's charm: Patrons like it just the way it is.

> **i** Don't worry: The Red Lion Lounge stocks aspirin, Tums, and peanut butter at their bar for all their loyal patrons' obvious needs. Why peanut butter? Well, it's for those who show up with or develop uncontrollable hiccups while there. Really.

ROGUE TAVERN
2312 2nd Ave. North, Birmingham
(205) 202-4151
www.roguetavern.com

As the slow revitalization of the city center progresses, Rogue Tavern is one more coup for the busy 2nd Avenue, an emerging entertainment district of its own. Voted Birmingham's 2009 "Best Restaurant," Rogue Tavern is located in a spacious downtown building full of old-city charm with plenty of tables and seats at the bar. They serve a full lunch and dinner menu of burgers and bar food with select entrees and eclectic alternatives. The bar is massive and the selection is impressive. Every weekend features live music with an emphasis on rock-n-roll with an occasional acoustic or non-traditional music act. Expect a $3 to $5 cover charge.

SPEAKEASY
1920 3rd Ave. North, Birmingham
(205) 251-1506
www.georgecowgill.roxer.com/
speakeasy

At happy hour, you might find the crowd at this downtown bar to be dressed in suits and ready to relax before heading home for dinner. At night though, things get looser and the ties disappear as locals head to Speakeasy, a faux–Prohibition era bar nestled in the commercial/loft area around the Alabama Theatre. As the name implies, Speakeasy focuses on spirits and does not serve food. There is usually a cover on the rare weekend night when Speakeasy hosts live music, but most weekends are spent socializing and enjoying the ambience of this amazing bar.

i Speakeasy is the perfect stop for a nightcap after a show at the Alabama Theatre (or the Lyric Theatre when the renovations are complete). It's also at the heart of the Sidewalk Film Festival. Taking the short walk to Speakeasy for a drink from either of these theaters is a reminder of what this once-vibrant area could become again someday.

STARZ KARAOKE LOUNGE
730 Valley Ave., Homewood
(205) 944-0077

When locals want karaoke, they head to Starz, a gritty lounge that offers an excellent sound system and a wide variety of songs for the karaoke star to play with. Located on Valley Avenue, the immediate area can be a bit sketchy at times, but that doesn't seem to stop the singing. People from all walks of life come to Starz to let off steam and sing the night away. Songs from an extensive range of genres are available to sing—the range of talent is just as wide. That doesn't stop the crooners from braving the mic and singing their favorite songs. Service and prices are reasonable considering the lounge's popularity. On late weekend nights Starz fills up

fast. There is usually a cash cover of around $5. An ATM is located in an adjacent building if all you have are cards.

SUPERIOR GRILL
4701 Hwy. 280, Hoover
(205) 991-5112
www.birmingham.superiorgrill.com

Tired of fighting 280 traffic on the afternoon drive home? Do what many do: Drop the commute and pick up a drink with friends at Superior Grill. It's 280's bar, no doubt about it. While you're there sample the fajitas, cheese nachos, and margaritas of this Tex-Mex dining and drinking destination. Live music Thurs, Fri, and Sat nights keeps the energy level up. During fall football, there's always a game on.

UPSIDE DOWN PLAZA
2012 Magnolia Ave., Suite R13, Birmingham
(205) 930-0333
www.angelfire.com/cantina/ theupsidedownplaza

Call it a dive, a smoky pool hall, trashy, or just a bar—locals simply call it "the Plaza." Hidden in the Five Points South area behind Sekisui and the entrance to the Hotel Highland, a flight of stairs leads you down into the depths of the Plaza. Graffiti covers walls surrounding a decent dance floor that often hosts live music acts in a space face-to-face with the audience. The busy bar usually has somewhere to squeeze in and order a drink. Pool tables, darts, a foosball table, and a bumper pool table provide diversion for those who enjoy a game with a drink. There aren't any gimmicks or promotions, just a simple atmosphere that continues to draw in locals year after year.

SPORTS BARS

KELLEY'S NEIGHBORHOOD SPORTS GRILL

720 29th St. South, Birmingham
(205) 323-9786

Like a tale out of a movie, when Lakeview favorite OT's closed down in 2008, Kelley Harris, a server at OT's with over a decade of experience, decided to invest in her dreams and buy the sports grill. Harris ended up completely remodeling the entire building and it shows. What she didn't change was the excellent service and the delicious down-home cooking that continues to make it a local favorite. Enjoy the weather out on the patio or take in some football on one of their many HDTVs. Kelley's features nightly drink specials and live music on most weekend nights.

ON TAP SPORTS CAFE

737 29th St. South, Birmingham
(205) 320-1225
www.ontapsportscafe.com

With locations in Lakeview, Hoover, and the 280 areas, On Tap has secured a place for itself as one of the best bars in Birmingham. Locals have responded to On Tap's classic pub and sports bar approach by consistently awarding it top honors in many local polls. All three locations each offer at least 50 different draft beer choices ranging from popular beers from major brewers to exclusive microbrews not usually available on tap. If you're ready to travel on a journey of draft goodness, any location of On Tap can take you there. The grill menu features fresh salads, pizza, burgers, and sandwiches as well as On Tap's incredible award-winning buffalo wings. A sports fan's dream, each location of On Tap also contains an astounding amount of HDTVs showing multiple sporting events.

Chances are, no matter where you're from, if your game is televised, On Tap probably has it. Additional locations are at 3440 Galleria Circle, Hoover (205-988-3203), and 810 Inverness Corners, Hoover (205-437-1999).

TILTED KILT PUB & EATERY

14 Perimeter Park South, Birmingham
(205) 972-0204
www.birmingham.tiltedkilt.com

Alabama was settled by plenty of Scots, so it's about time a Scottish pub set up shop here. Soccer and other sporting aficionados enjoy the Highway 280 location for the HD television sets with exclusive programming showing just about any game or match you could want. Other patrons enjoy the serving ladies decked out in their red and black short-short kilts and mid-drift exposing tops. Sure the Tilted Kilt is a chain that started in Las Vegas (shock), but its pan-British appeal has been embraced along the 280 corridor. So enjoy a black and tan (or black and blue), rotten pear, or a pint of draft Guinness or Smithwick's.

WINE BARS & MARTINI LOUNGES

BLUE MONKEY LOUNGE

1318 Cobb Lane, Birmingham
(205) 933-9222
www.bluemonkeylounge.com

If you want some of the best martinis in the city, the Blue Monkey is your next stop. Locals consistently rank this martini bar on historic Cobb Lane in Southside as one of the best bars in town. Don't be surprised if you think you recognize some of the patrons—celebrities and well-known locals often stop here for a martini and a cigar from their full cigar menu (cigar smoking is permitted throughout the bar). Wed nights through Sat, live piano music fills the bar.

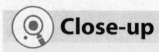

Close-up

Birmingham Live Team Trivia

Think you know it all? Test your trivia skills in the **Birmingham Live Team Trivia League.** This semi-competitive but always fun league offers Birmingham's "trivi-athletes" the opportunity to play for cash and prizes seven nights a week. Many area sports bars and restaurants offer the ever-popular trivia night. With over 30 participating locations, a real trivia maestro could play every night of the week at a number of different venues.

The League operates a spring and fall "season" at its participating venues. Teams of five earn points for placing first through fifth, and at the end of the three-month qualifying period, approximately 80 teams are invited to the playoffs. From there the participants are whittled down to a final 40 that compete for the whole magillah, a $2,500 prize and a 4-foot high trophy to be displayed at the winner's favorite bar for all to see. Sound like fun? Get some friends together, come up with a funny name (best team name wins a free pitcher of brew) and try your hand in the Birmingham Live Team Trivia League. For more information on the League or to find participating venues, visit www.facebook.com/birminghamtrivia.

The patio edges against the old cobblestone of Cobb Lane, giving patrons a relaxing view unencumbered by speeding traffic and the rush of the day. After work or after dinner, Blue Monkey Lounge is a consistently exceptional martini bar that shouldn't be missed. Street clothes are frowned upon, and a light dress code is often enforced (no sweats; tucked in shirts).

THE RARE MARTINI
2839 7th Ave. South, Birmingham
(205) 323-0008
www.theraremartini.com
Another popular Lakeview destination, The Rare Martini is one of Lakeview's more refined establishments with an elegant interior. Longtime site of the Bombay Cafe, The Rare Martini is located in the historic Avon Building on the corner of 29th Street and 7th Avenue. The dinner menu is mostly traditional American with a few seafood choices, but honestly, most people meet at The Rare

Martini for drinks. A small dance floor and stage area hosts live music Thurs, Fri, and Sat nights.

THE WINE LOFT
2200 1st Ave. North, Birmingham
(205) 323-8228
www.wineloftbham.com
Birmingham's franchise of this popular upscale chain doesn't look like a chain at all. Located in an expansive building in Downtown's Loft District, The Wine Loft is a beautiful wine bar with exposed brick walls and huge floor-to-ceiling windows that allow great views of the rapidly developing Loft District. Crowds are usually older professionals and trendy thirty-somethings out on the town. Seating is comfortable and spread out, encouraging mingling and socializing as you enjoy one of the best wine lists in town. The limited food options are exquisite but generally meant as an embellishment to the wine.

PERFORMING ARTS

For a town with a blue collar, steel-industry history, many new visitors mistakenly assume that Birmingham remains the city it was back in the mid-to-late 20th century. This could not be farther from the truth. The University of Alabama in Birmingham (UAB), the state's largest employer, helped create a strong intellectual life in the city by attracting some of the most brilliant minds in medicine, research, and science, a cultural vitality further augmented by Samford University as well as Birmingham-Southern College, one of the nation's premier liberal arts colleges. Alabama School of Fine Arts, a public high school located downtown, has been a wonderful incubator of young artistic minds since the 1970s in fields such as creative writing, dance, music, theater, and visual arts. In fact, the fine art departments at ASFA are consistently ranked among the most prestigious in the nation.

That sort of environment produces results. *Newsweek* magazine selected Birmingham as one of 10 "Hot Cities: America's Best Places to Live and Work," and the US Conference of Mayors also selected Birmingham as "America's Most Livable City." It's a testament to the many attributes the city enjoys, from a temperate climate to the affordable cost of living, but it is most certainly the strong presence of a number of fine performing arts venues, institutions, and organizations such as Cultural Alliance of Greater Birmingham, The Community Foundation of Greater Birmingham, and others that help push this mid-size city so high up in the national rankings. Music, theater, dance, visual, and the symphonic arts all thrive in Birmingham, drawn to the many excellent venues such as the Alys Robinson Stephens Performing Arts Center, Birmingham-Jefferson Convention Complex, and smaller innovative concert venues.

OVERVIEW

As one might expect, a number of artists of note hail from Birmingham such as musicians Emmylou Harris, Chuck Leavell, Lionel Hampton, Sun Ra, Cleveland Eaton, the Temptations, and Jimmy Carter, leader of the Grammy Award–winning gospel group The Blind Boys of Alabama. Indeed, a look at the who's who of television's *American Idol*—Taylor Hicks, Ruben Studdard, Diana Nicole DeGarmo, and Bo Bice—seems to indicate that being from Birmingham is in a contestant's best interests. There are visual artists such as Thornton Dial, Frank Fleming, and Lonnie Holley. Birmingham can also claim a host of writers and novelist such as Daniel Wallace, Walker Percy, E. O. Wilson, Fannie Flagg, Robert McCammon, Howell Raines, Warren St. John, Daniel Alarcón, and Tobias Wolff. Actors and directors like Courtney Cox, Kate Jackson, Louise Fletcher, and John Badham, director of *Saturday Night Fever, Dracula,* and *WarGames,* all hail from the Magic City.

But beyond the name-dropping, Birmingham is simply a city that supports the various performance arts, creating an environment where craftspeople can experiment and thrive. One only has to pick up a local newspaper or city magazine like *Black & White, Birmingham Magazine,* or *Birmingham Weekly* to look at the numerous weekly listings for theater, dance, performance art, and other special events to realize the city is very fortunate in this regard.

The venues and organizations listed in this chapter have established themselves as dependable, quality providers of professional entertainment. Are there other smaller community groups, cultural centers, and supportive organizations in Birmingham that contribute to the region's art scene? Certainly so, but there is simply not room or time enough to list them all. The phone numbers listed are typically for the box office, though some performing-arts events sell tickets through Ticketmaster and other ticket services. Most venues offer discounts for seniors, students, and groups. Call or see the websites to find out more.

Price Code

The price code includes one regularly priced ticket for admission for one adult. Call ahead to see if discounts apply to members of your party.

$	Less than $5
$$	$5 to $10
$$$	$10 to $20
$$$$	More than $20

DANCE

ALABAMA BALLET $$$$
2726 1st Ave. South, Birmingham
(205) 322-4300
www.alabamaballet.org

Headed by artistic director Tracey Alvey, an internationally recognized principal dancer and Royal Academy of Dance professional dance teacher, Alabama Ballet leads the state in professional dance performance, instruction, and community outreach. Joined by associate artistic director and resident choreographer Roger Van Fleteren, also an internationally renowned principal and soloist, the two have set a high standard for the organization. Celebrated music director Leslie Fillmer composes and conducts contemporary compositions and cherished classics for the company's wide variety of performances. Alabama Ballet brings a new spin to old stories with original creations like *Dracula* and *Dr. Jekyll and Mr. Hyde.* A repertory of standards and performances of some of the most challenging ballet works rounds out most of Alabama Ballet's traditional offerings.

Every Christmas season, Alabama Ballet is one of six companies in the world licensed to perform George Balanchine's *The Nutcracker,* widely considered to be the preeminent production of *The Nutcracker.* In addition to its top-flight ballet company, Alabama Ballet also offers a Royal Academy of Dance–accredited dance school that features professional classes for almost every age group. Children ages 3 to 18 can enjoy classes that range in level for both beginning and experienced dancers. Jazz, pointe, and tap classes are also available. Adults can participate in the Fun and Fit program, a combination of artistry and exercise with classes in ballet, tap, pilates, and jazz. Some Fun and Fit programs are open to ages 16 and older. Classes and some performances are located in Alabama Ballet's state-of-the-art facility in the Lakeview district of Southside. Other performances are held in many of the city's venues, including Sanford University's Wright Center and the Alys Robinson Stephens Performing Arts Center.

BIRMINGHAM BALLET $$–$$$
2198 Columbiana Rd., Suite 100, Vestavia Hills
(205) 979-9492
www.birminghamballet.com

Focused on providing professional quality cultural entertainment and training for aspiring dancers, Birmingham Ballet presents a full ballet season together with a ballet academy that conducts classes for every age and skill level. To her credit, in a relatively short time Executive and Artistic Director Cindy Free has assembled an established community ballet company with a professional repertory ensemble. In 2010 Birmingham Ballet introduced its own Professional Repertory Dance Company, a group of top dancers performing classical and contemporary works while building toward their professional careers. Semi-annual auditions for area dancers are conducted for those wishing to perform with Birmingham Ballet. From those selected, Birmingham Ballet organizes their Professional Ensemble, Senior Company, Junior Company, and Community Cast. The Family Series of performances features works like *Peter Pan, The Sleeping Beauty,* and *Hansel and Gretel.* Classes and some performances are held in the Birmingham Ballet facility. Major performances are held in the Birmingham Jefferson Convention Complex.

UMDABU DANCE COMPANY FREE
2016 2nd Ave. South, Birmingham
(205) 251-7158
www.umdabudance.org

Umdabu Dance Company entertains through riveting performances of South African dance with a focus on the Zulu people. The company's combination of dance, song, and audience participation also educates audiences on "traditional and contemporary South African history and culture." Presentations are offered throughout the Birmingham area and are often held at local libraries and schools and are free to the public. Classes are available for adults and children. A summer camp for children teaches traditional dances and songs along with conversational words from IsiZulu, a widespread South African language.

MUSIC

ALABAMA SYMPHONY ORCHESTRA $$$$
3621 6th Ave. South, Birmingham
(205) 251-7727
www.alabamasymphony.org

To be truly missed and appreciated, sometimes, sadly, one has to go away for a time. That was the case with the Alabama Symphony Orchestra. It's difficult to discuss the ASO without touching upon its bankruptcy and closing in 1993. Reborn in 1997, the ASO has reestablished itself as one of the South's finest orchestras. The ASO is led by Grammy-nominated music director and principal conductor Justin Brown, an internationally acclaimed conductor and solo pianist. Under Brown's masterful guidance, the ASO offers a tremendous range of concerts suited for many audiences. The Masterworks series features simply the best of classical music. The SuperPOPS concerts offer contemporary performances ranging from pop stars to Irish folk artists performing alongside the orchestra. The ASO also conducts family concerts, matinee "coffee" concerts, chamber music ensembles, seasonal shows, and unique events such as a country music review, a Charlie Chaplin retrospective, and world premieres of some of the best new orchestra music. The ASO's concerts are usually held at the Alys Stephens Center, although occasionally concerts are held at other prominent Birmingham venues.

i With the ASO's success many of the seasonal shows, unique concerts, and Masterworks performances often sell out months in advance. Check the website and call the box office to check ticket availability, and ensure you don't miss one of Birmingham's treasures.

BIRMINGHAM MUSIC
COOPERATIVE $$
1807 3rd Ave. North, Birmingham
(205) 322-6737
www.bhammusiccoop.org
This nonprofit administrative cooperative supports Opera Birmingham, the Birmingham Art Music Alliance, the Birmingham Chamber Music Society, and the Birmingham Music Club. These organizations offer a multitude of excellent performances in diverse genres. Opera Birmingham, the cooperative's most successful group, is one of the state's only professional opera companies. Together with an educational tour that serves to promote the arts in local schools, Opera Birmingham performs two major operas each year to rave reviews. An annual vocal competition draws some of the best in current opera singing to Birmingham for an extraordinary "reality" singing contest. Concerts are held at Samford University's Wright Center. The Birmingham Art Music Alliance has a "twofold mission of promoting music by Alabama composers

and presenting concerts of recently created art music." True to its mission, the alliance lists as its members Birmingham's best composers and performers. Featuring college professors, award-winning youth composers, and avant-garde performers, the alliance offers a wonderful opportunity to enjoy modern-art music at an affordable price. The Birmingham Chamber Music Society presents an annual performance by some of the world's best professional ensembles.

THEATER
✱BIRMINGHAM FESTIVAL
THEATRE $$$$
1901½ 11th Ave. South, Birmingham
(205) 933-2383
www.bftonline.org
Presenting cutting-edge theater that often features non-traditional, alternative themes, the Birmingham Festival Theatre is located in Southside's trendy Five Points South entertainment district. Since 1972 the BFT has challenged audiences with more than 250 plays that would usually never have the chance to be performed in Birmingham's more conservative theaters. It is intimate and exciting fare. With season tickets that include preferred seats and parking all for only $99, the BFT is an excellent choice for the budget-minded theater lover.

CITY EQUITY THEATRE $$$
1800 8th Ave. North, Birmingham
(205) 251-1206
www.cityequitytheatre.com
City Equity Theatre bills itself as "Birmingham's longest-running Equity theatre company," providing a place for some of the best union actors to display their talents. What does this mean to you? Audiences

are given the opportunity to experience theater crafted by dedicated professionals from around the country. Consistently well reviewed, the City Equity Theatre presents a yearly season that focuses on quality instead of quantity. Most shows are held at the Virginia Samford Theatre in the Highland Park neighborhood of Southside.

RED MOUNTAIN THEATRE COMPANY $$$$
3028 7th Ave. South, Birmingham
(205) 324-2424
www.redmountaintheatre.org
Formerly Summerfest Music Theatre, the Red Mountain Theatre Company is a nonprofit professional group that provides the only full season of musical theater in Alabama. The RMTC produces classics like *Cabaret* and *The Music Man* along with newer musicals from modern artists. Well known in the city for its high standards, shows produced by the RMTC continue to impress music-loving audiences year after year. Performances are held at the RMTC's own Cabaret Theatre in Downtown and also at the Virginia Samford Theatre.

i Have a child who's ready for the chorus line? RMTC is also recognized for its excellent musical theater programs for students ages 5 to 18. Call or check the website for information about their professional training program.

TERRIFIC NEW THEATRE $$$$
2821 2nd Ave. South, Birmingham
(205) 328-0868
www.terrificnewtheatre.com
Offering some of Birmingham's best modern theater, the Terrific New Theatre continues to thrive after more than 25 years in production. TNT has found its niche offering progressive theater produced and performed by some of Birmingham's best local talent. Terrific New Theatre is located in the popular Pepper Place downtown. Watch for "pay what you can afford" for Thurs evening performances.

THEATRE LJCC $$$
3960 Montclair Rd., Birmingham
(205) 879-0411
www.bhamjcc.org
The theater company at the Levite Jewish Community Center produces a family-friendly season of plays and musicals each year. Celebrating its 50th anniversary in 2010, Theatre LJCC continues to present the community with outstanding theater at inexpensive prices. Opportunities to work with the theater are available for volunteers, and a popular summer theater camp teaches the basics of theater in the comfort of the community center's impressive facilities.

THEATRE UAB $$-$$$
1200 10th Ave. South, Birmingham
ASC 255
(205) 934-3236
http://theatre.hum.uab.edu
Birmingham's largest university develops a full season of theater each year with a distinct focus on student involvement in all aspects of its productions. An acclaimed professional faculty engages students and the community in a program that embraces both established classics and controversial modern works. Theatre UAB also runs a touring company that performs for schools across the state. The theater's annual Festival of Ten-Minute Plays is a popular favorite that features plays written by student playwrights and continues to sell out every performance

each year. All performances are held in the Alys Stephens Center.

PERFORMING ARTS VENUES

ALABAMA THEATRE
1817 3rd Ave. North, Birmingham
(205) 252-2262
www.alabamatheatre.com

Opened as a silent film theater in 1927, the Alabama Theatre for the Performing Arts is the crown jewel in the state's performance art world. Step into the past as you enter one of the nation's oldest original theaters featuring one of the nation's oldest original Mighty Wurlitzer organs. The theater was actually the first public building in Alabama to have air-conditioning, a sure sign of its significance. Thoroughly restored to its original grandeur in 1998, the Alabama Theatre allows patrons to experience live performance in a stunning space that harkens back to the glory days of cinema in the United States. Dominated by gold leaf and the glow of the lighted dome ceiling, the interior of the theater resembles a European opera house more than a movie theater. Upstairs and downstairs bars serve the hallways and waiting areas outside the theater, and patrons are allowed to take their drinks to their seats in some shows (mostly movie viewings).

From the gilded box office to the detailed facade around the stage, the Alabama Theatre is a piece of art in itself. The original Wurlitzer organ often entertains audiences before the show and interested patrons can occasionally enjoy scheduled organ tours. The theater also includes many organ recitals as well as free organ shows and silent films accompanied by music, continuing the tradition of what must have been the theater's original offerings to the Birmingham public. The Alabama Theatre consistently offers regular viewings of popular contemporary movies, including seasonal classics, cult favorites, and some of the best films from a wide variety of genres. And when a popular musician books a show here, you can be certain that the 2,220-seat venue will often sell out.

The Alabama and Lyric Theatres

Located opposite one another at the corner of 18th Street and 3rd Avenue North the **Alabama and Lyric Theatres** were once the nexus of cinema and live performance in the city. While many know the Alabama Theatre, the Lyric, an equally grand and beautiful old gem, remains more of a mystery. Built in 1914 as a vaudeville venue, the Lyric attracted performers such as Jack Benny, Will Rogers, Buster Keaton, Mae West, and other such stars of the period. After the Great Depression the Lyric reopened as a movie house until it closed in the late 1980s after a less-than respectable run as the Foxy Adult Cinema. Closed for years, that dire neglect makes for slow restoration. But progress is being made. Watch for behind-the-scenes tours of the Lyric for rare glimpses inside to follow the restoration efforts and learn how you can help. Here's to two of the region's grandest old theaters coming back from the brink!

It is a wonderful place to experience intimate performances from artists that often perform in larger, noisier venues. Other events include dance recitals, drama, and yearly performances by the Alabama Symphony Orchestra. In a time when most performance art has moved to the Southside area, the Alabama Theatre provides an anchor for live art in downtown Birmingham.

✳ALYS ROBINSON STEPHENS PERFORMING ARTS CENTER
1200 10th Ave. South, Birmingham
(205) 975-ARTS, (877) ART-TIKS
www.alysstephens.uab.edu

Soon after opening in 1996, the Alys Robinson Stephens Performing Arts Center (or "Alys Stephens Center," as it is often called) quickly became the primary center for performing arts in the city. Indeed the ASC's superior design and accessibility make it one of Birmingham's leading entertainment venues. It hosts more than 250,000 people for more than 300 various events each year. A central feature of the University of Alabama at Birmingham, the ASC contains a 1,330-seat concert hall, 350-seat proscenium theater, 170-seat recital hall, and a black box theater. The ASC holds events for many of Birmingham's artistic institutions including the Alabama Ballet, the Alabama Symphony Orchestra, and Theatre UAB. Popular entertainers like Ellis Marsalis, Diana Krall, Itzhak Perlman, Queen Latifah, Mandy Patinkin, Natalie Cole, Willie Nelson, and Savion Glover perform in many of the ASC's sold-out mainstream concerts. The ASC also presents film and multimedia productions as well as a Kids' Club for the little ones. Spoken-word performances by modern storytellers such as Ira Glass and Henry Rollins together with hit comedy performers like Rickey Smiley and Joan Rivers prove that the ASC has quickly become

one of Alabama's first choices for artists from around the world. There is always something going on at the Alys Stephens Center.

BIRMINGHAM-JEFFERSON CONVENTION COMPLEX
2100 Richard Arrington Jr. Blvd. North, Birmingham
(205) 458-8400
www.bjcc.org

With over one million attendees in the 2008–2009 fiscal year, the BJCC is the city's largest space for concerts, banquets, trade shows, conferences, and other large functions. Centered in the heart of downtown Birmingham, the BJCC has a facility for any type of event, from the 17,000-seat arena to a 1,000-seat theater. The world's most popular musicians are guaranteed to play here when they come to Alabama. Events vary from the latest teen heartthrob singer, Broadway shows, and high school basketball games to Davis Cup tennis, Ringling Brothers and Barnum and Bailey Circus, and massive auto shows. It has hosted numerous Southeastern Conference, Sun Belt, and NCAA college basketball tournaments. The connected Sheraton Birmingham Hotel offers the best in guest accommodations with a convenient location to the entertainment options offered by the BJCC.

BOUTWELL AUDITORIUM
1930 8th Ave. North, Birmingham
(205) 254-2820

Set in the heart of the downtown Birmingham business district adjacent to Linn Park, Boutwell Auditorium has been at the center of arts and cultural entertainment since first opening its door in the 1920s. Though overshadowed by newer venues like the BJCC and Alys Stephens Center, the building still hosts Broadway plays, musicals, rock concerts, and other performing arts events.

CARVER THEATRE
1631 4th Ave. North, Birmingham
(205) 254-2731
www.jazzhall.com
As part of the beautiful Jazz Hall of Fame, the Carver Theatre continues a proud tradition of jazz performance downtown along with comedy, spoken word, theater, and dance. Many local artists perform in this historic art deco venue, making it a favorite for its intimate setting—there are no bad seats in the house. Touring the museum to discover more about Duke Ellington, Erskine Hawkins, Nat King Cole, as well as Birmingham's role in the jazz world makes for a delightful excursion. See the Attractions chapter for more information on the Carver Theatre and Alabama Jazz Hall of Fame.

SAMFORD UNIVERSITY
800 Lakeshore Dr., Homewood
(205) 726-2011
www.samford.edu/arts.aspx
Samford University, a small college set on a sloping hill in Homewood, presents performances and exhibitions that enhance the city's visual and performance art programs. From string quartets and solo recitals to dance and theater performances, the school's Brock Recital Hall and Harrison Theatre host events for both touring professional groups as well as Samford's School of the Arts and Department of Theatre and Dance. Check the School of the Arts site for information regarding events and tickets. The school also offers workshops and hosts exhibits.

VIRGINIA SAMFORD THEATRE
1116 26th St. South, Birmingham
(205) 251-1228
www.virginiasamfordtheatre.org
The Virginia Samford Theatre at Caldwell Park has served the Southside community for over 80 years. Named after the benefactor who saved the theater from closure in the 1990s, the VST (formerly known as the Little Theatre, Town & Gown Theatre, and Clark Memorial Theatre) serves as a facility for a number of local performing-arts organizations, underground musicians, and various groups. After the Metropolitan Arts Council helped restore and refurbish the distinctive Romanesque landmark, it reopened in 2002 to much acclaim. Enjoy a play in the spacious theater, an intimate acoustic performance in the smaller upstairs dance hall (with bar), or a chamber music recital on the outdoor terrace.

i The entrance of the theater connects to Caldwell Park, a popular urban park set in the graceful curve of Highland Avenue in Southside. Bring a blanket and a picnic basket and have a meal before the show. Parking for the theater is usually on the street only, so be sure to arrive early.

LITERARY EVENTS

When it comes to literary events and book signings in Birmingham, arguably no bookstore shines as brightly as the **Alabama Booksmith.** Literary luminaries such as Isabel Allende, Richard Russo, Sena Jeter Naslund, Pat Conroy, Edna O'Brien, and Anne Rice have all done book signings at the Alabama Booksmith. Alabama Booksmith frequently sells books at various literary events in different locations about town as well. Another locally owned independent bookstore just a few blocks away from the Alabama Booksmith, **Little Professor** frequently hosts signings, discussions, and literary events—just look on the glass entryway for the proliferation of flyers announcing upcoming events. There will typically be several signings each week, usually from local or regional authors. Alabama-owned **Books-A-Million,** a chain with more than 200 stores in 18 states, operates 7 stores in the Birmingham region and frequently hosts national and local authors for readings and in-store events. With two stores in the city, chain giant **Barnes & Noble** is another source for literary events.

ALABAMA BOOKSMITH
26 19th Place South, Homewood
(205) 870-4242
www.alabamabooksmith.com

BARNES & NOBLE
Summit Shopping Center
201 Summit Blvd., Suite 100,
Birmingham
(205) 298-0665

Patton Creek Shopping Center
171 Main St., Hoover
(205) 682-4467
www.barnesandnoble.com

BOOKS-A-MILLION
Multiple locations
(800) 201-3550
www.booksamillion.com

LITTLE PROFESSOR BOOKSTORE
2717 18th St. South, Homewood
(205) 870-7461
www.littleprofessorhomewood.com

MUSEUMS & GALLERIES

Birmingham's collection of museums and galleries is as diverse as its population. Whether it's art, sports, or history, Birmingham is home to a variety of museums and galleries to satisfy your intellectual curiosity. While the city features museums such as the world-class Birmingham Museum of Art and the internationally renowned Birmingham Civil Rights Institute together with galleries such as the Andy Warhol Foundation's Space One Eleven, you'll also find places that you never expected like the Karl C. Harrison Museum of George Washington or the Samuel Ullman Museum. Science museums like the McWane Science Center offer fun, educational programs that stimulate young students' minds and provide a lasting connection and interest with the natural world.

Art lovers of all kinds can find more traditional art that reflects the city's Southern roots as well as challenging and provocative installation pieces that push the boundaries. Considering the number of traveling shows and permanent collections in the city, a visitor to Birmingham can expect to see exhibits as varied as Leonardo da Vinci's drawings from the Biblioteca Reale in Turin, Africa-American portraits from the Smithsonian, contemporary Korean prints, Yale University's American art, or collected works of an intriguing multi-generational family of women artists from Selma, Alabama.

Of course the key to a healthy artistic environment is the support organizations that provide local arts education and community outreach. In Birmingham a number of fine, active galleries fill this function, whetting the public's appetite for the exciting promise of art. Alabama School of Fine Arts, a partially residential public school located downtown, enjoys a strong national reputation for its creative programs in creative writing, dance, mathematics and science, music, theater arts, and visual arts. That energy and enthusiasm translates into an enormous source of ever-new talent that infuses the arts scene in town. Local artists from Birmingham's artistic community fill the walls and spaces of the city's art galleries, keeping things happening at this, the most local of levels.

Keep an eye out for new and developing museums and galleries such as the proposed Museum of Urban Art, a planned addition to Birmingham's Downtown Business District, which will feature contemporary art that reflects life in urban America. Birmingham's increasingly international population combined with its rich local and regional traditions make for some stunningly brilliant productions by artists who call Birmingham home. From the world's largest collection of Wedgwood outside of England to the largest motorcycle collection in the United States, there is plenty to take in at Birmingham's museums and galleries.

Price Code

The price code includes one regularly priced ticket for admission for one adult. Call ahead to see if discounts apply to members of your party.

$.....................**Less than $5**
$$ ....**$5 to $10**
$$$ .... **$10 to $20**
$$$$ .... **More than $20**

MUSEUMS

ALABAMA HISTORICAL RADIO SOCIETY AND DON KRESGE MEMORIAL MUSEUM   FREE

600 18th St. North, Birmingham
(205) 822-6759
www.alabamahistoricalradiosociety.org

Located in the Alabama Power Building downtown, the Alabama Historical Radio Society (AHRS) and Don Kresge Memorial Museum have been providing lovers of old-time radio with unique events and exhibits for over 20 years. See the old radios from the early part of the 20th century and even listen to some of the old programs, such as *Dick Tracy,* that drew listeners to the speaker each week. The pride and joy of the museum, however, is the world's only surviving "Super-Flex" radio receiver manufactured right here in Birmingham in 1927. In addition to the cool old-time radios, the AHRS provides a series of interesting discussions on all things radio. Got an old radio you'd like to restore? This is the group for you. Parents will get a kick out of explaining to children raised in the iPod era just what these curious, funny-looking old devices of wood, cloth, and metal were used for.

ALABAMA JAZZ HALL OF FAME $

1631 4th Ave. North
(205) 254-2731
www.jazzhall.com

Perhaps the South's greatest artistic contribution, jazz has a rich history in the Magic City and in Alabama—and it is all captured at the Alabama Jazz Hall of Fame. Located at the Carver Theatre in Birmingham's historic Civil Rights District, the Alabama Jazz Hall of Fame features over 2,200 square feet of priceless memorabilia related to the history of jazz in Alabama and the greater southeast. Aside from photographs and memorabilia, the Alabama Jazz Hall of Fame also offers a number of fun and educational programs at no charge. Among the most popular of the programs is the "Free Saturday Jazz" series. These free classes are taught by the Jazz Hall's Director of Student Jazz Programs Ray Reach and Director of Education, Emeritus, Dr. Frank Adams and are free to the public.

In addition to "Free Saturday Jazz," the Jazz Hall also features a number of workshops and clinics taught by various jazz greats. Past guest instructors have included Thelonious Monk and Bill Goodwin, among others. Visit the Jazz Hall website for more information on upcoming workshops. Of course, once you've attended these clinics and have become a jazz master, don't just throw out your old instrument. Donate it to the Jazz Hall's Musical Instrument Recycling Program. This program takes used instruments and cleans and repairs them and gives them to budding young musicians in need of an instrument. The Alabama Jazz Hall of Fame is a wonderful place to inspire the next generation of musicians.

ALABAMA MUSEUM OF
HEALTH SCIENCE   FREE
Lister Hill Library
1700 University Blvd., Birmingham
(205) 934-4475
www.uab.edu/amhs

When the University of Alabama first opened its "Birmingham Extension Center" nearly 75 years ago to accommodate for students who were unable to make the trip to Tuscaloosa, the steel industry was booming. No one could have predicted that Birmingham would eventually be counted among the nation's top centers for medicine. Today, the University of Alabama at Birmingham is the largest employer in the state of Alabama.

The Alabama Museum of Health Sciences, housed in the Lister Hill Library on the campus of UAB, reflects Birmingham's transition from the steel industry to the present day. Complete with information and collections of artifacts marking 700 years of medical advancements, the museum features an assortment of historical instruments, equipment, and devices that illustrate the advancement of health sciences. Although the museum is free and open to the public, admission prices for exhibitions may vary. Visit the website for more information on upcoming events and exhibitions.

ALABAMA SPORTS HALL OF
FAME AND MUSEUM $
2150 Richard Arrington Jr. Blvd. North,
Birmingham
(205) 323-6665
www.ashof.org

Organizing a sports hall of fame may seem like no more than compiling an impressive list of names and collecting a few artifacts, but in a state as sports-crazy as Alabama, creating a sports hall of fame that matches the enthusiasm of its patrons is no easy task. The curators of the Alabama Sports Hall of Fame have done just that, however, creating a state-of-the-art facility in the heart of downtown Birmingham that records and interprets the athletic feats and accomplishments of Alabamians.

In Alabama sports are not just a diversion from the every-day life—they've been a catalyst for political change. It was Alabama's own Jesse Owens that shocked Hitler and the Nazi Party at the Berlin Olympics in 1936 when the sprinter won four gold medals. And although many have criticized Alabama coaching great Bear Bryant for not being more resolute on integration earlier, many minds were changed after African Americans began suiting up for the Crimson Tide on Saturdays—and winning, by the way. The Alabama Sports Hall of Fame reflects not only the passion of Alabamians in support of their favorite teams and players, but also the social transformation that sometimes followed.

Over 300 men and women are enshrined in the Alabama Sports Hall of Fame. In addition to Jesse Owens and Bear Bryant, the museum has honored legends such as Willie Mays, Hank Aaron, Bo Jackson, and Joe Namath. In fact, in the ESPN Sports Century list of the 100 greatest athletes of the 20th century, 5 of the top 15 are enshrined in the Alabama Sports Hall of Fame. One need not be an Auburn or Alabama fan to enjoy the museum. It has something for sports fans of all persuasions.

✳BARBER VINTAGE
MOTORSPORTS MUSEUM $$$
6030 Barber Motorsports Pkwy., Leeds
(205) 699-7275
www.barbermuseum.org

Representing the culmination of a dream of local dairy magnate George Barber, the Barber Motorsports Museum is one of the world's finest collection of motorcycles. The museum also showcases a number of sports autos including a magnificent collection of Lotus race cars. Located within the Barber Motorsports Park, one of North America's premiere raceways, the Barber Motorsports Museum is the place to be for auto-racing enthusiasts. Although the museum features racing autos of all types, Barber's preference is no secret: motorcycles. And with over 1,000 different makes and models, one could spend weeks ogling at the beauties. In fact, when Guggenheim's Museums in New York and Bilbao hosted the "Art of the Motorcycle" exhibit, Barber Motorsports Museum was its largest lender.

BIRMINGHAM HISTORY CENTER $
1731 1st Ave. North, Suite 120,
Birmingham
(205) 202-4146
www.birminghamhistorycenter.org
While most large cities in Alabama—Montgomery, Mobile, Huntsville—have museums or attractions that tell a narrative of the city's history, Birmingham has been late to the show for a variety of reasons. Visitors generally have to visit a variety of sites, museums, and attractions to piece together the full Birmingham story. In 2008 Birmingham businessman Thomas E. Jernigan Jr. pledged $750,000 to establish the Birmingham History Center for 10 years. Opening in the historic Young & Vann Supply building two years later, the museum's mission is to "collect, preserve and present the comprehensive history of the Birmingham region."

Accordingly, the history center possesses more than 4,000 objects that recount the story of Birmingham in what the center hopes will just be a temporary space. Displays include Birmingham during the Great Depression, local inventors, and the World War II era. The museum serves to protect an assortment of documents, books, clothing, photographs, machinery, and other historic items of significance to the city and surrounding communities. The majority of the museum's holdings are donations generously provided by local residents. It's early days yet, but the fruits of the excellent Birmingham-Jefferson Historical Society appear to be paying off.

✳BIRMINGHAM MUSEUM
**   OF ART**   FREE
2000 Rev. Abraham Woods Jr. Blvd.,
Birmingham
(205) 254-2565
www.artsbma.org
The Birmingham Museum of Art is the largest municipal art museum in the southeast, housing over 25,000 works of art from various periods and media. Through the generosity of local benefactors, the museum has amassed some impressive collections, such as the Dwight and Lucille Wedgwood Collection, the world's largest outside of England. The museum's permanent collections include works from around the globe and from various time periods. In addition to the museum's permanent collection, the BMA also hosts a number of exhibitions at any given time. Past exhibitions have included the popular "Pompeii: Tales from an Eruption" and European Masters, among numerous others. And when the Da Vinci exhibit, "Leonardo Da Vinci: Drawings from the Biblioteca Reale in Turin," ventured to North America, just two cities were honored to temporarily house the collection: San Francisco and Birmingham. Although the BMA's permanent collections are always free

and open to the public, the museum features many exclusive programs available only to members of the BMA. To learn more about the various exhibits coming through town, be sure to check the website.

i Among the BMA's most popular programs is "Art on the Rocks," held on Fri during the summer and featuring live music and refreshing drinks. Check the BMA website for dates, grab a friend, and join the rest of Birmingham's art-loving community at "Art on the Rocks."

*BIRMINGHAM CIVIL RIGHTS INSTITUTE $$$
520 16th St. North, Birmingham
(205) 328-9696
www.bcri.org

The Birmingham Civil Rights Institute has received considerable international acclaim for its efforts to promote human rights worldwide by drawing on the experience of the American Civil Rights Movement here in Birmingham. The BCRI has worked with a number of other prestigious human-rights organizations to spread the message of the Civil Rights Movement in Birmingham and help foster human-rights education. The state-of-the-art facility located in Birmingham's historic Civil Rights District faces Kelly Ingram Park and is flanked by the 16th Street Baptist Church, two additional civil rights attractions.

A walk through the museum features a number of moving images and displays beginning with Birmingham's own civil-rights struggle followed by an exhibition on the broader Civil Rights Movement in the United States. The tour concludes with a powerful gallery on international human-rights injustices and a plea for humanity to work together to respect the intrinsic rights of the individual to put an end to current human-rights violations. In addition, the BCRI also houses thousands of documents on and from the Civil Rights Movement in the Richard Arrington Jr. Resource Gallery.

Since 2002 the BCRI has awarded the Reverend Fred Shuttlesworth Human Rights Award annually to an individual displaying, "A philosophy of non-violence and reconciliation, courage, both moral and physical in the face of great odds, humility, leadership by example and an established commitment to human-rights activities." The award's first recipient was Reverend Fred Shuttlesworth, and has been followed by Congressman John Lewis, actor Danny Glover, and activist Dorothy Cotton, among others. The BCRI is open 6 days a week and closed on Mon. Admission is $15, but discounts are available to seniors and students. The Institute features a number of exhibitions and special events every year.

i If you happen to be in Birmingham on Martin Luther King Jr. Day, be sure to make a trip to the Birmingham Civil Rights Institute. Admission is free all day on MLK Day—plus it's the only Mon of the year that the BCRI is open.

KARL C. HARRISON MUSEUM OF GEORGE WASHINGTON FREE
50 Lester St., Columbiana
(205) 669-8767
www.washingtonmuseum.com

Located in probably the last place you'd expect, a unique collection of George Washington memorabilia is found at the Karl C. Harrison Museum of George Washington

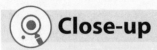

Close-up

Birmingham Artist Lonnie Holley

Known to many as **"The Sand Man,"** famed artist **Lonnie Holley** calls Birmingham home. Born the 7th of 27 children, Holley's first works included the tombstones for the deceased children of his sister, which he carved from sandstone. It would be easy to say that the rest is history, but as any artist can tell you, and as Holley will certainly attest, the road to success for an artist is never easy. Holley took some of his sandstone carvings to Birmingham Museum of Art director Richard Murray and the BMA immediately put several on display. In a short time a mention of Lonnie Holley soon became part of any discussion on southern art. His work includes paintings and recycled found-object sculptures. Today, Holley is one of the country's most highly respected and sought-after artists. Aside from the Birmingham Museum of Art, Holley's works have been featured in the Smithsonian American Art Institute, the High Museum of Art in Atlanta, and the White House, among others distinguished locations. His career came full circle in 2004 when the Birmingham Museum of Art organized his first major retrospective, *Do We Think Too Much? I Don't Think We Can Ever Stop: Lonnie Holley, A Twenty-Five Year Survey.*

in Columbiana, just south of Birmingham. Through the generosity of Charlotte Smith-Weaver, herself a direct descendant of Martha Washington, the museum began acquiring artifacts. Today, the Karl C. Harrison Museum of George Washington occupies its own wing of the Harrison Regional Library. Among the various items housed in the museum are a number of George Washington's personal effects including hand-written letters to his wife, Martha, and an original sketch of Mount Vernon by Samuel Vaughn. Open weekdays, the museum is a must-see for history buffs.

MCWANE SCIENCE CENTER   **$$**
200 19th St. North, Birmingham
(205) 714-8300
www.mcwane.org
Located next to the historic Alabama Theatre in the former Loveman's Department Store, the McWane Science Center is an interactive educational science museum. Although

most of the exhibits are geared towards children, it's not uncommon to catch Mom or Dad enjoying themselves while learning something new. And with four floors filled with fun and educational exhibits, there are plenty of new things to learn and discover. With everything from the "World of Water Aquarium" to the "Challenger Learning Center," the McWane Science Center covers most kids' intellectual curiosity—and then some. Also located within the McWane Science Center is Birmingham's only IMAX domed theater. In addition to educational documentaries, the IMAX also plays feature-films released in IMAX. Visit the website for more information on special events and to see a full list of all of the Center's permanent exhibits.

SAMUEL ULLMAN MUSEUM   **FREE**
2150 15th Ave. South, Birmingham
(205) 934-3328
www.uab.edu/sites/UllmanMuseum

Samuel Ullman, best known for writing the poem "Youth," was a German immigrant whose family came to the United States in the 1850s. Ullman lived in New Orleans, Louisiana, and Natchez, Mississippi, before finally settling in Birmingham where he lived for the last 40 years of his life. He achieved literary fame in Japan, of all places, before he was well-known in the United States, and it was through the efforts of the Japan-America Society of Alabama that his home was restored and made into a museum. Ullman's "Youth" has been quoted by countless speakers such as Robert F. Kennedy and General Douglas MacArthur, who was so fond of the poem that he had it framed and hung prominently in his office. It was because of MacArthur, in post-war Japan, that the poem grew in popularity. The University of Alabama at Birmingham currently operates the museum. Admission is free, and the museum is open weekdays.

SOUTHERN ENVIRONMENTAL CENTER $
900 Arkadelphia Rd., Birmingham
(205) 226-4934
www.myecoscapes.org
Found on the campus of Birmingham-Southern College, the Southern Environmental Center is devoted to promoting healthy, sustainable lifestyles with respect for the environment. The SEC is responsible for promoting and building numerous EcoScape urban gardens in vacant lots throughout the Birmingham area. The center is geared towards school-age children and features 5,600 square feet of interactive, environmental education exhibits showcasing our impact on the environment—and most importantly, what we can do to change it for the better. In addition to the center

itself, the Southern Environmental Center maintains a 4-acre EcoScape on the campus of Birmingham-Southern that features a miniature Mobile Basin wetland as well as edible and medicinal plants and herbs. For a hands-on good time, visitors can also make eco-art out of discarded plastic and wire.

SOUTHERN MUSEUM OF FLIGHT $$
4343 73rd St. North, Birmingham
(205) 833-8226
www.southernmuseumofflight.org
Appropriately enough, the Southern Museum of Flight resides on the property of the Birmingham-Shuttlesworth International Airport. It houses some of the world's most unique aircraft, and everyone from children to grandparents will be entranced by the power of flight. Established by the Birmingham Aero Club in 1965, the museum features artifacts from every American war since the dawn of aviation as well as special exhibits on the Tuskegee Airmen, Korean War jets, and Vietnam War helicopters. In addition to the various aircraft, the museum is also home to the Alabama Aviation Hall of Fame, a site dedicated to honoring the men and women from the state who have made great strides in flight.

VULCAN PARK AND MUSEUM $
1701 Valley View Dr., Birmingham
(205) 933-1409
www.visitvulcan.com
Overlooking the city from atop Red Mountain stands *Vulcan,* Roman god of the forge, which was first unveiled at the 1904 St. Louis World's Fair. The world's largest cast-iron statue was the creation of Italian artist Giuseppe Moretti whose companion piece to *Vulcan, Head of Christ,* accompanied the massive statue to remind viewers that Vulcan

was indeed a pagan god. Moretti considered *Head of Christ* his masterpiece, and it is on display at the Vulcan Museum. The museum not only tells the story of Vulcan, but of industrial Birmingham as well: The two are intrinsically linked. It was nearly 35 years after its unveiling at the World's Fair—and after Moretti had died—that *Vulcan* was finally installed atop Red Mountain in 1939. The statue you see today is still the original work of Moretti, but the statue and the surrounding park underwent a complete renovation recently. The museum itself is full of fascinating information and artifacts that tell the story of Birmingham, where it's been, and where it's going. The Vulcan Museum features a number of special events and exhibitions throughout the year. See the website for details. By the way, the observation deck provides the undisputed best view in town.

i Nothing to do on a lazy Sunday? Check out Vulcan AfterTunes, usually running from Aug through Sept and featuring live music in Vulcan Park. Good music and a stunning view. What more could you want?

GALLERIES

All the galleries listed below are free and open to the public.

ART ALLEY
109 Broadway St., Homewood
(205) 879-1105
www.artalley.net
Located in suburban Homewood just off Oxmoor Road in the Edgewood neighborhood, Art Alley features works from artists all over the world in a variety of styles and in a location where art authorities and amateurs

alike will feel welcome. Owner Jim Smith wants every type of person to feel comfortable walking into his gallery, whether they want to add to an already extensive collection, start a collection, or find a single piece to hang on a particular wall. Consequently, the gallery offers art ranging from $100 to $5,000. The gallery lives up to its name—part of it was, in fact, an alley between two buildings before a facade and roof were added. Whether you're looking for something in particular or just browsing, there's a good chance Art Alley has it—or can get it.

BETA PICTORIS GALLERY
2411 2nd Ave. North, Birmingham
(205) 413-2999
www.betapictorisgallery.com
One of the newest galleries in town, Beta Pictoris Gallery is like a shot of adrenalin for the more traditional world of Birmingham galleries. In the heart of the Loft District, the gallery may be on the small side but it occupies a great street-level storefront with a glass facade set among the historic old shops of 2nd Avenue. Beta Pictoris is one of the projects of Maus Contemporary, headed by art raconteur, Guido Maus. It infuses the art scene with a more contemporary take on the visual arts. Consequently, the artists and shows at Beta Pictoris all share an issue-driven approach to their work that is often challenging and experimental in nature.

For the visitor, this means art on the edge that is playful as well as risk-taking. The gallery's programming balances Alabama artists along with nationally recognized artists such as John Bankston from San Francisco or Bayete Ross Smith from New York. The gallery also emphasizes the importance of contemporary African-American art by bringing internationally renowned African-American artists to Birmingham. Other events such as collaborations with independent curators in alternative spaces, artist-in-residency programs, and upcoming participations in art fairs in Brussels, Belgium, and Vienna, Austria, keep Beta Pictoris on the creative edge of art in Birmingham.

COBB LANE GALLERY
1 Cobb Lane, Birmingham
(205) 967-2929
www.cobblanegallery.com
Cobb Lane, a quaint cobblestone drive lined with tables and chairs from local cafes, offers bar and restaurant patrons an escape in the fall and spring when the stifling humidity of summer is absent. The narrow little street could almost pass for some provincial French town. Maybe this is what makes Cobb Lane Gallery so appealing before you even set foot in the door. Take the spiral staircase from Cobb Lane Restaurant, and you've reached Cobb Lane Gallery. Inside you'll find works from local artists in a variety of styles that adhere to the gallery's mantra, "art at reasonable prices." What makes Cobb Lane different from other galleries, however, is that it isn't just a space for showing completed works. The gallery also doubles as a working studio, and on any given day you can see local artists such as Nan Eurton busily at work. This presents the customer with the opportunity to not only witness the finished work, but to also see the stages of development of the creative process.

i If you're planning on going down to Cobb Lane, don't just stop at the art; drop by Cobb Lane Restaurant for a bite to eat or have a drink at Blue Monkey Lounge or The J. Clyde.

BIRMINGHAM ART ASSOCIATION
1901 6th Ave. North, Birmingham
(205) 324-9127
www.birminghamartassociation.org
The oldest organization dedicated to promoting the arts in Birmingham, the Birmingham Art Association has been active in the area for over a century. The nonprofit, all-volunteer organization assists in putting on exhibitions at local galleries and also helps promote the works of local artists. Membership in the BAA is available to both artists and lovers of art alike. Membership provides the opportunity to meet both artists and arts supporters. For more information on upcoming events or on becoming a member, call or visit their website. BAA meets on the third Mon of the month at 6 p.m. at the Homewood Public Library.

DS ART
2805 Crescent Ave., Suite E, Homewood
(205) 802-4700
www.dsart.com
The works of local artist Don Stewart have become known the world over. Specializing in visual puns, Stewart plays on our own subconscious, or conscious, associations with objects and things, deftly pointing out the humor in items we often take much too seriously. At the same time, Stewart also likes to point out the seriousness of subjects we often take much too lightly. Stewart trained as a surgeon, receiving his MD from the University of Alabama at Birmingham, and trained at the Mayo Clinic before deciding to concentrate on his art full-time. That background is evident in the care and precision that he puts into his artwork.

His art is quick-witted and carefully executed—with a Papermate ballpoint pen. Most of Stewart's drawings follow the same formula: One large figure is composed of many smaller figures, and each is built around a particular theme, joke, or image. For example, a print entitled "Fast Food" is composed of pieces of food that together become a motorcycle. One called "Shoe Horns" is a woman's pump made of tubas, trumpets, French horns, and other similar instruments. Stop by his gallery for chat and a first-hand look at his intriguing creations.

i If you admire Don Stewart's artwork but can't decide which piece to purchase, you might try his book, *DS Art: The Visual Humor of Don Stewart.* Published in 2005 and available online, it's a fun, funny introduction to his particular brand of art.

GRIFFITH ART GALLERY
109 Hilltop Business Dr., Pelham
(205) 985-7969
www.griffithartgallery.com
Featuring over 2,500 works in various styles, media, and themes from artists everywhere from Peru to Russia, the Griffith Art Gallery is one of Birmingham's most comprehensive art galleries. The ground floor contains 3,000 square feet of art on display while upstairs there are more than 10,000 frames for sale, many of which were designed by the Griffiths and incorporate antique materials. Open since 1987 the gallery specializes in original oil and acrylic paintings. Twin brothers Rick and Dave Griffith provide local and regional art aficionados with hard-to-find works to adorn their homes and offices. The sheer volume of art at hand can be a bit overwhelming. If you're looking for something in particular, call Rick or Dave and if they don't have it, they can probably find it.

LORETTA GOODWIN GALLERY
605 28th St. South, Birmingham
(205) 328-1761
www.lorettagoodwingallery.net
Located in the popular Lakeview District just down the street from the Matt Jones Gallery, the Loretta Goodwin Gallery has been in the business of serving discriminating collectors in Birmingham for over 25 years. The steel gates and brick patio at the entrance set a cultured tone that is more than fulfilled by the gallery's display rooms. Featuring the works of artists both local and national, known and unknown, the Loretta Goodwin Gallery is not afraid to promote an artist it thinks has got "it." The gallery features a number of shows and exhibitions yearly.

✳MARILYN WILSON GALLERY
3908 Clairmont Ave., Birmingham
(205) 591-1150
http://208.75.85.114/
A staple of the Birmingham artistic community for over 35 years, the Marilyn Wilson Gallery features works in all styles from various local and national artists at its Forest Park location. Located just across the street from Naked Art, the Marilyn Wilson Gallery showcases various forms of artistic expression in everything from paintings to crafts. The gallery also offers museum-quality framing. While other galleries have come and gone, the Marilyn Wilson Gallery continues to grow, moving into a new 5,000-square-foot space recently. It is a testament to the gallery's support of local artists that is reciprocated by the artists and art patrons alike.

MATT JONES GALLERY
2830 6th Ave. South, Birmingham
(205) 521-6656
www.mattjonesgallery.com

Just down the street from the Loretta Goodwin Gallery in the Lakeview District is the Matt Jones Gallery. Featuring works from a number of artists in a variety of styles within its ample 7,500 square feet of exhibition space, the Matt Jones Gallery has drawn significant support from local art patrons in its short existence in the Magic City. For all of the magnificent art on display, perhaps the most significant feature of the Matt Jones Gallery is the building in which it is housed. Located in an old iron finery with high ceilings and natural light, the Matt Jones Gallery once again demonstrates Birmingham's successful transition from an industrial past to a promising future. The facility is available for wedding receptions, events, and parties.

MONTY STABLER GALLERY
1811 29th Ave. South, Homewood
(205) 879-9888
www.montystablergalleries.com
Located across from Homewood's SoHo district, the Monty Stabler Gallery offers works from well-known national and international artists as well as local artists. Visitors will find abstract and figurative paintings, botanical prints, sculptures, pottery, and more. Featuring respected artists such as Frank Fleming, Dorothy Gillispie, and Nieto, the well-respected gallery has been in business in Birmingham for nearly a quarter-century. The gallery holds monthly exhibits with new works from featured artists with "meet the artist" receptions. It also offers custom framing. Call or visit the website for more information on upcoming events.

✳NAKED ART
3831 Clairmont Ave., Birmingham
(205) 595-3553
www.nakedartusa.com
Art should be fun as well as instructive or inspiring. Located just across the street from the Marilyn Wilson Gallery, local favorite Naked Art takes that idea to a whole new level. Specializing in folk art and recycled art, Naked Art features works from the useful to the fashionable—with plenty of creative examples in between. Call it "art with an edge." Everything from duct-tape wallets to meticulously hand-crafted chairs and tables are on display and available for sale at very reasonable prices. Although Naked Art is a great place to pick up a unique gift for a friend or relative, it also exhibits the works of local and national artists and holds a number of events as well. For many husbands looking for a unique piece of wearable art for a birthday or last-minute anniversary present, Naked Art is a reliable old friend.

RED DOT GALLERY
1001 Stuart St., Homewood
(205) 870-7608
www.reddotgallery.com
Founded by artists Scott Bennett and Dori DeCamillis, the Red Dot Gallery offers art classes and studio space to local aspiring artists. With classes for children and adults, Red Dot teaches the principles and elements of various artistic styles whether you're 7 or 70. While Red Dot specializes in teaching, it also holds exhibits and features the works of its own teachers and students alike. Call or visit the website for more information on how to sign up for a class at this great community asset.

SPACE ONE ELEVEN
2409 2nd Ave. North, Birmingham
(205) 328-0553
www.spaceoneeleven.org

For 25 years Space One Eleven has cultivated and fostered artistic creation in downtown Birmingham with brilliant results, supporting such well-known artists as Darius Hill and Derek Franklin. Through its various arts education programs, Space One Eleven has fostered childhood creativity and contributed to the local community in the process. If you knew 2nd Avenue North before Space One Eleven, you might have a hard time recognizing it afterwards. Space One Eleven long ago recognized the implications for society if art is removed from our schools and communities and took it upon itself to ensure that Birmingham's children would not be without art. For their efforts SOE was honored as a member of the Andy Warhol Foundation for the Visual Arts, the first southern studio to be so honored. While Space One Eleven specializes in arts education, it also holds several exhibits a year on a variety of provocative, stimulating subjects. Call or visit the website for more information on events or to inquire about classes.

PARKS

It's a fun pastime for active residents of Birmingham to remind friends living in more chilly northern climes that they are playing tennis in Alabama in January in shorts and a T-shirt. Or that they've been hiking in the Appalachians or paddling on the river on a sunny 60-degree day in December. It may be a bit petty, but the truth hurts: Birmingham is a year-round outdoor playground. From Oak Mountain State Park on the outskirts of the city to Linn Park in the heart of downtown, Birmingham offers a multitude of parks that provide for the various outdoor needs of its residents and visitors. Sure, it gets plenty hot in July and August, but at least it's sunny.

Nestled at the southern end of the Appalachian Mountain range, Birmingham finally seems to be recognizing that its greatest natural resource is no longer the coal, iron ore, and limestone that formed its foundation during the city's formative years. The dramatic Ridge and Valley geographic environment, the many rivers and streams, the rich diversity of flora and fauna, and the tracts of undeveloped or underutilized land are what many now advocate as the future of the region. Instead of exploiting natural resources, it is in their preservation that the city has reason for hope in the future. Red Mountain Park, Railroad Park, and the ever-expanding system of greenways and trails in the area are solid proof of this movement.

On weekends, the parks come alive with a flurry of events. Linn Park's annual Birmingham Art Walk draws thousands of art lovers to downtown Birmingham every year, while over on the Southside, Caldwell Park's DoDah Day brings Birmingham's pets, with their humans in tow, together for a Frisbee-filled day of excitement (there's also live music for the non-furry). And don't miss Free Friday Flicks in suburban Homewood's Central Park on summer weekends. From canvases to tennis balls, Birmingham's parks offer a variety of activities that are both enjoyable and easy on the wallet.

And for something a little more adventurous, you need not look far. Just outside of Birmingham sits Oak Mountain State Park, an outdoor playground where park goers can camp, hike, fish, swim, and more. Spread out over nearly 10,000 acres of land, Oak Mountain State Park makes it very easy to forget that downtown Birmingham is just a 20-minute drive away. And with the 1,011-acre Ruffner Mountain Nature Center on the east side of the city and the new 1,200-acre Red Mountain Park on the west, Birmingham now has more park space per citizen than any city in the country.

STATE PARKS

BRIERFIELD IRONWORKS HISTORICAL STATE PARK
240 Furnace Pkwy., Brierfield
(205) 665-1856
www.brierfieldironworks.org
Like Tannehill, the Brierfield Ironworks were originally established by industrialists who saw the iron-laden soil that ran through Birmingham as an opportunity to make a fortune selling iron to the Confederacy. Like its sister park Tannehill, Brierfield also went up in flames as the Union forces rolled through the south. Today the restored historical park offers visitors a number of sites and activities from the old ironworks of the Confederacy to the pioneer-style homes. Brierfield also offers hiking trails and camping. The park is open 7 days a week from sunrise to sunset.

✳OAK MOUNTAIN STATE PARK
200 Terrace Dr., Pelham
(205) 620-2520
www.alapark.com/oakmountain
Just a short drive from Alabama's largest city sits Alabama's largest state park. Established in 1927 by the Alabama State Lands Act, Oak Mountain has long served as a haven for those hoping to escape the stresses that life in the city can sometimes bring without having to travel too far or pay too much. Within Oak Mountain's sprawling 9,940 acres lies an 18-hole public golf course, two 85-acre lakes for fishing, an additional lake for swimming and boating, 51 miles of trails for hiking and biking, horseback-riding facilities, and ample ground for camping. Oak Mountain is a playground with something for everyone loving the outdoors.

The **Alabama Wildlife Center** (www.awrc.org) also calls Oak Mountain its home and provides education and awareness about wildlife. Tour the facility and take a look at the local wildlife up-close and watch as injured animals are nursed back to health. And be sure to see the Treetop Nature Trail, an elevated boardwalk where kids delight in looking eye-to-eye with barred owls, vultures, red-tailed hawks, great horned owls, and other creatures. Within the park's two fishing lakes you'll find a number of species of local fish including largemouth bass, bream, catfish, and crappie. These lakes are open year-round and boats are available to rent. But please, don't feel obligated to take part in one of the park's many activities—relax along the lake-front beach and let your worries slip away for a while.

The park is open daily from 7 a.m. until sundown, but there are multiple campsites available for a weekend getaway. Ten fully equipped cabins are available for rent year-round and 85 RV sites are available for the road-tripper. Looking to "rough it"? Sixty tent sites are available for rent with fresh water nearby. There are also 10 pavilions available within the park that are ideal for family reunions. Call for rental prices and greens fees for the golf course.

TANNEHILL IRONWORKS HISTORICAL STATE PARK
12632 Confederate Pkwy., McCalla
(205) 477-5711
www.tannehill.org
Showcasing Birmingham's early industrial history, Tannehill Ironworks Historical State Park was once the site of an ironworks facility that produced iron for the Confederacy during the Civil War. As the War came to its end, Union forces raided southern industrial facilities, and Alabama and Tannehill were a major industrial target. In March of 1865,

General James H. Wilson ordered the Tannehill Ironworks to be burned to the ground. The 1,500 acres of land that once housed a Confederate ironworks now serves as a museum, campground, and hiking trail for visitors.

Tannehill is home to a number of unique events and activities. Each year, on Memorial Day weekend, the park plays host to a Civil War re-enactment and on Labor Day you can participate in a Moon Pie eating contest at the United Mine Workers' annual celebration. In addition to these annual festivities, the park also hosts Tannehill Trade Days on the third weekend of each month from Mar to Nov. The Trade Days are a great opportunity to find unique crafts made by artisans from across the state. Although the park is primarily for day use 7 days a week from sunrise to sunset, there is ample campground available for both RV-ing and tent camping. Call the park, or visit the website for more information.

COUNTY & CITY PARKS

Note: All city and county parks are open to the public from 6 a.m. to 11 p.m.

AVONDALE PARK
5th Avenue South between 40th and 42nd Streets South, Birmingham
As one of Birmingham's oldest parks, Avondale Park has served the community for over a century. Located on land that the Avondale Land Company purchased in 1887, the property, with its wading pools and cave, was soon converted into a public park. For years Avondale was the site of many of Birmingham's civic and recreational events. The city hosted its 50th anniversary at Avondale, and the park housed the Birmingham

Zoo during its early days. In the 1930s an amphitheater known as the "Villa" was completed and was the site of Birmingham Civic Symphonic Orchestra performances. In the 1960s young people congregated in Avondale Park for folk music performances. The spring (once known as King's Spring) is still flowing, though it is no longer the water source for surrounding homes.

By the 1970s, however, the park had fallen on hard times. Thankfully, in 1989 a group of civic-minded individuals calling themselves "Friends of Avondale Park" organized to renovate and restore the park. Their plans have been met with great success. Avondale Park and the amphitheater still host many sporting and cultural events such as Art in Avondale Park, an affair geared towards inspiring children to discover their artistic talents through a variety of art lessons and activities. When Ruffner Mountain Park—one of the country's largest urban nature preserves—was dedicated in 1977, it eclipsed the 40-acre Avondale Park as the largest park in the city. Today Avondale Park is once again one of Birmingham's most beautiful parks and is currently listed in the National Register of Historic Places.

✳BIRMINGHAM BOTANICAL GARDENS
2612 Lane Park Rd., Birmingham
(205) 414-3900
www.bbgardens.org
Within Birmingham's Lane Park is one of the south's finest botanical gardens and with over 350,000 visitors per year, the state of Alabama's most-visited free attraction,. Designed by former Montreal Botanical Gardens curator Henry Teuscher, the gardens were completed in the 1960s and have been supported by the Friends of Birmingham Botanical Gardens ever since. Featuring

over 10,000 varieties of plants on 67.5 acres of land—as well as the nation's largest public horticulture library—the gardens truly are an urban oasis and perfect retreat from a busy world. In addition to viewing the gorgeous plant life, the gardens also host a number of popular events such as Cocktails in the Gardens and Antiques in the Gardens. The fall and spring plant sales draw thousands of local gardeners eager to improve their own botanical gardens by purchasing plants in support of the organization. The gardens are open daily from sunrise to sunset, and admission and parking is free. Check the website for events such as lectures, plant sales, shows, dinners, classes, and other happenings.

CALDWELL PARK
26th Street South and Highland Avenue South, Birmingham

Located just off the Red Mountain Expressway along Highland Avenue is Caldwell Park. One of three parks in the Highland Park neighborhood near Birmingham's Five Points South (the other two being Rhodes Park and Rushton Park), Caldwell Park is one of Birmingham's most popular outdoor spots for events and social gatherings. It has also become a hub for outdoor fine-arts experiences, hosting the Alabama Symphony Orchestra's Sounds of Summer and the Park Players Theatre Company.

But the event that draws thousands of locals and their pets to Caldwell Park every year is the annual DoDahDay festival benefiting local animal charities. Since 1979, DoDahDay has grown from a few friends getting together with their pets to thousands of pet owners gathering in Caldwell, Rhodes, and Rushton parks for live music and refreshments in support of a good cause

(www.doodahday.org). Be sure to visit the Alabama Symphony Orchestra and Birmingham Park Players' websites for more information on their performances in the park at www.alabamasymphony.org and www.bhamparkplayers.com.

GEORGE WARD PARK
1871 Green Springs Hwy., Birmingham
(205) 322-9958
www.friendsofgeorgewardpark.org

Opened in 1925 as Green Springs Park, George Ward Park was renamed in 1952 to honor Birmingham's eccentric former mayor. This expansive park is one of the city's most unique. It holds the distinction of containing Birmingham's only official dog park and is home to the city's only disc-golf course, a 24-hole course totaling nearly 7,200 feet. The park also features 8 hard-surface tennis courts and 6 softball fields that host local teams and even professional events on occasion. In addition to the various activities that take place at George Ward Park, the facility also serves as an ideal backdrop for reunions and get-togethers with its spacious pavilion. The park connects to the Vulcan Trail greenway via Green Springs Avenue South, located just south of the park. Through the efforts of The Friends of George Ward Park, the park recently underwent a reforestation project to enhance the natural surroundings. Things are only getting better at George Ward Park.

✳HOMEWOOD CENTRAL PARK
1632 Oxmoor Rd., Homewood
(205) 332-6700
www.homewoodparks.com

In the heart of suburban Homewood sits one of the area's most-loved parks. The park, known to locals simply as Homewood Park, has many features that make it a favorite for the many residents that enjoy the greens-pace on a regular basis. Griffin Brook snakes through the park to provide a natural aes-thetic, and the gently banked streambed is a great spot for kids to get wet while looking for crawfish or admiring the herons that are often found doing the same. Following a $2.6-million renovation project that was com-pleted in 2003, the park is home to 6 pavilions for reunions and get-togethers, as well as an amphitheater, tennis courts, and a children's playground with a small shade tarp—a real boon in the hot summer months.

A number of events take place in the park each year as well. The Birmingham Park Players have performed at the park's amphi-theater and Free Friday Flicks have made Homewood Park the place to be on Fri-day nights in the summer. Additionally, the annual Chili Cook-Off and I Love Homewood Day bring hundreds of Homewood and Bir-mingham residents to the park to celebrate the community. Adjacent to the park is the Homewood Public Pool, one of the area's finest public swimming pools.

i For an inexpensive birthday party, reunion, or just a family get-together, the pavilions at Home-wood Central Park are available for rental for residents and non-Homewood residents (for a higher fee). It's a good idea to secure a reservation in advance to make sure you have the pavilion during the warmer months—they book up fast.

JEMISON PARK TRAIL
Mountain Brook Parkway, Birmingham
Along Mountain Brook Parkway in pictur-esque suburban Mountain Brook, runs the extensive Jemison Park Trail. Named for the famed architect Robert Jemison, who designed many of the homes in Mountain Brook, the Jemison Park Trail is ideal for walkers, joggers, and bikers. The trail runs alongside two creeks, Shades Creek and Watkins Creek, and thanks to the Friends of Jemison Park, the trail is marked with signs pointing out local plant and wildlife. For more on the Jemison Park Trail, see the Greenways chapter.

KELLY INGRAM PARK
16th Street North and Sixth Avenue North, Birmingham
Located directly across the street from the Birmingham Civil Rights Institute and diago-nal to the 16th Street Baptist Church in Birmingham's Civil Rights District is Kelly Ingram Park. Originally called West Park, it was renamed to honor the memory of Osmond Kelly Ingram, a Birmingham native who was the first American sailor to die in World War I. During the Civil Rights Move-ment, Kelly Ingram Park was the gathering point for of a number of protests against segregation. It was at this park that Public Safety Commissioner Eugene "Bull" Connor infamously ordered the use of attack dogs and fire hoses on non-violent youth demon-strators. Today the park serves as a symbolic reminder of the injustices carried out by state and local governments against African Americans during the Jim Crow era. Kelly Ingram Park features work by artists James Drake and Raymond Kasky honoring the memory of those who risked their lives for the cause of justice and freedom.

LINN PARK
7th and 8th Avenues North, Birmingham
Arguably the city's most notable urban park, Charles Linn Park is located in the heart

of downtown Birmingham. Originally called "Capitol Park" when Birmingham leaders had hopes of luring the Alabama state capitol away from Montgomery, the park was renamed Woodrow Wilson Park and Central Park before Charles Linn, a Finnish immigrant who became a prominent local industrialist and banker, was finally chosen as the namesake. One of Birmingham's oldest parks, Linn Park has been at the center of Birmingham culture for well over a century. Birmingham's "Semi-Centennial" was celebrated in Linn Park and featured then-President Warren G. Harding. The park also served as a site for film screenings. Today the park is still frequented by residents and visitors alike and hosts a number of annual events like the ONB Magic City Art Connection, Mercedes Marathon, and more.

Situated in the park's center is a large fountain that sends a stream cascading downhill through the park—it's a cool spot where kids often frolic in the summertime. Located near this fountain is a steel pavilion where park goers can relax in the shade. Recent renovations have made the park more appealing than ever before, but with the changes, the park has earned something of a reputation as a hangout for panhandlers. Linn Park also features two prominent statues: the *Eternal Flame of Freedom* and the *Mary Cahalan Statue*. The Eternal Flame of Freedom was established by the American Legion and dedicated in 1969. It burns for the Jefferson County veterans of war. Sculpted by famed Italian artist Giuseppe Moretti (who also sculpted Birmingham's famous *Vulcan*), the *Mary Cahalan Statue* honors this famous Birmingham teacher. Just across 8th Avenue is the Birmingham Museum of Art. In the southeast corner is the Linn Henley Research Library, a limestone-clad neoclassical gem built in 1927. Sneak a peek inside, if only to admire the murals.

OVERTON PARK
Overton Road, Mountain Brook

Snuggled away off Highway 280 just down the road from the Summit Shopping Center is Mountain Brook's Overton Park. Known to many locals simply as "Overton," this charming little park right next to the Mountain Brook fire station is ideal for children and pets. The 2.5-acre pocket park was recently improved and renovated and has found a new lease on life. Fenced-in, and therefore easy to keep an eye on the kids, Overton is a popular choice for birthday parties at its pavilion. But the park is not for children only. With tennis courts and basketball goals, adults also frequent the park for a little exercise. On nice weekends, young adults kicking the soccer ball or throwing the football are often found enjoying Overton.

✳RAILROAD PARK
1601 1st Ave. South, Birmingham
(205) 223-4013
www.railroadpark.org

If Birmingham had a river, Railroad Park would be the city's river walk. As it is, the railroad has long been the river of commerce passing through the city's downtown core. The park marks a fresh, new start for this area of downtown Birmingham. Another newcomer to the scene, this downtown 8-block city park with walking trails and an elevated walkway is a lovely space with big dreams. Opened in late 2010, the current park covers 19 acres between 14th and 18th streets South, running parallel to the railroad tracks that slice through downtown Birmingham.

Nine of the acres are open park space, and the pond covers approximately 2 acres.

A mixture of more than 600 hardwoods, flowering trees, and evergreen were planted, including more than 50 Princeton elms. Much of the seating area as well as the walls were built from hand-cast bricks and cobblestone found at the site during the park's construction. In a similar "green" vein, the pond and wetland area filters rainwater at the site to be reused for irrigation. The park makes for a great destination for recreation, concerts, cultural events, or just passing the time of day while enjoying a novel view of the city skyline. The park also serves as an elegant corridor that connects Birmingham's downtown with Southside and the University of Alabama campus.

The Railroad Park Dining Car, a small bistro run by the nearby B&A Warehouse, offers a weekday lunch that changes seasonally. Play areas for children, a climbing dome, and a small skate park area offer fun diversions, as does a movie series during warm months. Rangers patrol the park, and security is present 24 hours a day. Free Wi-Fi is available on the grounds.

RED MOUNTAIN PARK
Lakeshore Parkway, just past West Oxmoor Road, Birmingham
(205) 202-6043
www.redmountainpark.org
Though not due to open until 2012, Red Mountain Park in the corner of southwest Birmingham has generated a great deal of enthusiasm and activity since the 4.5-mile long urban park was sold to a state-appointed commission at a tremendous discount by US Steel. When completed, the 1,200-acre urban park will include a large trail system, historic mining structures and heritage sites to explore, interpretive exhibits, and general recreational opportunities

like hiking and biking. Look for sneak peak tours run by Friends of Red Mountain Park. See the Greenways chapter for additional information.

RHODES PARK
Highland Avenue South, Birmingham
Named for *Birmingham News* founder Rufus Napoleon Rhodes, Rhodes Park is one of the three parks of the Highland Park neighborhood. Although not designated as an official dog park, it is popular among locals as a place to bring their furry friends. Rhodes Park also serves as co-host, along with nearby Caldwell Park, of the annual Doo-Dah-Day pet festival. There is a leash law in Birmingham, so be sure to keep your canine leashed. And because Rhodes Park is not fenced in, it's a good idea anyway.

RUFFNER MOUNTAIN PARK AND NATURE CENTER
1214 81st St. South, Birmingham
(205) 833-8264
www.ruffnermountain.org
With a dozen trails to choose from spread out over 1,000 acres, Ruffner Mountain is a hiker's dream and just minutes from downtown Birmingham. The park also features the state-of-the-art Tree Top Nature Center that looks out over the mountain and offers free educational tours for visitors. While the park has been a staple on the field-trip calendar of local schoolteachers for years, it also offers summer camp opportunities for young nature lovers. Ruffner Mountain Park and Nature Center is also currently in the process of creating an off-the-leash dog park for pet owners in need of a place to let their dogs roam free. The park is open 6 days a week and closed Mon. While the park is open to the public, a donation of $2 is suggested.

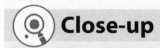

Close-up

Vulcan: A Birmingham Symbol

It doesn't get much more iconic than the largest cast iron statue in the world, an iron god of fire and forge, standing sentinel over the city of Birmingham from his perch atop Red Mountain. Originally commissioned by the Commercial Club of Birmingham, **Vulcan** was designed by Giuseppe Morettie and cast by the Birmingham Steel and Iron Company in 1903. After winning the Grand Prize at the 1904 Louisiana Purchase Exhibition in St. Louis, the 100,000-pound iron giant resided at the Alabama State Fairgrounds for many years before finding a permanent home overlooking Jones Valley in 1936 thanks to the Works Progress Administration. Ever since then, **Vulcan Park** has been the spot that locals most often take visitors to show off panoramic views of the city when not looking up and giggling over the fact that this god has no cast-iron underpants. Many locals fondly recall that for more than half a century, *Vulcan* held aloft his green neon torch signifying that there were no traffic fatalities that day. Commuters driving the Red Mountain Expressway that cuts through the mountain below *Vulcan* would look to see if the torch was lit red: If it was, that meant bad news for some unlucky driver.

In 1976 *Vulcan* made the National Register of Historic Places, but after a century of exposure to hot and cold temperatures—and some fairly nasty industrial pollution—even a god starts to look his age. Thanks to a $15.5-million renovation of the statue and 10-acre park, *Vulcan*'s 100th birthday made for a wonderful celebration, winning a National Preservation Honor Award from the National Trust for Historic Preservation. The old statue drew more than 100,000 visitors that first year after reopening. And it's much improved, with a new Vulcan Center Museum showing the story of Birmingham's founding through new interactive exhibits and materials relating to Birmingham's early days. The site also hosts numerous events such as the popular summer outdoor music series called Vulcan AfterTunes. *Vulcan* is now more relevant than ever. A side note: Locals nearly always refer to the statue and park as "*Vulcan*." When you hear someone say "the *Vulcan*," you can safely bet they're from out of town.

RUSHTON PARK
Highland Avenue South and 31st Street South, Birmingham

Rushton Park is a great place to take kids for a fun picnic or lazy afternoon throwing the Frisbee or football. Named for former Birmingham School Board President William J. Rushton, the park features a fenced-in playground area for children as well as a basketball goal. Like at Rhodes and Caldwell parks, many people bring their dogs to Rushton Park, but Birmingham's leash law still applies.

VULCAN PARK AND MUSEUM
1701 Valley View Dr., Birmingham
(205) 933-1409
www.visitvulcan.com

Atop Red Mountain stands Birmingham's iconic *Vulcan*. Sculpted by Italian artist Giuseppe Moretti in 1904, *Vulcan* has stood vigilantly above Birmingham for over 75 years as the world's tallest cast-iron statue. As recently as the late 1990s however, *Vulcan* was in grave disrepair and the park was closed off to the public. In 1999 an ambitious

$15.5-million renovation of both the statue and park began (followed by a very public criticism by Senator John McCain of Arizona for the US Department of the Interior grant that partially funded it). By 2003 *Vulcan* was once again on his perch overlooking Birmingham.

Vulcan Park has the undisputed best view in Birmingham. From the observation deck at the foot of the statue, one can look out over the entire city. While under renovation, additions were made to lengthen the walking trail that runs along the park and great pains were taken to salvage the marble originally used along the path of the trail. While at the park pay a visit to the Vulcan Museum and get an inside look at the history of *Vulcan* and the role of the steel industry during Birmingham's formative years. The park and observation deck on Vulcan are open daily. For more information, see the Vulcan Park and Museum entry under Attractions.

DOG PARKS

GREEN SPRINGS DOG PARK
George Ward Park
1871 Green Springs Hwy., Birmingham
(205) 322-9958
www.friendsofgeorgewardpark.org

After opening in 2009 the Green Springs Dog Park finally offered canine lovers in town an official destination to legally run, walk, and play off-leash in a controlled environment with their dogs. Accordingly there are three separate enclosures for dogs, one being a separate small-dog area. There's good shade under the trees during hot weather, but you'll want to bring your own source of water for your pet. The **Greater Birmingham Dog Park Association** (www .barkforapark.org) lends a helping paw to support the park while advocating for the construction of more dog parks in the area. Hours run from sunrise to sunset.

LOCH HAVEN DOG PARK
3469 Loch Haven Dr., Hoover
Loch Haven Park is a 17-acre neighborhood park located off Loch Haven Drive near Rocky Ridge Road on the dividing line between Hoover and neighboring Vestavia Hills. The park has walking trails, picnic areas, doggy water fountains, and an open field. The dog park opened in 2010 and offers an agility course, A-frames, pause boxes, teeter totters, tunnels, and other challenging obstacles for owners to exercise their dogs. The park is often called the "Hoover Dog Park" by residents.

RECREATION

Other than sports that involve snow and freezing weather, Birmingham is ideal for those who love the outdoors. From golf and kickball to swimming and biking, Birmingham offers a full range of recreational activities for just about every interest imaginable. With its ever-expanding green spaces and energetic residents, Birmingham is full of opportunities to compete, exercise, or simply get out and enjoy some fresh air. Before and after work and on weekends, you'll see Birmingham residents flocking to the gyms, golf courses, running trails and other recreational sites all over the city. It is not uncommon, particularly in the summer months, to see hordes of runners and cyclists jogging and biking together along the city's most popular routes (watch for the Wednesday-evening Trak Shak runners in Homewood).

In addition to these everyday activities, Birmingham and its surrounding areas also offer seasonal recreational activities of which residents take full advantage. Youth and adult soccer runs fall and spring. Kayaking and canoeing, while year-round options, tend to be best in the winter and spring months when the water level is highest. From basketball to softball to the increasingly popular kickball, Birmingham surely has a seasonal league that will interest you. Summer is for swimming, and you'll find a number of public and private pools in the area. State parks like Oak Mountain offer bow-hunting opportunities and Lake Guntersville, which has hosted the Bass Masters Classic, features some of the best fishing in the south. Be sure, however, to check local laws and licensing procedures on hunting and fishing before planning an outing.

Golf, as any aficionado will tell you, is a year-round sport in Alabama. Birmingham is dotted with beautiful award-winning public and private courses throughout the city and surrounding areas. From the exclusively private Shoal Creek, two-time host of golf's PGA Championship, to the public Ross Bridge, gem of the famed Robert Trent Jones Golf Trail, Birmingham is a golfer's paradise.

Whether you're into more traditional recreational pastimes or if more extreme sports like mountain biking and rock climbing help you find your focus, Birmingham has a course, court, field, or trail for you.

BIKING

Birmingham has a considerable population of cycling enthusiasts, led by the **Birmingham Bicycle Club** (www.bhambikeclub.org) and **BUMP** (Birmingham Urban Mountain Pedalers, www.bump.org), an active group of mountain bikers maintaining and building new trails. And while drivers on the road probably have noticed the growing number of bikers, the various cities and municipalities are just starting to take notice, thus there are very few bike lanes along Birmingham roads. Though drivers, for the most part, are generally courteous and willing to share the road, be mindful of the fact that many Birmingham motorists are only just now becoming aware that they must share the road with area cyclists—be prepared to yield to some of the more oblivious drivers. After all, your lightweight road bike is no match for an SUV. For these reasons, the Birmingham Bicycle Club, after years of riding around town, have discovered the best routes for a challenging ride while avoiding major traffic—see their site for a number of suggested road rides. There is always the Shades Creek Greenway in Homewood, popular among bikers, joggers, and walkers alike, a paved flat trail that goes through Homewood and connects with Mountain Brook via the Jemison Park Trail. As for mountain bikers in Birmingham, Oak Mountain State Park is a haven thanks to BUMP's instrumental role in creating a 21-mile loop through the park. BUMP has also established trails in Trussville and Tannehill as well.

Mountain-Biking Trails

DOUBLE OAK TRAIL AT OAK MOUNTAIN STATE PARK
200 Terrace Dr., Pelham
(205) 620-2520
www.bump.org/oakmountain
The gem of local mountain biking, the Double Oak Trail is a loop through scenic Oak Mountain State Park totaling 21 miles. Composed of 14 smaller trails, the Double Oak is an uphill battle, peaking at nearly 1,200 feet. Within the Double Oak, however, there are differing levels of difficulty, allowing for a day of family mountain biking at selected trails

or a treacherous, challenging push through the trails used for national mountain-biking competitions. Bikers are warned, however, to stay on Red Trail or face a fine from the park rangers. Also, be sure to watch out for pedestrians on the trail as it doubles as a popular route for day hikers.

TANNEHILL IRONWORKS HISTORICAL STATE PARK
12632 Confederate Pkwy., McCalla
(205) 477-5711
www.tannehill.org
Just off I-59 at Tannehill Ironworks, BUMP has completed 2 miles of trail, with an additional 10 miles under construction. While the biking trail is being completed, bikers are allowed to use a section of the hiking trail, but please be aware of hikers along the trail, too. Tannehill features a number of historical dirt roads that make for a very interesting bike ride. It's also a chance to combine a ride with a bit of local history at this popular state park.

FISHING

Southerners love to fish, and Birmingham is no exception. Flanked by the Black Warrior River to the West and the Coosa River to the East, you'll find plenty of great fishing opportunities in Birmingham's lakes, rivers, and streams. Within the rivers, streams, springs, and reservoirs of Alabama, you'll find over 450 species of fish, more than any other state or province in North America. Why does Alabama hold the richest repository of fish species on the continent? A combination of high rainfall, temperate climate, and a diverse geological setting means that not only does Alabama provide the perfect environment for this diversity of fish, it offers the perfect setting for those loving to fish. For more information on what types of fish you might find in Birmingham's water and what is considered legal game fish, visit **www.outdooralabama.com/fishing.**

Because of the amount of rainfall, drive in just about any direction within an hour and a half of Birmingham, and you are presented with numerous lakes, rivers, and creeks to fish. Throw a rock in any direction in Birmingham, and you're likely to hit someone who either has a lake house or knows somebody who owns one. The deep, clear waters of **Smith Lake** contain some of the best striped-bass fishing in the state as well as the opportunity to fish for trout below the tailrace. It is also among the cleanest lakes in North America. The list of fishing options is huge and for those willing to drive a bit beyond Birmingham, there are several great options: **Holt Lake** and **Bankhead Lake** (Warrior River), **Neely Henry Lake** (Coosa River), **Weiss Lake** (Coosa River, known as the "Crappie Capital of the United States"), **Lake Mitchell** (Coosa River), **Lake Jordan** (Coosa River), **Lake Guntersville** (Tennessee River), and **Lake Wheeler** (Tennessee River). If you are planning on fishing in Birmingham, or anywhere in Alabama for that matter, you must have a fishing license. These are easily obtainable and can be purchased at your local tackle shops, sporting goods stores, or online at **www.outdooralabama.com/dcnr_license.** Licenses are valid for one year, or you can purchase one for the week. Prices vary according to residential status.

FIVE MILE CREEK
www.fivemilegreenwaydistrict.org
Although most of Five Mile Creek is relatively shallow and more suited for canoeing or kayaking, there are quite a few pools along its 26 miles that make for excellent bank fishing. Through recent citizens' initiatives, the Five Mile Creek Greenway in Brookside makes for some fine bank fishing. At Brookside are some of the creek's deepest pools, ideal for fishing. Look for bass, sunfish, carp, and bream. You'll find these, in addition to many other species, in abundance. While in the past, Five Mile Creek had been one of the most polluted waterways in the state, in the past couple of decades the creek's status has been upgraded, establishing minimum water quality standards and ensuring the future protection of the creek for fishing and wildlife.

Readers of *Bassmaster* magazine recently voted Birmingham America's Bass Capital. Anglers were asked to submit their choice for the country's best big city basin. Ten major cities were in the running, with specifications including a major metropolitan population, healthy bass populations, enthusiastic bass-fishing communities, and opportunities for big fish.

*CAHABA RIVER
www.cahabariver.net/fishing
Counted among "Alabama's Ten Natural Wonders" for good reason, the Cahaba River is ideal for bank fishing, and for those wanting a little more adventure, canoe fishing. Home to 135 species of fish, not to mention countless plant species, the Cahaba River is indeed an ecological wonder. Among the most popular sport fish found in the Cahaba are the spotted and largemouth bass. The bass found in the Cahaba are much larger than northern bass and are known to some locals as "Alabama bass." You'll also find abundant populations of crappie and channel catfish. There are also a number

of fish species native to the Cahaba that have gained special conservation status that you'll want to avoid, notably the Alabama sturgeon, the Cahaba shiner, crystal, freckled, and goldline darters, and the frecklebelly madtom. Familiarize yourself with these fish by consulting www.outdooralabama.com and be able to recognize these rare beauties.

Among the most popular fishing spots along the Cahaba is the dam just off Highway 280, not too far from the Summit Shopping Center. Here you'll find surprisingly good fishing. And in Bibb County, about an hour outside of Birmingham, a section of the Cahaba deemed a National Wildlife Refuge by the federal government is available for fishing as well. Locals will attest that any day spent on the Cahaba is a good day and fisherman will agree that the Cahaba is one of those rare fishing spots: so naturally magnificent that you won't care what you did or didn't catch.

> **i** Typically the main forage in the region's lakes are crawfish and threadfin shad so anglers might want to take this into account when selecting their lures.

LAKE PURDY
www.lakepurdyfishing.com
Some fisherman feel the need to get far, far away from the city, out in the "middle of nowhere" in order to find a good fishing hole. Not so in Birmingham. Just 25 minutes from downtown Birmingham on Highway 119 sits Lake Purdy, a 990-acre reservoir created in 1923 to serve the citizens of Birmingham and its surrounding areas with fresh drinking water. Today, the lake still serves as a reservoir, but it is also available to the fishing public.

While anyone is allowed to fish along the banks of Lake Purdy, to get to the prized spotted bass and crappie that lurk in the lake, you'll want to take a boat out on the water. To protect the lake from foreign plant species, however, no private boats are allowed, but there are boats available to rent for as little as $15. You can bring your own outboard motor or rent one. All other auxiliary fishing equipment, such as a depth-finder, is available to rent as well, or you can bring your own. Nightly boat rentals are also available for nocturnal fishing. In addition to spotted bass, you'll find populations of large-mouth bass, bream, crappie, and catfish. Although there is good fishing to be had at Lake Purdy any time of the year, locals know that the best time to bring in a good haul is around February and March. And thanks to Alabama's mild winters, the weather is often just about right for a day on the water.

LAY LAKE
www.outdooralabama.com
Named for Alabama Power founder William Lay, Lay Lake is yet another fishing-rich reservoir close to Birmingham. It borders St. Clair, Talladega, Shelby, Coosa, and Chilton counties. Known for its spotted and large-mouth bass as well as crappie and bream, this 12,000-acre lake features some of the best fishing in the south. Spend a day on Lay Lake and you'll know why it has hosted the Bassmaster's Classic four times. There are 7 access points located along the lake. Beeswax Creek launch on Beeswax Park Road in Columbiana is the most popular launch for the Birmingham area. The Narrows in Shelby County is another option close to town. See the Alabama Department of Public Health website, www.adph.org, to stay abreast of fish consumption advisories on Lay Lake.

ℹ️ Lay Lake hosts the Marks Outdoor Bass Tournament annually, which attracts entries in excess of 1,000 anglers. Numerous other tournament events are held on Lay Lake weekly during the summer months. Local tackle shops are the best source for information for these events.

LOGAN MARTIN LAKE
www.outdooralabama.com

A popular getaway spot among locals, Logan Martin encompasses 15,263 acres along the Coosa River and sits just 30 miles east of Birmingham near Talladega along St. Clair and Talladega counties. Like many of Alabama's lakes, Logan Martin was the result of a hydroelectric dam built by Alabama Power. Within Logan Martin you'll find abundant populations of largemouth and the famous, hard-fighting Alabama spotted bass as well as crappie. A three-time host of professional fishing's Forrest L. Woods Championship, fishing in Logan Martin is a joy for both the experienced and beginning fisherman alike. There are several marinas on Logan Martin: Poor House Branch, which is just off I-20 at exit 165 and Lakeside Marina, just off I-20 in Cropwell, Alabama. Logan Martin is ideal for a day trip, but there are also houses available for rent and the Lake Front Motel if you'd rather just stay the weekend. And there's a good chance you will. Look for weekly tournaments during the summer. Be advised, however, that Logan Martin and Choccolocco Creek have fish-consumption advisories due to PCBs.

OAK MOUNTAIN STATE PARK
877 John Findlay III Dr., Pelham
(205) 620-2528 (Park Fishing Center)
www.alapark.com/oakmountain/fishing

On the seemingly endless list of recreational activities at Oak Mountain State Park is, of course, fishing. The park boasts two lakes reserved for fishing and stocked with largemouth bass, catfish, bream, and crappie. These two 85-acre lakes are open year-round and are great for those pleasant Alabama winter days. Private boats are allowed, but

---

Fish Advisories

It is a shame that in a state that takes its fishing so seriously, polychlorinated biphenyls (PCBs) are a worry to area fishermen and women wanting to catch and enjoy their game. On Lay Lake, PCBs mean "do not consume" status for striped and spotted bass. For Logan Martin Lake, there's a consumption advisory for all fish. PCBs from Monsanto Chemical Company in Anniston, Alabama, discharged waste into Snow Creek and open pit landfills, which then traveled downstream to Choccolocco Creek and finally into Logan Martin. In fact, there are a number of waterways across Alabama (and most other states, as well) also under fish-consumption advisories for mercury, a heavy metal that is difficult to clean up once in the water and into the fish. Check the consumption advisories found on the Alabama Department of Public Health website, www.adph.org. Look under "Fish Consumption Advisories" on the "A-Z Contents" page.

gasoline motors are not. Boats and electric motors are available for rent for with discounts available for seniors. Bait is available for sale at the Campground Country Store. The fishing center entrance is located off Highway 119, in the rear of Oak Mountain State Park. For more about Oak Mountain State Park, see the Parks chapter.

✳TANNEHILL HISTORICAL
STATE PARK
12632 Confederate Pkwy., McCalla
(205) 477-5711
www.tannehill.org

Boasting two of the Cahaba River's liveliest tributaries, fishing is one of the most popular activities at Tannehill Historical State Park. Within Roupes Creek and Shades Creek, both of which run through Tannehill before emptying into the Cahaba, you'll find rainbow trout. Imported from the Pacific coast and stocked in these creeks, these beautiful creatures are found few places in Alabama other than at Tannehill. In addition to the trout, Tannehill also features common native fish such as brim and crappie. Roupes and Shades Creeks are generally too shallow to navigate by boat, so only bank fishing is allowed. There are, however, many deep pools along the creek that make for great fishing spots. In order to fish at Tannehill, you'll need to purchase a fishing permit. These are available in the park's country store.

> **i** Because of Alabama's historically mild winters, there is really never a bad time to fish. Locals, however, will tell you that the best time to take to the water is around February and March. While it's still winter in other regions, in Alabama, things are just beginning to warm up.

GOLF

Birmingham and its surrounding areas are renowned for the stunning golf courses scattered about the hills and valleys. Private courses such as **Shoal Creek Golf and Country Club, Birmingham Country Club, Greystone Golf & Country Club,** and **Old Overton Club** are among some of the region's premier courses. While many of the city's best courses are at such exclusive and expensive clubs, there is plenty of great golf to be played at local public courses. From **Ross Bridge and Oxmoor Valley** along the Robert Trent Jones Trail to **Highlands Golf Club** in one of Birmingham's oldest neighborhoods, Birmingham is full of great golfing opportunities. When checking on or booking tee times, be sure to review your selected club's standard course policies such as soft spikes or hard spikes, required attire, etc., as this can differ from club to club. While a comprehensive description of all the courses in the area is beyond the scope of this guide, readers will find a listing of additional public courses at the end of the golf section.

Semi-Private

BALLANTRAE GOLF CLUB
1300 Ballantrae Club Dr., Pelham
(205) 620-4653
www.ballantraegolf.com

Named in 2005 as *Golf Digest's* "Best New Affordable Public Golf Course," Ballantrae has earned quite a reputation in the area. Designed by famed architect Bob Cupp and located just south of Birmingham in suburban Pelham, this semi-private club features 18 holes of gorgeous golf for a reasonable price, and the club offers varying levels of membership. Lined with endless southern pines, this wide-open course is described as being fast, friendly, and fun. Ballantrae is well suited for beginners but still presents a challenge to more seasoned golfers. Call or visit the Ballantrae website for tee times and information on club membership.

LIMESTONE SPRINGS GOLF CLUB
3000 Colonial Dr., Oneonta
(205) 274-4653
www.limestonesprings.com

Designed by former US Open Champion Jerry Pate, Limestone Springs has won multiple accolades from sources like *Golf Digest* and *Golfweek*. Located 30 miles north of Birmingham in Oneonta, this semi-private club features a majestic 18-hole course measuring nearly 7,000 yards. Nestled in its dramatic natural setting, Limestone Springs offers wonderful views of the Appalachian foothills as well as championship-level golf. While the club is open to the public, there are varying levels of membership for the golfer looking to return to Limestone Springs. And chances are you'll want to play this course again.

TIMBERLINE GOLF CLUB
300 Timberline Trail, Calera
(205) 668-7888
www.timberlinegc.com

Just outside of Birmingham in nearby Calera lies another Jerry Pate–designed course. Timberline Golf Club features 18 holes of golf marked by a picturesque wooded setting. This semi-private golf club is a challenge to long-time golfers yet friendly to beginners. Billed as "The True Golfer's Club," Timberline offers varying levels of club membership with benefits, but it is also open to the public. Call the club or visit the website for more information on membership or tee times.

Public

BENTBROOK GOLF CLUB
7900 Dickey Springs Rd., Bessemer
(205) 424-2368
www.bentbrook.com

Located just 8 miles from the Riverchase Galleria in Hoover, Bentbrook offers a unique golfing experience at a moderate price. Bentbrook features 27 holes of golf divided into three 9-hole courses: Brook, Graveyard, and Windmill. Play 9 holes or all 27, or choose two of the three to play 18 holes. Each 9-hole course is named for a characteristic feature found along its path. At the Brook you'll find a calming stream running along the course, while at the Graveyard you'll pass by, well, an old graveyard still intact. And in keeping with the trend, the Windmill course features Bentbrook's trademark windmill. The bent-grass greens and Bermuda fairways are complemented by the course's signature clubhouse, a converted barn that serves as the club's dining area and lounge. Because Bentbrook is one of the most popular public courses in Birmingham, it is recommended to schedule a tee time in advance.

EAGLE POINT GOLF CLUB
4500 Eagle Point Dr., Hoover
(205) 991-9070
www.eaglepointgolfclub.com

Just down Highway 280 in the Eagle Point subdivision is one of Birmingham's finest public golf courses. Named one of *Golf Digest*'s "Best Places to Play" for 2009, Eagle Point features 6,493 yards of wide open play in an easily accessible location. An 18-hole par 71, Eagle Point is a challenge for golfers of all skill levels. Although carts are available, Eagle Point is a fine walking course. And why not walk? With abundant pines and hardwoods all along the course, there is ample space for shade. Looking for a place to practice your swing after sundown? Eagle Point's lighted driving range allows golfers to work out the kinks after dark.

i Because of Birmingham's long summer days, many golf clubs feature "Twilight Bargains," a discounted rate after a certain hour of the day that will allow you to play as many holes as you can fit in before the sun goes down. Call or check the course websites for these deals.

HIGHLAND PARK GOLF COURSE
3300 Highland Ave. South, Birmingham
(205) 322-1902
www.highlandparkgolf.com

Established in 1903 Highland Park Golf Course is the oldest course in Alabama. Founded as the Country Club of Birmingham, the course was sold to the City of Birmingham when the club decided to move to suburban Mountain Brook in 1927. It opened to the public in 1955, and today Highland Park is one of two municipal golf courses managed by the City of Birmingham. Although it is referred to now simply as "Highlands," it was known for some time as the Boswell golf course after the famous former Alabama football star and World War II hero Charley Boswell, who lost his sight during battle.

Located in the scenic Highland Park neighborhood near Birmingham's Southside, Highland Park features 18 holes of par-70 golf for a reasonable price. Praised by the *Birmingham News* for having the "Best Greens," Highland also features a panoramic view of the Birmingham skyline at the course's highest points. Although many courses claim to, Highland Park really does offer public golf

with the look and feel of a private club. After a recent revitalization, it is looking better than ever.

OAK MOUNTAIN STATE PARK GOLF COURSE
200 Terrace Dr., Pelham
(205) 620-2520
www.alapark.com/oakmountain/golf

Of the many activities Oak Mountain offers, golf is surely one of the most popular. While other golf courses may attempt to recreate a natural setting, Oak Mountain truly has it. Surrounded by some 10,000 acres of Alabama's largest state park, it is difficult to find another course quite like Oak Mountain. Besides the remarkable scenery, the price is affordable—the downside is that for golfers used to the premium maintenance of most private courses, Oak Mountain may seem a bit rough around the edges. That could be why *Golf Digest* consistently ranks it among the top 50 to 75 public courses in the United States. The course is 18 holes stretched over 6,842 yards (from the longest tees) with Bermuda greens. After a round relax in the spacious clubhouse overlooking Oak Mountain. Senior and junior discounts are available. Walk-ons are welcome, but tee times are not accepted on the same day of play and should be reserved 5 days in advance.

OXMOOR VALLEY, ROBERT TRENT JONES GOLF TRAIL
100 Sunbelt Pkwy., Hoover
(205) 942-1177
www.rtjgolf.com/oxmoorvalley

One of eleven courses to make up The Robert Trent Jones Golf Trail (see Close-up) and, along with Ross Bridge, one of two located in Birmingham, Oxmoor Valley features 54 of the finest holes of golf you're likely to find. With 36 championship holes and an 18-hole short course, golfers can spend a day at Oxmoor Valley or just get in a quick 18 holes. Nestled under Shades Mountain on land previously owned by US Steel, Oxmoor Valley is as "Birmingham" a golf course as they come.

Designed by internationally celebrated course architect Robert Trent Jones, Oxmoor Valley utilizes its natural surroundings to perfection to make for a course that feels not as if it was built, but rather occurred naturally. Each of Oxmoor Valley's three courses offers something a little different to the golfer. The Ridge Course stretches to just over 7,000 yards and is an up-and-down monster of a course. Only the brave walk this one. Take a second to check out the exposed shale rock as you walk up to the par-five third hole and you'll get a good idea as to why Birmingham was once called the "Pittsburgh of the South." The Valley, at 7,005 yards, is only slightly shorter than the Ridge, but without all the hills of the Ridge, making it much easier on the knees. Of course, carts are available for both of these courses and the short course as well.

✳ROSS BRIDGE, ROBERT TRENT JONES GOLF TRAIL
4000 Grand Ave., Hoover
(205) 949-3085
www.rtjgolf.com/rossbridge
The latest addition to the Robert Trent Jones Golf Trail, Ross Bridge immediately took the golf world by storm and at the same time became one of Birmingham's hottest tourist destinations. Designed with the modern long-drive golfer in mind, Ross Bridge tops out at a whopping 8,191 yards, making it the third-longest course in the world. Built along Birmingham's undeveloped Shannon Valley,

the course features breathtaking landscapes in addition to two lakes that occupy the boundary along 10 of the course's 18 holes highlighted by a stunning 80-foot waterfall between the 9th and 18th greens. Some may find maintaining focus in the face of such natural scenery a challenge.

In addition to the world-class golf, Ross Bridge also features the thoroughly modern Renaissance Resort & Spa. An attraction all its own, the resort has become extremely popular among visitors and local "stay-cationers" alike. Named one of *Travel + Leisure* magazine's top 50 hotels in the world for 2008, the Renaissance is making splashes in the world of resorts just as Ross Bridge pleasantly shakes up the golf world.

Additional Public Golf Courses

BALLANTRAE GOLF CLUB
1300 Ballantrae Club Dr., Pelham
(205) 620-4653
www.ballantraegolf.com

BENT BROOK
6217 Harpers Dairy Loop, Bessemer
(205) 428-1999
www.bentbrook.com

CASTLE PINES COUNTRY CLUB
1600 Quail Ridge Dr., Gardendale
(205) 631-3140
www.castlepinesllc.com

EAGLE POINT GOLF CLUB
4500 Eagle Point Dr., Meadowbrook
(205) 991-9070
www.eaglepointgolfclub.com

HORSE CREEK GOLF COURSE
1745 Hwy. 78, Dora
(205) 648-1499
www.horsecreekgolf.com

LIMESTONE SPRINGS GOLF CLUB
3000 Colonial Dr., Oneonta
(205) 274-4653
www.limestonesprings.com

MOUNTAIN VIEW GOLF COURSE
3200 Mountain View Dr., Graysville
(205) 674-8362

RIVER OAKS GOLF AND COUNTRY CLUB
6396 Zeigler Rd., Leeds
(205) 699-4856
www.riveroaksgolfcourse.tripod.com

ROEBUCK GOLF COURSE
8920 Roebuck Blvd., Birmingham
(205) 836-7318

TIMBERLINE GOLF CLUB
300 Timberline Trail, Calera
(205) 668-7888
www.timberlinegc.com

TRUSSVILLE COUNTRY CLUB
7905 Roper Rd., Trussville
(205) 655-2095
www.trussvillecountryclub.com

GYMS

In addition to YMCAs, Birmingham has a number of gyms to help you stave off the effects of all the great local restaurants. Among the most well known of these are Gold's Gym and Riviera Fitness. There are also a host of smaller fitness centers located primarily in the Over the Mountain area. While it is impossible to list them all, some of the best-known are listed below.

ANYTIME FITNESS
4510 Overton Rd., Birmingham
(205) 957-2525
www.anytimefitness

CURVES
Multiple locations
www.curves.com

GOLD'S GYM
www.goldsgymbham.com

3427 Colonnade Pkwy., Hoover
(205) 583-GOLD

2244 Pelham Pkwy., Pelham
(205) 358-1330

1090 Montgomery Hwy., Vestavia Hills
(205) 823-4635

GRAVLEE FITNESS & BODY DESIGN
15 Dexter Ave., Mountain Brook
(205) 871-7128
www.gravleefitness.com

IRON TRIBE FITNESS
2809 Central Ave., Homewood
(205) 874-6300
www.irontribefitness.com

PLANET FITNESS
1839 Montgomery Hwy., Suite 40, Hoover
(205) 444-2282

RIVIERA FITNESS
www.rivierafitnesscenters.com

2310 Center Point Rd., Birmingham
(205) 853-8878

327 Palisades Blvd., Homewood
(205) 290-0000

1548 Forestdale Blvd., Forestdale
(205) 798-0098

SNAP FITNESS
2512 Rocky Ridge Rd., Suite 104, Vestavia Hills
(205) 822-4348

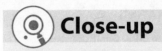

Close-up

Robert Trent Jones Golf Trail

The **Robert Trent Jones Golf Trail,** one of Alabama's most famous recreational attractions, features 468 holes of world-class golf divided along 11 sites spanning the state from Muscle Shoals in Alabama's northwest to Mobile along the Gulf Coast. Dr. David Bronner, CEO of Retirement Systems of Alabama, originally conceived of the golf trail idea to promote the state's recreational assets, temperate climate, and natural beauty to retirees and those considering relocation. The legendary golf course designer Robert Trent Jones Sr. soon joined Bronner, and together the two embarked on one of the most ambitious golfing projects in the country. Taking meticulous, artistic care to the details of each particular hole, Jones created his golfing masterpiece.

Educated at Cornell University, Robert Trent Jones is regarded as a pioneer of golf-course design. He designed his first golf course, The Peachtree Club in Atlanta, under the tutelage of legendary golfer, Bobby Jones (no relation). And like his mentor, Robert Trent Jones developed a respect for the ideals of the game of golf, namely self-discipline and focus, but above all he developed a respect and admiration for the natural environment that he deftly manipulated to build some of the most challenging and stunningly beautiful golf courses around the world. It's been said that of the hundreds of courses designed by Jones, none bring together these characteristics—daring design and natural grace and beauty—quite like the courses of the trail.

Each of the trail's 11 sites is noted for its challenging play and natural beauty, a trademark of Jones-designed courses. From the swamps of Muscle Shoals, to Birmingham's mountainous terrain, and finally to the Spanish moss–covered oaks of Mobile, each course incorporates the inherent natural elements of its location. The most impressive of the 11 sites is surely Birmingham's Ross Bridge. At 8,191 yards, Ross Bridge is the world's third-longest golf course and an ideal setting designed for both the modern golfer and spectator. Suitably enough, soon after opening, Ross Bridge played host to the Champions' Tour's Regions Charity Classic.

Described by *The New York Times* as, "Some of the best public golf on earth," and by the *Wall Street Journal* as, "Maybe the biggest bargain in the country," the Robert Trent Jones Golf Trail has already become a site of pilgrimage for devotees of the sport. Six of the trail's 11 locations feature hotels on-site, combining the golfing experience with Southern hospitality at its finest.

The 11 sites of the Robert Trent Jones Golf Trail (www.rtjgolf.com) are:

The Shoals, Muscle Shoals

Capitol Hill, Montgomery

Hampton Cove, Huntsville

Cambrian Ridge, Greenville

Silver Lakes, Gadsden/Anniston

Highland Oaks, Dothan

Oxmoor Valley, Birmingham

Lakewood, Point Clear

Ross Bridge, Birmingham

Magnolia Grove, Mobile

Grand National, Auburn/Opelika

STUDIO FITNESS

2900 Central Ave., Suite 110, Homewood
(205) 414-3644
www.studiofitnessllc.com

THE FITNESS CENTER

3900 Montclair Rd., # 210,
Mountain Brook
(205) 870-1121
www.thefitnesscenter.org

HUNTING

Hunting season in Alabama is perhaps second only to football season for the level of fierce anticipation it builds in devotees. Deer season typically runs from mid-November to mid-January and fills the void in the sportsmen's life from the end of the regular football season and the advent of post-season bowl games, just as nature intended. Some have even speculated that the annual Auburn and Alabama match was moved from the Saturday after Thanksgiving to Friday to allow for hunters to take advantage of the long weekend.

In addition to whitetail deer, you'll also find turkey, quail, dove, and even bear among Alabama's game. And recently, alligator has been opened up to the Alabama hunter on a limited basis, though this is only in the southern part of the state. You must enter into a lottery draw in order to hunt gator, however. Hunting licenses are necessary for hunting of any kind and can be purchased online at **www.alabamainteractive.org.** For more information on hunting, visit **www .outdooralabama.com/hunting.**

ICE SKATING

PELHAM CIVIC COMPLEX

500 Amphitheater Rd., Pelham
(205) 620-6448
www.pelhamciviccomplex.com

As Birmingham's only public skating rink, the Pelham Civic Complex is a popular destination for those in search of a winter wonderland any time of year. In addition to hosting recreational ice skaters on its two NHL-size rinks, the PCC is also the home of the Birmingham Figure Skating Club, the University of Alabama Hockey Club, and the Birmingham Adult Hockey Association and Youth League. At less than $10 per person, the Pelham Civic Complex Ice Skating Rink is one of the best deals in town for active indoor exercise and fun, and it's great for children's birthday parties. If you haven't skated in a while, get back in the swing of things with the Birmingham Skating School, led by respected instructor Danny Tate. These lessons are great for the beginning skater as well as the aspiring Olympian.

KAYAKING & CANOEING

With its diverse geography and physiography, Alabama contains a large variety of natural environments. For the paddler this means a host of canoeing and kayaking options, from mountain streams to coastal meanderings. In and around the Birmingham region, you'll find a number of paddling opportunities such as the **Cahaba River** and **Five Mile Creek.** Many of the best sites for canoeing and kayaking in Birmingham—and in the state for that matter—are found along the tributaries of the **Black Warrior River,** itself a tributary of the **Tombigbee Waterway.** Stretching over 175 miles, the Black Warrior has been channelized and shaped through a series of dams in order to connect barge traffic from the Gulf Coast and beyond to Birmingham.

While the once mighty Black Warrior River is now just a waterway thanks to these dams, area residents still have a few natural rivers to paddle along upstream, chiefly the **Locust Fork, Mulberry Fork** and **Sipsey Fork.** The Sipsey Fork, flowing from Bankhead National Forest, and the Locust Fork, from near Sand Mountain, both join the Mulberry Fork 20 miles west of Birmingham to form the Black Warrior. The Black Warrior's tributaries possess unrivaled natural beauty and scenic seclusion. For over 25 years the **Birmingham Canoe Club** has led efforts to stop the pollution of Birmingham's waterways and to encourage water recreation. The club offers a number of opportunities through membership and is a great resource for visitors to Birmingham who are interested in navigating these waterways by canoe or kayak. For more information visit **www.birminghamcanoeclub.org.**

ℹ️ The word "Tuscaloosa" is from the Choctaw *tashka,* "warrior," and *lusa,* "black." Another name for the Black Warrior River in the 18th century was *Apotaka hacha,* meaning "Border River" since it served as a boundary between Choctaw, Chickasaw, and Creek lands.

✳CAHABA RIVER
(205) 322-5326 (Cahaba River Society)
www.cahabariver.net

South of Birmingham, the Cahaba River is the longest undammed (largely) river remaining in the state. Aside from serving as the primary water supply for Birmingham, the Cahaba is an environmental treasure,

one of the nation's most biologically diverse and endangered rivers. With 131 fish species, the river contains more fish species per mile than any other river on this continent. At 191 miles, it is the longest free-flowing river in the state of Alabama. The Cahaba also holds the largest number of snail species in the entire Mobile River basin, itself the richest habitat of snail species in the world. The Cahaba is a recreational, biological, and geological treasure.

Winding gracefully around Birmingham from the east and then south, the Cahaba is the backyard playground for area canoeists wanting a peaceful day on the river. If you're looking for more than just a day float, it's not uncommon for canoeists to camp along the river, especially the lower Cahaba where long, graceful sandbars are frequent—but check beforehand as much of the land along the river is privately owned. The river's symbol, the Cahaba Lily, is native only to Alabama, Georgia, and South Carolina. The Cahaba Lily blossoms between May and June, so if you're scheduling a canoe trip around then, be on the lookout for this rare and beautiful flower. The **Cahaba River Society** also features a number of guided trips along the river. A schedule of these trips is available online at **www.cahabariversociety.org,** (205) 322-5326, and they usually run about $20.

The Cahaba is generally a calm river, but it can pick up dramatically after heavy downpours. This is when you'll find the more extreme kayakers (some might say foolhardy) out on the river to experience the Cahaba at white-water levels, even if only briefly. For put-ins along the river as well as further information, visit **www.cahabariver.net.** Grants Mill Road at the official Jefferson County canoe launch to either Old Overton

Road or Highway 280 is a flat, calm run good for families or smaller children. Farther south, the Piper Bridge (County 65) to River Bend Bridge (County 27) contains the last major drops in elevations before Hargrove Shoals near Centerville.

i For detailed notes on the Cahaba River (and most other area rivers) put-ins, John Foshee's *Alabama Canoe Rides and Float Trips* remains the definitive source. It offers detailed guides, maps, and other information paddlers rely on for fun, safe outings. lands, primarily for cultural and spiritual purposes.

✳LOCUST FORK

For serious canoeists and kayakers, it is the Locust Fork—a rocky, secluded, wild river with spectacular cliffs—that has long attracted whitewater-loving boaters from nearby states. In Blount County alone the river drops more than 500 feet, creating up to Class IV rapids. Before today's avid boaters used the river, pioneers— calling the region the Bear Meat Cabin Frontier—depended on the Locust Fork's many falls for power to grind their corn and wheat. The bears may be few and far between today, but kayakers aren't. Check out the annual **Locust Fork Whitewater Classic,** usually in Feb or Mar, to see the river and its sporting aficionados at their best. And to see why the National Park Service ranks the Locust Fork River in the top 2 percent of all rivers in the United States.

A rocky river that is remote and pristine, the first portion of the river near Wards Bridge on AL 79 has smaller shoals and pools that become progressively more challenging until the heavy-duty whitewater portions and waterfalls around US 231 to Swann Covered Bridge. With up to Class IV rapids, you should not attempt to paddle this portion alone or without skilled partners you can rely on in a jam. Again, see John Foshee's *Alabama Canoe Rides and Float Trips*. Look for dramatic cliffs at Skirum Bluff on the run to Nectar Covered Bridge— it's a great place to swim in the summer when the water is up.

The Cahaba Lily

Probably the best known of the Cahaba River's imperiled species is the **Cahaba Lily** (also known as the Shoals Lily, *Hymenocallis coronaria*). Once the lily prospered throughout the Southeast where clear water flowed over layered rock, but because of the destruction of its habitat—from water-quality problems to sediment smothering the lily's roots—the lily's most significant habitat today is the Cahaba River. In late May and early June, not far from the town of West Blocton, a yearly spectacle occurs in the river. Patches of green stalks jut out of the water two or more feet high; flower buds burst open on each stalk and wait patiently for the lily's primary pollinator, the Hawk Moth, to drift from lily to lily at night. The lilies come to life in brilliant white color. Each year hundreds of people make the pilgrimage to the Cahaba to view one of the finest remaining colonies of Cahaba Lilies in the world.

i The famous bridges of Madison County have absolutely nothing on the bridges of Blunt County! When out canoeing in the area, visit Swann Covered Bridge. Built in 1933 it stretches 324 feet across the Locust Fork. Horton Mill Covered Bridge near Oneonta stands 70 feet above the Calvert prong of the Locust Fork, making it the highest covered bridge above water in the country.

MULBERRY FORK

Beginning in Arab and flowing in a southwesterly direction until it joins the Sipsey Fork below Smith Lake, the Mulberry Fork combines beautiful scenic floats popular with both fishermen and canoeists. Much like its sister river the Locust Fork, it's one of the more popular rivers in the state for paddlers wanting a good, fun playful day on the water. Its upper reaches are narrow and shallow until the Duck and Broglen rivers nearly double the Mulberry's flow. The 22-mile stretch from Center Hill/Blountsville Road past Highway 31 to the bridge at I-65 is a scenic paddle with high bluffs and cliffs as well as a few Class I and II rapids. Below I-65, the current slows and it's a pleasant float.

Commonly divided into the **Upper Upper, Upper,** and **Lower Mulberry** (don't ask), the Upper Upper is mellow, the Upper can be a wild ride, and the Lower, starting below the old Highway 31 bridge, is a bit like the Upper Upper with lots of pools, small rapids, and play holes. The last rapid on the lower run, the famous Hawaii Five-0 Wave, is a popular park-and-play spot at the well-maintained Birmingham Canoe Club's take-out on Whitewater Bend Road.

At high water levels, Hawaii Five-0 Wave can reach Class III so have fun and take care! Look for the **Mulberry Fork Canoe and Kayak Race** in March, **www.alabamacupraces.com.**

✳SIPSEY FORK

Flowing south through the Sipsey Wilderness Area of Bankhead National Forest, the Sipsey Fork is a wonderland of hidden canyons, large waterfalls, and cave-like overhangs. Even after the hardest rains, the Sipsey runs clear and clean, supporting many rare species and old-growth forests. Smith Lake on the Sipsey Fork is the largest impoundment in the western Mobile basin (21,000 acres), and its deep, clear waters are well known by fishermen for their spotted and striped bass. As well as the headwater of Smith Lake, the Sipsey Fork is Alabama's only federally designated Wild & Scenic River.

If you want a fun, scenic narrow river-run in total seclusion, try the **Borden Creek** within the Sipsey Wilderness Area—one of the most beautiful hiking and camping spots in Alabama. Take Cranal Road (signage often reads "Cranal Road Access") and turn left on FS 224 which dead ends at Borden Creek and the put-in at the bridge. The run from Cranal Road/County 60 (often called the Upper Sipsey Fork) is almost equally scenic, with large cliffs and huge boulders as well as a Class I rapid (Class II during high water). The Lower Sipsey Fork begins at the Highway 33 bridge and is equally beautiful but certainly slows as the river widens. The takeout is at Grindstone Creek, a tough spot without four-wheel drive after a heavy rain.

RECREATION

FIVE MILE CREEK

For decades it seemed that Five Mile Creek would be yet another victim of Birmingham's industrial past. Many locals know the creek as "Chocolate Creek" or "Creosite Creek" because of its thick appearance and dark brown color, nicknames it earned as a result of years of careless pollution and waste. Thankfully though, due to the efforts of local officials and concerned residents, Five Mile Creek is in the process of transforming from an unhappy footnote in Birmingham's history into an environmental success story. Five Mile Creek is yet another sign of Birmingham's successful transformation from capitol of industry at the expense of the environment to a city that is working to become greener every day.

Perhaps Five Mile Creek is a bit of a misnomer, however. The creek actually runs a total of 43 miles before releasing into the Black Warrior River to the west of Birmingham. Five Mile Creek is open for canoeing and kayaking from Mar to Nov. Canoes and kayaks are available for rent and camping is available in Brookside along the Five Mile Creek Greenway. For more information on the **Five Mile Creek Greenway,** see Greenways or visit www.fivemilecreekgreenway.org or www.canoe5mile.com.

VALLEY CREEK

Yet another of the Black Warrior's gifts to Birmingham paddlers, Valley Creek winds 72 miles from Birmingham until it reaches the Black Warrior River west of the city. Valley Creek is a great opportunity to escape the hustle and bustle of the city and take in some fresh air while getting a little exercise. A generally calm creek, Valley presents very few challenges to the experienced paddler and is easily manageable for novices. Although it does pick up at a few sites along the way, on a typical day Valley Creek presents a relaxing and enjoyable ride atop the water with the chance to spot wildlife like herons, cranes, and otters.

Valley Creek is open to kayakers and canoers, but you must bring your own equipment because there is no rental available. In summer the water is generally too low for a successful float, as is the custom of most smaller creeks and streams in the area. A small fee of $3 is required for parking at **Clevenger's Marina** at 1395 Shortown Branch Rd. in Bessemer, (205) 491-6684. Launch points are located at the Powder Plant Road Bridge and at the John's Road Bridge near Bessemer. For more information on Valley Creek, call the Valley Creek Society at (205) 425-0962.

Outfitters

Alabama Small Boats
2800 Cahaba Village Plaza, Suite 250, Birmingham
(205) 977-7010
www.alsmallboats.com

Five Mile Creek Canoe and Company
100 Park Rd., Brookside
(205) 674-5550
www.canoe5mile.com

Limestone Park Canoes
1456 Limestone Pkwy., Brierfield
(205) 926-9672

LEAGUE SPORTS

Whether you're looking to channel your competitiveness or just interested in getting together with friends, Birmingham offers an array of adult sports leagues. Choose from bowling, flag football, basketball, soccer, and lacrosse, among others, or try a different one every season. There are enough sports leagues in town to keep you busy throughout the year. Of course, you don't have to join a league. Many facilities host pick-up games for all comers. Check which nights and ask about availability as some of these, such as pick-up basketball at the YMCA, can get very crowded.

Baseball

There are plenty of options for America's game in Birmingham. The City of Hoover Parks and Recreation Department provides competitive adult baseball with former college and high school stars adding to the level of play. For youth leagues, see area parks and recreation departments.

BIRMINGHAM METRO BASEBALL LEAGUE
(205) 901-6629
www.bmbl.org

CENTRAL ALABAMA BASEBALL ASSOCIATION
(205) 901-6629

YOUNG MEN'S BASEBALL LEAGUE
www.youngmensbaseballassociation.com

Bowling

Birmingham features seven bowling alleys, all open to the public. Each of these bowling alleys has leagues supported by the **United States Bowling Congress of Greater Birmingham.** The USBC offers a variety of different league formats to suit various skill levels and interest. For more information on the GBUSBCA and to check out the various leagues, visit **www.gbusbca.net.** All of these alleys have shoes available for rent and many feature cosmic bowling, a popular nightlife activity around town.

BRUNSWICK RIVERVIEW LANES
2908 Riverview Rd., Hoover
(205) 991-3900

HOLIDAY BOWL
4321 Bessemer Super Hwy., Bessemer
(205) 428-8461

LIGHTNING STRIKES CENTER
3600 Roosevelt Blvd., Trussville
(205) 655-4500

OAK MOUNTAIN LANES
300 Bowling Lane, Pelham
(205) 403-7466
www.oakmountainlanes.com

PINE BOWL
2015 Decatur Hwy., Fultondale
(205) 841-4353

SUPER BOWL
4416 Pinson Valley Hwy., Pinson
(205) 854-9159

VESTAVIA BOWL
1429 Montgomery Hwy., Vestavia Hills
(205) 979-4420
www.vestaviabowl.com

Kickball

Each year, kickball seems to grow in popularity as more and more young adults strive to relive their middle-school years without all the wedgies, bad haircuts, and general awkwardness. The **Birmingham Adult Kickball**

League features a number of teams around town, all playing for various local charities. Anyone can participate and the games are just as much fun to watch as to play in. With the phrase "desperate to be different" as their motto, the BAKL welcomes anyone who ever thought that middle school would never end. And well, who didn't? Playing every first and third Sun of every month at Avondale Park, be sure to check these guys and girls out. The 1970s period costume attire is *de rigueur*. For more information contact the **Birmingham Adult Kickball League** (www.desperatetobedifferent.com)

Lacrosse

A sport that continues to grow in popularity with each passing year, lacrosse hit the area in the late 1990s and now can count the number of boys and girls participating in the thousands. Fall, spring, and summer recreational leagues attract players from first grade through high school, though the most popular season is spring. Watch the **Greater Birmingham Youth Lacrosse Association** website for information on local camps and clinics throughout the year, as well as out-of-state lacrosse camps. Additionally, many local high schools now field lacrosse teams, a sure sign of its enduring popularity. For more information contact the **Greater Birmingham Youth Lacrosse Association** (www.byll.org).

Soccer

Birmingham is home to quite a few players of the beautiful game. On any given night you'll find pick-up games at parks across the city. Homewood's **Patriot Park** and Hoover's **Rocky Ridge Sports Park** are popular for

pick-ups, but the undisputed hub of Birmingham's footie fanatics is **Sports Blast.** Located just off Highway 280 in Shelby County, Sports Blast is the only indoor soccer facility in Birmingham. In addition to two indoor fields, Sports Blast also features several outdoor fields. Indoor leagues for all levels of play are held year-round, while outdoor leagues play during the spring and summer. Organize your own team or just get onboard with someone else.

There are numerous adult leagues in the city administered by the **Birmingham United Soccer Association, Homewood Soccer Association,** and **Central Alabama Independent Soccer League.** An amateur soccer association known as "La Liga" also operates in the city, primarily for the Latino population, though anyone is welcome to field a team. The listing below is only a partial accounting of the larger leagues and clubs, so check with area parks and recreation departments for information on the multitude of organized soccer opportunities.

Indoor Facilities
SPORTS BLAST
19220 Hwy. 280 East, Chelsea
(205) 980-1701
www.sportsblastsc.com

Regional Leagues & Clubs
ALABAMA YOUTH SOCCER ASSOCIATION
(205) 991-9779
www.alabamayouthsoccer.org

BIRMINGHAM UNITED SOCCER ASSOCIATION
(205) 981-6629
www.birminghamunited.com

CENTRAL ALABAMA INDEPENDENT SOCCER LEAGUE

(205) 957-1191

http://caisl.peregrinetech.net

HOMEWOOD SOCCER CLUB

www.homewoodsoccer.com

HOOVER SOCCER CLUB

Hoover Court, #215, Hoover

(205) 978-8663

www.hooversoccerclub.com

MID-ALABAMA RECREATIONAL SOCCER LEAGUE

www.marsleague.com

VESTAVIA HILLS SOCCER CLUB

1973 Merryvale Rd., Vestavia Hills

(205) 978-0182

www.vestaviasoccer.com

Hockey

Believe it or not, there are many who love hockey in Birmingham. For these loyal fans and athletes, the **Pelham Civic Complex** is home. The **Birmingham Adult Hockey Association** operates 2 leagues that consist of 6 teams, each with 15 to 18 players—if you are interested, sign up quickly as the spots are often filled quickly. Depending on the league, games run each Sun or Wed evening for a total of 15 regular season games plus playoff games. You'll get in plenty of hockey action.

BIRMINGHAM ADULT HOCKEY ASSOCIATION

500 Amphitheater Rd., Pelham

(205) 620-6448

www.bahainfo.com

Flag Football

Among the most popular adult recreational sports, various flag-football leagues operate throughout the city. Many churches, YMCAs, and locals colleges host flag competition. The **Birmingham Independent Flag Football League (BIFFL)** is perhaps the best-known league and plays its games at the intramural fields on the campus of the University of Alabama at Birmingham. If you've always wondered what it's like to play at the pace of the Arena Football League, join the **Sports Blast Flag Football League.** Because these games are held indoors, league sessions operate year-round. In fact it isn't uncommon for many people to participate in the winter session indoors and in the fall session outdoors to play flag football all year.

BIRMINGHAM INDEPENDENT FLAG FOOTBALL LEAGUE

www.eteamz.com/biffl

SPORTS BLAST FLAG FOOTBALL LEAGUE

www.sportsblastsc.com

Ultimate Frisbee

Known locally by its acronym, **BUDA,** the **Birmingham Ultimate Disc Association** enjoys a fiercely loyal following among the athletes that compete year-round on fields all across Birmingham. BUDA organizes as well as participates in local and regional tournaments. For more information contact the **Birmingham Ultimate Disc Association** (www.mudbowl.org).

ROCK CLIMBING

✳FIRST AVENUE ROCKS
2417 1st Ave. South, Birmingham
(205) 320-2277
www.firstaverocks.com
With nearly 4,000 square feet of world-class indoor rock-climbing equipment, First Avenue Rocks is the premier indoor rock-climbing facility in the state. Ideally located in the heart of Downtown Birmingham, First Avenue Rocks is a haven for the outdoorsman who finds himself suddenly trapped in the city. Whether it's exercise or stress relief you seek, First Avenue Rocks is the place to go from the beginner to the expert.

MOSS ROCK PRESERVE
617 Preserve Pkwy., Hoover
www.hooveral.org
For rock-climbing suburbanites, Hoover holds a hidden treasure: Moss Rock Preserve. This 250-acre nature preserve features Boulder Field, a climber's heaven with assorted rock formations ideal for bouldering. The preserve features rocks and boulders of various shapes and sizes to suit all climbers from beginner to advanced—visit the city of Hoover website to download a PDF map and detailed guide of the three distinct bouldering areas: Ozzy Area, Grass Man, and Lost Roof. The preserve is open from sunrise to sunset and is free to the public. You'll find most climbers from fall to spring. And don't miss the Moss Rock Festival each Nov at the Preserve. The Moss Rock Festival is devoted to environmental sustainability and features outdoor-themed artwork as well as live music and an environmentally themed design competition. Visit www.mossrockfestival.com for more information on this year's event.

HORSE PENS 40
3525 Co. Rd. 42, Steele
(256) 538-7439
http://horsepens40.tripod.com
Slightly beyond the Birmingham region, Horse pens 40 remains a top choice for bouldering daytrips from the city. At 1,500 feet above sea level, Horse pens' setting atop Chandler Mountain is the third-highest point in the state, but boulderers know the site for its great sandstone slopers. A historic outdoor nature park popular for hikers and boulderers alike, the natural stone fortress was used by Native Americans for thousands of years, dating back to the Paleolithic era. Today visitors will find rustic cabins, bluegrass and rock festivals, motorcycle rallies, and more. Night bouldering is allowed for registered campers. See the website for rules, operating hours, and other information. No pets are allowed.

ℹ️ Mountain High Outfitters, a local outdoors store, has partnered with Fox Mountain Guides and Climbing School, the Southeast's only American Mountain Guides Association Accredited Climbing School, to offer an assortment of climbing classes ranging from novice day trips or more advanced group excursions and multi-day courses. See www.mountainhighoutfitters.com or call (877) 557-5322 for details.

PALISADES PARK
1225 Palisades Pkwy., Oneonta
(205) 274-0017
www.blountcountypark.com
With its easy access and accommodating park rangers, the sandstone formations of

Palisades Park in Oneonta make for a good spot for beginners to learn the ropes. Rock climbing and rappelling options abound on the 70-foot cliffs. There is some bouldering to be done, and with nearly 100 routes, there's plenty to keep you busy for the day. Most routes can be top-roped. No bolts and no camping or overnight stays are allowed. Permits are required.

i For those interested in Alabama history and culture, when at Palisades Park, be sure to visit the fine restored buildings, Daniel Murphree cabin (1820), Blackwood cabin, and Compton schoolhouse (1904).

RUNNING

The world's oldest sport (or is that speed walking?) has an enormous following in Birmingham. On a spring or summer afternoon, don't be surprised to see a number of tank-top clad runners jogging all over the city and suburbs, particularly Homewood, one of the less steep of the suburbs. And in Nov and Feb, downtown streets close for the **Vulcan Run** and **Mercedes Marathon.** Both of these races attract thousands of participants and supportive observers cheering the competitors on.

On a typical day though, runners complete their routines then meet at the **Trak Shak** (205-870-5644, www.trakshak.com) in Homewood, fresh off their "runner's high." Runs start every Wed at 5:30 p.m. at their Homewood store and there are 3-, 5-, and 8.5-mile courses. Birmingham has a number of great jogging routes as well. One of the most popular, the **Jemison Park Trail** and the surrounding greenways, are pounded upon

by hundreds of joggers each day. For more information on routes, area races, or how to join a running group, visit the **Birmingham Track Club** at **www.birminghamtrackclub .com.** See the Greenways chapter for some excellent trails.

SWIMMING

The City of Birmingham operates 17 public swimming pools (www.birminghamal.gov/swimming-pools.aspx) throughout the summer months for a $1 admission fee. The pools are open from noon to 6 p.m. 6 days a week. Closed days vary by pool, so call or check the Birmingham Parks and Recreation website at www.informationbirmingham.com/swimming-pools before visiting a local pool. See the Kidstuff chapter for a description of two of the city's most popular public pools, Homewood Central Pool and Vestavia Hills Swimming Pool. Additionally, see the YMCA listing at the end of this chapter for more public pool options. There are also a number of private pools at area country clubs.

COOPER GREEN
111 Dorothy Dr.
(205) 925-9457

CRESTWOOD
5400 ½ Crestwood Blvd.
(205) 595-8523

EAST LAKE
116 84th St.
(205) 836-5312

EAST THOMAS
208 Bankhead Hwy. West
(205) 251-1964

E.O. JACKSON
601 15th Ave. North
(205) 323-8382

Camellia Road
(205) 853-0533

HARRIS
2720 Ave. West
(205) 787-0771

LEWIS
7500 66th St. South
(205) 595-5267

M.L. KING
529 43rd St. North
(205) 591-2033

MACLIN
2701 Huntsville Rd.
(205) 251-2278

MCALPINE
115 Ave. F
(205) 786-0025

MEMORIAL
524 6th St. South
(205) 252-0135

NORWOOD
2700 15th Ave. North
(205) 252-4943

ROOSEVELT CITY
2500 Warner St.
(205) 424-2751

UNDERWOOD
1021 26th St. South
(205) 930-0821

WIGGINS
3301 Jefferson Ave. Southwest
(205) 923-8977

WOODWARD
1220 McMillian Ave. Southwest
(205) 781-4965

Swimming Leagues

BIRMINGHAM SWIM LEAGUE
1025 Montgomery Hwy., Suite 106,
Vestavia Hills
(205) 823-5512
www.birminghamswimleague.org

HOOVER BLUE THUNDER
600 Municipal Dr., Hoover
(205) 979-8434
www.hbtswim.org

MAGIC CITY AQUATIC LEAGUE
(205) 541-4737
www.mcalswim.com

SHOOTING RANGES

There are quite a few places around town to practice your aim, whether with a bow, pistol, or rifle. Here is a listing of local shooting ranges that are open to the public. Fees may apply.

ALABAMA TRAINING INSTITUTE AND PISTOL RANGE
906 North 40th St., Birmingham
(205) 592-3004
www.alpistol.com

PLEASANT GROVE FOP RANGE
91 1st St. South, Pleasant Grove
(205) 744-2600
www.foprangeinc.com

TANNEHILL SPORTING CLAYS
Highway 11, Woodstock
(205) 938-3379
www.tannehillsportingclays.com

TENNIS

Birmingham features a number of tennis centers in the city as well as in the suburbs. Most of these are semi-private clubs that are open to the public for a small fee. Because of Alabama's generally mild winters, many of these centers operate year-round, and other than during a few times of severe cold, most courts are in use. Most city parks and recreation departments run programs and leagues as well, and there are a number of private individuals offering lessons for individuals or groups. Many local parks also feature tennis courts, and in the warm months, you'll find competitors playing late into the night. Although there are also a number of private tennis clubs in the Birmingham area, they are not included in this list. Visit the **Birmingham Area Tennis Association** at www.jltsfi.com to find out more.

EAST LAKE RACQUET CLUB
408 82nd St. North, Birmingham
(205) 833-2960

GEORGE WARD TENNIS CENTER
331 16th Ave. South, Birmingham
(205) 322-8745

HIGHLAND PARK RACQUET CLUB
3300 Highland Ave., Birmingham
(205) 251-1965
www.academytennis.com

JAMES LEWIS TENNIS CENTER
2800 Avenue K, Birmingham
(205) 788-0505
www.jltsfi.com

PELHAM TENNIS CENTER
315 Ballpark Rd., Pelham
(205) 620-6428
www.pelhamracquetclub.com

ALABAMA TENNIS ASSOCIATION
3300 Highland Ave. South, Birmingham
(205) 328-3984
www.alabamata.usta.com

YMCA

Birmingham features quite a few YMCAs dispersed throughout the city. Many of the local YMCAs feature basketball, softball, and swimming, among other popular sports leagues. Most of the various branches operate basketball leagues year-round and softball leagues in the summer. Call your nearest YMCA branch or visit the YMCA website at **www.ymcabham.org** to find out more.

DOWNTOWN BRANCH
2101 4th Ave. North, Birmingham
(205) 324-4563

MOUNTAIN BROOK BRANCH
2401 20th Place South, Mountain Brook
(205) 870-0144

NORTHEAST FAMILY BRANCH
628 Red Lane Rd., Birmingham
(205) 833-7616

SHADES VALLEY FAMILY BRANCH
3551 Montgomery Hwy., Birmingham
(205) 870-9622

WESTERN AREA FAMILY BRANCH
1195 Bessemer Rd., Birmingham
(205) 923-1195

YOGA

As yoga continues to grow in popularity, Birmingham yoga studios have thrived. No longer just seen as the practice of yogis and housewives, yoga studios in Birmingham are filled with a broad array of new and experienced yoga practitioners. Classes for Asthanga, Vinyasa Flow, Kundalini, and more are available at various studios. Here are a few of the top studios found in Birmingham. In addition to these studios, many YMCAs and local gyms also have yoga teachers on staff and offer classes. Find out what works best for you!

BIRMINGHAM YOGA
2417 1st Ave. South, Birmingham
(205) 427-2171
www.birminghamyoga.com

CRESTWOOD YOGA AND MASSAGE
5508 Crestwood Blvd., Birmingham
(205) 908-1247
http://crestwoodyogaandmassage
.blogspot.com

FIRST AVENUE ROCKS
2417 1st Ave. South, Birmingham
(205) 320-2277
www.firstaverocks.com

HEARTWOOD YOGA
700 Century Park South, Hoover
(205) 979-0019
www.heartwoodyoga.com

SOHO-PIYO
1830 29th Ave. South, Homewood
(205) 879-2710
www.soho-piyo.com

THE YOGA CIRCLE
1425 Richard Arrington Jr. Blvd. South,
Birmingham
(205) 266-7547
www.theyogacircle.net

GREENWAYS

There's no doubt about it, one of Birmingham's biggest assets is a climate that lends itself to year-round outdoor activities. Yes, you'll sweat in the dog days of July and August, but when you're running, walking, or biking on area greenways and trails on a sunny 55-degree day in January, don't forget to be grateful for what you've got.

The Olmsted Brothers, the nation's foremost park-planning architectural firm, finalized *A Park System for Birmingham* in 1925 that recommended numerous active and passive parks throughout the booming young city. It was a forward-thinking blueprint with a series of recreational green areas for the city's citizens that the planners thought would increase economic growth, connect communities, and promote better health and happiness for residents. Some of the plan was completed until the Great Depression, local dithering, world war, and subsequent recovery delayed much implementation. Yet today, recent additions like Ruffner Mountain Nature Preserve, Red Mountain Park, and Railroad Reservation Park are showing that Birmingham's unofficial tag line, as advocated by local environmentalist Roald Hazelhoff, "The Gateway to Nature," can still ring true.

The Olmsted Brothers' vision for Birmingham has never been as close to being realized as it is right now. The next few years could be crucial as many exciting greenway projects are currently funded and dozens of others are in the final drawing stages. "Other cities are making these greenway and pedestrian path connections, and considering the great natural advantages we have here, there's no reason Birmingham can't be a leading livable city," explains Jane Reed Ross, a landscape architect who developed the master plan for the Homewood Shades Creek Greenway as well as worked on the Our One Mile Greenway Master Plan for Jefferson County by the Freshwater Land Trust. "When this is all done, Birmingham will be a better city because of it."

OVERVIEW

But there's a flip side: In true Birmingham fashion, much of what has occurred in the way of greenways and pedestrian paths has been achieved through the perseverance and hard work of an assortment of individuals, advocacy groups, and individual municipalities. Concerted, consensus-building efforts across community lines have been perhaps talked about more than implemented in actual practice. But that, too, may be changing for the better.

That has started to change, most notably with the new $13.5-million grant awarded to the Jefferson County Health Department to combat tobacco use and obesity in the county. The **Freshwater Land Trust,** the entity administering the grant, is finalizing a comprehensive greenway master plan to fulfill the grant that identifies a workable network of over 100 miles of greenways, trails, and blueways. In 2010 the **Alabama Trails Commission** became a reality, advancing the interconnection of lands for trails of all sorts. Similarly, the Birmingham Metropolitan Planning Organization is working on an Active Transportation Plan that addresses and identifies ways to develop alternatives to motor vehicle travel in the region. It makes for encouraging times. All greenways and trails listed are free and open to the public.

CAHABA RIVERWALK GREENWAY
Grants Mill Road Bridge near Overton Road
www.cahabariverwalkfriends.com
The community of Irondale has long appreciated the ecological importance of the Cahaba River, the state's longest free-flowing river. The city developed the first section of the trail and plans extensions as well as additional parking on Overton Road. Access to the greenway is from a parking lot on Grants Mill Road next to the bridge. Plans for the neighboring community of Trussville to preserve nearly 1,500 acres along the river for a park and greenway connecting to the Riverwalk are in preliminary stages. Not to confuse matters, but Trussville Springs Village, a new planned community along the Cahaba River has also taken advantage of its location by creating a Riverwalk Park and 1-mile gravel trail.

i The Cahaba River contains a greater number of fish species per mile than any other river in North America. In fact 8 of the 131 fish species found here occur nowhere else in the world. It is a biological treasure, as well as Birmingham's primary water source.

FIVE MILE CREEK GREENWAY
(205) 264-8464
www.fivemilecreekgreenwaydistrict.org
For those who know Birmingham, Five Mile Creek has long been emblematic of the dark legacy of coal mining and coke-processing industries during the previous century. The stream was one of the state's worst polluted waterways and acquired a less than favorable reputation. For younger generations though, that negative image is changing thanks to the Five Mile Creek Partnership. Through agreements between Birmingham, Center Point, Fultondale, Tarrant, Graysville, and Brookside, $4.2 million in resources have begun a true transformation. A mobile home park has been converted to a new municipal park in Brookside, a plan for a network of greenways and parks along 28 miles of the creek is being implemented, hundreds of acres of land have been protected by the Fresh Water Land Trust (see their website for greenway details: www.freshwaterlandtrust.org), and cleanup of the creek is well underway.

For its part, The Five Mile Creek Greenway District is acquiring right of way on an abandoned CSX Railroad running through Graysville and Fultondale that happens to include the largest wooden trestle in the Eastern United States. Connections from the greenway to Village Creek and Ruffner Mountain—approximately 16.5 miles of greenways—are close to becoming a reality. Most encouraging is the tremendous amount of grassroots work being done in these small communities on the north side of Birmingham. The towns are not wealthy. They may not have the resources that other communities possess, but what they do have is a great deal of pride. Credit for the progress of the Five Mile Creek Greenway belongs squarely with the citizens along Five Mile Creek.

Our One Mile

One of the biggest single indicators of positive change is the **Freshwater Land Trust's (FLT)** work to acquire, conserve, and connect open space along rivers and streams in the community. From Red Mountain Park and Five Mile Creek to Turkey Creek Nature Preserve and Shades Creek projects, the FLT is mapping and protecting the places that matter most. The FLT's Our One Mile master plan identifies a system of over 100 miles of greenways in the region. Backed by a $13.5-million grant from Centers for Disease Control and Prevention, the **Our One Mile** project published a plan in 2011 that identifies the best locations for enhanced sidewalks, bike paths, soft-surface walking trails, rails-to-trails, and other connections near schools, churches, and community areas. The goal is to create a better physical, environmental, and social well being for Birmingham.

HOMEWOOD SHADES CREEK GREENWAY

Runs parallel to Lakeshore Parkway between Columbiana Road and Brookwood Village Mall, Homewood
www.homewoodchamber.org

It's not easy being a pioneer, as the city of Homewood discovered when they started building the multi-use trail for pedestrians and cyclists back in 1999. But despite the difficulties, the results are overwhelmingly positive—just try to get a parking space in the main parking lot during peak times! Shaded and cool under a canopy of oaks and sycamores, the "Lakeshore Trail" is popular with runners, cyclists, families, and those who just want a moment of peace beside a bubbling creek during their lunch hour. Running from Jemison Park in the east to Columbiana Road in the west, Phase I connects a university, a high school, a major shopping area, several residential neighborhoods, apartment complexes, sport complexes, churches, and office buildings. Phase II and III aim to continue the trail westward under I-65 along Shades Creek with a flyover connecting John Carroll Catholic High School and West Homewood Park. Ideally, a better connection with Jemison Park to the east will be constructed as well, and there is some discussion that the greenway could eventually connect with Moss Rock Preserve in Hoover.

Recently goldline darters, coal shiners, and the endangered Cahaba shiners were discovered by biologists in Shades Creek for the first time, perhaps a sign that streamside improvements, recent land acquisitions for permanent conservation, and other efforts are having a positive effect on the quality of water—and native life—along the little suburban creek.

*JEMISON PARK NATURE TRAIL

Mountain Brook Parkway near Mountain Brook Village, Mountain Brook
www.mtnbrook.org

In true Birmingham fashion one of the most pleasant running or walking environments started off a bit isolated and cut off from the wider community. Named after Robert

Jemison Jr., an entrepreneur who famously developed the exclusive Mountain Brook neighborhood, the park was dedicated in 1952. Modern improvements to the trail itself have made it a top destination for those wanting a good workout in beautiful surroundings. A wending, winding paved and gravel trail running 3 miles along Shades Creek and adjacent Watkins Creek has a wild, natural feel to it that draws runners and neighborhood families out walking their dogs. In fact, head to the trail after a good downpour and there's a good chance floodwaters may have risen to the trail itself. Recent excellent connections to the larger trail system of Mountain Brook extend the Jemison Trail beyond this isolated short section, making it much more usable for the larger community. See Village Trails for more information.

i Signs along the trail identify native plants and wildlife commonly found in the area. A list of birds spotted in the area is sometimes available in wooden boxes at both ends of the trail courtesy the Friends of Jemison Park. See www.mtnbrook.org for a complete listing.

OAK MOUNTAIN TRAILS
200 Terrace Dr., Pelham
(205) 620-2520
www.alapark.com/oakmountain
With over 50 miles of trails, Oak Mountain State Park is the largest state park in Alabama. Consequently, the Park Road—which cuts from one end of the park to another—is a highly popular destination for road cyclists since auto traffic is minimal and the winding road offers great variation as it passes through the forest. Additionally, a series of excellent trails—named Red, White, Blue,

Yellow, Green, and Orange trails—offer year-round hiking. The Red Trail or "Double Oak Trail" is a 17-mile-long loop trail for mountain biking and is maintained by the Birmingham Urban Mountain Pedalers (www.bump.org). It features large climbs and fast, technical downhills and is the only trail in the park specified for biking. The Orange Trail or "Horse Trail" is 10.7 miles long and is for horses only. It begins on Findlay Dr. at the horse stables.

✳RAILROAD PARK
1601 1st Ave. South, Birmingham
(205) 223-4013
www.railroadpark.org
A 8-block city park with walking trail and elevated walkway in the heart of downtown, Railroad Park marks the first step towards a planned linear park stretching from I-65 to Sloss Furnaces National Historic Landmark. Open since late 2010 it is one of the most exciting downtown developments in recent memory. With its proximity to Birmingham Central Station, the park is an important link to a multi-modal transport hub while connecting the downtown business district with the Southside. Many community leaders and politicians see Railroad Park as a transformative new initiative that could change the urban core by connecting Birmingham's downtown area with the University of Alabama at Birmingham campus. See the Parks chapter for more details.

RED MOUNTAIN PARK TRAILS
Lakeshore Parkway, just past West
Oxmoor Road, Birmingham
(205) 202-6043
www.redmountainpark.org

Perhaps the single largest environmental or outdoors coup in recent years, Red Mountain Park, located in the southwest corner of Birmingham is a 1,200-acre, 4.5-mile-long urban park stretching east to west along Red Mountain. The Phase I development plan currently underway includes construction of the 'Round the Loop Trail, a welcome center, and new access routes to the emerging park from Lakeshore Parkway on the south and Ishkooda Wenonah on the north. The loop will be a 6.8-mile-long 12-foot-wide paved trail that links the park's major attractions and connector trails. It is due to open in 2012 and will make Birmingham the country's greenest city in terms of total amount of public park space available to its citizens.

RUFFNER MOUNTAIN TRAILS
1214 81st St. South, Birmingham
(205) 833-8264
www.ruffnermountain.org
While Ruffner Mountain Nature Center, a 1,011-acre natural escape just minutes from downtown Birmingham, does not have trails accessible for cyclists, more than 12 miles of hiking/walking through forested trails with spectacular views of Birmingham in the distance make it a top outdoor destination. Ruffner Mountain plays a crucial role in connections to come as the Highline Trail, CSX Trail to the Railroad Park in downtown Birmingham, and greenways connecting the park to neighboring schools are underway. Be sure to start at the new LEED-certified Tree Top Visitor Center and Mountainside Pavilion Complex. The park is open 6 days a week and closed Mon. While the park is open to the public, a donation of $2 is suggested.

TURKEY CREEK NATURE PRESERVE AND GREENWAY
3906 Turkey Creek Rd., Pinson
(205) 680-4116
www.thecityofpinson.com
A 466-acre preserve in Pinson just outside of Birmingham proper, Turkey Creek was funded by the Jefferson County Greenways Program and other sources to protect three endangered species of fish: the Vermillion Darter, Rush Darter, and Watercress Darter (the Rush and Vermillion Darters occur nowhere else in the world other than Turkey Creek). The side benefit is a closed road great for a hike, bike ride, or stroll and picnic along the picturesque little stream and surrounding pine-hardwood forest. Bring your swimming trunks as you'll want to get wet and play at the falls on a warm day. For more details see the Freshwater Land Trust (www.freshwaterlandtrust.org), which along with Forever Wild, a community group called START (Society to Advance the Resources at Turkey Creek), and Southern Environmental Center, have made Turkey Creek possible.

VESTAVIA HILLS WALKWAY SYSTEM
(205) 978-0100
www.vestaviahills.net
Much has changed, and continues to change, in Vestavia Hills for the better with regards to greenways, trails, and frankly, even sidewalks. A true post-war suburb with all the sprawl that entails, Vestavia Hills is a town that couldn't exist without a car and a full tank of gas. Recognizing the need to improve connections between schools, neighborhoods, homes, and commercial districts, the city developed a Walkways Master Plan with Nimrod Long and Associates to

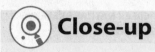

Close-up

City-wide EcoScapes

A novel approach to saving Birmingham, one **EcoScape** at a time, the Southern Environmental Center's program of reclaiming urban abandoned lots and turning them into community gardens has been spearheaded by the SEC's director, Roald Hazelhoff, a native of Holland and an energetic environmentalist-about-town. It started with the original EcoScape, a 4-acre outdoor environmental campus, at Birmingham Southern. In a nutshell, it's a tool to teach organic gardening practices and touch on water conservation issues like xeriscaping and non-point source pollution. The thing of it is, Hazelhoff did not stop there. Similar to the various greenway projects percolating at different points all over the city, the green oases of EcoScapes popping up throughout the city are reaching a critical mass.

By building—quite literally—on the success of the first EcoScape, Hazelhoff went to Woodlawn for the next garden, a first attempt to step beyond the college and into the greater Birmingham community. The gardens that followed targeted once-beautiful historic neighborhoods in a state of decline or fragile stasis. The basis of this model is that metro Birmingham has something on the order of 8,000 to 11,000 vacant lots. That's the setting. Migration to the suburbs in the 1960s and 1970s left communities like Norwood, Ensley, Woodlawn, West End, and North Birmingham with less and less of an economic base to maintain their neighborhoods. The sale of houses becomes difficult, and the residents who cannot afford to move out are often the elderly and the poor. The remaining homes that cannot be sold are rented, and the decline continues until public works has to take over the maintenance of the lots—an expensive prospect for the city of Birmingham.

Currently there are 11 EcoScapes scattered across the city. Some of the future EcoScapes will be botanical gardens, some playgrounds, some just for produce such as growing basil or cut flowers for profit. Others might just be for Frisbee enthusiasts or dog parks lined with native plantings. Hazelhoff is open to ideas on how Birmingham can turn unsightly abandoned urban lots into a benefit for all. Seed money comes from supportive groups like Community Foundation of Greater Birmingham, Little Garden Club, Red Mountain Garden Club, Legacy grants, and other organizations and individual donors. It is a step in the right direction.

increase pedestrian access in various areas of the city. Greenway projects in the Rocky Ridge–Little Shades Creek area as well as spots along the Cahaba River have been identified for future development. Most of the initial work focused on sidewalk projects along Highway 31, area shopping centers, and trails spoking out from neighborhood schools. A great example of this vision is the new Vestavia Hills Public Library, a wonderful LEED-certified building set in the woods near Central Elementary School that connects with the greater community through sidewalks and trails. Additional greenway efforts include the city partnering with the Freshwater Land Trust to secure lands for nature trails along Little Shades Creek as well as lands for a linear park in Cahaba Heights near the Cahaba Pumping Station east of I-459. The future looks brighter for Vestavia Hills. For more details see www.nimrodlong .com/urban_design.htm.

VILLAGE TRAILS, MOUNTAIN BROOK
www.mtnbrook.org

As far back as 1993, the city of Mountain Brook saw that creating corridors to connect their greatest assets—the three historic villages and Jemison Park—would improve the quality of life in the community. The wooded neighborhood linked by English Village, Mountain Brook Village, and Crestline Village is full of charm and with the implementation of a pedestrian walkway loop linking these villages, those assets are even more accessible for the city's active residents. With about 35 miles of the phased project completed, the Village Trail System still expects to add more than 20 miles of walkways and pedestrian connections. Routes for 5K and 10K races are also part of the master plan.

In many ways it's the continuation of developer Robert Jemison's original vision for the area back in 1929. The system connects several schools, as well as two golf courses, into what for pedestrians essentially becomes a beautiful park. The loops and interconnected nature of the system means that if you like, you can take a different route each time you put on your running shoes. Interestingly, some of the walkways were old horse trails—the one passing near the Civil War–era Irondale Furnace near Old Leeds Road is currently being renovated and improved. What was a forgotten, overgrown trail meandering several miles right above a pristine section of Shades Creek has been gloriously rediscovered. For more details see www.nimrodlong.com/urban_design.htm.

The Future

Currently, the list of funded greenway, bicycle, and pedestrian feasibility studies underway is encouraging, if a bit overwhelming. The list is impressive: Brookside's bike/hike trail corridor, Clay Community Greenway, Center Point Greenway, Dunnavant Valley Greenway, Fultondale Five Mile Creek Trail, Inverness Community Greenway, and the Oak Mountain Community Greenway to name a few. And there are more studies still in the works, from the Railroad Reservation Corridor, CSX Rails-to-Trails project, Cahaba River Greenway, Red Mountain Rail-to-Trail project and more. New bike lanes downtown are appearing, many of which provide connections to the new Railroad Park that opened in 2010. Existing bicycle lanes like Seventh Avenue South are being widened. And the Alabama Department of Transportation, perhaps not the most enthusiastic supporter of bicycling in the past, is getting on board, soliciting public comment on a draft of a statewide Bicycle and Pedestrian Plan they published in 2010.

VULCAN TRAIL
At the crest of Red Mountain on Richard Arrington Jr. Boulevard, Birmingham
(205) 933-1409
www.visitvulcan.com

Short and modest, yet with terrific historical and cultural significance, Vulcan Trail atop

GREENWAYS

Red Mountain is a popular route for joggers, cyclists, and families. Set on the site where iron ore was mined in the late 19th century, Red Mountain is very much a symbol of Birmingham's early days as a central location where the industrial "holy trinity" of coal, iron, and limestone were found—materials that allowed Birmingham to become the leading producer of steel and iron. Today's trail runs along the L&N railroad line built by the Birmingham Mineral Branch and was used to transport heavy materials for early furnaces below in the valley. The line ran along the side of the mountain from Bessemer to Trussville and beyond and was active until the 1930s. The trail is 2.8 miles in length, paved, and at an elevation of nearly 1,000 feet, offers spectacular views of downtown Birmingham looking north. Good shade from hardwoods keeps it cool in the summer; pesky kudzu on the hillside adds a bit of local panache. A parking lot exists at the crest of the mountain on Richard Arrington Jr. Boulevard/21st Street South.

CIVIL RIGHTS

That Birmingham was home to some of the most significant events in the Civil Rights Movement of the 1950s and 1960s comes as no surprise to most people. It has been a long time coming, but that black eye the city took—even though it was mostly self-inflicted—has gone through a long, slow, painful healing process.

"The past is never dead," novelist William Faulkner famously wrote. "It's not even past." This much-quoted and perhaps even more puzzled-over statement resonates in Birmingham as much today as it did nearly 60 years ago. Faulkner was writing in 1951, and while he was not addressing the long journey to equality that African Americans have taken in this country, he might as well have been.

In Birmingham the past has often not even been past. Still, Birmingham may have had its Eugene "Bull" Conner, but it also had its Fred Shuttlesworth and a host of others—many of whom were young children—who bravely took up the cause at the most local level. And at great risk to themselves. The struggles of the citizens of Birmingham, along with leaders like Martin Luther King Jr., began a modern human-rights movement that emerged to stake a claim on the nation's conscience. It transformed the city, the country, and arguably the world in its wake.

Consequently, visitors from all over the country and from around the globe come to the city—and often travel down the road to Selma and Montgomery—precisely to see where history happened in Alabama. The Birmingham Civil Rights District, the area downtown where most events took place, refers to a six-block area designated by the city in 1992 as a special area deserving preservation. Kelly Ingram Park, Carver Theatre, 16th Street Baptist Church, and the historic Black Business District itself all serve as reminders of the past—and starting in 1993 with the opening of the Birmingham Civil Rights Institute, the district now also serves as a guide for the future.

It's an irony that Birmingham, a city founded after the Civil War, would be a crucial battleground for the Civil Rights Movement. Looking at the journey from Civil War to civil rights, it's clear that neither of them were that civil, yet they are both part of the American portrait. Birmingham is slowly realizing that telling its own story is a vital step in coming to terms with the past—and moving forward to the future together.

*BIRMINGHAM CIVIL RIGHTS
INSTITUTE
520 16th St. North, Birmingham
(205) 328-9696, ext. 203
www.bcri.org

Few participants in Birmingham's civil-rights struggles of the 1950s and 1960s—on either side of the conflict—probably thought there would come a day when an interpretive museum and research center would be

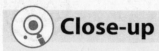

Close-up

Eugene "Bull" Conner: Right Man, Right Time

Obstinate, autocratic, and hot-tempered, Birmingham Public Safety Commissioner **Eugene "Bull" Conner** was the right man at the right time as far as the Southern Christian Leadership Conference (SCLC), Martin Luther King Jr., and Fred Shuttlesworth were concerned. In an attempt to highlight the bigotry and racism inherent in American life and Southern cities in particular, the SCLC deliberately chose to protest the racist Jim Crow laws via Birmingham in large part because of Conner's propensity to overreact. To illustrate the harsh police tactics often used against African Americans, civil-rights organizers needed a willing participant. When planning their 1963 Project "C" (confrontation) campaign in the city, Conner's spectacular miscalculation was part of the plan.

Ironically, his brutal response to what was a relatively mild protest was the key to gaining national and international media attention. Connor's decision to use fire hoses and police attack dogs against protesters elevated the campaign to a symbolic level that led to major social change in the coming months and years. President Kennedy intervened, and eventually, facilities were desegregated in Birmingham following the protests. The passage of the Civil Rights Act of 1964 by Congress was perhaps the crowning achievement of the civil-rights struggle.

built on that bloody battlefield. The difficulty of exhibiting the city's past in a non-divisive environment was a challenge the city decided to embrace. Opening its doors in 1992, the Birmingham Civil Right Institute saw more than 25,000 visitors during its first week, a sure sign of immediate success. Permanent exhibits highlight the city's contribution to the movement while multimedia installations present the larger history of African-American life in the past. Special exhibits and traveling exhibitions frequently change. Educational programs available at the institute also offer resources for individuals, schools, groups, and researchers.

One of the museum's biggest success stories is the way it manages to illustrate and explain that it was not just Martin Luther King Jr. and other prominent leaders who overthrew segregation in Birmingham, it was also the ordinary citizens of the city

who put their beliefs into action. There is admission for adults and minimal admission for children. Be sure to also visit two other important civil rights sites adjacent to the institute, Kelly Ingram Park and 16th Street Baptist Church.

BOUTWELL AUDITORIUM
1930 8th Ave. North, Birmingham
(205) 254-7797

Not too many visitors (or probably residents, for that matter) in Birmingham think of Boutwell Memorial Auditorium in connection with the civil-rights struggle, but that is a mistake. The historic structure, the first city structure built on the government campus surrounding what was then called Woodrow Wilson Park (now Linn Park) is rife with social significance. Ku Klux Klan rallies and car shows, wrestling matches, and the Southern Conference for Human Welfare in 1938 all have been held in the auditorium. This conference is significant because it brought together white and black progressives working for a more equitable society. The integrated affair is still remembered for the confrontation between First Lady Eleanor Roosevelt and other progressives in attendance and Birmingham City Commissioner T. Eugene "Bull" Connor over audience segregation.

In 1956 Alabama native Nat King Cole sang for an all-white audience at Boutwell and was attacked in an apparent kidnapping attempt by a newly formed white supremacists group. Calling themselves the White Citizens Councils in Alabama, the group was campaigning against "black music" like rock-n-roll. Never mind that Cole was a jazz pianist and singer—racists are hardly known for recognizing subtlety. In a bizarre side note: Though he was not actually present the night of the concert, one of the council's more active leaders was Alabama native Asa

Earl Carter, the author of *The Education of Little Tree* and *The Rebel Outlaw: Josey Wales*.

The touches of Lombard architectural influences seen in the exterior of the building are largely obscured by the marble, glass, and aluminum from the major modernist facelift the building received in 1957. In 2007 the mayor put forth proposals to demolish the building, but for now, the historic building remains in use for performing arts and sporting events, concerts, galas, and parties. It is not officially open for tours, but inquisitive visitors can often peek inside.

FREEDOM RIDES
1900 block, corner of 4th Avenue North and 19th Street North, Birmingham
Historical marker
The 1961 Freedom Ride that left Washington, DC, on May 4th arrived in Birmingham on May 14th en route to its final destination of New Orleans. The ride's goal was to end discrimination and segregation on buses.

Fred Shuttlesworth

Everyone knows Martin Luther King Jr. as the hero of the movement, but what many visitors to this city learn is that **Reverend Shuttlesworth** led the civil-rights campaign in Birmingham. And he led it bravely as perhaps the most militant non-violent agitator in the movement. His home was bombed in 1956. His church was bombed on three occasions. He was beaten and his wife stabbed during the attempt to integrate the all-white Phillips High School in 1957. Water from a high-pressure fire hose broke his ribs as he led the attempt to end segregation in Birmingham in 1963. Founder of the Alabama Christian Movement for Human Rights and pastor of Bethel Baptist Church in north Birmingham, Shuttlesworth's statue stands in front of the Birmingham Civil Rights Institute, giving one of the great civil-rights figures his full due—visit the Institute to learn more about his life. President Bill Clinton presented him with the Presidential Citizens Medal. Bethel Baptist Church is at 3233 29th Avenue North. Phillips High School, the city's first high school, is at 2316 7th Avenue North. The Birmingham-Shuttlesworth International Airport is named after him.

In 1956 the Supreme Court ruled that segregated seating on interstate buses was unconstitutional, and after a 1961 Supreme Court decision desegregating bus terminal facilities, this new set of Freedom Rides began.

Alabama native John Lewis, a future US congressman from Georgia, embarked on the ride organized by the Congress of Racial Equality. There were attacks on the Freedom Riders in South Carolina and a bus was set on fire in Atlanta. Similar violence occurred in Anniston, Alabama. When a new group of riders from the Student Nonviolent Coordinating Committee reached the Birmingham bus terminal, a mob armed with blackjacks and bicycle chains attacked, beating several protesters until they were unconscious—the Birmingham Police Department had apparently made a deal allowing the white supremacists 15 minutes to attack before they would arrive. The group returned the next day attempting to board a bus to Montgomery but none would take them. The ride was briefly abandoned, but a few days later, the protesters started again in Birmingham. Several were arrested and spent the night in jail before the Freedom Ride continued on to Montgomery, Alabama, and beyond. It took intervention from President John F. Kennedy and his brother, Attorney General Robert F. Kennedy, to order federal marshals to protect the riders.

A historical marker for the Freedom Riders is located at the site of the former Trailways bus station (now a Wachovia branch bank) where the riders were attacked on 4th Avenue North between 19th and 20th Streets North. The current Greyhound station at 618 North 19th is in the same location where the Freedom Riders departed from in 1961.

i Bars from the jail cell where Martin Luther King Jr. wrote "Letter from a Birmingham Jail" are on display at the Birmingham Civil Rights Institute across the street from Kelly Ingram Park. "Injustice anywhere is a threat to justice everywhere," is one of the most often quoted lines from the famous epistle.

KELLY INGRAM PARK
16th Street North and 6th Avenue North, Birmingham

Looking at Kelly Ingram Park today, the lack of drama seems almost anticlimactic. The quiet 4-acre park at the heart of the Birmingham Civil Rights District lies just across the street from the Birmingham Civil Rights Institute. During the 1960s it served as a crucial staging ground for demonstrations, boycotts, and protests organized by local and national civil-rights leaders. But what seared itself into the American consciousness were the events that took place here in the spring of 1963 when Birmingham firemen turned their hoses on young marchers. This was just after Martin Luther King Jr. penned his "Letter from a Birmingham Jail." Tensions were high and Public Safety Commissioner Eugene "Bull" Conner dealt with protesters with mass arrests, but the young men and women, many of them children, kept coming. Conner ordered firemen use their hoses on the protesters. Eventually city officials gave ground, negotiating with King and others so that the last of the "whites only" signs, colored water fountains, and other vestiges of racist Jim Crow laws were removed. It wasn't over, but it was a slow, painful start. Renovated in 1992 the park has several sculptural pieces related to the civil-rights struggle, as well as statues of King,

Fred Shuttlesworth, and other luminaries of the movement. Audio tours of the park are available at the Institute.

i For those interested in knowing more about the 16th Street Baptist Church bombing, Spike Lee's 1997 historical documentary film *4 Little Girls* is a poignant study of the tragic event. Through rare family photos, historical footage, and access to Christopher McNair, whose young daughter, Denise, died that morning, Lee presents a searing look at domestic terrorism and race.

16TH STREET BAPTIST CHURCH
1530 6th Ave. North, Birmingham
(205) 251-9402
www.16thstreetbaptist.org
As far as a powerful symbol of Birmingham goes, 16th Street Baptist Church is almost without parallel for the scope of its tragic role. The Ku Klux Klan bombed the church September 15, 1963, killing four young girls that Sunday morning: Addie Mae Collins, Cynthia Wesley, Denise McNair, and Carole Robertson. It wasn't the first stick of dynamite throw by Klansmen and white

supremacists in the city, but it crossed a line that put the city at risk of outright racial contagion. It also was a shocking act of depravity that could not be ignored by the rest of the country and provided major media exposure for the cause of civil rights. Martin Luther King Jr. returned to Birmingham from Atlanta to offer the eulogy. Before the bombing the church was a headquarters for rallies and meetings during the civil-rights movement. Speaking of the past not even being past, it wasn't until 2002 that the last living man thought to be responsible for the bombing, Bobby Frank Cherry, was finally convicted of the crime.

Founded in 1873 as the First Colored Baptist Church of Birmingham, this was the first black congregation in the young city. The church's present structure, the 16th Street Baptist Church, was built in 1911, designed in the Romanesque and Byzantine style by African-American architect Wallace Rayfield. The site became a National Historic Landmark in 2006. A display in the basement explains the church's role in the civil-rights movement. Tours may be scheduled in advance, but with a few polite words and permission, some visitors find a quick peek inside is not out of the question.

SPECTATOR SPORTS

Birmingham is a sports town. That may seem an exaggeration coming from a place with no professional football, baseball (only minor league), or basketball team, but take a quick sampling of local talk-radio chatter or office water cooler topics and chances are, it's sports that are on the agenda. From the college ranks to the high school level, area residents love to take in a good game. And as any Alabamian can tell you, no game compares to the storied football rivalry between the state's two largest universities, Auburn University and the University of Alabama, otherwise known as the Iron Bowl (see Close-Up). Don't be surprised if, upon your arrival in Birmingham, you are confronted with three very important words, "Auburn or Alabama?" Neither school is in Birmingham but that doesn't make a lick of difference: From September to January (and again during spring training), Alabama and Auburn football dominates sports in town.

In fact many sports fans in the city blame the undying loyalty of Auburn and Alabama's respective supporters for the failure of the various professional football teams that the city has hosted over the years. Yet at the same time, there also exists in Birmingham a respect and admiration for the amateur athlete that is rare in the era of free agency and multi-million-dollar contracts. High school sports are followed with an intensity and enthusiasm that many colleges would envy while college football is elevated to near religious status.

Although Auburn and Alabama football dominate the headlines of the sports pages of the *Birmingham News*, sports coverage on local television, and call-in sports radio, Birmingham actually has college teams of its own. The University of Alabama at Birmingham, located on Birmingham's Southside (better known as UAB), plays an exciting brand of basketball and has made a number of memorable runs in the NCAA tournament. UAB also has an up-and-coming football team, and a nationally ranked men's soccer team. Even Birmingham-Southern College, a small but excellent liberal arts school, now has a football team as well. Just south of downtown is Samford University where the Bulldogs football team, competing at the Football Championship Sub-division of the NCAA's Division I, are coached by former Heisman Trophy winner and star Auburn quarterback, Pat Sullivan. And of course, the Birmingham Barons minor league baseball organization maintains a rich tradition that can be traced all the way back to the 1880s. Many of the game's greatest players, most notably Birmingham native Willie Mays and even basketball legend Michael Jordan, have worn the Barons' uniform.

OVERVIEW

Birmingham has had difficulty maintaining a professional sports franchise, however, the city has been remarkably successful at hosting a number of yearly professional sporting events such as the Champions Tour's Regions Charity Classic and NASCAR's Amp Energy 500 at the Talladega Superspeedway. In addition to these annual events, Birmingham has also hosted top draws like the PGA and Champions Tour, FIFA men's and women's World Cup qualifiers, Davis Cup tennis, IndyCar Series races at the Barber Motorsports, US Men's Olympic Marathon Championship, Olympic soccer, and other events that reflect the varied tastes of Birmingham's sports palette and enthusiasm towards sports of all kinds.

Price Code

The price code includes the cost of one, regularly priced adult ticket. Most venues offer discounts for groups or for children ages 12 and under, as well as special offers.

$	Less than $5
$$	$5 to $10
$$$	$10 to $20
$$$$	More than $20

COLLEGE

Football

SAMFORD UNIVERSITY BULLDOGS $$
Seibert Stadium
800 Lakeshore Dr., Homewood
(205) 726-2050
www.samfordsports.cstv.com
Samford football offers a smaller and more family-friendly atmosphere for the Birmingham sports fan who wishes to see quality competition in a more intimate setting. Located in suburban Homewood on Lakeshore Drive, Samford is a picturesque university campus, but don't let the quaintness of the grounds fool you; there is quality football to be seen at Samford.

Samford boasts a rich if understated football history. Coaching legend and Birmingham native Bobby Bowden played for Samford, then known as Howard College, and later coached the Bulldogs as well. His son, and former Auburn head coach, Terry Bowden coached the Bulldogs in the late 1980s and early 1990s when Jimbo Fisher, current Florida State head coach, played quarterback for the Bulldogs. In 1971 Samford claimed an NCAA Division II, then known as the "College Division" of the NCAA, regional title. In 2007 Samford hired former Heisman Trophy winner and Birmingham native Pat Sullivan as head coach, raising interest from sports fans across the state. Following Sullivan's first season, Samford joined the Southern Conference in 2008 with such FCS powerhouses as Appalachian State, Wofford, and Furman. With the arrival of Pat Sullivan, a new era began at Samford, and plans were made to upgrade the athletic facilities. In 2009 construction was completed on the Bulldogs' all-new Cooney Family Fieldhouse.

i Samford head coach and Heisman-winning former Auburn quarterback Pat Sullivan graduated high school from Birmingham's John Carroll Catholic, which, after moving from the Highlands area downtown in 1992, is now located just 4 miles down Lakeshore Drive from the campus of Samford University.

There is no doubt that big things are happening on Lakeshore Drive. Individual tickets range from $5 to $20 with season ticket packages ranging from $60 to $80. Discount packages are also available.

High School Football

One of the hottest tickets on a Birmingham Friday night is to a local high school football match-up. Birmingham and its surroundings areas have become a hot-bed of college football talent, and fans relish the opportunity to see tomorrow's stars today, if only to say, "I saw him when . . ." It was only a few years ago that the country was enamored with the testosterone drama of Hoover High School's football stars on the MTV series "Two-a-Days." Now, to accommodate its enormous following, **Hoover High** plays its home football games at Regions Park, home to the Birmingham Barons. The best way to find Friday night's hottest match-up is to simply pick up a Friday edition of *The Birmingham News*. Each Friday, the paper devotes an entire portion of the sports section to that evening's best games and players. Find the one nearest you or drive a ways to see the next all-American for your favorite college football team.

UNIVERSITY OF ALABAMA AT BIRMINGHAM BLAZERS $$$
Legion Field
400 Graymont Ave. West, Birmingham
(205) 975-UAB1
http://uabsports.cstv.com

It is hard to imagine that the UAB football program has only competed at the Football Bowl Sub-Division (FBS) level of the NCAA's Division I since the mid-1990s, but it has grown from its humble beginnings as a club sport on Birmingham's Southside to become the occupant of the famed Legion Field on Saturdays in the fall. While many critics long ago said that UAB would only be a third wheel to Alabama and Auburn, the university has gained a substantial following in its own right.

Following the success of the UAB men's basketball program, which shot to stardom as an NCAA tournament darling in the early 1980s and quickly became the talk of Birmingham's basketball community, the Blazers' athletic department, at the time directed by head basketball coach Gene Bartow, hoped to follow suit with a venture into the world of major college football. Prior to their first season as a full-time FBS member, UAB hired former Vanderbilt head coach Watson Brown to lead them into big-time college football. Success in football, however, would not come as quickly for the Blazers as it did in basketball.

UAB's first years as an FBS member saw them accumulate more losses than wins and were marked by a constant struggle for their own identity in the shadow of Alabama and Auburn. In 2000, though, things would finally begin to look up for the young Blazers program. That was the year that UAB upset Nick Saban's (current Alabama head coach) LSU Tigers in Baton Rouge in dramatic

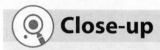 **Close-up**

Iron Bowl

From the final whistle of this year's game until next year's kickoff, nothing dominates conversations in Birmingham quite like the **Iron Bowl,** the annual football rivalry between the **Tigers of Auburn University** and the **University of Alabama Crimson Tide.** Although the game is no longer played in Birmingham where it earned the name the "Iron Bowl" due to the city's industrial past, much of its rich history still resides in the Magic City.

The very first match-up between the Tide and Tigers took place at Birmingham's Lakeview Park in 1893. For the next five match-ups, the game would alternate between Montgomery, near Auburn, and Tuscaloosa, home to the University of Alabama. The schools finally settled on Birmingham as a permanent site in 1904 (there was no game from 1895 to 1900). Due to disagreements between the two universities, however, there would be no game played for 41 years after 1907, leaving neither Tigers nor Tide supporters with bragging rights for four decades.

Finally, after a resolution by the Alabama State House of Representatives (yes, politicians became involved), the two schools set aside their differences and agreed to renew the rivalry. Birmingham's Legion Field, with seating capacity of 44,000 at the time, was chosen as the site of what would soon be called the Iron Bowl. Legion Field would remain the host for the annual Iron Bowl for the next 40 years, expanding its seating capacity to 83,000 to accommodate the game's intense popularity. Many of the rivalry's most memorable moments took place in Birmingham, such as "Punt Bama Punt," Bear Bryant's record-setting 315th victory, "Bo over the top," and "The Kick" among many others.

In 1989, after Auburn expanded seating capacity in Jordan-Hare Stadium, the Iron Bowl was played outside of Birmingham for the first time in four decades. For the next 10 years, the Iron Bowl would alternate between Auburn and Birmingham. In 1998 Legion Field hosted its final Iron Bowl, and in 2000 the rivalry was played in Tuscaloosa for the first time since 1902. In 2008 Alabama stopped a six-game winning streak for Auburn, and their victory in 2009 eventually led to Alabama winning the national championship that year. The game may no longer be played at Legion Field, but the heart of this famous rivalry still resides in Birmingham.

fashion. Suddenly football fans, not only in Birmingham, but also across the south, began to take notice of this rising program. The Blazers reached another milestone in 2004 by winning a bid to play in the Hawai'i Bowl on Christmas Eve, their first bowl game.

The current UAB Blazers have been led by head coach Neil Callaway since 2006 and although they still struggle for headlines in

the sports pages with Auburn and Alabama, they represent another option—and one much closer to home—for sports fans in Birmingham. Individual tickets range from $12 to $30 and season tickets go for $150. Various discount and family packages are also available.

i Though the museum dedicated to University of Alabama coach Paul "Bear" Bryant is in Tuscaloosa, if you're on pilgrimage to his grave in Birmingham's Elmwood Cemetery, you're in luck. Attendants at the cemetery gave up and painted a crimson red line from the entrance to his grave in Block 30. Auburn fans like to joke this is because Alabama fans can't follow directions.

Basketball

UNIVERSITY OF ALABAMA AT BIRMINGHAM BLAZERS $$$

Bartow Arena
617 13th St. South, Birmingham
(205) 975-UAB1
www.uabsports.cstv.com

Right from the start in 1978, UAB basketball set a course for excellence that it has yet to depart. UAB first made waves in the late 1970s by luring John Wooden successor and two-time NCAA Final Four head coach Gene Bartow away from UCLA to build the infant UAB basketball program. Within three years the Blazers were the darlings of the 1981 NCAA tournament where they defeated powerhouse Kentucky before bowing out to eventual National Champion Indiana in the Sweet Sixteen. The following season, much to the dismay of critics who denounced UAB's previous post-season run as a fluke, the Blazers advanced even further in the NCAA tournament. The fourth-seeded UAB Blazers avenged their loss to Indiana by defeating the defending National Champions in the second round and followed that victory by upsetting the top-seeded Virginia Cavaliers before eventually being eliminated by Louisville in the Elite Eight.

Bartow would lead the Blazers to another seven NCAA tournament appearances before retiring in 1996. His son, Murry Bartow, was tapped as his successor but would prove unable to match the level of accomplishment achieved by his father. In 2002 UAB hired Arkansas assistant and Birmingham native Mike Anderson to lead the program. By Anderson's second season, the Blazers were back in the NCAA tournament where they would once again surprise the college basketball world by upsetting top-seeded Kentucky. Following two more successful seasons, marked by appearances in the NCAA tournament, at the helm of UAB, Anderson would leave for the University of Missouri.

In 2006 the Blazers hired Fayette, Alabama, native and former University of Alabama star Mike Davis as the basketball program's fourth head coach. The Davis era at UAB began with optimism, but despite winning over 20 games in each of the last three seasons, the Blazers have been unable to return to the NCAA tournament. Fans, however, remain hopeful that UAB will regain the status that the program held under Bartow and Anderson. Individual tickets range from $12 to $20 and season tickets start at $215. Discount packages are also available.

i The football rivalry between UAB and the University of Memphis is known as the "Battle of the Bones" for the two cities' affinity for good barbecue. The winner takes home a 100-pound Bronze rack of ribs that is presented at halftime of the equally fierce basketball rivalry between the two schools. Get your tickets early for this one, as it usually sells out.

PROFESSIONAL

Auto Racing

*BARBER MOTORSPORTS
  PARK $$$–$$$$
6040 Barber Motorsports Pkwy., Leeds
(205) 699-7275
www.barbermotorsports.com

Designed by internationally renowned racetrack architect Alan Wilson, the Barber Motorsports Park opened in 2003 to rave reviews from journalists and race fans alike. The course's brilliant design, combining form with function while maintaining an aesthetic grandeur, has earned it the nickname "the Augusta of race tracks" in reference to the famous Augusta National Golf Club, host of The Masters. And people have begun to take notice.

With the intention of expanding into the southern market, the IRL IndyCar Series decided to hold an official IRL race at the Barber Motorsports Park, and in April 2010 the Barber Motorsports Park hosted the inaugural Porsche 250 Indy Grand Prix of Alabama. The race was met with great excitement and did not disappoint as thousands of interested spectators saw Indy Racing great Helio Castroneves win his record-setting 23rd IndyCar event, putting him in first place all-time among Brazilian IndyCar drivers. Such an event quickly brought notoriety to the Barber Motorsports Park from the international racing community. Alabama has long been known as NASCAR country, but with the addition of the Barber Motorsports Park, perhaps it is also F-1 country, too. As if driving at crazy speeds on four wheels weren't enough, in 2010 the Barber Motorsports Park also played host to the AMA Superbike Championship.

Not content to merely watch while other drivers take to the course at break-neck speeds? Grab the wheel at the Porsche Sport Driving School. At the only official Porsche Sport Driving School in North America, you can choose from a fleet of over 40 Porsches designed by Germany's top auto engineers. Also, don't forget to check out the world's largest collection of motorcycles at the Barber Vintage Motorsports Museum located on the grounds of the Barber Motorsports Park. Prices vary according to event. Museum admission ranges from $10 to $15 with discounts available with proof of AAA membership.

TALLADEGA SUPERSPEEDWAY
3366 Speedway Blvd., Talladega
(877) 462-3342
www.talladegasuperspeedway.com

Every year hundreds of thousands of race fans flock to the "Big One," the Talladega Superspeedway. And although the track earned its nickname because of its tight turns, with a seating capacity of 175,000, it is indeed the "Big One." Located approximately 30 miles east of Birmingham, the Talladega Superspeedway hosts a number of NASCAR and other auto-racing events each year. In addition to the Amp Energy 500, known to many as the Talladega 500, and the Aaron's 499, both on the NASCAR Sprint Cup Series, the superspeedway also hosts the Aaron's 312 on the NASCAR Nationwide Series, the Mountain Dew 250 of the NASCAR Camping World Truck Series, and the Food World 250 on the ARCA RE/MAX Series.

Designed by NASCAR pioneer Bill France Jr. in 1969, the Talladega Superspeedway quickly became one of the most popular tracks among race fans. Due to its tight, high-banked turns, races at the Superspeedway were often very competitive and featured a number of crashes. While this made the track popular among fans thinking in gladiatorial terms, many drivers came to fear Talladega. In fact, due to the unfortunate deaths of a number of drivers at Talladega, fans and drivers alike have begun to refer to the "Talladega Curse" as the reason for these unfortunate events. Explanations for the cause behind the curse vary and because the area was largely inhabited by Native Americans centuries ago, some have come to the conclusion that the track must have been built upon a Native America burial ground. Of course, this and other theories have never been substantiated, but it does make for amusing conversation and adds to the legend behind the track. While in Talladega be sure to stop by the International Motorsports Hall of Fame and Museum located right beside the Talladega Superspeedway. This fascinating facility not only covers NASCAR, but Formula One Racing, Sport Boat Racing, and other motorsports as well. Ticket prices vary according to the event.

Baseball

BIRMINGHAM BARONS $$
Regions Park
100 Ben Chapman Dr., Hoover
(205) 988-3200
www.barons.com

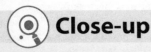 **Close-up**

Birmingham Black Barons

Among the most storied of the old Negro Leagues is the **Birmingham's Black Barons.** Led by baseball legends like Satchel Paige and Willie Mays, the Black Barons became a force in the Negro Leagues they participated in such as the Southern Negro League, Negro National League, Negro Southern League, and the Negro American League.

Locked out of Major League Baseball, many of the game's greatest players found their competitive outlet in the Negro Leagues. And the Black Barons soon became a favorite among Negro League supporters. The golden era of the Black Barons was the 1940s. As members of the Negro American League, the Black Barons participated in the largest and most competitive of the various Negro Leagues. Owned by T.H. "Tom" Hayes from 1940 to 1950, the Barons roster was stacked with great ball players like Mays, Sam Hairston, and Lyman Bostock, who would lead the club to three pennants in the decade, each followed by a World Series clash with Josh Gibson's Homestead Grays.

Following Jackie Robinson's debut for the Brooklyn Dodgers and Major League Baseball's gradual acceptance of African Americans, Negro League baseball became less and less necessary. The Black Barons remained until 1960, when the Negro National League, with only five clubs left, officially disbanded. Its service to Birmingham and the rest of the sports world would not go unnoticed. Thanks to clubs like the Black Barons and other Negro League teams, generations of African Americans, who were otherwise banned from Major League Baseball, were allowed to participate in the great American pastime.

Professional Football in Birmingham: A Look Back

One might think that with a city as football-mad as Birmingham, surely a professional football franchise would have no trouble settling in. Birmingham has had a number of memorable forays into the world of professional football, yet like many of the start-up leagues themselves, those adventures have flamed up brightly . . . then faded away into sporting oblivion. A brief primer:

Birmingham Vulcans, Dixie Professional Football League, 1961–62. After going 1-6-1 in its first season, the Vulcans fold after the first two games of the '62 season, both losses.

Birmingham Americans, World Football League, 1974. The most successful of Birmingham's pro football franchises, the Americans went 17-5 and won the WFL title in their only season.

Birmingham Vulcans, World Football League, 1975. Birmingham reemerged as the Vulcans for the 1975 WFL season, but as fate would have it, the entire league would fold before the end of the season.

Alabama Vulcans, American Football Association, 1979. The Vulcans went 13-6 before being eliminated in the first round of the playoffs in their only season in the short-lived AFA.

Alabama Magic, American Football Association, 1982. The Magic went 6-4 in the final season of the AFA.

Birmingham Stallions, United States Football League, 1983–1985. In three seasons in the USFL, the Stallions compiled a 36-18 record with two playoff appearances. What could've been?

Birmingham Fire, World League of American Football, 1991–92. Led by current Buffalo Bills head coach Chan Gailey, the Fire went 12-9-1 and made the playoffs in both of the World League's seasons.

Birmingham Barracudas, Canadian Football League, 1995. The Barracudas went 10-9 in the CFL's American expansion season before the league retracted.

Birmingham Thunderbolts, Xtreme Football League, 2001. Led by former LSU head coach Gerry DiNardo, the Bolts went 2-8 in the infamous XFL's only season.

Alabama Steeldogs, Arena Football League 2, 2000–07. The Steeldogs maintained a decent fan following before the AFL2 fell apart in 2008.

With the Barons, sports fans in Birmingham have no trouble filling the void between the end of basketball season in the spring and the beginning of football season in fall. And with promotions like "Belly Buster Monday" and "Thirsty Thursday," Barons games are both a fun and inexpensive way for the whole family to spend an evening in Birmingham while taking in some serious baseball action.

The Barons have called Hoover's Regions Park (formerly the Hoover Met) home since 1988 when they moved away from historic Rickwood Field. Dating back to the 1880s, the Barons are one of the most storied franchises in all of minor league baseball and have been a launching pad for some of the game's greatest players including Reggie Jackson, Frank Thomas, and Willie Mays, who played for the Birmingham Black Barons during segregation. And in 1994 packed stadiums saw basketball legend Michael Jordan don the Barons' black-and-white uniforms during his sabbatical from the NBA and his short foray into professional baseball.

The team is an affiliate of the Chicago White Sox since 1986 and Barons fans have seen a number of their former players go on to star for the parent club on Chicago's South Side. Prior to its affiliation with the White Sox, the Barons were affiliated with the Oakland As, at the time owned by Birmingham native Charles O. Finley. Birmingham had been without a professional baseball club for one season before Finley, who grew up a short distance from Rickwood Field as a boy, brought it back in 1967, winning the Southern League title with many of the same stars that would go on to win multiple World Series in Oakland. In addition to the White Sox, the Barons have been affiliated with a number of big-league teams such as the Boston Red Sox, New York Yankees, and Detroit Tigers.

The current Barons still play in the Southern League of double-A minor league baseball where they consistently finish at or near the top. The Barons made the playoffs a record six consecutive seasons from 2000 to 2005, winning the Southern League title in 2002 with a lineup that featured many of the players that would lead the White Sox to the World Series title three seasons later in 2005, and in 2009 the Barons set a club record for regular season winning percentage, winning 66.2 percent of its games. Individual ticket prices range from $7 to $12 while season tickets range from $90 to $420. Various discount packages are also available.

ℹ️ The Birmingham Barons are known for their promotions, the most popular of which include "Belly Buster Mondays" (all you can eat) and "Thirsty Thursdays" (all beverages only $1). Be sure to arrive early to avoid long lines at the concession stands.

Roller Derby

TRAGIC CITY ROLLERS $$$
Zamora Shrine Temple
3521 Ratliff Rd., Birmingham
www.tragiccityrollers.com
Like your sporting entertainment pierced, tattooed, bruised, and ready to kick you in the you-know-what? Well, then roller derby just might be for you. Straight out of a bad 1970s movie, roller derby is back with an underground vengeance in Birmingham and other cities across the country. But don't underestimate these ladies: They take

the sport seriously, often training three to four times a week preparing for competition. There are rule tests and skating assessments that the women must pass before anyone can play—and there is nothing staged about what they do. It's an energetic sport where the fans feel like an active participant as they scream their support for the home team or vociferously boo the out-of-town team. Attending it is an event in itself. With names like Black Eyed Tease, Motley Kruel, and Sookie Smackhouse, the women skating in circles while elbowing and jockeying for position have the temperament to live up to their inventive names. It's a combination of fun play and fairly serious intent. Don't be surprised if the emergency medical personnel attending each game are utilized at some point. It's serious fun for all.

ATTRACTIONS

I t is always mildly surprising to hear visitors talk in astonished tones about the Magic City after an initial visit: "It's so green!" "It's so hilly!" "There are so many things to do!" Happily, it is all true.

Set in the Appalachian foothills, Birmingham roughly lies between the Cumberland Plateau to the northwest and the Piedmont to the southeast in a geological region called the Valley and Ridge. Called "America's monster of biological diversity" by the *Nature Conservancy,* Alabama's choice location means we enjoy one of the most diverse ecological systems in the country. In fact, not too long ago, biologists discovered seven plant species previously unknown to science—a similar find might be significant though not totally unexpected in the Brazilian rainforest, but such a discovery in North America today is remarkable. It also means Birmingham is a city of views, of winding roads, of hills, creeks, rivers, and lots of greenery. It is pretty here, there's no denying that.

In that lovely setting, there are a host of activities for passing the time. This chapter focuses on some of the more established attractions—some of them outdoors, some of them indoors. The list below is certainly no comprehensive accounting of all there is to do in town. Bike rides and outdoor adventure options are covered in the Parks & Greenways chapters. You'll find even more in the Day Trips & Weekend Getaways chapter, as well as a few extra fun items listed under Festivals & Annual Events. And of course, a lot of fun for the young ones in the Kidstuff chapter.

Price Code

The price code includes one regularly priced ticket for admission for one adult. Many sites offer discounts for children and seniors. Call ahead to see if discounts apply to members of your party.

$....................Less than $5
$$ ....$5 to $10
$$$ .... $10 to $20
$$$$ .... More than $20

ALABAMA ADVENTURE WATER AND THEME PARK $$$$
4599 Alabama Adventure Pkwy., Bessemer
(205) 481-4750
www.visionland.com
Combining the best of both worlds, Alabama Adventure is an amusement park (Magic City USA) with rides plus all the fun activities one would expect from with a water park (Splash Beach) replete with slides, wave pool, and activities. It is the

largest such park in the state. The water park is open May to Sept and the theme park is open Apr to Sept. Check for concerts and special events held in a cooled indoor space, a concession to the region's warm summers. Street vendors selling food congregate on Celebration Street, a shopping and dining area where families tend to hang out in between activities, catching their breath before more fun ensues. A children's area called Marvel City caters to kids with more age-appropriate attractions. Season passes are available. It is one of the state's most popular tourist destinations.

ALABAMA JAZZ HALL OF FAME $
1631 4th Ave. North, Birmingham
(205) 254-2731
www.jazzhall.com
Hosted in the historic Carver Theatre in the Fourth Avenue Black Business District, the Alabama Jazz Hall of Fame preserves and promotes the heritage of jazz music in the city and state beyond. The museum itself contains more than 2,200 square feet of exhibits while also offering educational program to help cultivate the next generation of jazz musicians. The location in the Carver Theatre is more than appropriate: Legends like Duke Ellington, Lionel Hampton, and other luminaries have graced the stage while today the restored art deco theater hosts numerous concerts, entertainment, and special events.

Exhibits focus on local jazz greats such as Erskine Hawkins, composer of "Tuxedo Junction," Alabama native Nat King Cole, as well as Sun Ra, another well-known local musician and eccentric character with a strong cult following. Guided tours are available with Dr. Frank Adams, Director of Education Professor at the museum. An inductee and renowned

musician in his own right, Adams has been at the museum since its founding in 1993 and shares many first-hand anecdotes of the heady days of jazz. "Jazz is like a gumbo, a varied group of ingredients all mixed up together," explains Adams. "It's a language of improvisation spoken among a diverse assortment of people, not just one group."

ALABAMA SPORTS HALL OF FAME $
2150 Richard Arrington Jr. Blvd. North, Birmingham
(205) 323-6665
www.ashof.org
Sports in Alabama, especially on the collegiate level, have often been compared to religion for the heartfelt emotion and passion they elicit. For many fans, that's probably selling their devotion to sports a bit short. Without professional franchises in the state (except for temporary forays into non-NFL league football teams mainly in the 1970s and 1980s), college sports are the end-all-be-all for devotees. Perhaps that's why the Alabama Sports Hall of Fame (ASHF) has been such a success since its founding in 1967. The 33,000-square-foot building houses over 5,000 sporting artifacts from Alabama legends such as Hank Aaron, Jesse Owens, Joe Louis, Willie Mays, Satchel Paige, and Carl Lewis. Indeed, football luminaries from Alabama alone could fill their own museum: Bart Starr, Paul "Bear" Bryant, Joe Namath, Bo Jackson, Bobby Bowden, Pat Sullivan, Kenny Stabler, to name a few. Each year the ASHF inducts new sports personalities at an annual banquet. The facility is, appropriately, across the street from the Southeastern Conference headquarters (this highly successful college athletic conference distributed a remarkable $209 million to its members in 2009–2010).

*ALABAMA THEATRE $$
1817 3rd Ave. North, Birmingham
(205) 252-2262
www.alabamatheatre.com

Worth a trip, if only to admire the architecture, the 2,500-seat Alabama Theatre has been the premier cinema in Birmingham since it opened in 1927. French, Belgian, and Italian marble—as well as terra cotta from New York and granite from Minnesota—was lavished on the construction. The Spanish Revival style facade with tall columns framing the three-story windows make the entrance something to savor. Lyle Lovett, playing a concert here in the 1990s, was dead-on when he stopped in the middle of a song, paused and looked up at the thousands of lights set in the ornate ceiling and remarked, "You know, sometimes you just have to stop and look at the ceiling." When it was built the Alabama had one of the most expensive ceilings in any theater in the country. It has more than 12,000 individual effect light bulbs.

Now called the Alabama Theatre for the Performing Arts, the venue hosts live concerts, classic films, and musicals. The summer movie series shows vintage and contemporary classics—be sure to leave time to arrive early (the theater opens an hour before showtime) to tour the restored theater and gape. The Mighty Wurlitzer, the theater's pipe organ and a relic from the silent movie era, slowly rises from the stage and is a delight to witness. A side note: Restoration is underway on the Lyric Theatre, a 1914 vaudeville venue across the street, that attracted performers such as Jack Benny, Will Rogers, Buster Keaton, and Mae West.

AMERICAN VILLAGE $$
3727 Hwy. 119, Montevallo
(205) 665-3535
www.americanvillage.org

Located 30 minutes south of downtown, American Village is the ideal school civics field trip. Encouraging visitors to experience the journey of independence and the call to liberty, it offers an annual catalog of school programs detailing the civic, history, and other curriculum available on the 113-acre campus. But it makes for an engaging family trip as well. Items of interest include a full-scale replica of the Oval Office, rooms and a building patterned after George Washington's Mt. Vernon, and a room inspired by the assembly room of Independence Hall in Philadelphia. Costumed historical interpreters such as George Washington, Thomas Jefferson, and Benjamin Franklin frequent the grounds, offering one-on-one conversations to bring history alive.

And there's more. A church inspired by the Bruton Parish Church of Williamsburg, Virginia, from colonial days is a popular site for weddings. Replicas of Williamsburg's 1770 courthouse, the Concord Bridge, and of George Washington's house when the capital was in Philadelphia (the only replica of it in the United States) complete the grounds. As a means to introduce children to the basics of democracy, the constitution, and the fundamentals of United States citizenship, American Village is an ideal destination. It is history you can see and touch.

ARLINGTON ANTEBELLUM HOME AND GARDEN $
331 Cotton Ave., Birmingham
(205) 780-5656
www.informationbirmingham.com/arlington/index.htm

Since Birmingham itself is a post–Civil War town, it's no surprise that the city does not abound with grand old Antebellum homes; however, Arlington, a two-story frame structure dating from 1845, is a lovely example of the architecture of the time. Set on 6 acres near downtown Birmingham, the Greek Revival home was built by Judge William S. Mudd, one of the city's founders. Union troops occupied the home and planned the burning of the University of Alabama while staying there. As flocks of Birmingham school children well know, the home holds examples of 19th century furniture, silver, and other period pieces and makes a great excursion for kids and parents alike. Each Thurs June through Aug, Arlington offers guests the chance to enjoy lunch in the garden room followed by a tour of the home and surrounding gardens. Arlington is closed Mon. For tours with a docent, advanced reservations are required.

✳BARBER MOTORSPORTS PARK
6040 Barber Motorsports Pkwy., Leeds
(205) 298-9040
www.barbermotorsports.com
When it opened in 2003, Barber Motorsports Park instantly raised the profile of Birmingham among racing enthusiasts as the 2.38-mile long track on a 740-acre site just outside of the city was, and is, undoubtedly world-class. In fact, the Porsche Driving School was so impressed, they immediately relocated to Birmingham to take advantage of the course. Former 500cc world champion Kevin Schwantz recently moved his motorcycle riding school to Barber Motorsports Park as well. The dream of a top-quality track came from local automobile enthusiast George W. Barber, owner of Barber Dairies, who

funded the project with around $54 million of his own milk money. From Grand-Am and Vintage Racing Series to AMA Superbike and now the IRL IndyCar Series Grand Prix, the park is now host to numerous racing events, a clear validation that Barber succeeded. As a spectator the park is a delight with trees shading the perimeter of the course and grassy slopes perfect for a blanket and a picnic. Kids 12 and under are admitted free to races—but don't forget your earplugs. All that screaming horsepower can get loud!

BARBER VINTAGE MOTORSPORTS
   MUSEUM   **$$$**
6040 Barber Motorsports Pkwy., Leeds
(205) 699-7275
www.barbermuseum.org
Like the adjacent Barber Motorsports Park, the vintage museum is a product of Birmingham native and dairy magnate George Barber. A former race-car driver himself, Barber began collecting and restoring classic motorcycles in the 1980s. He opened a small museum in 1995 in Birmingham's Southside that displayed 325 vintage motorcycles from around the world—though his total collection was more than 500. Needing more space to house his collection, the museum relocated to its new home at the Barber Motorsports Park in 2003. There a museum more fitting to the extensive collection displays about 700 motorcycles at a time in a dramatic, open design that makes viewing something of an event itself. Children and adults alike who are fascinated by motorcycles will enjoy the restoration facilities, which are walled with glass so visitors can watch the work in progress. The collection now has more than 1,200 vintage and modern motorcycles—one of the largest

collections of its type in the world—as well as an equally impressive array of Lotus race cars. More than 200 different manufacturers from 20 countries are represented.

*BIRMINGHAM BOTANICAL
   GARDENS   FREE
2612 Lane Park Rd., Birmingham
(205) 414-3950
www.bbgardens.org

An oasis in the city, Birmingham Botanical Gardens is a well-loved treasure appreciated by locals and visitors alike since its opening in 1963. Set on the southern slope of Red Mountain next to the city's zoo, the 69-acre gardens are visited by more than 350,000 people annually. There are few places in Birmingham that offer so many private spots to enjoy a picnic lunch and read a book in solitude. Or to pass the time in beautiful seclusion in some quiet nook. A wide variety of individual garden collections are spread out over the grounds, including rhododendron, fern, hosta, camellia, vegetable, iris, Alabama woodlands, lily, old-fashioned rose, and the popular Dunn Formal Rose Garden and Japanese Garden. When the weather is nice and families want to pass the time in beautiful surroundings, the botanical gardens are often the destination of choice.

Amateur and professional photographers intent on capturing the perfect flower in bloom also frequent the grounds. Educational programs for children, adults, and the whole family are offered year-round, including internships, field trips, photography, and special member-only classes. Perhaps one of the more unappreciated aspects to the gardens is its library, which holds the largest public horticultural collection in the southeast—some 6,000 books, DVDs, and

magazines. Holders of a Jefferson County library card may check out materials. The wonderful Leaf & Petal Gift Shop housed at the gardens is a popular spot to shop for jewelry, garden items, children's toys, home decor, and more. Admission is free, and the gardens are open daily from dawn to dusk every day of the year.

BIRMINGHAM CIVIL RIGHTS
   INSTITUTE $$$
520 16th St. North, Birmingham
(205) 328-9696, ext. 203
www.bcri.org

One of the state's top tourist destinations—and certainly one of Birmingham's must-see attractions—the Birmingham Civil Rights Institute is a soul-stirring experience regardless of one's background or knowledge of the city's role in the civil-rights struggle of the 1950s and 1960s. Locals and out-of-town visitors mingle inside with a reverent sense of awe at the events that unfolded in Birmingham and other cities during the movement. In fact, a side trip to Selma, Montgomery, and Tuskegee, Alabama, is a great way to understand this crucial time in the United States' history. See the Civil Rights chapter for more details.

*BIRMINGHAM MUSEUM
   OF ART   FREE
2000 Rev. Abraham Woods Jr. Blvd.,
Birmingham
(205) 254-2565
www.artsbma.org

There is no doubt—Birmingham and the neighboring communities are fortunate to have a city museum of such quality. Whether wandering through an impressive arrangement of Asian art, Renaissance and

Baroque paintings, decorative arts, or more contemporary art by John Singer Sargent or Frederic Remington, the museum rewards investigation—don't miss Albert Bierstadt's "Looking Down Yosemite Valley, California" (1865), one of the country's most significant landscape paintings. Founded in 1951 the Birmingham Museum of Art has long been recognized as one of the premier collections in the region. This is largely due to the sheer number of objects, more than 24,000, in the museum's collections that represent a wide range of cultures and periods. Its collection of Vietnamese ceramics is one of the best in the world. And of course, the collection of Wedgwood is the largest outside of England. That recognition, however, also represents an active set of educational programs, curated exhibitions of note, and changing programs based on the museum's permanent collection and special events. In the summer, for instance, the highly successful Art on the Rocks! social event draws a young, vibrant crowd of a couple thousand each evening for live music, gallery scavenger hunts, and cocktails.

A destination inside the museum, Oscar's restaurant offers fresh fare sourced locally from Jones Valley Urban Farm and other nearby purveyors (www.oscarsthe museum.com). Need a curious, artsy gift for a friend? The museum store is a good resource for finding that special item for a special person (www.birminghammuseum store.org). The museum is closed Mon and major holidays. Admission is free—as is the parking in the museum lot behind the building—but why not drop a gracious dollar (or $5) in the collection at either entrance? You'll be happy you did.

BIRMINGHAM ZOO $$$
2630 Cahaba Rd., Birmingham
(205) 879-0409
www.birminghamzoo.com

For kids in Birmingham and beyond, a trip to the Birmingham Zoo is something one doesn't forget. Those from the area may remember when it was called the Jimmy Morgan Zoo with its Monkey Island and train ride through the tunnel. Today's zoo is not that zoo—fun as it was. In 1999 the Birmingham Zoo became an independent 501(c)(3) organization, and 5 years later, following the zoo's first capital campaign, the new Children's Zoo opened. This zoo within a zoo, a $15-million exhibit dedicated to wild animals of Alabama, trumpeted the zoo's new direction and energy. The zoo became the number-one tourist attraction in the state the next year and joined the Association of Zoos & Aquariums, placing the zoo in the top 10 percent of animal-holding facilities in the nation. And it is only getting better.

Animals on exhibits range from primates to predators, from waterfowl to reptile. Currently, the "Trails of Africa" initiative, a mixed-species exhibit with an elephant herd, kudu, red river hogs, zebras, rhinos, and other African animals, will make the zoo a national leader in the care, breeding, and conservation of threatened elephants. Aerial and ground observation points, botanical, and even cultural immersion are all a part of the new program, which seeks to support wildlife conservation. The zoo offers educational programs such as summer camps, homeschooler programs, and classes for teachers and students. But yes: Kids can still ride the miniature locomotive around the grounds and through that tunnel. And see lots of monkeys. Across the street from the zoo is the Birmingham Botanical Gardens.

KARL C. HARRISON MUSEUM
OF GEORGE WASHINGTON   FREE
50 Lester St., Columbiana
(205) 669-8767
www.washingtonmuseum.com

Modest and perhaps overlooked the Karl C. Harrison Museum of George Washington is one of those curious little gems that delight the visitor upon discovery. Focusing on artifacts from the colonial period up to the Civil War, the collection holds art, letters, furniture, and house wares, much of it from the Washington family and their descendants. It provides a glance at our first first family. Calera resident Charlotte Smith-Weaver, a sixth-generation granddaughter of Martha Washington, donated the items for the museum and local banker Karl C. Harrison founded the museum in 1982. Items of note include Martha's prayer book, George Washington's writing instruments and tools, an original sketch of Mt. Vernon, and the last tintype taken of Robert E. Lee, a descendant of Martha Washington. Admission is free.

*MCWANE SCIENCE CENTER $$$
200 19th St. North, Birmingham
(205) 714-8300
www.mcwane.org

Bugs. Dinosaurs. Robots. Mr. Potato Head. Cretoxyrhina (a 25-foot shark skeleton from the ancient Alabama oceans). There is so much to choose from for children, a visit to the McWane Science Center is easily an all-day affair. A temple to kids' enduring curiosity, creativity, and sense of fun, the McWane Science Center opened in 1998, an outgrowth of the Red Mountain Museum and The Discovery Place. Funded by the McWane family and McWane, Inc., the McWane Science Center is part science museum, part research archive, but to children the center is all about fun. From the aquarium to the 280-seat IMAX Dome Theater, most of the center provides hands-on learning experiences for children of all ages. Summer camps, traveling exhibits, and special programs keep the museum fresh for repeat visitors. Housed in the historic 1935 Loveman's department store building, the opening of the center in the refurbished building served as a pivotal urban renewal project downtown. Open seven days a week, 360 days a year.

RICKWOOD FIELD   FREE
1137 2nd Ave. West, Birmingham
(205) 458-8161
www.rickwood.com

As far as old-school baseball goes, Rickwood Field is it. One hundred years old as of 2010, the 10,800-seat Rickwood Field is the world's oldest surviving baseball park. That's right. The world's oldest. Built for $75,000 a century ago, the stadium in West End hosted both the Birmingham Barons and the Birmingham Black Barons of the Negro Southern League, as well as stalwarts of the game such as Ty Cobb, Babe Ruth, "Shoeless" Joe Jackson, Dizzy Dean, Leroy "Satchell" Paige, and of course, Willy Mays, who grew up just outside of Birmingham. In fact, more than 100 members of the Baseball Hall of Fame have played at Rickwood. The Rickwood Classic, an annual event at Rickwood Field where a regulation baseball game is played between teams in authentic period uniforms, occurs every June. If baseball is more than just a game, then Rickwood Field is more than just a field. For devotees of the game, it is a site of pilgrimage. There is no admission to enter the Rickwood Field on non-event days, but one should call to confirm it is open before visiting. See the Spectator Sports chapter for more information about the Birmingham Black Barons.

ROBERT TRENT JONES
GOLF TRAIL $$$$
Multiple locations
(800) 949-4444
www.rtjgolf.com
You don't have to be a golfer to know the Robert Trent Jones Golf Trail, an assortment of 468 holes of championship-level golf at 11 sites across the state. The brainchild of Dr. David Bronner, CEO of the Retirement Systems of Alabama, the trail began in the 1980s as a way to diversify the state's pension fund while improving Alabama's tourism offerings. He succeeded on both counts: The 100 miles of golf courses designed by Robert Trent Jones Sr. in some of the state's most beautiful locations has become well known in golfing circles and destination for aficionados of all levels of play. See the Recreation chapter for more details.

SLOSS FURNACES NATIONAL
HISTORIC MONUMENT $$
20 32nd St. North, Birmingham
(205) 324-1911
www.slossfurnaces.com
The mighty Sloss Furnaces created iron for close to a century, fueling the industrial engine that saw Birmingham rise from sparsely populated hills and valleys to become one of the region's leading cities in a few brief decades. After the Civil War the area around Jones Valley was known to be rich in the minerals and resources needed to make iron. James Withers Sloss, a merchant and investor, convinced the L&N Railroad to complete the rail line through the valley,

effectively jump-starting the town. In 1880 he founded the Sloss Furnace Company. By World War I, Sloss-Sheffield Steel and Iron (as it was renamed) was one of the largest pig iron producers in the world. By World War II nearly half of Birmingham's workforce was in the iron, steel, and mining industries—and more than two-thirds of these workers were African American.

Today, Sloss Furnaces is a unique repository of Birmingham's rich cultural and industrial history. It is currently the only 20th-century blast furnace being preserved and interpreted as a historic site, making the site the only publicly held industrial site in the world. Consequently, Sloss has become a model for preservation efforts of similar sites around the world. Currently, a master site plan is being developed to house a visitor center and exhibit gallery. In the meantime Sloss offers all sorts of educational activities for students and teachers as well as offering welding, iron and bronze casting, and blacksmithing workshops, preserving and promulgating the rich heritage this historical site holds. Self-guided or cell phone tours are available, and admission to the grounds is free. There is a charge for guided tours. Iron pours (exactly what it sounds like) occur in the spring and fall on Wed and the occasional weekend—make reservations in advance.

SOUTHERN ENVIRONMENTAL
CENTER $
900 Arkadelphia Rd., Birmingham
(205) 226-4934
www.bsc.edu/sec
The largest educational facility of its kind in Alabama, the Southern Environmental Center (SEC) on the campus of

Birmingham-Southern College is an interactive museum combined with an EcoScape garden that amuses while it introduces kids (and parents/teachers) to the importance of building sustainable communities. Water quality, urban sprawl, air pollution, and other complex issues are broken down so that kids can easily understand. And giggle at. For example, in the 5,600-square-foot center, a giant sewage pipe slide exiting a dramatically oversize fake toilet illustrates—squarely on the elementary and middle school level—just how water quality and our actions are interlinked. The 4-acre EcoScape gardens nearby is an edible outdoor classroom with medicinal plants, herbs, and various mini-EcoScapes that illustrate sustainability put into practice. It is one of eleven EcoScape gardens the SEC has constructed in vacant lots throughout the city. Several more are in the design stage while the SEC also maintains one demonstration farm and the Turkey Creek Nature Preserve in Pinson. Call before visiting to arrange a tour of the museum or schedule birthday parties. Visits to the EcoScape garden are free, though guided tours are also available for a small fee.

SOUTHERN MUSEUM OF FLIGHT $$
4343 73rd St. North, Birmingham
(205) 833-8226
www.southernmuseumofflight.org
For those interested in jets, bombers, and anything that flies, the Southern Museum of Flight is the first stop in Alabama to get your fix. The 68,000-square-foot facility located, appropriately enough, near the airport, holds more than 75 aircraft and numerous associated aviation items, covering the 20th century's winged history. Soviet MiG, "Blackbird" spy plane, Wright Flyer, B-25 Bomber,

biplanes, helicopters, and assorted experimental aircraft are just a few of the pieces on display at the museum. Popular with all ages are the flight simulators that give visitors a chance to gain a first-hand sense of what flying is all about. Of special interest is a diorama exhibit of Alabama's Tuskegee Airmen, the United State's first black military pilots. The museum is also home to the Alabama Aviation Hall of Fame.

TANNEHILL IRONWORKS
  HISTORICAL STATE PARK $
12632 Confederate Pkwy., McCalla
(205) 477-5711
www.tannehill.org
A collection of some 45 historical structures from dogtrot cabins to the beautifully preserved Sadler Plantation House, Tannehill Ironworks is a lovely little state park (well, if you can call 1,500 acres "little") full of activities, events, and attractions. Civil War reenactments, a dulcimer festival, rock and gem shows, trade days, and woodcarvers show are just a few of the activities that keep the park busy year-round. A central attraction is the Alabama Iron and Steel Museum, and of course, the Tannehill Furnaces, one of the nation's best-preserved Civil War landmarks. If you're looking to rent a restored log cabin from the 1800s, this is the place. See the Parks chapter for additional details.

✳VULCAN PARK AND MUSEUM $$
1701 Valley View Dr., Birmingham
(205) 933-1409
www.visitvulcan.com
The world's largest cast-iron statue, *Vulcan*, sits atop Red Mountain, the source of the iron ore that fueled the furnaces that built the city during the late 19th century. It's difficult to

get more emblematic of Birmingham, its history and its pride (and sense of humor), than a massively tall iron guy wearing no underwear.

A site for picnics, wedding, receptions, and reunions, the facility gets heavy use now—it is perhaps the go-to spot for locals to bring out-of-town friends for a fun introduction to their city. In the fall Vulcan After-Tunes concert series is a popular event, as is the Thunder on the Mountain 4th of July Fireworks Extravaganza, the largest display of pyrotechnics in the state. Admission to the park—an official welcome center for Birmingham—is free but there is a charge for the museum. For children interested in Birmingham's history, visit the Vulcan website for downloadable educational activities for each exhibit in the museum. See the Parks chapter for more details.

KIDSTUFF

Every parent has been there. It's a rainy day or it's too hot. You and the kids have been inside too long and the first warning signs of stir-crazy are beginning to manifest themselves. It's time to act! You need something constructive and fun for the children to do.

Part of the attraction of Birmingham and the reason for its high quality of life is the many great offerings aimed at children that can be found in the area. Some are of an educational bent while some are just plain silly, aimed at making a child laugh—or wear them out with some healthy exercise and active play. Most cultural organizations have outreach programs that provide ways for kids to get involved and most importantly, have a good time. From museums and dance to art and energetic fun, there are certainly plenty of kid-themed options around to fill an entire weekend.

While there's no way to mention every single destination or activity, don't overlook area libraries and bookstores that present story hours, book discussions, Lego clubs, and other child-focused programs on a daily basis. They are free and make for a great learning experience to stimulate your child's developing mind. In terms of seasons, fall and spring seem to bring a host of outdoor activities like fruit picking, harvest events, and festivals to entertain the young ones. For a more complete listing, see the Festivals & Annual Events chapter. When the weather is accommodating, look for farms in almost any direction outside of Birmingham and you're all set for a family-pleasing outing. When the weather turns downright hot in the summer, cool down with a refreshing H_2O-based activity. All kids like to get wet, so a couple of the top public pools are singled out while the rest may be found in the Recreation chapter. Also, consider a float along the Cahaba River or a picnic at a public lake.

OVERVIEW

While parents will have no difficulty scheduling after-school activities, weekend programs, and events that kids will love, there are also plenty of simple, even old-fashioned things that kids in and around Birmingham can do that have nothing at all to do with over-scheduling a four-year old. Every neighborhood, especially Over the Mountain, has a wonderful park or two where kids can just be kids and play to their heart's content. Let them roam free in a safe environment to play with old friends or make some new ones. Accordingly, we've mentioned a few parks worth knowing, though there are certainly plenty more out there (see the Recreation chapter). Sometimes the best plan for a kid is no plan at all.

Price Code

The price code refers to the cost of admission for one child. Admission to some attractions can vary based on which activities the child plans to participate in and the child's age. Call ahead to verify times and prices for your party.

$.....................Less than $5
$$ ....$5 to $10
$$$ ....$10 to $20
$$$$............ More than $20

ANIMALS, ANIMALS, ANIMALS

✳**BIRMINGHAM ZOO** $$–$$$
2630 Cahaba Rd., Birmingham
(205) 879-0409
www.birminghamzoo.com
One of Alabama's top tourist destinations, the Birmingham Zoo houses approximately 750 animals from 6 continents in a 122-acre modern facility. Most importantly for the boys and girls, the zoo offers a multitude of interactive, educational activities for kids of all ages. Daily events offer travelers guaranteed shows year-round including sea lion training sessions, giraffe and rhino viewings, and a glimpse into the workings of a lorikeet aviary. Among a variety of other conservation efforts, the Zoo plays a vital role in Alabama's dedication to repopulating the nation's endangered bald eagles. In 2010 the Birmingham Zoo's two nesting bald eagles hatched the only two eaglets born in an accredited zoo that year. The Predator Zone features training sessions with the zoo's two African lions while the new and exciting Trails of Africa allows visitors to enjoy a train ride through the zoo's mixed-species recreation of the African tundra in an area that features elephants, antelopes, zebras, giraffes, and ostriches.

The Birmingham Zoo is also an ideal birthday party or group destination, offering catering, private party rooms, guided tours, overnight stays, classes, summer camps, and more. Deluxe birthday party packages come with a party coordinator as well as admission, zoo-themed cake and goodies, and a train and carousel ride followed by private animal demonstrations. Plan your day on the website's detailed map before you visit to ensure you don't miss anything. Also check on monthly events like a Teddy Bear Clinic where kids can learn about veterinary medicine or a Zoo Olympics display that compares human physical ability to those of some of the Zoo's animals. The Birmingham Zoo is open 9 a.m. to 5 p.m. every day. Admission is half-price on Tues! Extended hours run in the summertime and during special events.

OAK MOUNTAIN STATE PARK
PETTING ZOO $–$$
200 Terrace Dr., Pelham
(205) 620-2520
www.alapark.com/oakmountain/attractions
When Birmingham residents want some time away from the city but don't have time for an extended vacation, they turn to Oak Mountain State Park and its bevy of outdoor activities. The park's petting zoo is the perfect place to bring the kids for a healthy dose of interaction with nature. The petting zoo features goats, sheep, and other animals, providing a rural farm-like setting that is often fascinating to children more used to an urban/suburban environment. Open Wed through Sun. The top of the barn can be rented for birthday parties.

EDUCATIONAL FUN

✳BIRMINGHAM CHILDREN'S
THEATRE $$–$$$
2130 Richard Arrington Jr. Blvd. North,
Birmingham
(205) 458-8181
www.bct123.org

Have a child who loves to put on plays or impromptu performances around the house? Now in its 63rd season, the Birmingham Children's Theatre (BCT) produces 8 professional shows each year that are focused on bringing young audiences' imagination to life. Shows like *The Frog Prince, Hansel and Gretel, Zorro,* and *Beauty and the Beast* captivate children, reminding them in the most fun fashion that their need for television screens just might be exaggerated. The BCT also provides school and community support through their educational outreach program. Know a 4-year old who wants to dress up in costume and pretend to be someone else? The BCT Academy of Performing Arts offers classes featuring individual instruction for children ages 3 to 18 in a variety of theatrical fields. There are no auditions: It is a chance for children to gain confidence and have a good theatrical time. Special accommodations for birthday parties are available for reservation. Performances usually run weekdays starting between 9:30 a.m. and 1:30 p.m. Additionally, the BCT offers fun birthday parties before performances where the actors come visit the children.

HEART OF DIXIE RAILROAD
MUSEUM $$$–$$$$
1919 9th St., Calera
(205) 280-0820
www.hodrrm.org

Tired of cartoon trains and popup books about railroads? Take your kids on a ride powered by a real 1951 diesel locomotive! Thirty minutes south of Birmingham, The Heart of Dixie Railroad Museum "is dedicated to the preservation, restoration, and operation of historically significant railway equipment." The area outside the museum houses the fleet of locomotives, cars, and cabooses the museum continues to restore and operate. Inspect these old beauties or take a ride in one of them during their season of annual events, usually held on weekends. Riders can choose their seats from a selection of passenger cars from the past lovingly restored to their original glory. Take in the view from a Long Island Railroad commuter car from the 1950s styled in retro orange and beige or bask in the antique beauty of the Frisco Coach built in 1910. Inside the museum proper visitors can tour a room filled with authentic treasures from railroad history and try to keep their kids from the gift shop stocked with train-themed toys and clothes. But if it's a beautiful day, you shouldn't have any problem keeping children outside as they wander through the huge machines surrounding the museum—it's a treat to watch their faces light up. For the locomotive-inclined birthday parties that feature a ride in one of the trains can be arranged.

✳MCWANE SCIENCE
CENTER $$$–$$$$
200 19th St. North, Birmingham
(205) 714-8300
www.mcwane.org

The McWane Science Center is an incredible non-profit interactive science museum and IMAX theater with four floors of all sorts of fun activities for the whole family. Alabama dinosaur skeletons stand beside an anatomically correct crawl-through bass fish complete with internal organs. Almost everything about the McWane Center is focused on hands-on activities, allowing children to physically explore science in a variety of ways, including touching sharks and manta rays in the Touch Tank, graphic examples of the theory of persistence of vision, and wielding automatons that draw three-dimensional shapes. And that's just the tip of the iceberg. The IMAX dome theater projects the latest 3-D children's movies and family-friendly scientific documentaries. Featured exhibits like the "Adventures of Mr. Potato Head" and the "Science of an Oil Spill" make science appealing and topical. The McWane Center offers rental space for 5 to 5000, including full catering and birthday options, day and overnight camps, a cafe with multiple dining options, and a gift store filled with an assortment of educational gifts and fun souvenirs. The McWane Science Center is open every day and during most holidays. When the weather is unpleasant, McWane is one of the most popular destinations for parents looking for something to do with stir-crazy kiddies.

SLOSS FURNACES   **FREE**
20 32nd St. North, Birmingham
(205) 324-1911
www.slossfurnaces.com
Sloss Furnaces is not just for adults keen on concerts, festivals, and special events. It offers kids a tactile opportunity to learn about Birmingham's history as the most powerful industrial center in the south. Walking among the huge blast furnaces and preserved century-old machinery of the plant inspires and educates children as they learn about the heavy metal past of Alabama's largest city. Kids can enjoy a short instructional video about the furnaces and take a self-guided tour through the facility. Since the grounds

are extensive and facilities are minimal, this tour might be more appropriate for older children who won't mind exploring the facility on foot. However, many parents find it a pleasant afternoon when you can let the kids roam about and explore the grounds. Guided tours are available for a fee ($) for groups smaller than 10 on Sat and Sun at 1 p.m., 2 p.m., and 3 p.m. Keep on the lookout for new exciting changes coming, like the new visitor center. For those older kids wanting a fun scare, try Sloss' annual Halloween haunted attraction, "Sloss Fright Furnace."

VULCAN PARK AND MUSEUM   **$**
1701 Valley View Dr.
(205) 933-1409
www.visitvulcan.com
Although Vulcan Park and Museum are mentioned at length in both the Attractions and Parks section of this guide, it would be deficient not to include a mention of *Vulcan* and his appeal to children. A visit to the public park itself is free, and kids love to play in the shadow of *Vulcan* as they enjoy both the view of the city and the giant statue. Inside the museum kids will be entranced by the interactive exhibits and *Vulcan* and Birmingham-related collection covering the history of the city and its most visible landmark. Heck, they might even learn something. See the Attractions chapter for more details.

FOR THE ARTISTS

CHILDREN'S DANCE FOUNDATION   **$$$**
1715 27th Court South, Homewood
(205) 870-0073
www.childrensdancefoundation.com
Their mission is straightforward: "To provide comprehensive dance education, enriching

the spirit, enlivening the imagination and celebrating community." Serving more than 2,000 students weekly, Children's Dance Foundation (CDF) uses a professional staff of dancers and musicians to teach kids about the power of dance. Classes are offered for a variety of ages and interests, from the-ater and special performances to adult/child classes or for those with special needs. Birth-day parties include a CDF dance instructor and musician who will lead the children in fun, creative movement based on the theme your child prefers.

RED DOT GALLERY $$$$
1001 Stuart St., Homewood
(205) 870-7608
www.reddotgallery.com
A small, welcoming gallery in the Edgewood district of Homewood, Red Dot is a work-ing studio and teaching facility owned by Dori DeCamillis and Scott Bennett. Here, kids (and adults!) can indulge their creative sides through painting, pottery, and drawing classes with the artists. The space, located off the busy Oxmoor Road is open and full of activity as students range from the young-est of beginners to practicing artists with advanced degrees. Check the website for listings of special events and exhibits.

i After a session at the Red Dot Gallery, walk the kids to Sam's Deli and Grill for delicious Middle-Eastern fare—or one of the city's best cheeseburger and fries. It's a neighbor-hood favorite. Then head to Edgewood Creamery for ice cream.

THE PINK HOUSE $$$
817 39th St. South, Suite B, Birmingham
(205) 591-6683
www.mybabymusic.com
One of the most established places in town for teaching young children to love music, The Pink House is all about play, singing, and making music. The Kindermusik stu-dio certainly helps develop early literacy and math skills, but try telling that to the newborns, toddlers, and preschool age kids banging on drums and playing with pup-pets and streamers while engaging with musical fun. For them it's all about having a blast with Mom or Dad and music. Classes are organized by age and designed to foster a love for music while stimulating the kids' imaginations. The Pink House also offers piano instruction that integrates computer technology with traditional piano education. Yoga classes are available for parents and kids. And of course, The Pink House offers interactive music parties for birthdays and special events on Fri, Sat, and Sun.

HAVE A BALL

ALABAMA ADVENTURE WATER
AND THEME PARK $$$$
4599 Alabama Adventure Pkwy.,
Bessemer
(205) 481-4750
www.visionland.com
Alabama's biggest theme park is always a hit with younger children. Compared to larger parks the theme park area isn't as appealing to roller-coaster fanatics and adult speed freaks, but the offerings for kids are excellent. All the things that make the big theme parks such a hassle for parents of small children are absent from Alabama Adventure. The lines are short, the facilities are visible and

accessible, and the crowds are usually not as packed. Numerous seating areas throughout the park offer parents hassle-free places for a pit stop. Both the theme park and water park offer a variety of rides for children or children accompanied by adults. The theme park has a dedicated children's area called Marvel City with 7 exhilarating children's rides. The water park has a slide for children only that's a summertime favorite. It may be smaller than other parks, but that makes Alabama Adventure a better fit for parents of smaller children.

IJUMP $–$$
157 Resource Center Pkwy., Suite 109, Inverness
(205) 981-2696
www.ijumpinc.com
Yes, it is full of screaming kids running about, bouncing on inflatable play slides and obstacle courses. Yes, the decibel level might be of a pitch that can damage the brains of those over 21 years of age, but the point is: Kids love it. Every screaming, bouncing, sliding moment of it. With 20,000 square feet of indoor play, iJump is a popular one-stop spot for birthday parties and more where kids can play until they are exhausted, refuel on cake and ice cream, and then return for more fun. Thankfully, there's a parents' lounge with a flat screen television that always seems to have a football game on. Count your blessings.

KIDS GYM $–$$
2826 Columbiana Rd., Hoover
(205) 822-2332
www.kidsgymvestavia.com
For kids ages 3 months to 8 years, Kids Gym offers a one-of-a-kind experience in movement that explores different ideas of dance and gymnastics. Classes feature a distinct gymnastics program that utilizes individual and group activities, educational props, and music. Birthday parties can be booked at the facility and the second Fri of each month Kids Gym hosts an incredible Parents Night Out your child won't want to end. Kids Gym isn't your typical dance studio, and the benefits of time spent here go beyond the typical lessons learned in normal dance classes.

PUMP IT UP $–$$
2724 Chandalar Place, Pelham
(205) 663-4646
www.pumpitupparty.com
Don't forget your socks! It's not called a jumping party for nothing. With two locations on the periphery of Birmingham (the second is at 4623 Camp Coleman Rod., Suite 101, Trussville; 205-661-5557), Pump It Up is a surprisingly fun birthday destination filled with inflatable rooms that are irresistible to kids. The bouncing is contagious, so don't be afraid to jump in and act like a kid yourself. The facilities available for parties include food, drinks, music, and more. Special weekly events are listed on the website. A popular site for birthday parties, Pump It Up is also available for $5 per session for kids who just want to jump to their heart's content.

SKATES 280 $$–$$$
7043 Meadowlark Dr., Inverness
(205) 991-3611
www.skates-280.com
Hit the rink for some weekend fun in this full-service skating facility. Bring the kids for free skating lessons every Sat from 11 to 11:45 a.m. Perfect for birthday parties and other group gatherings, Skates 280 accepts reservations for parties numbering 10 and larger and includes a private party room and

servers for the event. Nostalgic adults can turn back the clock during the 17 and older night skating from 11 p.m. to 1 a.m. every Fri and Sat night. Prices for admission and skate rental top out at $10. Free Wi-Fi is also available throughout the building. Seasonal schedules apply so check the website or call for hours. Facilities are open during many school holidays.

TRUSSVILLE PLAYSTATION $$–$$$$
411 Waterson Lane, Trussville
(205) 655-1800
www.trussvilleplaystation.com

A short trip beyond Birmingham proper leads to this one-stop kid wonderland with something for every child: state-of-the-art roller skating, video arcade, two-story laser tag arena, batting cages, large go cart track, and an 18-hole miniature golf course. Round out that list with support for parties up to 100 people and a generous concession menu, and you've got one of the best entertainment values for the family. Party features go beyond traditional venues to include "lock-ins" that allow large groups to bring their own music and food, semi-private and private parties, and unlimited use passes at an affordable price during regular hours. Be advised that Trussville Playstation does have a detailed dress code for patrons ages 7 and older that includes restrictions on garments like tank tops, untucked shirts, hats and headgear, and skirt lengths. A full listing of the dress code is available on the website.

SPLASH!

HOMEWOOD CENTRAL POOL $
1632 Oxmoor Rd., Homewood
(205) 879-5012
www.homewoodparks.com

While there are certainly no shortages of exclusive country clubs in Birmingham, those just wanting a great pool to share with their neighbors or a place to bring visitors could hardly do better than these two community favorites. Homewood Swimming Pool, located at the parks and recreation main facility at Central Park is a warm-weather gathering place for those living in the surrounding community. Ironically referred to as "Homewood Country Club" by locals, it's a family-oriented spot to meet friends, catch up on neighborhood gossip, and play with the kids. In fact, it's so relaxed, many residents from neighboring communities visit on a regular basis, all blending in and having a good time. A kiddie pool entertains toddlers and younger children while the main pool has a gently sloped ramp for older kids still testing out their confidence in the deeper water. The mushroom waterfall is a big attraction. It opens at the close of Homewood city schools for summer break and closes on Labor Day.

VESTAVIA HILLS SWIMMING POOL $
513 Montgomery Hwy., Vestavia Hills
(205) 978-0166, (205) 823-5512
www.vestaviahills.net/citydepartments

Located in the Wald Park complex and surrounded by tennis courts, baseball fields, and a walking track, the Vestavia Hills swimming pool (also called the Wald Park Pool) is at the heart of summertime activity in Vestavia and is open from Memorial Day through Labor Day. Call (205) 978-0172 to reach the pool directly. With 6 lanes 25 yards long, it is large enough to accommodate all ages and interests. Thanks to the air dome, when summer is over, the Birmingham Swim League administers the pool for their various competitive swim teams and practices. The pool is still available for free swim, water aerobics, and parties most days, though check the website for hours or phone them directly, (205) 823-5512. More information on the Birmingham Swim League can be found at www.bslswim.org.

TAKE AIM

FORT RED ROCK $$$–$$$$
223 Mountaintop Industrial Dr., Bessemer
(205) 424-3223
www.fortredrock.com
Fort Red Rock is the premier paintball facility in the Birmingham-Hoover Metropolitan area. From atop a small, secluded mountain only 25 minutes from downtown, players can enjoy multiple paintball fields featuring a variety of terrain and obstacles like piled logs, wooden sheds, and massive concrete pipes. For those inclined to picnic, the facility permits outside food and drink and offers covered seating, tables, and a charcoal grill. Drinks and snacks are also available for purchase. Don't feel the desire to run around in the woods and get covered in paint? Spectator masks are available free of charge. Frankly, watching the action can be almost as fun as participating yourself. Kids of all ages are welcome to watch, but they have to be older than 10 to play. While weekday and night play is available, it is only by reservation for groups of 16 or more. During daylight hours on weekdays, play is open to groups of 10 or more.

TOYS & MORE

✳HOMEWOOD TOY & HOBBY SHOP $–$$$$
2830 18th St. South, Homewood
(205) 879-3986

Located in the heart of the Homewood shopping district, Homewood Toy & Hobby Shop is a Birmingham institution that's been in business for nearly 30 years. Despite the multitude of big-box toy stores, this family-owned store has continued to thrive by offering the best selection of classic toys along with a wide range of educational toys suitable for kids of all ages. The staff is always willing to answer questions and help search for that special toy you've wanted since you were a kid. The hobby section of the store is a modeler's dream, housing shelf after shelf of the finest model kits available together with a complete line of supplies.

i A Birmingham institution, Homewood Toy & Hobby is a place parents can literally spend hours with their kids, watching them wander down every aisle in amazement, inspecting the model kits, building blocks, animal toys, and more. You'll be back sooner than you think.

NORD'S GAMES $$–$$$$
2000 Riverchase Galleria, #120, Hoover
(205) 986-4263
www.nordsgames.net
Nord's Games in the Riverchase Galleria is a one-stop board game and miniature gaming shop that offers an immense selection of board games for every age group. That's apparent just from the fun store exterior that resembles a castle fortress. Kids will love the selection of non-traditional board games available alongside the well-loved classics like Monopoly and Risk. If it's a board game you need—parlor, adventure, card, or family—Nord's probably has it. Nord's also sells the latest and greatest collectible card games that are in demand. Pewter

miniatures and painting supplies round out the excellent variety for sale.

✳SMITH'S VARIETY TOY
& GIFT SHOPPE $–$$$$
2715 Culver Rd., Mountain Brook
(205) 871-0841
www.smithsvarietyshop.com

Like Homewood Toy & Hobby, Smith's Variety is an independently owned toy store with a selection all its own that distinguishes it from larger chain stores. A destination for kids and parents since 1950, Smith's Variety, as it is called, is a fun jumble of toys and games practically bulging from shelves. Bringing the kids here is an adventure as children hurry across the wooden floors to discover toys they've never seen or dreamed of before. The old time feel of the shop makes shopping here relaxing compared to the sterile bright white of the superstore. Once you bring the kids to Smith's, they might not be able to settle for a chain store again.

YOUTH SPORTS LEAGUES

Parks and recreations departments in individual towns throughout the Birmingham-Hoover area offer organized sports for children and adults, as do the proliferations of local sports clubs. Leagues cover everything from soccer and lacrosse to swimming and football. See the Recreation chapter for more on leagues, YMCAs, and other organized sports for children.

YUMMY

ALABAMA FARMERS' MARKET $–$$$$
344 Finley Ave. West
(205) 251-8737
www.alabamafarmersmarket.org

Being the big city in a primarily rural state means that Birmingham residents can enjoy locally grown produce without having to pay premium prices. The Alabama Farmers' Market represents the best of Alabama's agricultural heritage by offering an incredible assortment of local produce direct from the farmers who grew it. Bring the kids and walk through aisles of every fruit and vegetable imaginable freshly picked and available in any quantity. Whether you're here for the sights and a few pieces of succulent fruit or for the week's produce, the friendly farmers and the quality food won't disappoint you. Since 1956 the farmers' market on Finley Avenue has provided the metropolitan citizens of Birmingham with the opportunity to purchase fresh Alabama produce without having to go through the inflated middleman of the grocery store. Open daily year-round.

BUD'S BEST FACTORY TOUR FREE
2070 Parkway Office Circle, Hoover
(205) 987-4840, (800) 548-1504
www.budsbestcookies.com/tours

All aboard the Cookieland Express! Stop by this ultra-modern cookie-making facility and take the kids on the free motorized train tour through the plant. In the mid-90s, Bud's Best revolutionized the cookie industry with its high-quality bite-size cookies. Their factory tour allows cookie-lovers a look behind the scenes at the creation of these delicious treats. Kids will be both inspired and hungry as they witness the power of a plant that can bake a million cookies an hour. If your kids love dessert (and don't they all?), this tour is a guaranteed hit that will create severe anticipation for the free samples at the end of the tour. Call the numbers listed above to schedule a tour.

GOLDEN FLAKE FACTORY TOUR   FREE
1 Golden Flake Dr., Birmingham
(800) 239-2447
www.goldenflake.com/walkingtour.html
No, potato chips aren't exactly the healthi-est food around for kids, but boy, they are tasty. And Golden Flake is ours. Starting as a snack food company in 1923, Golden Flake eventually became known specifically for its delicious potato chips and built a large manufacturing facility in 1958 in the heart of Birmingham. Since then Golden Flake has grown into a multi-state snack-food provider that has become one of Birmingham's most widely known locally founded companies. Some 25,000 visitors visit the facility annu-ally. The factory tour takes kids through each step of the chip-making process from potato peeling to bagging. Kids can snack on samples from Golden Flake's wide range of products as they learn about the cre-ation of one of the most popular foods in America. The tour is a walking tour through a food processing plant, so remember to wear comfortable shoes that are fully enclosed (no sandals or flip flops). Check the website for specific tour days and times.

PEANUT DEPOT $–$$$$
2016 Morris Ave.
(205) 251-3314
www.peanutdepot.com
This small business in the heart of the city has been roasting peanuts for over a cen-tury. The roasters cook their peanuts without added oils or preservatives in antique roast-ers resulting in the perfect peanut. Children will enjoy the weathered roasting machines and the rustic building while they chomp down on the best peanuts around. Peanuts are sold in a variety of quantities and pack-ages including gift boxes and old-fashioned burlap bags. Although the facility isn't large and doesn't qualify for an extended trip, the magnificent peanuts sold here demand that you at least stop by and purchase a bag of legumes as you explore historic Morris Avenue.

ANNUAL EVENTS & FESTIVALS

No matter the weather, no matter the time of year, it's rare that a weekend passes without some event tempting residents out of their home for a fun gathering downtown or in the peripheries of the city. Neighborhood festivals, outdoor excursions, school benefits, art shows, gala, golf tournaments, and races—there is no end to the great options to while away your Saturdays and Sundays in Birmingham. From events like the ONB Magic City Art Connection and the Vulcan Run to races at the Barber Motorsports Park and Greek and Lebanese food festivals, you can eat, watch, run, and admire art to your satisfaction: often all in a single weekend.

Spring and fall alike are special times in Birmingham as the pleasant weather brings people back outdoors in great numbers. But for some reason, the fall is literally jam-packed with festivals, art shows, and outdoor cultural events—it must be the relief of knowing that another hot and humid summer is nine months away. It's almost too much to keep track of: St. Nicholas Russian Food Festival, Artwalk, Moss Rock Festival, Magic City Classic, Bluff Park Art Show, and the Sidewalk Moving Picture Festival, an event *TIME* magazine recognized as a "Film Festival for the Rest of Us." And proof that the city also knows how to have fun, Birmingham's annual "Mr. & Miss Apollo Pageant" is now the second oldest continuously running drag queen pageant in the country (see Mystic Krewe of Apollo, www.mkabirmingham.com, for details).

Many festivals and events are geared towards having a good time, but look closely and there is often more to them than meets the eye. Birmingham has always been a community that gets behind a good cause. In fact, according to a recent study that tallied the largest metropolitan areas, Birmingham is demonstrably the most generous city in America, giving a higher percentage of household income to charities than any other city. So don't be surprised if a great number of the festivals and events listed here donate a portion (or all) of their proceeds to a worthy cause.

This certainly is not a comprehensive list of every festival or annual event in and around Birmingham. Look under the Parks chapter for other state parks and outdoor destinations that often host events. See the Recreation and Spectator Sports chapters for more active sporting events. And for keeping the younger ones entertained and engaged, the Kidstuff chapter holds many options.

JANUARY

BIRMINGHAM BOWL
Legion Field
www.birminghambowl.com

Formerly known as the Papa John's Bowl, the Birmingham Bowl continues the grand tradition of post-season football in Birmingham where it belongs: Birmingham previously hosted the Dixie Bowl (1947–1948), the Hall of Fame Bowl (1977–1985), and the All-American Bowl (1986–1990). In the few years since the tradition began in 2006, the bowl has grown each year and generated an economic impact of more than $41 million dollars. The game also supports charities such as the Crippled Children's Foundation, which in turn supports a number of area charities. An exciting match-up between the Southeastern Conference and Big East Conference, the 2010 game between the University of Connecticut and the University of South Carolina drew more than 42,000 fans. ESPN owns and operates the bowl. Tickets are $30 for corners and $50 for sidelines.

MARTIN LUTHER KING JR. DAY
Numerous locations and events
www.bcri.org
www.16thstreetbaptist.org
www.yourcitycenter.com
www.gbm.org

Officially observed in every state for the first time in 2000, Martin Luther King Jr. Day means a variety of activities and gatherings in Birmingham. That morning Operation New Birmingham (205-324-8797), along with the Southern Christian Leadership Conference, National Conference for Community and Justice, Greater Birmingham Ministries, and the NAACP, host the Dr. Martin Luther King Jr. Unity Breakfast at 7:30 a.m. at the Birmingham Jefferson Convention Complex. The Breakfast Committee also holds an essay contest each year to honor Dr. King, and winners are presented and honored at the breakfast. The 16th Street Baptist Church, just across the street from the Birmingham Civil Rights Institute, also is the focus of further holiday programs such as the Southern

Christian Leadership Conference Rally and Program. The Birmingham Civil Rights Institute offers free admission for the holiday.

BIRMINGHAM BOAT SHOW
Birmingham Boat Show
www.birminghamboatshow.com

If inboard and outboard engines float your boat, the Birmingham Boat Show is likely an event you look forward to every January. A fixture for four decades, the show was the first public event held at the new Birmingham Jefferson Civic Center back in 1972. With 250,000 square feet of the newest boats, fishing gear, motors, and more, the show resembles a giant-size toy store for adults. Local and regional dealers are present, as are professional fishermen, guides, and other marine experts offering seminars and free events for patrons. Look for grand prize giveaways such as Yamaha Waverunners. The event runs Thurs through Sun, and admission is $9.

FEBRUARY

ARTBLINK GALA
The Kirklin Clinic
2000 Sixth Ave. South, Birmingham
(205) 934-0034
www.uab.edu/artblink

For more than a quarter-century, the Comprehensive Cancer Center Advisory Board has hosted this charitable event to support cancer research and patient and family services. Its success is a testament to the giving nature of Birmingham's citizens who are always quick to get behind a good charitable cause. The idea of the ArtBLINK Gala is that several of Alabama's top artists create a new work of art in 90 minutes right before the eyes of the Gala attendees. A celebrity host then auctions off the art. Of course, there is live music, cocktails, and fine dining to accompany the evening's festivities. Proceeds benefit the University of Alabama at Birmingham (UAB) Comprehensive Cancer Center. Dress is black-tie optional, which really means black tie in a city as formal as Birmingham can be. Tickets are $150.

✴MERCEDES MARATHON
Linn Park
P.O. Box 59260, Birmingham 35259
(205) 870-7771
www.mercedesmarathon.com
The 2011 Mercedes Marathon marked the 10th anniversary of this much-beloved run. First organized to fund The Bell Center, a nonprofit that supports parents with children born prematurely or with Down syndrome and other genetic disorders, the marathon event has grown significantly, hosting the 2003 USA Men's Marathon Championships in preparation for hosting the 2004 USA Men's Marathon Olympic Trials. It's an all-around fun time for runners as well as their families and friends as the multi-loop course makes for an exciting, spectator-friendly route. In fact, the loop course idea was so successful, that both the New York and Boston Marathons recently employed it. Runners and fans dress up in silly costumes, and bands will often play to rouse the runners along the route. Volunteers provide great support throughout the race, and whether you're a professional marathoner or just a weekend warrior, expect numerous festivities. The race, with more than 9,000 participants each year, has raised around $2 million for local charities. Look for the marathon, half-marathon, marathon relay, 5K, and kids' marathon over the event weekend.

MARCH

BIRMINGHAM HOME & GARDEN SHOW
Birmingham-Jefferson Convention Complex
2100 Richard Arrington Jr. Blvd. North, Birmingham
(205) 458-8400
www.homeandgardenshow.tv
For nearly 40 years the four-day Birmingham Home & Garden Show has been the event in Alabama for both consumers and businesses focusing on making their home a more perfect place to live. Numerous exhibitors display the latest trends and newest products for bath, spa, windows, siding, green living, security, landscaping, and more—if it has anything to do with the home or garden, expect to find solutions at the show. Look for celebrities like Ty Pennington, Chip Wade, Christopher Straub, and other household names from HGTV and Lifetime sharing their unique perspective while seminars led by industry notables educate and inform you about the latest tips and trends in everything from home decor to going green. Admission is $10 for adults, under $5 for children 6 to 12.

APRIL

LEBANESE FOOD AND CULTURAL FESTIVAL
Saint Elias Maronite Catholic Church
836 8th St. South, Birmingham
(205) 252-3867
www.stelias.org
Birmingham enjoys a strong Lebanese tradition since the earliest days of the city when many immigrants living in the Northeast migrated south. Many peddled fruits and vegetables, eventually becoming wholesalers and retailers of groceries or selling linen

and dry goods. The Maronites, a sect of Catholics founded by Maron, a monk from Syria during the 5th century, soon established themselves in Birmingham. The food festival celebrates more than a century of Lebanese life and culture in Birmingham through food, music, and culture. Delicious items like baked kibbee, grape leaves, falafel, baklava, flat bread, harrissi, and other items are reason enough to participate. Church tours, traditional dancing, commemorative items, and a heritage room present the best of Lebanese culture. There is no admission charge to attend.

✳ONB MAGIC CITY ART CONNECTION
Linn Park
ONB Magic City Art Connection
1128 Glen View Rd., Birmingham
(205) 595-6306
www.magiccityart.com

One of the city's cultural highlights, Operation New Birmingham's Magic City Art Connection is perhaps the premier art festival in the city, attracting local and national artists. From painting and photography to clay and furniture, the range of styles and mediums are broad enough to appeal to most patrons' interests. Many a home in Birmingham hangs original artwork purchased at Magic City Art Connection. Workshops for children in subjects such as painting, clay, dance, pastels, collage, and more may be enjoyed in the Imagination Festival for Kids, a large area dedicated to the delights of the youngest attendees. Corks & Chefs, an annual food-and-wine tasting event showcases the culinary talents of numerous independently owned restaurants in the area. Separate tickets to the event are sold—arrive early to guarantee samples of all the tasty items on display as Corks & Chefs typically is a heavily attended affair. Magic City Art Connection runs Fri through Sun, and admission to the park is free.

SCHAEFFER EYE CENTER CRAWFISH BOIL
www.schaeffercrawfishboil.com

What started as a crawfish boil in the backyard nearly 20 years ago has blossomed into one of Birmingham's largest outdoor musical festivals, generating over $450,000 for local charities in the process. Imagine tons upon tons of delicious crawfish prepared for several thousand of your closest friends while you listen to some of the bigger names in music. That's what the Schaeffer Crawfish Boil is all about: good food, friends, and music. Recent artists include Fergie, Train, Snoop Dogg, Katy Perry, Jason Mraz, LL Cool J, Goo Goo Dolls, and many other pop, rap, and contemporary rock acts. Recently, the event has been held outside at the Birmingham Jefferson Convention Complex. General tickets are $20 in advance, and VIP tickets are $75 per day. Tickets cover all artists' performances. Nope, admission to the festival does not include a plate of hot Louisiana crawfish, potatoes, and corn—but nice try.

ALYS STEPHENS CENTER WOMEN WHO ROCK FESIVAL
Alys Robinson Stephens Performing Arts Center
1200 10th Ave. South, Birmingham
(205) 975-2787
www.alysstephens.org

The first week of April, UAB's Alys Robinson Stephens Performing Arts Center celebrates women making significant contributions to the arts with a week of performances, lectures, discussions, and events. The week culminates with the southeast's most elegant celebration of the arts, the VIVA Health Starlight Gala, a black-tie evening that has featured headliners such as Diana Krall, Queen Latifah, The Pointer Sisters, Natalie Cole, and Frederica van Stade. Admission to festival events varies.

MAY

DO DAH DAY
Caldwell and Rhodes Parks, Highland Avenue, Birmingham
www.dodahday.org

How to explain Do Dah Day? From a small party more than 30 years ago to benefit local charities like the Birmingham Zoo and Avondale Library to a full-blown festival for animal lovers and their four-footed friends, Do Dah Day in historic Caldwell and Rhodes parks regularly draws 40,000 people from all over the country. Look for the Do Dah Eve Party, a kickoff event held the night before the festival, where the Do Dah Day King and Queen are crowned. Unlike traditional politics those running for King and Queen can buy the election: Raise the most money for charity and the title is yours. Bands play throughout the day, but the highlight for most is the parade that starts promptly at 11:01 a.m. Sat. Children will love the fun costumes, dressed-up dogs and cats, and general frivolity. Kids will enjoy face painting, hair weaving, crafts, T-shirt art contest, and other children's activities. Since 1992 the festival has raised more than $500,000 for local animal shelters. Admission to the event is free but donations are welcome.

✴PEPPER PLACE SATURDAY MARKET
Pepper Place
2829 2nd Ave. South, Birmingham
(205) 802-2100
www.pepperplacemarket.com

Starting in the middle of May and running until Oct, the Pepper Place Saturday Market pairs up nicely with Alabama's extended growing season: Sure, it's a "Summer Market," but the folks don't get too fussy about the terminology. Expect the best chefs and local purveyors to put on cooking demonstrations and seminars during the market time, from 7 a.m. to noon, rain or shine in the summer time. Live music is always on hand, usually on multiple stages at the same time. But don't let the dates fool you: The overwhelming success of the Saturday market means a Spring Market (mid-Apr to early May) and a Fall Market (mid-Oct to the first Sat in December) keep the tradition alive and growing! In the spring, look for the seedlings and young plants you need to get your garden on at home. In the fall, it's all about fresh apples, squash, pumpkins, and other items you'll want for your harvest table.

REGIONS TRADITION
(205) 967-4745
www.regionstradition.com

Renamed the Regions Tradition (formerly the Regions Charity Classic), this major stop on the Champions Tour is a Birmingham event that draws some of the biggest names in golf. It is the first of five major championships on the Champions Tour. As Birmingham is known for its support of the sport of golf, the event is a hot ticket in town. The tournament was previously played at the Robert Trent Jones Trail at Ross Bridge in Hoover, Alabama, but in 2011 organizers changed both the location as well as the event's name. Past champions of the Tradition include greats like Jack Nicklaus, Raymond Floyd, Tom Watson, and Lee Trevino. Shoal Creek, a Jack Nicklaus–designed golf course, hosted two PGA Championships in 1984 and 1990. It is widely recognized as one of the country's great courses. Children's Hospital of Alabama is the primary focus of the event's charitable contributions.

WE LOVE HOMEWOOD DAY
Patriot Park or Central Park
1632 Oxmoor Rd., Homewood
(205) 332-6700
www.homewoodparks.com
A celebration of the history and heritage of this small Birmingham suburb, We Love Homewood Day is just what it purports to be: an opportunity for residents to sound their own horn a bit and show what a great place the city is to live. Usually alternating between Patriot Park and Central Park, the day of festivities includes a colorful parade from the Homewood Public Library to the Edgewood Business District where a Quality of Life award is given to a local citizen of note. Children line the parade route waiting for the inevitable candy thrown from passing antique cars and trucks. A festival with carnival rides, games, and fun is held in the park. A Family Street Dance with live music in Edgewood at the intersection of Broadway Street and Oxmoor Road is the culminating event as the streets are closed to traffic and hundreds in the nearby neighborhoods walk and push strollers to Edgewood to join in the festivities.

JUNE

ALABAMA SPORTS FESTIVAL
Various locations
www.alagames.com

Held in Birmingham for the past few years, the Alabama Sports Festival is a massive weekend of athletic competitions in a variety of sports. Archery, basketball, bass fishing, disc golf, flag football, gymnastics, soccer, swimming, taekwondo, track and field, volleyball, and wrestling are just a few of the sports represented in what has been called "Alabama's Olympics." The athlete of the year is selected from the participants, and the event also hands out scholarships for qualifying students. The Alabama Sports Festival has awarded more than 300 academic scholarships for a total of more than $200,000 to young students. By placing first, second, or third in the festival, participants are qualified to compete in the State Games of America, a national competition among states that is usually held in San Diego.

BUMP 'N GRIND
Oak Mountain State Park, South Trailhead
877 John Findlay III Dr., Pelham
www.bumpngrindrace.com
It's hot, sweaty, and buggy, but that's just part of the attraction of the Bump 'N Grind mountain bike race at Oak Mountain State Park. The course start is easy to find: Head past the beach and canoe rental area to the last parking lot before the road up to Peavine Falls. Exciting changes are afoot as Birmingham Urban Mountain Pedalers (BUMP) expanded Oak Mountain's mountain-bike trails in early 2010, completing a new 3.5-mile-long singletrack with exciting turns and downhill action. Bump 'N Grind spectators must pay a $3 entrance fee for the park. Race participants must register in advance—there are no race day registrations. Participants are required to hold a USA Cycling license. The racing entry

fee for riders is $45 with discounts given for early-bird registrations.

i The best places for families and friends to watch loved ones flying down the trail at the Bump 'N Grind are Blood Rock and Johnson's Mountain. But really, any comfortable spot in the shade where you can see riders is probably fine. Bring your own water.

MAGIC CITY BREWFEST
Sloss Furnaces Historic Landmark
20 32nd St. North, Birmingham
www.magiccitybrewfest.com

With the massive industrial setting of rusting metal and tall smokestacks, Sloss Furnaces is an ideal outdoor/indoor spot to host beer and food festivals like Magic City Brewfest. The number of beers from around the world available to sample, typically more than 200, is truly amazing. Beer samples are in two-ounce pours. Now that the Free the Hops' Gourmet Beer Bill passed in 2009, beers with an alcohol by volume (ABV) of greater than 6 percent are now legal in Alabama. This huge step in bringing the world's best beers to Alabama has meant Magic City Brewfest can offer the high-quality beer that aficionados love. Tickets are sold online as well as at retail locations in Birmingham, and patrons have a choice between "beer only" sampling tickets ($26 in advance or $34 at the gate) or "beer and food" sampling tickets ($36 in advance or $44 at the gate) for each of the festival's two nights. Be aware that the event's overwhelming success has meant that "beer and food" tickets often sell out. There is a nominal fee for parking.

RICKWOOD CLASSIC
Rickwood Field
1137 2nd Ave. West, Birmingham
(205) 458-8161
www.rickwood.com

Rickwood Field, the oldest baseball professional baseball park still in use, has seen its share of stars. Babe Ruth, Ty Cobb, "Shoeless" Joe Jackson, Dizzy Dean, Leroy "Satchell" Paige, and Birmingham's own Willy Mays all played in the historic ballpark in West End. The Rickwood Classic, an annual event at Rickwood Field where a regulation baseball game in this historic park is played between teams in authentic period uniforms, is a major fundraiser for the park, attracting nearly 10,000 baseball supporters. Organized by the Friends of Rickwood, the game is a vintage affair, a throwback to the romanticized days of baseball's youth and the country's fascination with "America's Game." Indeed, down to the faux vintage signage in the outfield, recreated advertisements from American Cast Iron Pipe Company, US Steel, Grape Ola, and others. Be sure to take the time to wander the field and admire the posters, photos, and historic memorabilia.

i For beer-lovers in Birmingham, no organization has been so beneficial as Free the Hops, a grassroots non-profit organization trying to bring the highest-quality beers in the world to Alabama. If you support that cause, see www.freethehops.org to learn how you can help.

TANNEHILL GEM, MINERAL, AND JEWELRY SHOW
Tannehill Historical State Park
12632 Confederate Pkwy., McCalla
(205) 477-5711
www.tannehill.org

For those not acquainted with the Tannehill Gem, Mineral, and Jewelry Show, it may seem an obscure, minor side note. Don't tell that to the Alabama Mineral & Lapidary Society that presents the weekend show (www.lapidaryclub.com) or any of the zealous collectors on hand for this popular regional event. The 2011 event marked the 38th annual show. Hourly door prizes, gem and mineral exhibits, gemstones, beads, fossils, lapidary working techniques, as well as events and areas just for the children are just a few of the items of interest at the show. In fact, this show is for every young boy and girl who ever brought home a rock to save. The event is free with a paid $3 admission to Tannehill Historical State Park in McCalla. Admission for children ages 6 to 11 is $1.

i If you're a fan of gems, rocks, tools, knives, and other treasures, be sure to visit Tannehill Trade Days Mar through Nov on the third weekend of each month. Bring goodies to trade and barter!

JULY

THUNDER ON THE MOUNTAIN
Vulcan Park and Museum
1701 Valley View Dr., Birmingham
(205) 933-1409
www.visitvulcan.com
If it is the evening of July 4th and you are in Birmingham, chances are you are looking up at Red Mountain waiting for the Thunder on the Mountain fireworks display to begin. Under *Vulcan* professional pyrotechnics set up some $40,000 worth of rockets that blast exciting patterns and colors into the Birmingham sky. Several local radio stations typically broadcast the specially recorded musical soundtrack that accompanies the 20-minute Fourth of July fireworks celebration. Local Fox affiliate station Fox6 WBRC also broadcasts the fireworks show. Just about anywhere in Homewood's downtown or Southside's Five Points South offers superb vantage points, as does Highway 31 as it rises uphill into Vestavia Hills.

AUGUST

BIRMINGHAM ARTS AND MUSIC FESTIVAL
Various locations
www.baamfest.com
A week-long celebration advancing the city's cultural and musical arts scene, Birmingham Arts and Music Festival (BAAM) takes place in a wide variety of venues in the city. Modeled on Austin, Texas' enormously successful South-by-Southwest festival, BAAM draws patrons to art centers, nightclubs, bars, and theaters that expose new audiences to some of the best entertainment Birmingham has to offer. Live music, films, drum and guitar clinics, children's workshops, open mics, even working seminars on the business side of music are all on display.

STOKIN' THE FIRE BBQ AND MUSIC FESTIVAL
Sloss Furnaces National Historic Landmark
20 32nd St. North, Birmingham
(205) 324-1911
www.slossfurnaces.com
Barbecue and rock-n-roll are two items best served hot, and that's what patrons get at Stokin' the Fire BBQ and Music Festival at Sloss Furnaces in July. Grills are fired up, the sweet smell of chicory and pork wafts across the grounds, and smoke is rising as

more than 70 professional barbecue teams from around the country compete for tens of thousands of dollars in cash and prizes. This is not the place for vegetarians. A world-class BBQ competition sanctioned by the prestigious Kansas City Barbeque Society, Stokin' the Fire also features as many as 50 amateur teams grilling pork, chicken, and beef to claim the top prizes. Rock bands, children's areas, and lots of good eats complete this two-day affair. Take the time to wander the grounds and gaze in amazement at the souped-up BBQ rigs and trailers that the contestants bring: This is serious business for those competing in the festivities. Admission is $10 for Fri, $15 for Sat. There is a nominal fee for parking in the Sloss Furnaces lot.

SEPTEMBER

ARTWALK
Various downtown locations
Loft District, Birmingham
www.birminghamartwalk.org
A juried art show displaying all over downtown Birmingham, Artwalk is unique in that artists show their work in an assortment of ground-level businesses and residences, primarily clustered around the Loft District along 1st and 2nd avenues. The work of more than 100 visual artists, musicians, and street performers are on display in a festival atmosphere. In the past couple of years, more than 10,000 people have attended. It's a clever way to attract visitors to the area to see the increasing number of galleries, businesses, lofts, and restaurants and bars now found within a few square blocks. If you haven't been here in awhile, you'll probably be surprised to find establishments like Urban Standard, Rogue Tavern, What's on 2nd, Beta Pictoris, and others. The event

is free, though the cost of the artwork on display ranges wildly.

BIRMINGHAM SHOUT GAY + LESBIAN FILM FESTIVAL OF ALABAMA
Various downtown locations
2310 1st Ave. North, Birmingham
(205) 324-0888
www.bhamshout.com
In previous years Birmingham SHOUT Gay + Lesbian Film Festival ran independently of the Sidewalk Moving Picture Festival, showing features, documentaries, and short films of interest to the GLBT communities. Artists and filmmakers both established and new interact with attendees while panels on subjects such as diversity in filmmaking, documentary filmmaking abroad, digital rights, and more offer substance. But most of all, for fans of cinema, SHOUT offers a fresh look at some of the most innovative new films that appeal to the GLBT communities. Look for special SHOUT opening night parties, award shows, and more. If one wishes to participate, volunteers are always needed.

✳GREEK FOOD FESTIVAL
Holy Trinity–Holy Cross Greek Orthodox Cathedral
307 19th St. South, Birmingham
(205) 716-3086
www.birminghamgreekfestival.net
After close to 40 years of delicious food, festive music and dancing, and Greek culture, the Greek Food Festival needs no introduction to anyone who has lived in Birmingham for even a few years. For those who have not experienced this three-day weekend celebration, now is the time. Begun in 1972 by the Ladies Philoptochos Society, the event has grown to massive proportions and draws

visitors and volunteers from neighboring states. Held downtown at the Holy Trinity–Holy Cross Greek Orthodox Cathedral, the food-ordering process marches along in military-like precision.

Be sure to head upstairs to sample the desserts like baklava, loukoumathes, melomakarona, and of course, the kourambethes, Greek wedding cookies sprinkled with powdered sugar. If you are sweet, maybe the nice ladies who cooked the desserts will share a recipe with you—be sure to make it because they'll certainly remember you next year and inquire about how it turned out! Yes, for those on the run, there is a take-out line—for orders of 10 or more items, call or use the printable online menu to fax the order. The frozen pans of pasticho to go are a popular tasty takeaway. Opa!

i In recent years, the city has taken to partially closing off 19th Street South to accommodate the Greek Food Festival spillover crowds, so be aware that tables may be set up in the street for dining. If the crowd is too large for your taste, buy takeout and walk to the nearby Railroad Park 2 blocks north on 1st Avenue South.

*SIDEWALK MOVING PICTURE FESTIVAL
Various locations downtown
2310 1st Ave. North, Birmingham (office)
(205) 324-0888
www.sidewalkfest.com
A celebration of independent cinema, Sidewalk Moving Picture Festival in downtown Birmingham has been embraced by the greater community since its founding in 1999. The festival attracts national and international filmmakers like John C. Reilly and John Sayles as well as highlights the best of independent cinema in the region. There are panels, meet-and-greets, workshops, and films for children. Birmingham, a city of over a million, has plenty of new multiplex theaters but not one active independent theater, a potential reason residents enjoy a look at fresh, new films that will in all likelihood never be seen on a large screen in the state (other than Montgomery's excellent Capri Theatre, www.capritheatre.org). Identified by *TIME* magazine as a "film festival for the rest of us," the festival is a must-see for film fans. Showings are held in the Alabama Theatre, Carver Theatre, Birmingham Museum of Art, Civil Rights Institute, and other venues.

WHISTLE STOP FESTIVAL
1912 1st Ave. North, Irondale
(205) 297-9897
www.irondalewhistlestopfestival.com
The 1987 Fannie Flagg novel, *Fried Green Tomatoes at the Whistle Stop Cafe,* popularized Irondale, a small railroad town east of Birmingham. Both the book and the movie of the same name are loosely based on the city of Irondale and the Irondale Cafe. The Whistle Stop Festival, set right in the downtown that is split by the railroad tracks, is the kind of small-town gathering most communities would trade their eyeteeth for. Live music, vintage fire engines, funnel cakes, old cars, children's games, and plenty of good food are just a few of the many attractions and activities in this great little town during the festival. Yes, you can get plenty of fried green tomatoes at the Irondale Cafe!

OCTOBER

ANTIQUES AT THE GARDENS
Birmingham Botanical Gardens
2612 Lane Park Rd., Birmingham
(205) 414-3950
www.bbgardens.org/antiques

A three-day event, Antiques at The Gardens: Heirlooms in Bloom, is Birmingham Botanical Gardens' largest annual fundraiser. Sophisticated antiques dealers from across the country present their rugs, furniture, artwork, jewelry, silver, and more. Each year a lecture series features nationally renowned floral arrangers, event planners, and interior designers. The events are an excellent opportunity to solicit expert gardening advice from both fellow attendees as well as The Gardens' staff. Prior to the antiques show, an elegant black-tie First Look Party honors donors and sponsors, as well as the committee that organizes the events. The last Antiques at The Gardens raised more than $291,000 for educational programs at The Gardens, exposing thousands of Birmingham area school children to nature in the Alabama's most-visited free attraction.

BARBER VINTAGE FESTIVAL
Barber Vintage Motorsports Museum
6030 Barber Motorsports Pkwy., Leeds
(205) 699-7275
www.barbervintagefestival.org

For anyone who loves vintage motorcycles, the Barber Vintage Festival is for you. Really, it's like seeing thousands of adults as happy as kids to be discussing, viewing, learning, and riding some glorious old motorcycles among friends. A moonlight benefit dinner and live auction generates funds for the Barber Vintage Motorsports Museum. Need parts? Bring your used parts, literature, or gear to the Swap Meet and trade with over 400 vendors with motorcycle gear and goods. Expect racing on the Barber track, tech seminars, cross-country races, vintage motor cross, an air show, and more vintage vehicles than one can imagine. There's even the Century Race, a motorcycle race among bikes that are at least 100 years old! Visitors can tent camp or park their motor home at the park for the duration of the festival; just be sure to purchase your camping pass in advance. Day passes are available starting at $20 and 3-day admission is $45.

BLOUNT COUNTRY COVERED BRIDGE FESTIVAL
Downtown Oneonta
(205) 274-2153
www.blountoneontachamber.org/
covered-bridge-festival

The Blount County Covered Bridge Festival, set in downtown Oneonta some 30 miles northeast of Birmingham, set out nearly 3 decades ago to highlight the wonderful old covered bridges of this wooded, mountainous region. From the treasures like Swann Covered Bridge and Horton Mill Covered Bridge to the Easley Covered Bridge and the ghostly abandoned Stracener Bridge over the Locust Fork of the Black Warrior River, the range and beauty of these bridges is remarkable. Swann, a lattice truss spanning 324 feet across the Locust Fork, is the longest covered bridge in the state and one of the longest in the country. Horton Mill is the highest covered bridge in the United States. The festival itself, with a quilt show, river walk, golf tournament, arts and crafts, pancake breakfast, 5K run, car show, and Miss Covered Bridge Pageant has plenty of activities to entertain just about anyone. Downtown Oneonta is covered in vendors selling everything from handmade jewelry to festival food. The bridges of Blount County are one romance novel away from being world-famous.

✳BLUFF PARK ART SHOW
Bluff Park
517 Cloudland Dr., Hoover
(205) 822-0078
www.bluffparkartassociation.org
What started in 1963 as a small fundraiser for the Bluff Park Elementary School library (and raised $600) now attracts some 30,000 people from across the country for the one-day event. The Bluff Park Art Show, held the first Sat in Oct, has become a rite of fall for many Birmingham residents. The park itself, set on 4 wooded, rocky acres atop Shades Mountain, makes for a delightful setting for the 100-odd artists invited to show their work. The artists work in a variety of mediums: painting, jewelry, clay, sculpture, photography, fiber, mixed media, glass, and more. Today, the show's success means the Bluff Park Art Association donates significant funds to entities such as the Birmingham Museum of Art, the Alabama Symphony, Space One Eleven, as well as local public school libraries and music programs. The show runs from 9 a.m. to 5 p.m. Admission is free.

i Since Bluff Park Art Show is one day only, arrive early if you plan on parking anywhere near the park itself. But no worries for late-comers: The barbecue and bake sales will still be going strong but you will need to use the free shuttle buses that regularly ferry patrons to and from the show.

FIESTA
Regions Park
Stadium Trace Parkway, Hoover
www.fiestahbc.com
A celebration of Hispanic culture, Fiesta started in 2001 as a project of the Hispanic Business Council of the Birmingham Regional Chamber of Commerce (now the Birmingham Business Alliance) to promote the customs and traditions of the many Latino people who call Birmingham and Alabama home. The goal was to educate the mainstream public about the art, music, food, dance, and culture of the many Hispanic countries represented here. After many years hosting the event downtown, the organizers relocated to Regions Park in Hoover, a city well represented by a large Hispanic population. The one-day event attracts more than 20,000 attendees, many of which represent the 20 countries showcased in this community experience. Admission is $5, and children under 12 are free. Bring an appetite, an open mind, and expect to have fun.

MAGIC CITY CLASSIC
Legion Field
Alabama Sports Foundation
100 Grandview Place, Suite 110,
Birmingham
(205) 967-4745
www.themagiccityclassic.com
Since 1924 the Magic City Classic has featured a gridiron battle for bragging rights between Alabama A&M University and Alabama State University, two of Alabama's historically black universities. It has been played annually at Legion Field since 1946. It's an intense but good-natured affair (Alabama A&M holds a slight advantage in the

series) but one of the main attractions is the parade and Battle of the Bands fiercely waged between each school's marching bands. The parade, which runs along 19th Street North to 4th Avenue North then loops back through the Civil Rights District, is an affair to behold: Numerous middle and high school band strut their stuff. Recent ambassadors and parade grand masters include Earvin "Magic" Johnson, LL Cool J, Sinbad, Evander Holyfield, and other celebrities and sports figures of note. Tickets to the Classic start at $20.

MT. LAUREL HARVEST FESTIVAL
Mt. Laurel Avenue, Mt. Laurel
(205) 408-8696
www.mtlaurel.com
Located on Country Road 41 just south of Double Oak Mountain, Mt. Laurel is a self-contained, planned New Urbanist community with schools, restaurants, shops, and businesses all within a short walking distance from each other. Planned as an antidote to modern sprawl, Mt. Laurel has its own 25-acre organic farm, and the Harvest Festival is a chance to show off their farmers' market, restaurants, local artisans, and shops. Look for fresh cabbage, broccoli, winter squash, and if the weather's right, maybe even some late-fall tomatoes hanging on in Alabama's warm climate. Kids will enjoy the usual run of fun inflatable playgrounds, fresh-squeezed lemonade, and other activities. Look for the corresponding spring festival in Apr. Admission is free.

NOVEMBER

MOSS ROCK FESTIVAL
The Preserve, Hoover
www.mossrockfestival.com

With 15,000 visitors the Moss Rock Festival has continued to grow each year since its inception in 2005. With artwork, green living ideas, products and services, live music, delicious food, geocaching, fuel-efficient car exhibitions, and more, Moss Rock is the festival for those concerned with the environment and their place in it. Indeed, the eco-ideas on LEED certification, recycling, and the many green exhibitors makes the festival a fun and informative alternative to just another great cultural event. For parents, your children will not even know they are learning something about their environment: They'll just be having fun. Parking and free shuttle bus service is available in the nearby Regions Park (6000 Stadium Trace, Hoover). Admission is free.

NATIONAL VETERANS DAY PARADE
National Veterans Day in Birmingham
Downtown parade
(205) 325-1432
www.nationalveteransday.org
The traditions of the National Veterans Day Parade are strong in Birmingham. The November 11th parade, which has as many as 5,000 participants, typically centers on a 1.5-mile route that includes 20th Street North and surrounding blocks and features veteran organizations, Boy Scouts, Girl Scouts, military units, and various marching bands and school groups. People march, walk, and ride on cars and float while residents line the parade route to honor veterans past and present. It's an event that draws school children from all over the city and suburbs to join in celebrating our nation's veterans as only Birmingham does.

The Nation's First Veterans Day Parade

There is a reason Birmingham's Veterans Day parade is such a big deal: A World War II veteran, Raymond Weeks, a native of Birmingham, organized the first celebration using the term "Veterans Day." Weeks wanted to honor the people who served during World War II, so he organized the first Veterans Parade in Birmingham in 1947, which led to the passage of a Congressional bill in 1954 renaming November 11th as Veterans Day in honor of all American servicemen and women.

ST. NICHOLAS RUSSIAN/SLAVIC FOOD FESTIVAL

St. Nicholas Russian Orthodox Church
105 Pastor St., Brookside
(205) 674-1325
www.stnicholasbrookside.org

Commonly known as the Russian Food Festival, this delightful little event is a fundraiser for the Russian Orthodox Church in the former mining town of Brookside. Settled by immigrants in the 1880s from Western Ukraine (what's now Slovakia), Brookside today is making a comeback with developments along the adjacent Five Mile Creek Greenway. The charming church, with its cupola topped by an onion-shaped dome, indicates immediately to visitors that Brookside has a singular history and culture. But for attendees, it's the stuffed holupki (cabbage), klobasa and kraut, potato dumplings, baked piroshki (meat pie), borscht, piroshky, and other delicious Slavic foods that cause the line to run out the church door and down the steps outside. End your meal with some spiced Russian tea or tea from the samovar and some kolach, baked goods, and other delicious sweets. While you're waiting for the Russian dancing to begin, be sure to tour the old temple building.

VULCAN RUN

Linn Park
Vulcan Run
P.O. Box 59349, Birmingham, 35259
www.vulcanrun.com

Since the first race in 1975, the Vulcan Run has been Birmingham's premier 10K running event, not only due to its longevity as the city's longest running road race but also because of its immense popularity. The race started when running was just taking off in the mid-1970s and today more than 2,000 people run it annually. The race starts at 8 a.m. and by 9 a.m. runners are enjoying a beer, massage, and barbecue in Boutwell Auditorium, listening to music and talking about how they could have shaved off some seconds from their time. It's a fun community event and a chance to talk, meet new and old friends, or run as fast as you possibly can. At 9:30 a.m. the Magic City Mile, a one-mile fun run kicks off, giving kids a chance to follow in their parents' footsteps. The race benefits Vulcan Park and Museum as well as the Birmingham Track Club. The race starts and finishes in Linn Park at the heart of downtown Birmingham. Cost is $30.

DECEMBER

**JINGLE BELL RUN/WALK FOR
  ARTHRITIS**
Underwood Park
1021 26th St. South, Birmingham
Arthritis Foundation
(800) 283-7800
www.arthritis.org/jingle-bell-run
One of many such events across the country, the Jingle Bell Run/Walk is a fun and festive 5K and one-mile fun run fit for the whole family. In fact, the sillier your Christmas costume—think reindeer antlers, jingling bells, and Santa Claus hats for starts—the better. The popular Santa Chase is a 100-yard dash for children 12 and under. The race starts and finishes at Underwood Park, located on the Southside behind St. Vincent's Hospital on 26th Street South and 10th Avenue South. Registration starts at $30. The Santa Chase is $25. But don't let that stop you from forming your own fundraising/racing team to raise as much money as you can to support the Arthritis Foundation.

SHOPPING

Birmingham residents have recently been recognized for being as stylish as we've always known we've been. Magazines like *Traditional Home* have celebrated the fine homes—and furnishings available for them—located in the city. The fashion magazine *Lucky* has singled out a handful of women's boutiques, and *GQ* and *Esquire* have both given a nod to one of our local menswear stores. We have a century-old jewelry store that's been a tastemaker, and required bridal registry, for four generations of Alabama couples. Our burgeoning food and farm community, as well as our internationally celebrated chefs who rely on the local food produced here, have made food and ingredients something to shop for in Birmingham. Pottery. Antiques. Books. Art. Birmingham is chock-full of remarkable shops, boutiques and galleries that attract not only locals, but also residents from throughout the state and region. From luxury stores not found within 150 miles to tiny nooks where locals still practice a craft and sell their handmade wares, Birmingham has it all.

The region is also blessed with clusters of walkable shopping districts, be they historic, new, or within large malls, that make the shopping experience especially pleasurable. From the many villages of Mountain Brook to downtown Homewood, the old-fashioned storefronts still promote toys, gifts, jewelry, clothing, linens, sporting goods, shoes, furniture, hardware, and groceries—just as these old communities always have. One can park in one spot and spend the day strolling the sidewalks, stopping for breakfast, lunch, coffee, drinks, or dinner, and never have to move the car.

OVERVIEW

New shopping centers like The Summit are completely walkable, or navigable by shuttle, and feature national high-end chain stores and department stores. Large malls, such as the **Riverchase Galleria,** maintain the indoor shopping concept, and offer seemingly endless shop and food choices in a controlled climate. But the newest big addition to Birmingham's retail scene is **The Shops of Grand River,** a $127-million outlet mall off I-20 in Leeds. With high-end shops like Brooks Brothers, Talbot's, DKNY, Coach,

and Jos. A. Bank, as well as favorites such as Nike, Ghirardelli, Izod, and Polo Ralph Lauren, the new mall has something for everyone.

Whatever you're searching for, in whatever environment you prefer, you can find it in Birmingham, and you'll meet some incredibly friendly people and have a great time to boot. Birmingham is a great shopping town, but remember, this listing is only a survey of the range of stores and shops in the area—it is by no means comprehensive.

ANTIQUES

5TH AVENUE ANTIQUES
2410 5th Ave. South, Birmingham
(205) 320-0500
www.5thavenueantiques.com
Located in Southside's antiques district, 5th Avenue Antiques is a large building filled with booths managed by multiple sellers. Look for estate jewelry, furniture, books, rugs, and other finds. With more than 30,000 square feet of space, it's one of the largest antique malls in the area. More than 100 antique dealers sell their goods in the store.

✳ARCHITECTURAL HERITAGE
200 28th St. South, Birmingham
(205) 322-3538
www.architecturalheritage.com
A unique store specializing in architectural salvage, this treasure trove is located in the Pepper Place shopping district and is filled to the rafters with old doors, windows, furniture, statuary, lighting, and hardware. The 6,500-square-foot warehouse is complemented by an adjacent garden with more distinctive architectural elements. Look for limestone mantels from France, terra cotta tile from Europe, planters, baptismal fonts, and more.

> **i** Since new crates full of items arrive on a regular basis at Architectural Heritage, check their website's homepage for a convenient link to view the contents of the latest new container that arrives.

ARGENT
2949 18th St. South, Homewood
(205) 871-4221
www.argentantiques.com

Specializing in silver and other fine metals, Argent is well known in the city not only for its antique inventory but also for its appraisal services. Antique tea services, complete place settings, jewelry, furniture, accessories, paintings, and watches are found inside this one-of-a-kind store, located in the heart of downtown Homewood. Close to dozens of other shops and restaurants within a short walking distance, Argent regularly get new shipments of antiques from the United Kingdom and France—check their website for posted pictures of new items as they arrive.

ON-A-SHOESTRING
601 Shades Crest Rd., Hoover
(205) 822-8741
Perched high up on the ridge of Shades Crest Mountain in the historic enclave of Bluff Park, On-A-Shoestring promises a few hours of happy discovery to the customer who made the drive up the hill. With an old caboose parked out front and rows upon rows of old windows and other finds nestled about the property, this slightly ramshackle, but utterly charming, rambling building won't disappoint. Be sure to grab lunch at the diner across the street or at the Tip Top Grill, with its jaw-dropping views of the Shannon and Oxmoor Valleys below.

✳SOHO RETRO
2805 18th St. South, Homewood
(205) 870-7655
So named for the large SoHo development in the heart of Homewood, this new shop is also inspired by the funky boutiques of the New York landmark neighborhood. Recently opened by two long-time fans and collectors of mid-century modern furniture and accessories, Soho Retro has the Danish Modern sofa, shag rug, mirrored bar, and

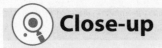 **Close-up**

Museum Gift Shops

If you're looking for a truly remarkable item with a significant connection to Birmingham, be sure to visit one of the fine museum gift shops in town, including **Vulcan Park and Museum, The Birmingham Museum of Art, The McWane Science Center,** or **The Birmingham Botanical Gardens.** Whether you're seeking a toy for the kids, a gift for a loved one, or just something special for yourself, don't miss these beautifully stocked, gracefully organized shops, most of which are staffed by local volunteers who will be happy to not only direct you to the right thing but to tell you a little more about their home town. Residents know that these boutiques are great shopping resources and regularly add them to their rounds.

At Vulcan you'll find miniatures of the God of the Forge, as well as books, T-shirts, and other miscellany celebrating Birmingham's industrial heritage. The Birmingham Museum of Art has lovely glassware, ceramics, art kits, books, and home-decor items inspired by its permanent or rotating collections. Don't miss the jewelry case or the kids' gift ideas. The McWane Science Center gift shop is a dream for any science lover—no matter their age. Educational toys and books, stuffed animals, chemistry sets—it's all there. And lastly, for garden-lovers, there is no place better than **Leaf & Petal** at The Gardens. From living plants to garden accessories to garden-inspired stationery, kids' toys, clothing, jewelry or artwork, there's something wonderful inside this lovely shop located at the entrance to The Birmingham Botanical Gardens.

driftwood lamps you're looking for. Don't miss the jewelry collection near the counter, the antique table linens, and the fabulous lawn furniture out back.

TRICIA'S TREASURES
2700 19th Place South, Homewood
(205) 871-9779

There's so much inside the large building that houses Tricia's Treasures that you're almost overwhelmed when you walk in. But take a deep breath and begin your journey of discovery, making sure to look up, down and in between, otherwise you'll miss an amazing find. From architectural salvage outside the front door to furniture, light fixtures, rugs, books, artwork, findings and fixtures, toys, and even vintage clothing, one could easily pass several hours inside

Tricia's Treasures without realizing time had passed. Across the side street from The Alabama Booksmith, Tricia's could be one half of a blissful day for the book and antique lover.

WHAT'S ON SECOND
2306 2nd Ave. North, Birmingham
(205) 322-2688

This funky emporium resides along the trendy block of 2nd Avenue North in downtown Birmingham that's also home to the hip Rogue Tavern, Urban Standard coffeehouse, Pale Eddie's Pour House bar, Faith Skate Supply, and Charm jewelry boutique. What's On Second has become a key destination not only for downtown workers looking for a fun way to pass a lunch hour, but a serious stop for young hipsters searching for vintage clothing and home accessories.

Look for T-shirts from the '70s, old toys and equipment, fantastic lamps, and the odd outdoor furniture set, often displayed on the sidewalk out front.

BOOKSTORES

2ND & CHARLES
1705 Montgomery Hwy., Hoover
(205) 444-0509
www.2ndandcharles.com
A novel new take on the used bookstore theme, 2nd & Charles is located in a strip mall across from Riverchase Galleria at the I-459 and Highway 31 intersection. It's something of have-one-trade-one, need-one-buy-one shop for books, DVDs, game systems, audio books, vinyl records, and CDs. Drop off up to 3 bins of used items per customer per day, go shop around while the employees evaluate your books or CDs, then look for your claim number on one of their screens spread around the store to learn the value of your items. You can take cash, store credit, or, if you aren't satisfied, take all your used goodies back and go home.

✳ALABAMA BOOKSMITH
26 19th Place South, Homewood
(205) 870-4242
www.alabamabooksmith.com
When it comes to literary events and book signings in Birmingham, no bookstore shines as brightly as the Alabama Booksmith. Known for its collection of Birmingham- and Alabama-related literature as well as its signed first editions club, the store is the first place to go if you're looking for a signed copy of Harper Lee's *To Kill a Mockingbird* or the latest from Isabel Allende, Richard Russo, Sena Jeter Naslund, Pat Conroy, Edna O'Brien, and Anne Rice—all of whom have done book signings at the Alabama Booksmith. Alabama Booksmith frequently sells books at various literary events in different locations about town as well. Owner Jake Reiss (whose son opened the well-known A Cappella Books in Atlanta's bohemian Little 5 Points district), has found his niche in Birmingham and has been rewarded with a loyal local following.

BARNES & NOBLE
Patton Creek Shopping Center
171 Main St., Hoover
(205) 682-4467
www.barnesandnoble.com
With two stores in the Birmingham area, the book giant bookends two of the larger shopping areas on either side of I-459 in Birmingham: Patton Creek/Riverchase Galleria (address above) and The Summit (201 Summit Blvd., Suite 100; 205-298-0665). A variety of programs are offered, such as book signings by local and international authors and story-time activities for preschoolers and older children. Complimentary Wi-Fi is available throughout both stores, making their open cafe and lunch counter a popular spot for students and businessmen and women on the go. The children's section includes a large colorful stage for special presentations and readings, and the music section offers listening stations. The Summit location seems to consistently have more programs and events scheduled.

BOOKS-A-MILLION
Multiple locations
www.booksamillion.com
This Birmingham-based book chain, the third-largest bookstore chain in the country, is headquartered here in town. In addition to more than 200 stores nationwide, there are several stores in the Birmingham area. Each

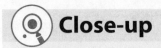

Close-up

Birmingham's Literary History

To define terms, Birmingham literature is simply literature by Birmingham writers as well as literature about Birmingham. This would include Tobias Wolff *(This Boy's Life)*, Edward O. Wilson *(The Ants, The Diversity of Life)*, even Martin Luther King Jr. *("Letters from a Birmingham Jail")* if you stretch it. It would include Pulitzer Prize–winner Walker *Percy (The Moviegoer, The Last Gentleman)*, who was born in Birmingham and lived here until his teens. John Beecher *(Report to the Stockholders, To Live and Die in Dixie)*, a member of the prominent New England abolitionist family, was born in Birmingham in 1902 and was blacklisted during the McCarthy era. Barry Hannah *(Geronimo Rex)* and Richard Yates *(Revolutionary Road)* taught at the University of Alabama, and Gay Talese *(A Writer's Life)* also attended UA. Richard North Patterson *(No Safe Place, Eyes of a Child)*, an attorney in Birmingham, took creative writing at UAB and has since sold over 40 million books. Other Birmingham writers include Charles Ghigna *(One Hundred Shoes)*, Daniel Wallace *(Big Fish)*, and Fannie Flagg *(Fried Green Tomatoes at the Whistle-Stop Cafe)*.

There was a minor literary revival in Birmingham's Southside neighborhood in the 1960s and 1970s when Gene Crutcher's City Lights Bookstore helped create an intellectual cafe society for a generation of young writers like Allen Barra *(Yogi Berra: Eternal Yankee)*, Steven Ford Brown, Dennis Covington *(Salvation on Sand Mountain)*, Mark Childress *(Crazy in Alabama)*, and Michael Swindle *(Slouching Towards Birmingham)*. Over the past decade or so, the Civil Rights–inspired novels and autobiographies by local writers such as Pulitzer Prize–winning Diane McWhorter *(Carry Me Home)*, Sena Jeter Naslund *(Ahab's Wife, Four Spirits)*, Paul Hemphill *(Leaving Birmingham: Notes of a Native Son)*, Leah Rawls Atkins *(Alabama: History of a Deep South State)*, Howell Raines *(My Soul is Rested,* Executive Editor of *The New York Times)*, and others who experienced the turmoil of 1950s and 1960s in Birmingham seems to signify another renaissance.

stocks a strong local and regional selection of titles as well as maintains a format similar to other large bookstore giants. The bookstores are large and roomy with plenty of seating for those who wish to browse before they buy. There's usually a family area in the children's section so adults can sit and find a peaceful moment while the kids play with the train sets and other toys set out for their amusement. As befitting a local business, Books-A-Million frequently hosts signings and other events with local and national authors. Look for small gift items, stationery, pens, and other literary-inspired products.

i Join the Millionaire's Club to save up to 46 percent off bestsellers at Books-A-Million. By purchasing the club discount card for a small fee, members save an additional 10 percent off all purchases in the stores or online for a year.

LITTLE PROFESSOR BOOKSTORE
2717 18th St. South, Homewood
(205) 870-7461
www.littleprofessorhomewood.com
Conveniently located in downtown Homewood on busy 18th Street, Little Professor is

a great spot to linger when you have a few minutes to kill browsing the latest blockbusters, literature, and children's selections. Upstairs contains a wide range of magazines as well as a token collection of used books, while adjacent to the main bookstore downstairs is Crape Myrtle's Cafe. The helpful and knowledgeable staff is good about making recommendations or running down obscure titles for customers. Little Professor offers a 20-percent discount on book club titles for the groups that order through the store; consequently if you're curious about what the book club crowd is reading in Birmingham, have a gander at their book club selection shelves.

✳REED BOOKS
2021 3rd Ave. North, Birmingham
(205) 326-4460
www.jimreedbooks.com
One of the more original bookstores one is likely to come across, Reed Books is part bookstore, part museum. The full name, Reed Books: The Museum of Fond Memories, pretty much says it all. Owned by author and bibliophile Jim Reed, the store is a jam-packed gallery of books, magazines, newspapers, movie posters, and assorted literary odds and ends. There are some 45,000 items listed on their online inventory, but as Reed will tell you, he has around a quarter of a million more items for sale that are not even catalogued. For those who get a thrill from the neat, orderly organization of the big box bookstores, Reed Books is delightfully antithetical: Piles of books and old magazines cover the store, making it the perfect place to spend a few hours some rainy afternoon. It is a Birmingham original.

CLOTHING

Baby

ONCE UPON A TIME
2900 18th St. South, Homewood
(205) 870-7776
www.onceuponatimellc.com
More traditional and certainly elegant, Once Upon a Time, located in Homewood with another location in Crestline Village in Mountain Brook (229 Country Club Park, 205-870-7772), appeals to those moms who are looking for the lace-and-batiste gowns and silver cups and spoons that so commonly signify babyhood in the south. The shop has furniture, bedding, clothing, gifts, and keepsake pieces that are so fine and lovely you can't help fingering the fine materials. They can also help with monogramming and smocking services—other must-have elements in Birmingham baby wear.

SWADDLE
2825 18th St. South, Homewood
(205) 870-3503
www.swaddleonline.com
Trendy and fun, this little boutique in downtown Homewood hits the sweet spot for young families or mothers-to-be looking for something slightly different from what's for sale at the big-box stores. Owner Marisa Mitchell, herself a mom to two young children, knows full well what hip young mothers are looking for—be that strollers, bedding, clothing, gifts and toys, or home accessories. Upscale moms can get their own designer clothing at neighboring boutiques and stop in to Swaddle to make sure baby is outfitted just as perfectly.

Where Do Tom Cruise, Jay Leno, and Sammy Hagar Buy Their Bikes?

Confederate Motorcycles, (205) 324-9888, www.confederate.com, formerly a New Orleans–based avant garde motorcycle design and construction company, relocated to Birmingham after Hurricane Katrina destroyed their offices. Bad rides in B120 Wraith, P120 Fighter, or the new C3 X132 Hellcat will make you seriously cool-looking. The Wraith features an astonishing throwback design that harkens to the 1930-era styling details. Many of the elements are proprietary designs. When Tom Cruise, Jay Leno, and other customers come to test drive a bike, they head out to Barber Motorsports Park.

Children's

JACK 'N JILL SHOP
2918 18th St. South, Homewood
(205) 879-7681

Located next door to the always-busy family institution that is Sikes Shoes, Jack & Jill is something like stage two for the traditionally clothed southern child. The baby who wore smocked batiste gowns and monogrammed linen will grow into Jack & Jill, known around for their coordinating sets. (Siblings are often dressed similarly in Birmingham, with sister wearing a plaid dress and brother wearing the same plaid for his shorts.) Special-occasion clothing is also a big seller at Jack & Jill: Easter outfits, velvet Christmas dresses and jumpers—all easily matched to a new pair of shoes in the adjoining Sikes.

✳SOCA GIRL
2815 18th St. South, Homewood
(205) 870-1285
www.socagirl.com

Owned by Jeff and Kathleen Tenner, who have the very popular Soca Clothing across the street, Soca Girl brings the same designer style to pre-teen girls who want to be as trendy as their moms and big sisters. The clothes are colorful and fun, and if they could be somehow magically enlarged, would no doubt be snatched up by full-grown women looking for a wardrobe update. The "Soca Girl" is a young woman who knows what she likes and what looks good on her, and also knows where to shop.

Men's

HARRISON'S LIMITED
2801 Cahaba Rd., Mountain Brook
(205) 870-3882
www.harrisonlimited.com

Located at one of the "spokes" of the wheel that makes the five-point intersection in Mountain Brook Village, Harrison's appeals to the traditional man who still appreciates a camel overcoat, a tweed sport jacket, a fine pair of flannel pants, and a pair of Italian loafers. The clothes are not fussy but are extremely well made and will last for years. This is classic menswear, very southern in style and in some ways are only updates to what men in Birmingham wore 50 years ago. If you're looking for a seersucker suit, this would be a good place to start.

MOBLEY & SONS

112 Euclid Ave., Mountain Brook
(205) 870-7929
www.facebook.com/mobleyandsons

A new location for the Tuscaloosa-based menswear store, Birmingham's Mobley & Sons is managed by Hunt Mobley, the latest in the family to take up the mantle. Mostly traditional but not at all stuffy, Mobley & Sons prides itself on its service and ability to custom-fit a man perfectly—in a suit, a pair of slacks, or a fine pair of shoes. Men can browse the off-the-rack selections or meet with a sales associate to choose fabric for a new suit. The tie selection is outstanding.

✳SHAIA'S

2818 18th St. South, Homewood
(205) 871-1312
www.shaias.com

The Shaia family immigrated to Birmingham from Lebanon several generations back and was known for their general mercantile in downtown Homewood. Family descendant Leo Shaia and his son Ken have, over the years, morphed the old store into one of the finest menswear boutiques in the entire region, and are regularly recognized by men's fashion magazines for their taste and style. The very latest designs—in suits as well as casual wear—made by outstanding American and European manufacturers, are standard in Shaia's inventory. The deeply experienced sales staff, some of which have been at Shaia's for decades, can ensure the perfect fit.

Women's

BETSY PRINCE
608 Brookwood Blvd., Homewood
(205) 871-1965

The Perfect Father's Day Present: The Porsche Sport Driving School

You never forget your first Porsche, even if you have to hand over the keys after two exciting days of thrills. The **Porsche Sport Driving School,** (888) 204-7474, www.porschedriving.com, shut down its Florida and Georgia tracks and relocated to Birmingham in 2004 after local milk magnate George Barber built a world-class racing track for his collection of more than 1,200 vintage and modern motorcycles. Thus, the **Barber Motorsports Park and Vintage Motorsports Museum,** www.barbermotorsports.com, was born. Driving Boxsters, 911 Turbos, Carreras, and four-wheel Cayennes on the 16-turn, 2.38-mile circuit is a demanding exercise. Additionally, if the boys get tired of driving their $75,000 toys, the striking museum holds over 1,000 vintage and modern motorcycles and race cars, and is one of the largest such collections in the world (See the Attractions chapter). For those women who understandably want to avoid all the guys in macho overdrive, the school also offers a "Women's Only" two-day course.

This is a shop like no other. Located in the bottom floor of Colonial Brookwood Village, what seems like a standard women's boutique is something completely different, once you walk inside. It's alternative—but highly stylish and trendy—women's fashion. Think Paris, or Milan, or New York. The clothes and accessories of Betsy Prince might push you outside your comfort zone, but will push you into a fantastic new look. Ask the knowledgeable sales staff for help, and don't miss the sale racks—some of the best in town.

EARTH CREATIONS
(800) 792-9868
www.earthcreations.net

When visiting friends out of town (or out of country), you always want to bring a gift that distinctively says "Birmingham" if you can. Wife/husband business partners, Joy Maples and Martin Ledvina, solved that problem with Earth Creations, eco-friendly clothing made in a sustainable manner. Ledvina, a native of the Czech Republic, was intrigued when he noticed that the Alabama red dirt they got on their clothes when mountain biking stubbornly resisted coming out in the wash. With his background in chemistry, Ledvina solved that problem by staining T-shirts with red clay from the area. The "Alabama Dirt Shirt" was born. While that first T-shirt is still a big seller, the duo have branched out into a full line of organic clothing that carries a bit of Alabama with you wherever you go. Order online or purchase at Whole Foods Market off Highway 280, 3100 Cahaba Village Plaza, (205) 912-8400.

✳GUS MAYER
The Summit, Birmingham
(205) 870-3300
www.gusmayer.com

Another long-time Birmingham shopping institution, Gus Mayer is owned by the Pizitz family, which also ran their namesake department store chain for generations. Gus Mayer left its Brookwood Village location for The Summit, hoping to remind an upscale shopping community of the sophisticated clothing, shoes, and accessories they've long been known for. Their shoe department is one of the best in the entire region, and their shoe sales draw long lines of shoppers waiting for a bargain. Regina, a jewelry store located inside Gus Mayer, is also top-notch. This is elegant Birmingham style at its best.

LULIE'S ON CAHABA
2724 Cahaba Rd., Mountain Brook
(205) 871-9696
www.luliesoncahaba.com

Lulie's is a new boutique in Mountain Brook that has quickly gained a following. It's funky and a little edgy, with a great selection of party wear, denim, adorable dresses, and great accessories. Lulie's clothes are unlike most others in town and will certainly make a statement—look for great tops in billowy fabrics accentuated with subtle detailing that sets them apart—ribbons, embroidery, and sequins. If you're going out to a gallery opening, drinks with friends, or one of the big social events in town (like Art on the Rocks at the Birmingham Museum of Art), Lulie's is a great place to get that hip new outfit.

MARELLA/VILLAGE SPORTSWEAR
2415/2421 Montevallo Rd.,
Mountain Brook
(205) 879-5748

These twin shops, owned by the same person and located side by side in Mountain Brook Village, can complete a woman's wardrobe. Filled with the latest styles in clothing, accessories, and shoes, Marella serves a slightly more contemporary client while Village Sportswear appeals to the more traditional dresser. But regardless of which shop you prefer, you'll know that you're buying from one of the most popular, well-respected boutiques in town. The clothes are simply gorgeous.

MIA MODA BOUTIQUE
1425 Montgomery Hwy., Suite 105,
Vestavia Hills
(205) 824-9441
www.miamodaboutique.com

After languishing in its former hidden location in Vestavia, Mia Moda recently moved farther south on Highway 31 to a much more visible, much larger space and their business is suddenly booming. Lush fabrics define the inventory—ruffled cardigan sweaters, velvet tops, sequin skirts, and great bags and other accessories. Mia Moda has a bit of fun to it—the vibe is relaxed and the staff is helpful and friendly, not intimidating like other boutiques in town can be. It's also a little more affordable than other high-end women's shops.

✳THEADORA
2821 18th St. South, Homewood
(205) 879-0335

Owned by two Birmingham sisters of Greek ancestry (Birmingham has a large and vibrant Greek community), Theadora has a distinctly European feel, from the styling of the logo and shop itself to the clothing and accessories inside. With a mission to celebrate global designers that are lesser known in the US, the Sarris sisters have built a reputation in town as style mavens with unique taste and sensibility. After a profile in *Lucky Magazine*, their reputation soared to national heights. The store has gotten raves from women's fashion magazines and also has a secret gem inside: the Abbeyluxe shoe store.

> ℹ️ For thoughtful men wishing to find their wives, girlfriends, whatever, fantastically original clothes at a bargain price, be sure to check Theadora's sales rack. From cute dresses to blouses, it's a great spot for last-minute gifts.

COMIC BOOKS & COLLECTIBLES

KINGDOM COMICS
1425 Montgomery Hwy., Vestavia Hills
(205) 978-0600
www.kingdomcomics.comicnet.net

The Birmingham market has been especially brutal to comic and collectible stores in the past, so it's a testament to the quality operation at Kingdom Comics that they've been able to establish themselves in such a tough area. For over 7 years, Kingdom Comics has offered a substantial collection of comic books, board games, figurines, and movie-related merchandise to their loyal customers. The staff at Kingdom Comics serves their customers by stocking the best current independent and mainstream comics in addition to offering some of the best knowledge about this growing art form.

LEGION GAMES & COMICS
3248 Cahaba Heights Rd., Vestavia Hills
(205) 970-0999
www.myspace.com/legioncomicsand
games

With locations in Vestavia and Hoover (1564 Montgomery Hwy., 205-979-0299), Legion is the oldest and largest comic book seller in the city. Legion doesn't stop at comics, though—their anime selection is possibly the best in the state with exclusive import titles of some of the most popular Japanese shows. Their Vestavia store is a tabletop and role-playing gamer's paradise full of miniatures, books, and gaming supplies for almost every game. The board-game selection features some of the most popular games together with a remarkable amount of hard-to-find modern board games. The Vestavia store also contains multiple large gaming tables available for use free of charge to gamers. Each weekend the Vestavia store hosts popular Magic the Gathering tournaments as well as long-running campaigns of Dungeons and Dragons and World of Darkness. Both the Hoover and Vestavia stores feature comics, books, anime, collectible cards, figurines, and music. Owing to its nature as a long-running local comic store, things in the Vestavia store can sometimes be chaotic. Don't be afraid to ask for help from any of the knowledgeable employees, who are always ready to assist you in finding that favorite issue from your childhood or the rare new game you've been dying to bring to game night.

ECLECTIC & BOUTIQUE

CHARM
2329 2nd Ave. North, Birmingham
(205) 322-9023
www.charmonsecond.com
When this shop opened, downtown denizens waited with bated breath to see if a jewelry store/boutique could make it on the booming block of 2nd Avenue North, already home to an architecture studio, a skateboard shop, a coffee shop, two bars, and an antique store. Charm is unlike most other jewelry stores and certainly almost any other downtown shop—you'll find folks of all ages inside looking at the accessories, including bags and scarves. You'll also find vintage items, art, and other fun gifts. A must-stop for anyone in the mood for the unusual.

LAMB'S EARS, LTD
3138 Cahaba Heights Rd., Vestavia Hills
(205) 969-3138
www.lambsearsltd.com
Locate in a converted old gas station in Cahaba Heights, Lamb's Ears is full of antiques and reproduction furniture, china, hand-painted pottery, artwork, and more. They also stock a wide selection of infant and children's clothing, in addition to bedding, cribs, accessories, and other items for youngsters. During the Christmas season the store offers a host of yuletide items such as decorations, ceramic figures, art, Santa figures, china, and more.

☀ZOE'S CONSIGNMENT
3900 Clairmont Ave. South, Birmingham
(205) 595-9049
www.zoeshop.com
The ultimate vintage clothing store, Zoe's has long been a staple of the Forest Park neighborhood. After moving out of its original converted bungalow to a larger location across the street, the store's profile has only grown. From designer-label consigned clothes and shoes to the rack upon rack of the coolest vintage clothing anywhere, Zoe's is everything from a weekly stop for regulars who watch the inventory for new finds to the once-a-year visit for those looking for a memorable Halloween costume. There's even a men's section for the savvy guy on the hunt for a slim-fit suit with peg pants or a newsboy cap from back in the day.

FARMERS' MARKETS

It seems like new farmers' markets are springing up constantly in and around the Magic City, offering fresh and often organic alternatives for area residents. The following is just a smattering of the places one can buy fresh fruits, vegetables, organic meat, local cheeses and flowers, and other farm products. **Jones Valley Urban Farm (JVUF),** www.jvuf.org, a community-based non-profit in downtown Birmingham has been instrumental in the growth of the farm-to-table movement in the city. JVUF grows organic produce and flowers while running educational programs for children and adults.

The **Farmers Market Authority,** www.fma.alabama.gov, is a good central source for markets, roadside stands, u-pick operators, nutritional programs, and more in the state of Alabama. The hours and dates of many markets change season to season, so check the websites for the most updated information.

EAST LAKE FARMERS' MARKET
7753 1st Ave. South, Birmingham
(205) 836-3201
www.peerinc.org
Open every Sat May through Oct from 8 a.m. to noon.

FINLEY AVENUE MARKET
344 Finley Ave. West, Birmingham
(205) 251-8737
www.alabamafarmersmarket.org
Open 24 hours daily, year-round. Vendors open from 5 a.m. to 8 p.m. in summer; from 6 a.m. to 5 p.m. in the off-season.

FRESH MARKET ON THE GREEN
2101 Grand Ave., Hoover
(205) 680-5372
Open the first and third Sat of each month, June through Sept, from 8 a.m. to noon.

JONES VALLEY URBAN FARM
701 25th St. North, Birmingham
(205) 322-0542
www.jvuf.org
Open May through Oct, Mon through Fri from 8 a.m. to 6 p.m.

MT. LAUREL FARMERS' MARKET AND CRAFT SALE
1 Mt. Laurel Ave., Mt. Laurel
(205) 408-8696
www.mtlaurel.com
Open every Sat June through Oct from 8 a.m. to noon.

OAK STREET LOCAL MARKET
115 Oak St.
(205) 870-7542
www.oakstreetgardenshop.us
Open Mon through Sat, year-round, from 9 a.m. to 5:30 p.m.

PEPPER PLACE SATURDAY MARKET
2829 2nd Ave. South, Birmingham
(205) 802-2100
www.pepperplacemarket.com
Open every Sat May through Nov, from 7 a.m. to noon.

URBAN COOKHOUSE FARMERS' MARKET
2846 18th St. South and 29th Ave., Homewood
Open every Sat May through Sept from 7 a.m. to noon.

FLORISTS

*DOROTHY MCDANIEL'S FLOWER MARKET
2560 18th St. South, Homewood
(205) 871-0092
www.dorothymcdaniel.com

Dorothy McDaniel built something of a land-mark when she opened her larger shop in Homewood a decade ago. Sitting right at the intersection of 18th Street and Rosedale Drive, the shop is front and center for anyone coming into Homewood from Mountain Brook, the 280 Corridor, or downtown. If you get caught at the traffic light, you have the pleasure of staring into the shop's beautifully designed window installations. Inside, you'll find a large space filled with fresh flowers, pre-made arrangements, gifts and acces-sories, and a talented staff ready to create a special design for a small gift or large event.

HOTHOUSE DESIGN STUDIO
518 29th St. South, Birmingham
(205) 324-2663
www.hothousedesignstudio.com
Known for designs that are a bit edgier than other local florists, Hothouse Design Studio has made a name for itself in a city that has long-standing relationships with established companies. Committed to their downtown location and willing to try new things, this little shop has built a following for their weddings and event installations. They also sell pretty, pre-made arrangements for the downtown crowd who'd like to pick some-thing up for small celebrations and gifts.

NORTON'S FLORIST
401 22nd St. South
(205) 313-1900
www.nortonsflorist.com
Owned by Gus Pappas, Norton's reflects its owner's gregarious and lively personality. Its downtown shop is painted a sunny golden yellow and sports a large iron sunflower out front—certainly ensuring that it stands out from the ordinary buildings around it. Over many years of service, Norton's has become

a local institution, and for good reason: Their designers do beautiful work and the entire crew offers wonderful service. From large events to small custom arrangements, Nor-ton's can do it all. With multiple locations Gus Pappas' formula continues to prove successful.

FURNITURE

BIRMINGHAM WHOLESALE FURNITURE
2200 2nd Ave. South, Birmingham
(205) 322-1687
www.birminghamwholesale.com
Don't let the name confuse you. This is no discount warehouse. Birmingham Wholesale Furniture is one of the finest furniture stores in the city, carrying high-end brands and sporting a staff of professionals who can walk you not only through your furniture purchase, but the redesign of your entire space. Elegantly appointed and filled with top-quality furniture handmade in the US and abroad, Birmingham Wholesale Furni-ture is where you go to find the future heirloom piece. Proudly hanging on to its longtime downtown location, the store has seen the surrounding blocks enjoy a minor renaissance, which will only ensure its con-tinued success.

HILLCREST FURNITURE
2808 18th St. South, Homewood
(205) 874-6680
This new shop in downtown Homewood is owned by a family from the Montgomery area that relocated their store when they saw opportunity in the state's largest city. Specializing in upholstered furniture, dining room sets and accessories, the inventory at Hillcrest reflects not only the tastes (and smaller bungalows) of Homewood—where

more contemporary, smaller-scale furniture is in vogue—but also the larger suburban homeowners with the space to handle a large sectional or table for 12.

MAZER DISCOUNT SUPERSTORE
816 Green Springs Hwy., Homewood
(205) 591-6565
www.mazers.com

You can't miss Mazer's—it seems larger than some small towns. Located on the western side of Homewood in the Green Springs community, Mazer's has been serving Birmingham since 1932 and is a mecca for shoppers from all over the state looking for everything for the home. Sofas, chairs, tables, kitchen and dining sets, bedroom suites, mattresses, kitchen cabinetry, appliances, lighting, flooring—it's all inside the massive and sprawling Mazer's complex. Affordable prices and regular sales make it an even more attractive destination for anyone looking to redo a room—or rooms.

SCANDINAVIAN DESIGN & LEATHER GALLERY
3075 John Hawkins Pkwy., Suite A, Birmingham
(205) 985-4507
www.scandesigngallery.com

Contemporary furniture is popular again, and Scandinavian Design Gallery is one of Birmingham's best stores for the sleek, modern look so many homeowners are seeking. Updated Danish modern styles, in sofas, dining sets, accessories and more, fill the large upstairs space, located right across Highway 150 from the Riverchase Galleria. If you're looking for a well-crafted piece of furniture—think high-end IKEA—this is the place for you.

GARDEN SHOPS

ANDY'S CREEKSIDE NURSERY
3351 Morgan Dr., Vestavia Hills
(205) 824-0233
www.andysgardencenter.com

Starting as a small roadside garden shop in 1997, Andy's Creekside has now grown into a huge garden center with a nearby farm market and another combination farm market and garden center in Hoover. Andy's also offers a full range of landscaping services including design and maintenance. The fruits and vegetables at their farm markets provide Over the Mountain residents with nearby access to the freshest local produce direct from the grower. Whether you want to grow it or eat it, if it's a plant, Andy's is the place for all your needs.

GARDEN SHOP OF HOMEWOOD
307 Oxmoor Rd., Homewood
(205) 445-1010
www.gardenshopofhomewood.net

Located at the busy Oxmoor Road and Green Springs Highway intersection, the Garden Shop of Homewood is owned and run by the helpful, knowledgeable Pam Clark. From landscape design and installation to raised bed gardening, Pam offers a range of organic gardening and lawn-care solutions both in and outside her shop. It's also a great local source for organic items, taking up the slack left by long-time environmental goods store Red Rain's closing. For organic fertilizers, Alabama-grown heirloom vegetables, and a range of Alabama-made products like honey and soap, the Garden Shop is one of the best spots in town. If you need a creative, decorative pot or window box in a hurry, ask about Pam's container gardens to go: Pick a container and the Garden Shop will fill it with colorful flowers and foliage to last all season.

HANNA'S GARDEN SHOP
5485 Hwy. 280, Birmingham
(205) 991-2939
www.hannasgardenshop.com
Found near Greystone just past the Highway 119 intersection, Hanna's is Birmingham's largest landscaping plant store, but the reason local lawn and landscaping businesses as well as residents continue to frequent Hanna's is their expert service. The grounds at Hanna's are a maze of 4 acres of healthy, beautiful plants that are ready to be packed up and loaded in any quantity. Don't worry about getting lost—employees happily guide customers through the rows of plants as they help determine exactly the type of plant you need and advise customers on plant care.

GOURMET SHOPS & GROCERIES

THE GENERAL STORE
212 29th St. South, Birmingham
(205) 202-5661
www.pepperplacegeneralstore.com
For those looking for uniquely Alabama gifts, The General Store at the popular Pepper Place offers one of the city's largest selections of local products. Now partnering with AlabamaGoods.com, the online retailer, the store offers items baked, crafted, and grown in the state. Look for distinctive original pottery and metal art, as well as a range of sauces, marinades, meats, barbecue, gift baskets, books, and more. If it's about Birmingham or Alabama, The General Store likely stocks it.

✳V. RICHARDS MARKET
3916 Clairmont Ave. South, Birmingham
(205) 591-7000
www.vrichards.net
Nestled in the Forest Park shopping district, this family-owned upscale market and restaurant has long been a staple for residents who want the best culinary experience possible. The grocery stocks fine olive oil and balsamic vinegar, cheese, truffles, fresh baked goods, exotic tea and coffee, gourmet chocolate, and local honey. If the ingredient is exotic, V. Richards is one of your best bets in town. Known for their meat and seafood department, those hard-to-find cuts of beef, lamb, and pork—including delicious heritage breed pork from Madison, Alabama's Fudge Family Farms, (256) 652-7440, www.fudgepork.com. If you need a quick lunch or dinner on the go, stop by the cafe for a range of delectable items you can take with you for a picnic or eat in at the restaurant's conditioned outdoor seating.

WHOLE FOODS MARKET
3100 Cahaba Village Plaza,
Mountain Brook
(205) 912-8400
www.wholefoodsmarket.com/stores/
birmingham
Residents of Birmingham are proud of their Whole Foods Market. As Alabama's only location of the now international natural food supermarket, the Whole Foods in the Vestavia Hills/Mountain Brook area is one of the city's most popular gourmet destinations. Yes, it's a chain, but Whole Foods makes an effort to incorporate local produce and products into the store and supports many area environmental non-profits such as the Jones Valley Urban Farm and the Southern Environmental

Center. They are dedicated to offering products that are natural, organic, and unprocessed. The combination of social responsibility and high-quality grocery items available from Whole Foods deserves mentioning. With a focus on local agriculture and products made from sustainable resources, Whole Foods serves the community and the customer.

JEWELRY

BARTON-CLAY FINE JEWELERS
2701 Cahaba Rd., Mountain Brook
(205) 871-7060
www.bartonclay.com

Located in Mountain Brook Village, Barton Clay has direct competition in Bromberg's, located just a block away. Like Bromberg's, Barton Clay is family owned and prides itself on its carefully selected inventory and outstanding customer service. Although it has not been around as long as Bromberg's, Barton Clay has built a solid clientele and dedicated following that it works very hard to maintain. Its fine jewelry collection is stunning, as is its selection of watches. With two remarkable jewelers in such close proximity, it's the shopper who benefits.

*BROMBERG'S
131 Summit Blvd., Birmingham
(205) 969-1776
www.brombergs.com

Established in 1836 in Mobile by Prussian merchant Frederick Bromberg, the jewelry, crystal, and silver retailer is the oldest family-owned business in Alabama. Many of the world's foremost names in jewelry and timepieces—David Yurman, John Hardy, Michele, Mikimoto, and TAG Heuer—are represented in the two Bromberg's locations. All of the staff members hold an AGS title, from Certified Gemologist Appraiser to Graduate Sales Associate. For those looking for the finest jewelry and gift items money can buy, Bromberg's is the destination of choice. A second location is in Mountain Brook at 2800 Cahaba Rd. (205-871-3276).

DIAMONDS DIRECT
2800 Cahaba Circle, Suite 150, Birmingham
(205) 972-8994
www.diamondsdirectbirmingham.com

The newcomer to town, this North-Carolina-based company is working hard to cut into the business of the highly respected, family-owned jewelers in the city. In a town like Birmingham, that cherishes personal relationships, family ties, and traditional ways of doing things, Diamonds Direct is taking a different approach, emphasizing lower prices on diamonds and other fine jewelry, Located in Mountain Brook, home to two of the city's top jewelers, Diamonds Direct is going after the city's wealthiest shoppers. Time will tell if price beats out tradition.

LEVY'S FINE JEWELRY
2116 2nd Ave. North, Birmingham
(205) 251-3381
www.levysfinejewelry.com

Levy's is an institution. Another of the city's longtime, family-owned jewelry stores, Levy's has maintained its downtown location when others have moved to wealthy suburbs. Located in an unassuming building on 2nd Avenue North, it's filled with a wonderful collection of both new and estate jewelry, as well as other fine pieces such as watches, china, and silver. Rhoda, the family matriarch, has developed a cult following for her radio advertisements. What you find at Levy's is sure to be unique.

LEATHER

TRILOGY LEATHER SHOP
1001 Oxmoor Rd., Homewood
(205) 871-9468

When Tony Pardi and Sam Sicola opened Trilogy Leather Shop in Edgewood's 1920s commercial district, they probably didn't suspect they'd still be crafting custom leather goods some four 4 decades later, but here they are. Expect belts, wallets, purses, bags, and hand tool belts among other leather items for sale in the small shop. Trilogy also works with alligator, shark, and other exotic skins and does various leather repair for customers. If it has to do with leather, there's a good chance the friendly Tony or Sam can help.

SHOPPING AREAS

COLONIAL BROOKWOOD VILLAGE
780 Brookwood Village, Homewood
(205) 871-0406
www.shopbrookwoodvillage.com

Known locally as "Brookwood," this mall is nestled at the bottom of beautiful Shades Valley in Homewood. While it's not on the same large scale of the Galleria or the sprawling Summit, that just may be the point. Shoppers at Brookwood enjoy a relaxed atmosphere that seems more like an indoor main street than a typical mall. Brookwood is smaller than the other malls in the area, but the variety of quality stores and food options combined with the calmer surroundings makes shopping here a local favorite. As part of a renovation in the early 2000s, Colonial Properties, owners of the mall, created an outdoor shopping area with multiple entrances to the mall. While most of the mall's locations are chains like the popular upscale **Brio Tuscan Grille,** the mall

features a number of unique stores in addition to the typical shops found in most malls. Brookwood contains some of the city's only locations for many trendy select chains including **Z Gallerie,** www.zgallerie.com, a trendy modern furniture store, **Gus Mayer,** www.gusmayer.com, a designer department store with some of the latest and most expensive fashions and accessories, and **O'Henry's Coffees,** www.ohenryscoffee.com, a branch of one of the city's most favorite coffee houses. Pay attention mall-rats: Brookwood is home to the city's only location of **Hot Topic.** The mall also houses **Macy's, Belk,** and a large **Books-A-Million,** www.booksamillion.com, a Birmingham-based chain of bookstores. Across from the mall, active residents enjoy the **Lakeshore Trail,** listed in the Greenways chapter.

RIVERCHASE GALLERIA
3000 Riverchase Galleria, Suite 1000, Hoover
(205) 985-3020
www.riverchasegalleria.com

With over 200 stores Riverchase Galleria is the biggest mall in Alabama. Located at the intersection Highway 31 and I-459, the mall ranks as the most-visited free tourist destination in the city. Known locally as **"The Galleria,"** residents of Birmingham often spend as much time here people-watching as they do shopping. Much of the mall's elaborate ceiling structure makes up an enormous nine-story glass atrium enclosed by the world's largest skylight. The shops here are almost universally mid-to-upscale chain stores and restaurants with a few exceptions. What the Galleria does offer are the largest and best-stocked locations of these chains in the state. From **Belk** to **JCPenney, Express** to **Gap,** and **Brookstone**

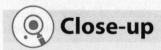 **Close-up**

The Villages of Mountain Brook

Mountain Brook is a municipality made up of winding tree-lined residential streets with some of the oldest and most notable homes in the city. It is dotted by historic commercial villages that contain most of the city's retail and dining options. Each village has a distinct style and offers an eclectic mix of exclusive upscale options alongside everyday neighborhood favorites. All the villages are pedestrian-friendly although the parking can get crowded during prime hours. The villages aren't very far apart from each other but the hilly terrain means a walk from village to village probably wouldn't be advisable. Mountain Brook and Crestline Village offer the most variety of shopping and each contains local and chain pharmacies and banks as well as a grocery store.

MOUNTAIN BROOK VILLAGE

The main village in the city is named for the city itself. Mountain Brook Village is centered at the busy five-way intersection of Cahaba Road and Montevallo Road. Enjoy a short walk by taking in the **English Tudor architecture** of the development. This village features some of the city's finest stores including **Barton-Clay Fine Jewelers,** a number of trend-setting women's boutiques like **Stella Blu, Kiki Risa,** and others. But it's not all high fashion and Rolex watches—local residents depend on the **Western Supermarket** and **Little Hardware** store for many everyday needs. With one of the only old-time soda fountains in town, the famous **Gilchrist Drugs** lunch counter serves some of the best sandwiches and sodas in the city.

ENGLISH VILLAGE

Heading north up Cahaba Road from Mountain Brook Village, after winding a short way up Red Mountain you'll reach English Village, a smaller shopping area with its own set of interesting destinations. This village is set up in the Tudor style to create the best in old world atmosphere. For nightlife and dining, **Billy's Bar & Grill** and **Chez Lu Lu** (see Nightlife and Restaurants, respectively) are popular locations prized by locals for their unique charm. **Brogue & Cruff Clothiers** offer some of the city's finest menswear available with options for custom tailoring and ready-to-wear clothing including their popular office and home service, which brings the tailor, and clothing come to you. **Joe Muggs Cafe** offers a quick cup of java along with a good magazine selection for a pick-me-up.

CRESTLINE VILLAGE

The most low-key of the three main villages, Crestline Village is Mountain Brook's family-friendly village. With a host of stores for kids and grown-ups alike, Crestline Village has something for everyone. A number of popular neighborhood restaurants can be found in this village including **Dyron's Lowcountry, Fire, Surin of Thailand,** and **La Paz.**

to **Sears,** the stores in the Galleria are situated to serve the crowds of people that shop there each day. Locally owned **Mountain High Outfitters,** www.mountainhighoutfitters.com, operates one of their four outdoor stores in the Galleria while local table-gaming experts **BumperNets,** www.bumpernets.com, supplies the best billiard, table tennis, and other game tables in their incredible store. Be sure to embrace the Auburn-Alabama football rivalry by stopping by **Bama Fever Tiger Pride,** a store that sells every piece of apparel and trinket associated with the two teams.

THE SUMMIT
I-459 at Highway 280
(205) 967-0111
www.thesummitonline.com/birmingham
The Summit represents an inside-out approach to the traditional mall. Instead of a large building surrounding a multitude of shops, The Summit is a shopping area—essentially a large, upscale shopping plaza or strip mall—built to maximize the generally beautiful weather in Birmingham.

Anchored by **Belk** department store and Alabama's only **Saks Fifth Avenue,** www.saksfifthavenue.com, The Summit's shopping options are a mix of upscale stores like the state's only **L'OCCITANE,** http://usa.loccitane.com, a high-end fragrance and skincare boutique, and regular mall standards like **American Eagle.** On a nice day The Summit is a great place to enjoy a plethora of retail choices without being cooped up inside. The Summit also features some of the area's most-popular restaurant chains—don't show up on a Friday or Saturday night and expect a table without a wait. The **Barnes & Noble,** www.barnesandnoble.com, in The Summit is one of the largest locations of this popular bookstore in the state.

The Summit has plenty of parking and even offers a shuttle service to make sure you can conveniently access all your favorite stores. Click on the "Services & Amenities" tab on the homepage to find a map of all shuttle stops as well as other services including baggage check, Wi-Fi, and personal shopping.

DAY TRIPS & WEEKEND GETAWAYS

Antebellum mansions, old town squares, expansive canoe trails, civil-rights sites, hiking excursions, educational fun, beach retreats, and nearby city escapes—with Birmingham as your starting point, the opportunities for idling away a day or a weekend are too numerous to count.

Living in Birmingham already places you at the heart of Alabama with regard to culture, entertainment, transportation, attractions, and general activity. It's the largest city in the state by far, and as such, possesses an unparalleled energy and excitement. However, the city is also not too far from the geographic center of the state (around Montevallo, Alabama, 30 miles to the south) and so is the perfect launching point for day trips and fun weekend excursions to places nearby.

In fact, as all interstates in the state converge in Birmingham—head any direction and it's all interstate, all the way to the nearest cities. Drive south on I-65 for 4.5 hours, and you're on the beach in Gulf Shores, Alabama. Head north on I-65 and in 3 hours you reach Nashville, Tennessee. Chattanooga, Tennessee, is a scant 2-hour drive northeast along I-59, and if you continue another couple hours you're in Knoxville, only a short jaunt to the Great Smoky Mountain National Park. The megalopolis Atlanta, Georgia, with all its great attractions (and traffic!), is just a couple hours east along I-20. Memphis is 3.5 hours away on I-22. The great city of New Orleans is 5 hours away on I-59.

Because of the state's wonderful physiographic diversity, The Nature Conservancy has called Alabama "America's monster of biological diversity" because of the massive range of flora and fauna that inhabit the area. Living in such a fortunate region, one doesn't have to travel far to enjoy canoeing the Sipsey or Conecuh rivers, exploring the world-class caving sites of northeast Alabama, rock climbing at Horse Pens 40, whitewater kayaking the Locust Fork, backpacking in Little River Canyon Preserve, hang gliding at Lookout Mountain, or bird watching on one of several popular Alabama birding trails.

OVERVIEW

But part of the point of any day trip or getaway is to get off the beaten path, to leave the interstates and the chain food options. Try something different. Visit quiet historic sites out in the countryside. See some of Alabama's great natural wonders for an active excursion all to yourself. Drive around at lunchtime in some small Alabama town, and look for where all the locals' cars are parked at some nondescript diner at noon: That's where you want to eat. There are so many interesting nooks and crannies to explore that the most difficult aspect to day tripping beyond Birmingham is narrowing down your options. Best of luck!

DAY TRIPS

Adventures

CANOE & KAYAKING

From a gentle day paddling on the river with family and friends to serious a whitewater kayaking adventure with experts, the Locust and Mulberry forks and the Cahaba River run the gamut of the type of experiences Alabama's waterways hold. All rivers are a short drive from Birmingham. The Black Warrior River's Locust and Mulberry forks are both located north of Birmingham, while the Cahaba River skirts the city to the south, flowing in a southwesterly direction. The Cahaba makes for a great leisurely float, and below Centreville where its character changes dramatically, there are long white sandbars that make excellent overnight camping spots. The Locust and Mulberry forks are known for their wilder, more adventurous natures, and some of the stretches should only be attempted by advanced paddlers in the company of equally skilled compatriots. See the Recreation chapter for complete details and information.

CHEAHA STATE PARK

The Society of American Travel Writers recently named the Talladega Scenic Drive one of the 10 most beautiful drives through scenic America. The bulk of the 26-mile drive follows Highway 431 just east of Talladega. It passes by small towns, rock outcrops, and the Talladega National Forest. Here in **Cheaha State Park** (800-ALA-PARK, www.alapark.com/cheaharesort) in the southernmost Appalachian Mountains is **Mt. Cheaha,** Alabama's highest point at 2,407 feet. For those wanting to stay longer than just a drive, there are spots to camp, fish, picnic, and hike, such as the excellent **Pinhoti National Recreation Trail,** Alabama's longest foot trail, www.pinhotitrailalliance .org. Cheaha has some excellent sandstone cabins dating back to the days of the Works Progress Administration and Civilian Conservation Corps during the Great Depression that were recently totally renovated. On the west side of Talladega National Forest in Childersburg, **DeSoto Caverns Park,** (800) 933-2283, www.desotocavernspark.com, offers guided tours in the underground caverns which start in a room 12 stories high and larger than a football field. It's a great experience for families. The park also runs a slightly kitschy Family Fun Park above ground with gemstone panning, moon walks, games, and a maze. Cheaha State Park is 60 miles from Birmingham.

✳**CHIEF LADIGA TRAIL**

Alabama's first rails-to-trails project, the **Chief Ladiga Trail** (www.chiefladiga.com), is a 33-mile jaunt from Anniston, Alabama to the Georgia state line. Named after a Muscogee chief who signed away his tribe's land in 1832, the trail passes through a former CSX railroad corridor. Though mostly flat the Chief Ladiga Trail travels through a variety of landscapes from small towns and open fields, to pine and hardwood forests as well as wetlands. Towns like **Weaver, Jacksonville,** and **Piedmont** offer bikers the chance to stop off for a snack or explore the environs. As the trail progresses closer to the Georgia line, it enters the southern Appalachians, **Dugger Mountain** and into the **Talladega National Forest.** The surface is asphalt, and

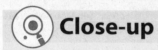

Close-up

A Word about the Black Warrior River Watershed

The **Black Warrior River** and its many tributaries, the northern sister system to the treasured Cahaba River, extend throughout the north portion of Birmingham. It encompasses a number of smaller tributaries such as Hurricane Creek, Turkey Creek, Village Creek, North River, Dry Creek, Duck River, Inland Lake, Five Mile Creek, and Valley Creek. It includes the magnificent Mulberry and Locust forks, then stretches north and west to include the Sipsey River and finally flows past Tuscaloosa and on to Demopolis. The system starts in the Appalachian Mountains and ends in the coastal plain, flowing through a bewilderingly diverse landscape. It stretches 178 miles, but its total drainage area is 6,275 square miles, a hefty portion of north central Alabama. Along with the Cahaba River, the Black Warrior can rightly be called Alabama's heart river, central to the state both in its geographical course as well as in the number of biological treasures it contains.

Yet the Black Warrior system, which makes up one of the longest channelized waterways in the United States, has in the past often been overlooked and under-valued by the people living in the watershed. A major supplier of drinking water for Birmingham and surrounding communities, there is a continual threat of unnecessary and damaging dams on the Duck River and especially the Locust Fork River—one of Alabama's few remaining free-flowing rivers and a priceless treasure for the state. While the lower Black Warrior River, a waterway that does the unglamorous work that Alabamians require of it, transports industrial goods like coal, chemicals, coke, wood, and steel, by contrast the unparalleled beauty of the Locus Fork is a pristine stretch of river to cherish and preserve. The great variety within this one watershed ironically has meant that the general public is just beginning to realize the entire Black Warrior watershed is a treasure and a river system to protect. The **Black Warrior Riverkeeper,** (205) 458-0095, www.blackwarriorriver.org, a non-profit group founded in 2001 that protects and restores the Black Warrior River and its tributaries, is a large part of this effort.

the trail is open to activities like biking, inline skating, mountain biking, and walking. On the same railroad corridor as **Georgia's Silver Comet Trail** (www.silvercometga.com), the two trials are now connected, creating a continuous 90-mile stretch from Atlanta to Anniston. If the current amount of use is any indication, this bike trail will only continue to grow in popularity as more and more people in the region learn of its existence. For transportation variety—and to entertain the kids—one could always hop the Amtrak from nearby Anniston back to Birmingham,

though it would involve some creative scheduling. Anniston is located just off I-20, approximately 65 miles east of Birmingham.

✳LITTLE RIVER CANYON NATIONAL PRESERVE

The term "little" is a misleading adjective to describe **Little River Canyon** to the uninitiated; its scale goes far beyond the idea such a word plants in the imagination. That one of the deepest gorges east of the Rocky Mountains would be in Alabama is virtually unknown both inside and outside the state. Snuggled amid the mountains of the **Cumberland Plateau** and ringed with forest, the canyon and river seem designed to remain a secret for the lucky few whom have seen it. Named an **Alabama Natural Wonder** by the Alabama Environmental Council and now a National Park Service designated National Preserve, www.nps.gov/liri, the canyon is finally gaining the attention it deserves. The canyon is located a few miles east of I-59, some 90 miles from Birmingham.

Starting on top of **Lookout Mountain,** several smaller streams join to make the Little River one of the few rivers in the country that form and flow almost entirely on top of a mountain. In **DeSoto State Park,** the river drops over 100 feet at **DeSoto Falls** below the town of **Mentone.** Farther along its course, the river drops another 45 feet into the canyon itself at **Little River Falls** and eventually empties into **Weiss Lake.** Though its origins lie in Georgia, it is here in Alabama's 14,000-acre **Little River Canyon National Preserve** that the most striking aspects of the Little River are found. Located in the northeast corner of Alabama in DeKalb and Cherokee counties, the canyon is 18 miles long, .75 mile at its widest point, and nearly 700 feet at its highest point. The nearest town to the canyon, **Fort Payne,** Alabama, about 2 hours northeast of Birmingham on I-59, sits at the foot of the mountain, roughly 10 miles away.

The canyon holds oaks, hickories, blackgum, yellow poplar, and American beech as well as dogwood, sourwood, sassafras, and huckleberry trees. Wild azaleas and mountain laurel dot the canyon walls, as do the beautiful blooms of the Catawba rhododendron found here at the southern end of its range. In the spring kayakers and canoeists come to try their luck at class IV and V rapids

during a particularly risky section near the canyon mouth and campground. The rapids can be lethal. During heavy rain, the river may rise as much as 20 feet in a short period of time, making it extremely dangerous. In low water, tributaries often dry up and the river is broken into smaller isolated pools of water.

But for most visitors, a drive along the canyon rim is as close to danger as they will get. Several overlooks with names such as **Hawk's Glide** and **Crow Point** make the twisting, turning road well worth a mild case of carsickness. In the fall when the hardwoods turn their brilliant, myriad of autumnal colors, the canyon has an unparalleled beauty that attracts the more dedicated souls. And for the few who truly know Little River Canyon—arguably, some of the world's greatest swimming holes are found in its depths—for the most part,

Go-To for Your Getaway

When wondering how to spend a day or two rambling about Alabama, a good guide is **www.800 alabama.com,** the official travel and tourism website for the state. There you'll find various travel tools, vacation packages, and general ideas and information to plan any trip, short or extended. The official site of the Alabama Department of Conservation is **www.OutdoorAlabama.com.** It's a great go-to for hunting, fishing, wildlife watching, and state park information.

they aren't telling. There's limited camping at the National Preserve, so some head to nearby **Cloudland Canyon State Park** in Georgia, (706) 657-4050, www.gastateparks .org/info/cloudland, or look for accommodations in Fort Payne, the nearest city or the resort town of Mentone. **Jacksonville State University**'s new multi-million-dollar **Field School,** (256) 845-3548, www.jsu.edu/epic/field_schools.html, opened in 2009 and offers a host of programs for students and visitors and is open to the public.

MARION

Marion is one of those fascinating small towns that are often overlooked. That's a shame. If you are looking for a short, active getaway, travel 80 miles southeast on Highway 5 to the sleepy little hamlet of Marion, about a 1.5-hour drive south of Birmingham. With its old county courthouse standing tall in the center of the square, it's just about the perfect template many have for small-town living. Accordingly, out-of-towners from Birmingham to Atlanta are buying up lovely old homes for retirement or weekend getaway spots. A closer look, though, reveals a town fixing up facades and renovating downtown structures that date to the 1830s. If it is still a bit on the sleepy side, then that's just a better reason to enjoy a day of walking about and admiring the old homes and structures, and learning more about Alabama history.

County seat of Perry County, and home to **Judson College** (1838) and **Marion Military Institute** (1842), Marion is certainly proud of the fact that Sam Houston, President of the Republic of Texas, was married here—well, for the second time, at least. It is also home to the remarkable **Lincoln Normal School** (1867). Founded by freed slaves, it was a groundbreaking educational

center for African Americans that lasted over 100 years and eventually spawned Alabama State University in Montgomery. The first Confederate flag and uniform were designed here in the town that came close to becoming the state capital before Montgomery got the final nod.

Marion's roots in the Alabama civil-rights movement run deep. **Coretta Scott King,** wife of Rev. Martin Luther King, is from Marion and graduated from the Lincoln Normal School. **Albert Turner Sr.** a civil-rights leader who worked alongside Martin Luther King, is from the area. The town was a pivotal site in Alabama civil-rights history as **Jimmy Lee Jackson** was shot here in 1964, galvanizing the pivotal march from Selma to Montgomery that proved so decisive a victory in that struggle. Jackson is buried just outside of town. In more recent history Jean Childs, daughter of Idella Childs, who was a prominent member of the Lincolnite Association here, married former Atlanta mayor, Ambassador Andrew Young. Marion has made an impact beyond the town's limits, that is certain.

Book a room at the 1840 Greek Revival **Myrtle Hill Bed & Breakfast,** (334) 683-9095, www.bbonline.com/al/myrtlehill. Surrounded by 5 acres of Victorian gardens and within a short walk of the town square, the B&B is a great place to spend some down time. Head out to nearby **Perry Lakes Park,** www.perrylakes.org, to visit some of the most original architecture going on in the country, thanks to Auburn University's acclaimed **Rural Studio** program, www .ruralstudio.com. Visit the Perry County Pavilion and the Perry Lakes Pedestrian Bridge to get closer to the surrounding cypress swamps rich in ecological diversity. The Rural Studio's newest addition to the park is an observation tower for watching wildlife. And since the swamps connect to the Cahaba River, bring a canoe or kayak to bird watch, fish, and explore the wonderful oxbow lake.

"Alabama's 10 Natural Wonders"

(Courtesy of the Alabama Environmental Council.)

1. Bankhead National Forest
2. Bartram Trail
3. Bon Secour National Wildlife Refuge
4. Cahaba River
5. Choctawhatchee River
6. Little River Canyon
7. Mobile-Tensaw Delta
8. Monte Sano State Park & Mountain
9. Sipsey River Swamp
10. Talledega Mountains

Passive Touring

ALABAMA'S COTTON COUNTRY

Earning its name from the rich, dark topsoil that stretches in a crescent shape across much of the lower third of the state, Alabama's Black Belt was the economic foundation for the cotton economy that made this region some of the nation's most expensive real estate from the 1830s to the start of the Civil War. Ninety miles south of Birmingham lies **Montgomery,** the state's capital since 1846. Montgomery may be the Black Belt's largest city, but it is off among the rolling

fields, small Antebellum towns, and Greek Revival plantation homes that visitors will find the heart of this fascinating region.

Set amid rolling pastures and rich agricultural land, **Lowndes County** is home to scenic, peaceful county roads passing barns, historic homes, and rural beauty. Finished in 1858 the **Lowndes County Courthouse** is the focal point of the quiet, charming town of **Hayneville.** Built in the Greek Revival style, the structure reflects the tremendous plantation-based wealth of Antebellum Lowndes County. Highway 80, which connects Selma to Montgomery, is home to three memorial trails: the **Jefferson Davis Highway,** www.fhwa.dot.gov/infrastructure/jdavis.cfm, the **De Soto Trail,** www.drivetheost.com/history, and the **Selma to Montgomery Civil Rights Trail,** www.nps.gov/semo, that Martin Luther King Jr. and hundreds of others took in 1965.

Just across Highway 80 lies the town of **Lowndesboro,** a treasure-trove of old homes and churches dating back to prestatehood. Amusingly enough, years ago while taking some out-of-town friends on a tour of the Black Belt, we noticed some perennials growing along an old dirt road across from a cotton field. We parked and followed the road on foot, coming to what was clearly a palatial old plantation home now in ruins, the roof caved in and only the shell remaining. Hardy flowers, many of which may have dated back a century or more remained growing about the grounds. Years later we saw the copy of *Vanity Fair* magazine that featured Natalie Portman in an Annie Leibovitz photo shoot at a broken down, yet luxurious ruined manse, and the location of the shoot? Lowndes County, at the same caved-in mansion we found. What is routine for Alabamians is often perceived as exotic to others. For those interested in Antebellum mansions, try **Gaineswood** in Demopolis, (334) 289-4846, www.preserveala.org, and **Magnolia Grove** in Greensboro, (334) 624-8618, www.preserveala.org.

AVE MARIA GROTTO

Cullman's **Ave Maria Grotto,** www.avemaria grotto.com, is something one has to see in order to believe. Located 50 miles north of Birmingham on I-65, Ave Maria Grotto in an old quarry near St. Bernard Abbey, the park and garden is the life's work of Brother Joseph Zoettl, a Benedictine monk from Germany who spent the last five decades of his life creating more than 125 famous miniature reproductions of famous religious buildings like the St. Peter's Basilica, ancient Jerusalem, and Our Lady of Lourdes, as well as seemingly arbitrary structures like the Leaning Tower of Pisa, German castles, exotic shrines, and Hansel and Gretel's Temple of the Fairies. The collection covers more than 3 acres. Admission is $7.

BLACK BELT PRAIRIES

For many people the concept of prairies in Alabama is nearly as foreign an idea as oceans in Iowa, yet there is more truth to the notion than most realize. It should not really be that great of a surprise, though: Alabama remains one of the most biologically diverse states in the nation. That Alabama contains a wealth of prairies that rival the Midwest—if not in size, then certainly in species—is simply par for the environmental course. At the time of European settlement, perhaps as many as 1,000 square miles of what is now Alabama was tallgrass prairie, extending in an arc from Phenix City to Cahaba to Livingston above a deep layer of dark chalk commonly referred to as Selma Chalk. The prairies here are home to a great variety of plant life, many species of which are typically found hundreds of miles away in places such as the great grasslands of the Midwest. Indeed, during the Ice Age, Black Belt Prairies may have served as a refuge for the tallgrass prairies of the west, preserving species of grasses and wildflowers that otherwise would have been lost. Dominated by Little Bluestem, yellow Indiangrass, white prairie-clover, Compass Plant, Big Bluestem, Side-oats Grama, Eastern Gamagrass, Purple Prairie-clover, Scaly Blazing-star—the Black Belt Prairie is a defining feature of Alabama's natural landscape.

It is thought that during the Holocene Era from 9,000 to 4,000 years ago, the prairies of the Coosa Valley probably were extensive enough to support large animals such as the bison. Yet while the larger herbivores may be gone, today there remain rare and declining species to protect such as the Lark Sparrow, Bobwhite Quail, Grasshopper Sparrow and Bachman's Sparrow that inhabit the prairies' shrubby edges. Rare plant species such as Celestial Lily, White Lady's-slipper, Three-flowered Hawthorn, Great Plains Ladies' tresses, Nutmeg Hickory, Old Cahawba rosinweed, and others survive because of the remaining Black Belt Prairie patches. **Kathy Stiles Freeland Bibb County Glades Preserve,** www.nature.org, a 480-acre preserve near Centreville, is 60 miles south of Birmingham. Protected by **The Nature Conservancy,** it offers good opportunities to see some 61 rare plant species. The Nature Conservancy also protects **Pratt's Ferry,** (205) 251-1155, www.nature .org, another area along the Cahaba River that is home to several rare wildflowers.

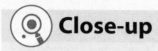 **Close-up**

Demopolis' Vine & Olive Colony: Bonapartist Refugees in the Alabama Territory

With Napoleon Bonaparte's final defeat and exile, a group of his supporters fled France and, strangely enough, found refuge in the newly formed Alabama Territory in 1817. The US Congress granted the group of nearly 400 families four townships near the junction of the Black Warrior and Tombigbee Rivers. They first called it White Bluff but later settled on **Demopolis,** Greek for "city of the people." In time, Demopolis would become just that—only not for the French settlers.

That the colony was a failure from the start should have surprised no one. Made up of Napoleonic officers, merchants, and their wives, few had any agricultural experience and even less knowledge of the new environment they were thrust into. After clearing land, planting their vineyards and olive trees and building cabins, they found they had mistaken the boundaries of their land grant and had to move. In addition American squatters often took French land illegally, refusing to give up their claims. The French paid too much for hired labor, and suffered fever, water shortages, and high prices for provisions. One story from 1822 explains their dismal efforts at clearing land. A man climbs a tree and fastens a rope to the top. A dozen men then pull hard on the rope while others take an ax to the tree in turns. When the tree came down, it killed two and crippled several. After this singular experience, the French didn't clear land anymore.

Like oil and water were the aristocrats and the Alabama frontier. Neither the vines, the olive trees, nor the Bonapartists thrived. By 1830 most had moved on to New Orleans or Mobile. Some even returned to France. What they left behind are names like Demopolis, Aigleville, Arcola, and Marengo—as well as a brief period when the rugged character of a young state possessed a singular, cosmopolitan flair. Never again will the Alabama wilderness witness French gentlewomen hoeing vegetable gardens in their tattered parlor gowns.

COVERED BRIDGES OF BLOUNT COUNTY

With more historic covered bridges still standing in a single county than any other state in the country, it's no surprise that **Blount County** would be known as the **"Covered Bridge Capital of Alabama."** Of Alabama's 11 remaining covered bridges, 3 of those are within the county and all 3 are listed in the National Register of Historic Places. Located 50 miles northeast of Birmingham off US 231 near Oneonta, at 95 feet, the **Easley Bridge** is the oldest and shortest covered bridge. It has been in steady use since 1927. **Swann Bridge** at 324 feet is the second longest covered bridge in the state, and spans the Black Warrior River's Locust Fork. Built in 1933 it is near the town of Cleveland off Highway 79. Just north of Oneonta, 220-foot-long **Horton Mill Bridge** spans the Calvert Prong of the Black Warrior River, and, at 70 feet high, is the highest covered bridge above water in the United States. Watch for the **Blount County Covered Bridge Festival** in October in Oneonta, www.blountoneontachamber.org.

MERCEDES-BENZ US INTERNATIONAL FACTORY TOUR

You don't have to own a Mercedes to be curious about the history of Daimler-Benz. The **Mercedes-Benz Visitor Center,** (205) 507-2252, www.mbusi.com, in Vance, Alabama, is some 50 miles southwest of Birmingham. It's the first factory of its kind outside Germany and tells the story of the company that created the first automobile way back in 1886 (beating Henry Ford to the punch). For racing enthusiasts to safety enthusiasts, there's something for just about anyone remotely interested in the world's premier auto manufacturer. Concept cars, 19th-century Mercedes motorcycles and motor carriages, as well as the full range of cars and sport utility vehicles made in Tuscaloosa at the factory are all on display.

MOUNDVILLE ARCHAEOLOGICAL PARK

Moundville Archaeological Park, (205) 371-2234, www.moundville.ua.edu, found 70 miles east of Birmingham, preserves 320 acres of what was the most powerful Native American community of its time. The **Jones Archaeological Museum** houses an excellent collection of Mississippian artwork found at the site, including the amazing **Rattlesnake Disc,** Alabama's official state artifact. And each fall, beginning the last Mon in Sept, the annual **Moundville Native American Festival** attracts thousands of people from across the region for a week-long celebration of the heritage of Southeastern Indians. Called the "Big Apple of the 14th century" by scholars, at its height in AD 1300, Moundville was the continent's largest single community north of Mexico. At the time, the walled city of Moundville was a ceremonial and commercial center whose trade routes stretched across the entire southeastern United States. The Mississippian Indians built some 29 mounds that vary in height from 3 to 60 feet. A massive 10-foot-high palisade wall enclosed the 185-acre town on 3 sides. It contained 1,500 inhabitants but received tribute from as many as 10,000 people in surrounding villages. Moundville and the Cahokia Mounds in Illinois are about the closest thing to pyramids that the United States possesses.

✳OLD ALABAMA TOWN

Old Alabama Town is the closest thing it gets to living, breathing, and working in 19th-century Alabama. The south's premier historical village, Montgomery's Old Alabama Town contains over 6 blocks and 50 buildings of restored 18th- and 19th-century structures. It's the best way to learn what life was like in the 1800s. The town's buildings present a cross-section of Alabama's past: a dogtrot house, a blacksmith's and woodcarver's shop, a drugstore museum, a 19th-century tavern, an 1874 meeting house, a black Presbyterian church, a one-room school house, and an 1820s log cabin to name a few. Developed by the City of Montgomery and the Landmarks Foundation, Old Alabama Town first opened in 1971. Since then the site has expanded rapidly and is open 361 days a year for interpretative tours, (334) 240-4500, www.oldalabamatown.com.

✳SELMA TO MONTGOMERY NATIONAL HISTORIC TRAIL

About 105 miles south of Birmingham, midway between Selma and Montgomery on Highway 80, is the **Lowndes County Interpretive Center,** (334) 877-1984, www.nps.gov/semo. The center provides what has been missing for years: a place to start for

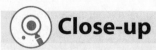

Close-up

The March from Selma to Montgomery

After years of strenuous efforts by the Dallas County Voters League and the Student Non-violent Coordinating Committee (SNCC), by the early 1960s the prospects were so that many civil-rights activists had written off Selma, Alabama. And with some foundation: Less than 1 percent of Dallas County's black citizens were registered to vote. But in late 1964 Martin Luther King Jr. and the Southern Christian Leadership Conference (SCLC) accepted the invitation of Selma activists to base a major voting rights campaign there. Soon, protests and mass meetings began to erupt across Alabama's Black Belt in Montgomery, Marion, and rural Lowndes County. In February 1965 the death of Jimmy Lee Jackson, who was shot by an Alabama state trooper in Marion, brought matters to a head: The idea to take Jackson's body to the Alabama State Capital steps in protest evolved into a march to petition the Alabama governor. Selma would be the starting point.

The first march began March 7, 1965, when the SNCC's John Lewis and the SCLC's Hosea Williams led some 600 marchers out of Brown Chapel AME Church in Selma. Just over the Edmund Pettus Bridge, Alabama state troopers blocked the way. When marchers ignored an order to disperse, the non-violent protesters were met with tear gas and clubs. That night the nation watched in horror as newscasts depicted the "Bloody Sunday" beatings of citizens seeking a basic democratic right. Across the country demonstrations sprang up. Carloads of supporters converged on the Selma. On March 8th, local whites attacked and fatally beat Rev. James Reeb, a Unitarian minister from Boston. Over the next week tensions mounted as beatings and arrests followed many protests. By March 16th, a federal order permitting a march from Selma to Montgomery was issued that directed state and federal governments to provide protection to the marchers. Finally, on March 21th, marchers began making their way on foot to the capital. In Montgomery carloads and busloads of demonstrators joined the final stage of the march, so that by March 25th, more than 25,000 people from as far away as Canada and Europe gathered to listen to King and others speak from the capitol steps. King delivered the climatic speech, saying, "We are on the move now, and we are not about to turn around. Segregation is on its deathbed."

By the mid 1960s public transportation, public accommodation, and public education were legally accessible to all Americans. But the right to vote was yet to be won. In response to the Selma to Montgomery March, on August 6, 1965, President Johnson signed the Voting Rights Act into law, guaranteeing for all the fundamental right of American democracy—the right to vote.

those interested in the civil-rights movement in Alabama. In fact, the center opened in 2007, and even today, many people are surprised to learn that the National Park Service manages the location. The first of three planned National Park Service visitor centers along the 54-mile Selma to Montgomery National Historic Trail route, the Interpretive Center is nestled in an open prairie surrounded by oak and hickory trees. This is the heart of the Black Belt that was home to prosperous cotton planters in the

1840s and 1850s. The epicenter of the slave-based plantation system a century before, it was the perfect site for civil-rights organizers to choose to protest the intransigence of state and local officials in the 1960s who prevented African Americans from registering to vote. The trail links places in Selma like the National Voting Rights Museum, www.nvrm.org, and the Edmund Pettus Bridge with those in Montgomery like the **Rosa Parks Museum,** www.montgomery .troy.edu/rosaparks, **Dexter Avenue King Memorial Baptist Church,** the **Civil Rights Memorial,** www.splcenter.org/civil-rights-memorial, and the **Alabama State Capitol.** In the center of the trail, the interpretive center's excellent introductory film, moving photography, and interactive exhibits provide the setting for understanding the 1965 Voting Rights March that culminated in the Voting Rights Act of the same year, one of the great campaigns for human rights in the United States.

i **At the Battle of Mabila between Hernado De Soto's forces and those of Chief Tascaluza, 82 Spaniards and possibly as many as 4,000 to 5,000 native men and women perished. It was not a battle but rather a slaughter. Remarkably, it was destined to be the bloodiest battle on American soil until Shiloh during the Civil War some 332 years later.**

SELMA & OLD CAHAWBA

Selma, about 90 miles south of Birmingham, makes for a great day trip. It is a fascinating old Alabama town known for its wealth of historic homes and buildings. In fact, it holds the state's largest contiguous historic district with over 1,250 structures. Be sure to see the **Old Town Historic District, Sturdivant Hall,** (334) 872-5626, www .sturdivanthall.com, and **Old Live Oak Cemetery,** www.selmaalabama.com. Housed in the Old Depot, the **Selma/Dallas County Museum of History and Archives,** (334) 874-2197, preserves a wealth of information, articles, and items from the Black Belt region's past. Photographs taken from the 1890s to 1905 marvelously record rural black culture among the Black Belt plantations of the day. The restored **St. James Hotel,** (334) 872-0332, www.historicstjameshotel .com, overlooking the Alabama River and the Edmund Pettus Bridge, is the best option for lodgings in the historic downtown area.

Old Cahawba, Alabama's first permanent state capital, is a short 13 miles from Selma, and may be the closest Alabama ever gets to ruined castles, fallen-in monasteries, and abandoned cathedrals. Set beside the Cahaba River as it flows into the mighty Alabama River, the city's ruins are a stark reminder of what could have been one of Alabama's greatest cities. Today, it is known as **"Alabama's most famous Ghost Town." Old Cahawba Archaeological Park,** (334) 872-8058, www.cahawba.com, is a fascinating interpretive site to wander about the abandoned streets, caved-in cellars, and vine-clad columns, and explore the picturesque remains what once was one of Alabama's wealthiest towns. An interesting side note: The route Spanish conquistador Hernado De Soto took when he made his way across the region in 1540 is not known for certain; however, a group of scholars recently suggested Dallas County near where the Cahaba joins the Alabama River at Old Cahawba. They posit the location as a possible site for the disastrous Battle of Mabila between De Soto's forces and those of Chief Tascaluza, the Native-American leader attempting to resist the invading Spaniards.

TUSKEGEE NATIONAL PARK SITES,

The **Tuskegee Institute National Historic Site,** www.nps.gov/tuin, on the campus of historic **Tuskegee University,** is a short 2-hour drive from Birmingham and holds a variety of attractions for those interested in this part of American history. At Tuskegee Institute National Historic Site, visitors learn about **Tuskegee Normal School for Colored Teachers,** established in 1881 in Alabama by a former slave and a former slave owner to educate recently freed African Americans. Later renaming itself **Tuskegee Institute,** the school would become a major political force in the country educating African Americans. **Booker T. Washington,** the school's first president, helped Tuskegee become vitally important, educating African Americans for self-sufficiency. Later, in the mid-20th-century when the struggle for equal rights progressed on to ending the practice of segregation, the right of all people to an equal education would take center stage. **George Washington Carver,** the renowned educator, scientist, and innovator, spent more than four decades on the campus at Tuskegee furthering the school's international reputation. That legacy and that journey continue today on the campus of Tuskegee University, where the park site is located. Other items to see include the **George W. Carver Museum** and **The Oaks,** home of Booker T. Washington.

Nearby, the **Tuskegee Airmen National Historic Site,** www.nps.gov/tuai, preserves the cultural legacy of the African-Americans pilots who, during World War II, challenged the United States government to reexamine its institutional segregation of African Americans in the military. Because of the Institute's flight program, the US military selected Tuskegee Institute as a place to train African-American pilots for the war effort. More than 1,000 aviators from across the country came here to become distinguished combat pilots in the nation's war effort. See the **Hangar #1 Museum,** historic **Moton Airfield,** and the visitor center to learn more about this era.

WEEKEND GETAWAYS

Beach Trips

✳APALACHICOLA, FLORIDA

A true gem on the Florida Gulf Coast, **Apalachicola** is a historic Antebellum town dotted with live oaks fringed with Spanish moss. Founded in 1831 the town has over 200 historic homes and buildings on the National Register. Biking through the district is a great half-day activity. The town is almost entirely devoid of chain restaurants. Surrounded by the last great expanse of pinewoods on the Gulf, this remote region is not called the **"Forgotten Coast"** for nothing. Try the **Coombs House Inn,** (850) 653-9199, www.coombshouseinn.com, a turn-of-the-century Victorian mansion, for lodgings with character. **Papa Joe's Oyster Bar & Grill,** (850) 653-1189, www.papajoesoysterbar .com, the local hangout, has plywood floors and the city's most notable oyster shucker in James Hicks. For a fun and productive day on the Apalachicola Bay or river, try **Book Me a Charter,** www.bookmeacharter.com, which leads fishing trips in the area. Apalachicola is 330 miles from Birmingham.

i For one of the best little bookstores in the Panhandle, try Downtown Books & Purl, (850) 653-1290, on Apalachicola's Commerce Street. Specializing in Florida history and fiction, it also offers yarn and accessories for knitters in the fantastic old structure.

MOBILE, ALABAMA

From early statehood until the Civil War, **Mobile** *was* Alabama in many respects. The point of entry for most goods from abroad, a source of world news, and the entryway for the latest fashions from Paris and London, Mobile was one of the most cosmopolitan cities in the region. While some of that has changed, Mobile, www.mobile.org, is still a fascinating city—look closely and you'll see its French and Spanish roots showing through, albeit with a particularly Southern-American flair. From the oldest Mardi Gras in the country to the south's easiest vacation cruise port, the city has loads of fun and excitement to offer. Try the **Gulf Coast Science Center Exploreum,** www.exploreum.net, which offers kids a chance to entertain themselves with a variety of hands-on educational activities. Don't miss **The Museum of Mobile,** www.museumofmobile.com, perhaps the ideal city history museum. If you're overnighting, the **Battle House Renaissance Mobile Hotel & Spa,** (251) 338-2000, www.historichotels.org/hotel/Battle_House, a legendary 1852 downtown hotel recently completely renovated and refurbished, is a delight. But really, of all Alabama cities, Mobile may be the only truly pedestrian-friendly one. With a comfortable pair of shoes, you can tour the city's historic districts and see just about all there is to see on foot. To soak up Mobile's great nightlife, take a stroll down **Dauphin Street:** You

Alabama's Biodiversity

A glance at any physiographical map of North America will tell the story of Alabama. The diversity of land forms—mountain, valley, plateau, coastal plain, highlands—create a great diversity of riverine environments from coastal marshes and swamps to broad rivers to narrow, rocky mountain streams. And in turn, because of such a wide range of habitats, Alabama's Mobile Basin alone contains more aquatic species than nearly any other drainage area of comparable size in North America. The fantastic natural riches this region can claim has sustained and allowed those settling here—from thousands of years ago through the present—to flourish. Alabama's rivers also serve as an ark of biodiversity for North America. The Cahaba River alone—just 190 miles long—contains more fish species than the entire state of California. Alabama rivers contain a staggering 38 percent of North America's fish species, 52 percent of it freshwater turtle species, 43 percent of its freshwater gill-breathing snails, and 60 percent of its freshwater mussels. Consequently, many of Alabama's rivers hold more species of fish, mussel, snails, and other fauna per mile than most other rivers in North America. With more than 47,000 miles of streams and rivers flowing year-round, Alabama can justifiably lay claim to an unparalleled abundance of water.

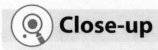

Close-up

Callaghan's Irish Social Club

Yes, St. Patrick's Day is in March, but that's no reason not to visit **Callaghan's Irish Social Club,** 916 Charleston St.; (251) 433-9374; www.callaghansirishsocialclub .com; in Mobile's Oakleigh Garden historic district. Whether it's Sunday brunch, a pint of Guinness with a friend after work, or better yet, the best hamburger you've ever had, Callahan's is the place to go. The burger is not fancy, it's just plain fresh ingredients: red onions, fat, tasty tomato slices, large sesame-seed bun. And a huge, juicy piece of meat—and applewood smoked bacon, if you like. There are no fries, so you choose between homemade potato salad, pasta salad, coleslaw, or, the best, a tart vinegar-laden tomato and cucumber salad. On Wed Callaghan's serves the "L.A. Burger" (think Lower Alabama rather than Hollywood), which employs some ground-up Conecuh sausage. Bad for your heart? Maybe, but good on your stomach. *Esquire* magazine featured Callaghan's in their Best Bars in America but don't worry: It's not that kind of a bar. Patrons range from college students to seniors, from friendly locals that walked to their neighborhood pub to French and German tourists who have heard this is the place to grab a hamburger and enjoy the Oakleigh district atmosphere.

---

never know what you'll turn up—fancy bistros, tattoo parlors, delicious Creole restaurants, and late-night bars. Mobile is a gumbo of culture and customs. It will surprise you. Mobile is 260 miles from Birmingham.

NAVARRE BEACH, FLORIDA

While Hurricane Ivan gave the barrier island a hammering in 2004, **Navarre** has come back strong. The rebuilt **Navarre Beach Fishing Pier,** a landmark destroyed by Hurricane Ivan, reopened in 2010. The 1,500-foot-long pier is the longest in the Gulf of Mexico. With a new visitor center, numerous new boardwalks over the dunes, rebuilt beaches, and one million sea oats recently planted, this lesser-known spot is ready for its close-up. Navarre enjoys 8 miles of undeveloped, pristine beaches courtesy of **Gulf Islands National Seashore,** www.nps.gov/guis, making this the longest section of continuously protected beach in the Panhandle. You'll find

historic forts, trails through fresh-and saltwater marshes to explore, and numerous bird species to observe. Start with the **Santa Rosa County Visitor Information Center,** (850) 939-2691, www.beaches-rivers.com, for vacation guides and local information. Navarre is 250 miles away from Birmingham.

In case that's not enough, nearby **Navarre Beach State Park** offers an additional 130-acres to ensure Navarre's best beach bragging rights.

ROSEMARY BEACH

The fact that New Urbanism visionaries Andres Duany and Elizabeth Plater-Zyberk (architects of Seaside fame, also on Highway 30A) designed the meticulous **Rosemary Beach,** (866) 348-895, www.rosemarybeach .com, might not impress your kids. The cultured, architectural hints of St. Augustine, the West Indies and traditional southern beach towns colored in warm earth tones

10 Things to Do in the Florida Panhandle

1. Experience the singular beauty and native wildlife of **Wakulla Springs State Park,** the world's largest single-vent freshwater springs.

2. Dine in white linen restaurants such as **Fish Out of Water** at **Water-Color Inn, Owl Cafe** in Apalachicola, and **Great Southern School of Fish** in WaterSound, where local flavors are the star attraction.

3. Scallop in **St. Joseph Bay,** where you'll see almost as many sea horses as the blue-eyed scallops.

4. Taste the unique flavor of **Wewahitchka's Tupelo Honey,** made only along the Chipola and Apalachicola river valley. It's the only honey in the world that will not granulate.

5. Watch the **Blue Angel flight team** perform amazing feats of aeronautics just outside **Pensacola's National Museum of Naval Aviation,** where visitors can see some 140 planes and learn what it was like for the crews who flew them.

6. Canoe the crystal clear **Econfina Creek** in Bay and Washington counties and swim in Gainer Springs, one of this continent's few first magnitude springs.

7. Drive back in time along the live oak-lined **Canopy Roads** that follow the same route today as they did when first Native Americans and then the Spanish followed these same trails.

8. Take one look at the color of the Gulf's waters along the western Panhandle, and you'll immediately understand why the region is known the world over as the **Emerald Coast.** Bring your shades because of the brilliantly, blindingly white-sand beaches.

9. Bring your binoculars and visit one of nearly 80 sites in the **Panhandle Section of the Great Florida Birding Trail.** Who knows, you might even spot the **Ivory-billed Woodpecker,** reportedly rediscovered in the Panhandle after decades of presumed extinction.

10. Join local residents at **Papa Joe's Restaurant** in Apalachicola to watch oyster shuckers pry open and serve on the half-shell what just may be the best oysters in the world.

and natural materials probably will be lost on them, too. As will the native plantings and flora. But the beautiful pools, impeccable beaches, grassy public parks, and ideal biking opportunities will certainly entertain the kids. And the many secret pathways and footpaths will only add to Rosemary Beach's charms for children. If that doesn't work, take them to **The Sugar Shack,** a youth hangout with more sweets than an adult can fathom. Comfortable cottages and carriage houses accommodate everyone from small families to large reunions, all in luxurious style. Shopping and dining, a great wine bar, and a bike rental shop mean you never even have to leave the town. Perhaps best of all, the online concierge services means parents can make requests before their arrival for everything from cribs and groceries to tee times and romantic dinner reservations at local restaurants ("romantic" because Rosemary Beach has a babysitting service). Rosemary Beach is 260 miles from Birmingham.

ℹ️ **The Northwest Florida Beaches International Airport, http://ifly beaches.com, connects the Panhandle with a host of new cites. The airport includes service by Delta Airlines and Southwest Airlines, www.southwest .com/ecpservice.**

✳SCENIC HIGHWAY 30A

When visitors to the Gulf Coast say they holiday "on 30A," what they are indicating is more suggestive of a general experience rather than any specific place. **Scenic Highway 30A,** a 19-mile road that hugs the coastline in **South Walton County, Florida,** passes by rare coastal dune lakes and some of the most brilliantly white-sand beaches in the country (all of 30A's beaches are certified Blue Wave Beaches), as well as the area's chic New Urbanist beach communities like **WaterColor,** www.watercolorresort.com, **Seaside,** www.seasidefl.com, **WaterSound,** www.watersoundvacationrentals.com, **Alys Beach,** www.alysbeach.com, and **Rosemary Beach,** www.rosemarybeach.com. All are among the finest planned resort communities in the nation. Sandwiched between these pristine destinations is the funky, organic town of **Seagrove Beach,** a refreshingly untidy collection of lovely homes, restaurants, and eclectic shops. Seagrove is a

popular spot for families to rent a home for the week. Also along the route is the historic old Florida neighborhood of **Grayton Beach,** home to the infamous **Red Bar,** several blocks of wonderful old homes and cottages, a number of charter fishing boat companies, and the fantastic breakfasts at the **Hibiscus Cafe,** within the larger **Hibiscus Guesthouse** (offering rooms and small cottages to rent). But the common denominator for the 30A experience is that the highway is flanked on either side for much of the way by bike paths, meaning vacationers can park their cars and walk or bike to most restaurants, seafood markets, state parks, beaches, coffee houses, and tourist attractions. Expect the gamut of distractions, from wine festivals to deep-sea-fishing opportunities, from top-notch white-linen dining experiences to atmospheric local oyster bars, boutique galleries, and the trademark roadside souvenir shops. And it's only 4.5 hours from Birmingham. For Birmingham residents 30A has become a home-away-from-home.

ST. ANDREWS STATE PARK, FLORIDA

St. Andrews State Park, (850) 233-5140, www.floridastateparks.org/standrews, in **Panama City,** is one of the most popular outdoor recreation spots in Florida. The park's uplands are characterized by rolling, white-sand dunes separated by low swales of either pinewoods or marshes. Dunes covered with sea oats abound. Dunes found farther inland are covered with sand pines, scrub oaks, rosemary and other hardy plants that help prevent soil erosion. Visitors are encouraged to hike the **Blue Heron Trail** that starts at a reconstructed Cracker turpentine still and winds through a number of plant communities. Freshwater and

Best of 30A

"Best of" lists are always limiting—what to leave out, what to leave in?—but here's a starting point for some of 30A's top attractions:

Best Art Gallery: Zoo Gallery, www.thezoogallery.com

Best Breakfast Spot: Hibiscus Cafe, www.hibiscusflorida.com

Best Coffee Joint: Amavida Coffee, (850) 231-1077

Best for Kids: Gigi's Fabulous Kids' Fashion & Toys, www.gigisfabkids.com

Best Golf: Camp Creek Golf Club, www.campcreekgolfclub.com

Best Live Music and Beer: Red Bar, www.theredbar.com

Best Old Florida Lodging: Seagrove Villas Motel, www.SeagroveVillas.com

Best Oyster Bar: Hurricane Oyster Bar & Grill, Facebook

Best Romantic Spot: Caliza Restaurant, www.calizarestaurant.com

Best Sunset Drink: Bud and Alley's, www.budandalleys.com

Best Seafood Market: Goatfeathers Seafood Market, (850) 267-3342

Best Specialty Foods: Modica Market, www.modicamarket.com

Best Shopping District: Seaside, www.seasidefl.com

Best White Linen Restaurant: Fish Out of Water, www.watercolorresort .com/resort_dining.aspx

saltwater marshes teem with wildlife and birds. The **Gator Lake Trail** provides visitors with a beautiful vantage point for spotting alligators and a variety of waterfowl, wading birds, and other small animals. **Button Bush Marsh** is a favorite feeding place for a variety of birds including herons and ibis. The 1,260-acre park is located on the island of **Panama City Beach** and has over 1.5 miles of beach on the Gulf of Mexico and the Grand Lagoon. *Travel Magazine* named it the "World's Best Beach" in 1995—you'll be delighted to find that very little has changed in the intervening years. Panama City is 270 miles from Birmingham.

City Destinations

✳ASHEVILLE, NORTH CAROLINA

For delicious food, funky arts, and outdoors fun, **Asheville** is unrivaled in the south. From the **Black Mountain Center for the Arts,** the **Folk Art Center,** and the **Museum of the Cherokee Indian** (in nearby Cherokee, NC) to the **Blue Ridge Parkway**—surely one of the most scenic byways in the country—as well as a host of other cultural sites like the **Thomas Wolfe Memorial** site, Asheville is more than just another town in the mountains. The concentrated mix of sophistication and culture that is Asheville seems to exist almost because of rather than in spite of its remote location at 2,120 feet. Everyone knows about **Biltmore Estate,** the grand Vanderbilt home in town, and it's certainly worth a visit. But Asheville is so much more. Recently, Asheville has become a food mecca. Local farm-to-table restaurants dot the culinary scene, as do vegetarian and organic spots, as well as a number of award-winning local breweries—think Portland in miniature. And it's hard to imagine a more pleasant sidewalk cafe town. At the nationally recognized **Tupelo Honey Cafe,** (828) 255-4863, www.tupelohoneycafe.com, on busy College Street, expect healthy southern favorites like blackened catfish and grits served with a twist. Try the **Princess Anne Hotel,** (828) 258-0986, www.princessannehotel.com, a boutique B&B nestled in a three-story shingle style hotel built in 1924 in Asheville's **Chestnut Hill National Historic District.** Wonderfully restored recently, it is only minutes from downtown by foot. Eat breakfast at **Over Easy Cafe.** If you're driving the 6 hours from Birmingham, be sure to end your trip in Asheville the way you began it—on the magnificent Blue Ridge Parkway.

ATLANTA, GEORGIA

For sheer size **Atlanta** is an unusual proposition. There's really no way to encapsulate all the fantastic weekend possibilities of this city of more than five million located only 150 miles east of Birmingham. If you want professional sports, there are the Braves, Falcons, Hawks, and Thrashers. Attractions like the **World of Coca-Cola, Georgia Aquarium, Children's Museum of Atlanta, High Museum of Art, CNN tours, Stone Mountain Park, Margaret Mitchell House,** and more offer round-the-clock entertainment for everyone. Atlanta's Midtown is hopping with chic hotels, clubs, and posh restaurants. The **Buckhead** area is home to upscale shopping and fine nightlife. **Quaint Virginia Highlands** is home to young families and professional types who appreciate their fine neighborhood boutiques, restaurants, and bars—and are willing to share them with visitors, too. For the bohemian set, **Little 5 Points** offers a fresh alternative with art, theater, shopping, and dining options. **East Atlanta Village,** a thriving community, is the perfect place to park your car and walk with

Georgia Aquarium

Leave it to Atlanta to one-up Chattanooga, water-wise: the **Georgia Aquarium,** (404) 581-4000, www.georgiaaquarium.org, opened at the end of 2005 as the world's largest aquarium with some 8 million gallons of fresh water and, oh, 100,000 animals, give or take. It encompasses more than 9 acres of prime land adjacent to Centennial Olympic Park. What's great for kids—and curious adults—is that 25 percent of the floor space is dedicated to education, ranging from interactive displays and creative technologies to make for a great travel destination when in Atlanta. Sixty aquatic habitats are covered, including those of whale sharks and beluga whales. A spectacular underwater tunnel allows kids an up-close view into the whale shark habitat. Open 365 days a year, aquarium tickets may sell out for any given day, so reserving ahead is a good idea.

the family to shops, restaurants, nightlife, and parks. Be sure to visit www.atlanta.net for visitor guides, hotel packages, CityPass, calendar of events, and their 50 Fun Things to Do list.

MEMPHIS, TENNESSEE

Home of the blues, birthplace of rock-n-roll, **Memphis** certainly has it going on with regard to music. Their barbecue ain't that bad, either (that's a friendly joke, as the city's excellent barbecue reputation is earned, setting the stage for the friendly barbecue rivalry between Birmingham and Memphis). From Delta greats like Muddy Watters, Howlin' Wolf, Johnny Cash, and Elvis Presley to the Stax Records soul heritage, the city is an astoundingly fun place to catch the best live rock, soul, blues, and alternative music. For the faithful there's **Graceland.** For the partying set there's **Beale Street.** For a taste of Memphis' still vibrant music scene, try the **Hi-Tone,** (901) 278-8663, www.hitonememphis.com, in Midtown—it offers the best of local rock, as well as occasional international acts such as Elvis Costello, Robin Hitchcock and the Posies. For local color with a beer, try the **Lamplighter Lounge,** (901) 726-1101, also in Midtown. For the bizarre, there are voodoo shops like **Tater Red's Lucky Mojos** and **Voodoo Healing.** Stay downtown in the boutique **Madison Hotel,** (901) 333-1200, www.madisonhotelmemphis.com, or the stately **The Peabody,** (901) 529-4000, www.peabodymemphis.com.

If you've only a short 24 hours in town, you've got your work cut out for you. Here's your perfect Memphis day: Start at the original **Cafe Eclectic** in Midtown for breakfast. Spend the morning just down the road at **Overton Park,** home of the **Memphis Zoo,**

Brooks Museum of Art, and plenty of green space. Have barbecue at the world-famous **Rendezvous,** then grab a coffee at **Otherlands.** Check out **Stax Museum of American Soul Music** then dine at **Tsunami** in Cooper-Young for dinner. Cross your fingers that a cool band is playing at **Wild Bill's,** then head back downtown to Beale Street and enjoy watching the tourists. Explore www.memphistravel.com for hotels, dining, coupons, events, and an overview of the city's great offerings. Memphis is 240 miles from Birmingham.

✳ CHATTANOOGA, TENNESSEE

Nestled between Missionary Ridge, Lookout Mountain, and Signal Mountain, **Chattanooga** has always benefited from its dramatic setting. But the city has also undergone a renaissance over the last few years, transforming from industrial blight with some of the worst air quality in the country to an outdoor-lover's green destination. New parks and recreation spaces have been created that take advantage of the city's natural setting as well as the Tennessee River, which twists and turns through the metropolitan area. Warehouses and old department stores are being restored, an electric shuttle silently spirits visitors through downtown, and a pedestrian bridge over the river connects with both green and blueways. When the turnaround began, an *Utne Reader* cover story hailed Chattanooga as one of the "Ten Most Enlightened Cities in America." There is much more to this town than just the Chattanooga Choo-Choo.

The world's largest freshwater aquarium, the **Tennessee Aquarium and IMAX Theater,** and the nearby **Creative Discovery Museum** alone are reason enough for a visit. Civil War buffs will find ample

---

Adventure Time Chattanooga!

If you love the active outdoors, there are numerous adventured-based excursions on-hand in and around Chattanooga:

Extreme rafting on the nearby Nantahala and Ocoee Rivers (class IV), www.noc.com

Caving/spelunking with High Country Adventures, www.hcrivers.com

Hang gliding at Lookout Mountain Flight Park, www.hanglide.com

Skydiving with Skydive Chattanooga, www.skydivechattanooga.com

Kayaking the Tennessee River Blueway Trail or whitewater adventure at one of several nearby options such as North Chickamauga Creek (class III–V), www.outdoorchattanooga.com

Stellar sandstone bouldering at Rocktown on nearby Pigeon Mountain, www.rockcreek.com

Rock climbing at multiple locations with The Adventure Guild (also offer ropes courses, caving, paddling, and other adventure-based trips and educational experiences), www.theadventureguild.com

---

entertainment at **Chickamauga National Park,** the nation's oldest military park, as well as several other nearby sites. And the retro kitsch of **Rock City, Ruby Falls,** and the **Incline Railway** never really goes out of style. Voted one of America's top family weekend getaways by *Southern Living*'s Reader's Choice Awards, Chattanooga also places you within striking distance of the **Smoky Mountains National Park** and a host of scenic hiking opportunities and day trips. Try www.outdoorchattanooga.com and www.chattanoogafun.com for more weekend ideas. Chattanooga is 150 miles northeast of Birmingham.

NEW ORLEANS, LOUISIANA
Everyone knows **New Orleans** is different. That "moonlight and magnolia" backdrop of romance and myth is certainly there, as is the tropical setting. But the Big Easy's hedonistic excesses—largely confined to **Bourbon Street**—are often exaggerated. Beyond the **French Quarter,** New Orleans is a city full of quaint, colorful districts and wards begging to be explored by foot or bike. Huge, stately live oaks line the city's broad avenues, extending their ancient branches over the streets and sidewalks that lead past stately mansions, charming shotgun houses, and neighborhood cafes and restaurants. And when the rest of the country shivers December through February, high temperatures in the Big Easy hover in the pleasant mid-60s. Begin in **Bayou St. John** and the petite plantations that date back to 1784. After a visit to **St. Louis Cemetery #3,** head to the French Quarter for a required stop in **Jackson Square** for beignets and cafe au lait at **Cafe du Monde,** (504) 525-4544, www.cafedumonde.com, one of the oldest cafes in the country. It is open 24 hours a day, a New Orleans perk.

After a break hop the ferry to the **Gretna Historical District** across the Mississippi River for a delicious late lunch at a tiny local hangout, **Gattuso's Neighborhood Restaurant,** (504) 368-1114, www.gattusos deli.com, famed for their crab and corn bisque, shrimp or fish po' boys, sweet potato fries and other Louisiana delicacies. Then head back across the Big Muddy to gawk at the **American Sector of the Garden District,** replete with Antebellum and Victorian mansions. For dinner try the colorful **Jaques-Imo's Cafe,** (504) 861-0886, www .jacquesimoscafe.com, in the Riverbend neighborhood, or **Mandina's,** (504) 482-9179, www.mandinasrestaurant.com, where locals tend to take their out-of-town guests to show them New Orleans. Follow that by a lively evening of jazz at **Donna's Bar & Grill** in the French Quarter, (504) 596-6914, www .donnasbarandgrill.com, or **Preservation Hall,** (504) 522-2841, www.preservationhall .com, a venue that preserves the authentic jazz spirit and feel of New Orleans' past. Every tourist does the French Quarter and Pat O'Brian's: Visit more of the real New Orleans. For guides, accommodations, calendars, and travel tools, see www.neworleansonline.com or www.neworleanscvb.com. New Orleans is 340 miles from Birmingham.

The Great Outdoors

BARTRAM CANOE TRAIL

Want to test your navigational skills the way naturalist William Bartram did here in 1775? Then the **Mobile-Tensaw Delta** is for you. Start at the **Five Rivers Delta Resource Center,** the terminus facility for the **Bartram Canoe Trail,** one of the longest canoe trails in the country. Located a short drive from Mobile, Alabama (250 miles south of Birmingham), Five Rivers contains exhibits, a widescreen theater, rentals, and outfitting, as well as a knowledgeable staff for trip planning. But bring your GPS: The 250,000-acre expanse of rivers, streams, lakes, sloughs, and bayous of this, the nation's second-largest river delta, snakes back and forth upon itself in a maze of waterways. There are 6 overnight trails, along with 4 floating covered platforms for camping. Times to avoid? Alligator mating season in the spring when the cold-blooded critters get downright frisky. They'll sometimes venture right up to your canoe just to see how friendly you are!

RECREATIONAL & SPORT DIVING, GULF OF MEXICO

For the adventurous the Florida Panhandle offers many great diving options, including spear fishing, reefs, manatee-watching, and shipwreck and historic underwater parks, www.museumsinthesea.com. Four of Florida's **Underwater Archaeological Preserves**—the USS *Massachusetts,* SS *Tarpon, Vamar,* and *City of Hawkinsville*—are located within a half-day drive from Birmingham. Once one of the most powerful battleships on the planet, today the **USS *Massachusetts*** rests serenely in 26 feet of emerald green water just waiting to be explored. Among the oldest existing American battleships, the USS *Massachusetts* is located south of Pensacola The 350-foot battleship was decommissioned in 1921 and used for target practice until it sank, creating an artificial reef attracting fish, fishermen, and of course, divers intent on exploring one of the area's archaeological treasures. Located nearly 4 miles off the shore of Mexico Beach, the ***Vamar*** is another popular underwater preserve. Rear Admiral Richard E. Byrd reconditioned and renamed the *Chelsea* to make it the first metal-hulled vessel to be

---

Sample Bartram Canoe Trail Itinerary

Day 1: Start in Mobile, founded in 1702, with a helicopter ride from the USS *Alabama* battleship in Mobile Bay to survey the marshlands you'll soon be paddling. Enjoy comfy historical B&B lodgings at Kate Shepard House, (251) 479-7048, www.kateshepardhouse.com, or My Victorian, (251) 219-9961, www.myvictorianbedand breakfast.com, before hitting the water. Dine at Wintzell's Oyster House on Dauphin Street, (251) 432-4605, wintzellsoysterhouse.com, for a fresh dozen and a cold one—break the record for oysters consumed in an hour (403!), and you eat free. Good luck with that.

Day 2: The light tannin-stained waters of Rice Creek are an ideal launching point. Head to Jug Lake platform to overnight and explore the cypress-tupelo swamps. Bring along Stan Tekiela's *Birds of Alabama* field guide: With over 300 species recorded here, this is prime bird-watching territory.

Day 3: Paddling to Two Rivers Campsite, you pass Jasmine Bayou—in the spring it is one of the prettiest spots in the Delta. Bottle Creek Indian Mounds, a large Mississippian complex inhabited from AD 1200 to 1450 is the closest thing the country has to pyramids.

Day 4: Didn't see enough gators? Head back to the city and take an airboat tour in the lower delta for a sure sighting, and then wind down in pampered luxury at The Battle House Renaissance Mobile Hotel & Spa, (251) 338-2000, www.historichotels.org/hotel/Battle_House.

---

used in Antarctic waters during his famous expedition there in 1928. But years later in 1942—and renamed *Vamar*—the ship sank in mysterious circumstances off the coast. Did saboteurs sink it to block the channel? Or was it just a simple case of negligence and overloading? No one may ever know. Though not an official archaeological preserve, the **Mighty O** is something of a pilgrimage site for divers. Off the coast of Pensacola lies the **USS *Oriskany*,** a massive aircraft carrier that was sunk in 2006 to create the world's largest artificial reef and dive site, www.divemightyo.com.

CAVE DIVING, FLORIDA

Cave diving is another sport, altogether. **Jackson Blue Springs,** www.cavediving.com/where/florida, located 240 miles from Birmingham, just outside of Marianna, Florida (about an hour west of Tallahassee) is regarded by many as one of Florida's best cave dives. Limestone formations, fossils, shells, and extensive offshoot provide enough entertainment for days of diving. For those with a boat, nearby **Merritt's Mill Pond** offers more dive options. Be sure to check in at the sheriff's office in Marianna with your C-card.

CALLAWAY GARDENS, GEORGIA

Much like the explosion of natural beauty every spring and summer, the esteemed **Callaway Gardens** in Georgia is undergoing a mild renaissance where the well-known traditions of the past are joined by new development and change. After all, it's been more than 55 years since the resort first opened. Callaway, (706) 663-2281, www.callawaygardens.com, found 150 miles from Birmingham, is the 40-acre azalea garden in Pine Mountain, Georgia, with some 3,400 varieties sporting purple, pink, and white blossoms. Equally well known is the vegetable garden demonstration area famous as the setting for the PBS television show, *The Victory Garden*. What many people take for granted is the vast extent of walking trails and scenic bikeways to explore. If gardens aren't your thing, there are several golf courses and a gun club offering both skeet and sporting clays. And the butterfly center, a Leadership in Energy and Environmental Design (LEED)-certified building and the continent's largest glass enclosed tropical conservatory, holds hundreds of butterflies to observe and enjoy—a favorite activity for children. The centerpiece and new hub amid all the changes is the **Lodge and Spa at Callaway,** a new 150-room facility opened in late 2006 that offers luxury guest rooms and suites, restaurants, conference facilities, and a saltwater pool. The spa's 13 treatment rooms and full menu is a nice complement to the resort's more traditional offerings.

NATCHEZ TRACE

It's the original road trip. The 444-mile long **Natchez Trace,** (800) 305-7417, www.nps.gov/natr, is essentially a story of migration, from the Choctaw, Natchez, and Chickasaw Indians that hunted along the paths that make up the Trace to the French, Spanish, and American settlers that used the route for settlement and getting products to market in Natchez or downriver to New Orleans. Today, the Trace is a leisurely and scenic drive from Nashville to Natchez taking the visitor through Tennessee, Alabama, and Mississippi. It's also a great destination for a family road trip with educational and recreational opportunities as well as interesting side trips found along the way. For those that want to stretch their legs, you'll find 63 miles of **Natchez Trace National Scenic Trail,** a **Chickasaw Village,** numerous overlooks, and small towns en route. There are Civil War sites such as **Brices Cross Roads National Battlefield Site** where Union forces lost five men to every southern casualty as Confederate General Nathan Bedford Forrest strove to break up General William Tecumseh Sherman's supply lines. And of course, there are miles of quiet parkway roads for teenagers aspiring to acquire

---

Trout Fishing

Since the waters below **Lewis Smith Dam** stay in the 50- to 65-degree range all year, the Sipsey offers Alabama's only year-round trout fishing. Some 3,000 to 3,500 rainbow trout are stocked every 60 days. For access on the east side of the Sipsey Fork, a paved road runs north off Highway 69. For the next 2 miles there are many good spots to access the river. The **Riverside Fly Shop** on Highway 69 is a good source of information, (256) 287-9582, www.riversideflyshop.com.

their driver's license. The park service offers 3 free, first-come, first-served campgrounds along the Trace: **Jeff Busby, Meriwether Lewis and Rocky Springs Campground.** Near Tupelo, Mississippi, the **Parkway Visitor Center** at milepost 266 is a good place to orient yourself. Try www.scenictrace.com for news and new offerings regarding the trace. The National Park Service's Parkway Visitor Center is found in Tupelo, Mississippi, some 135 miles from Birmingham.

i Located between Marianna and Panama City, the crystal-clear springs of Econfina Creek are not to be missed when paddling in the regions. Start at the Econfina Creek Canoe Livery, (850) 722-9032, www.canoeeconfina creek.net, to catch the 11 springs and 36 vents along the creek. Bring your snorkel.

PANHANDLE PADDLING

Few think of the Florida Panhandle as a kayak or canoeing option, but an elevation loss of more than 300 feet in the 40 to 50 miles from the Alabama state line to the Gulf of Mexico translates to some swiftly flowing coastal rivers. White-sand beaches, clear-flowing artesian springs, the occasional alligator or red shouldered hawk—and near utter seclusion—makes for a great weekend excursion. The great longleaf pinewoods of the **Blackwater State Forest** offer the chance to see one of the last remaining expanses of these magnificent trees. Paddle the crystal-clear Coldwater Creek into the dark, haunting tannin-infused waters of the **Blackwater River.** Dark as English breakfast tea, the Blackwater

is a rare sand-bottom river full of towering white sandbars ideal for overnight camping. Try the **Juniper Creek** as well, conditions permitting: When the Sweetwater and Juniper's levels are just right, the Blackwater can be dangerously high and unrunable. If you're not bringing your own boat, **Adventures Unlimited,** (850) 623-6197, www.adventures unlimited.com, offers rentals, lodgings, and river trips on Coldwater and Juniper creeks and the Blackwater River.

SIPSEY WILDERNESS AREA

If it's just recharging your spiritual batteries, there is arguably no prettier place in Alabama than 28,000-acre **Sipsey Wilderness Area** in **Bankhead National Forest,** www.fs.fed.us/r8/alabama, about 80 miles northwest of Birmingham. Often called the **"Land of a Thousand Waterfalls,"** it is full of hiking trails weaving through lush canyons cut from the limestone of the **Cumberland Plateau.** The nearest town of any size, **Double Springs** is the gateway to the wilderness area—and the last chance for food and supplies. The **Sipsey Fork,** Alabama's only National Wild and Scenic River, is a wonderful canoe trip waiting to happen. A tributary of the **Mulberry Fork** (part of the Black Warrior River), the **Upper Sipsey Fork** is Alabama's only stream designated as a National Wild and Scenic River, so expect seclusion. Good floats include runs from the Thompson Creek access off FR 208, down to Winston County Road 60. The run from here to the WT Mims' Family Public Access Point at Highway 33 is also a popular one. After this point paddlers are entering Smith Lake.

LIVING HERE

In this section we feature specific information for residents or those planning to relocate here. Topics include real estate, education, health care, and much more.

RELOCATION

There's a host of great reasons to call Birmingham home. New arrivals come for the temperate weather. They come for medical, dentistry, optometry, and other health-related education or careers. They gravitate to Over the Mountain schools for their excellence. They see big-city amenities with a small town's relative lack of traffic and congestion. They see easy access to interstates and an approachable airport.

There's no end to the reasons, but next comes the difficult part: where to live? The ease and convenience of Vestavia Hills, Mountain Brook, and Homewood are matched by their solid school systems, walkable neighborhoods, and charming homes. Down-town loft living is, despite the economic downturn, still drawing those empty nesters or young hipsters who want to be where the action is. They enjoy some of the best that city life has to offer. Talk to those choosing suburbs and small towns beyond the city's core, and they'll likely argue how pleasant it is to live in your own self-contained community removed from the hustle and bustle of the city. Of course it also depends on your job location and your commute. Fortunately, there are plenty of options.

THE MARKET

It will come as no surprise that home prices and real-estate sales slowed in the region in response to the nationwide economic recession starting in 2008 when the downturn truly reached the area. Price declines have been driven by a weak economy rather than on foreclosures, still, the average price per square foot in the city increased 10 percent in 2010 when compared with the same period the previous year—an encouraging sign. Popular neighborhoods in the city of Birmingham include Highland Park, Redmont Park, and Forest Park, with average listing prices of $286,623, $485,254, and $336,617, respectively. The Birmingham-Hoover metro area ranked 201 among the 303 largest metropolitan areas in the country in the Federal Housing Finance Agency's 2010 data, appreciating only 5.46 percent

over the last 5 years. Translation: That's not great news, but it certainly could be worse. Just look at nearby Atlanta or Mobile.

Of course price appreciation varies quite widely depending on city and neighborhood. In general the most expensive homes are in Over the Mountain communities and gated communities like Shoal Creek and Greystone. The farther you get south of town, the less expensive the homes prices, generally speaking.

In Birmingham your first choice in location, if you have children, probably comes down to school systems. Redmont Park, Forest Park, and Highland Park offer lovely homes in desirable, safe neighborhoods, but since they are zoned in the city school system, many people choose to go the private school route, adding a layer of expense to your final reckoning. Just over Red Mountain the communities of Homewood and Mountain Brook offer sidewalk communities with exceptional public school systems. There is a premium to pay for these older, charming homes, but many feel the quick access to parks, shops, and restaurants—as well as their close proximity to downtown—make it more than worth the extra cost. Up the next hill on Shades Mountain begins Vestavia Hills, a newer suburb dating back to the 1950s and 1960s. While it bears many of the hallmarks of a post-War suburb (sprawl, lack of sidewalks, highway-oriented, racial homogeny), it is also a safe, friendly community with an excellent school system. Homes are typically spacious, and residents of Homewood's older cottages often eye the roomy closets and basement garages of their Vestavia friends with mild envy. You will find few complaints from those living in Vestavia Hills.

Farther south along I-65, the fast-growing city of Hoover is an attractive location for those wanting the suburban experience with all the amenities, from malls, new shopping developments, large national chain stores, and plenty of entertainment options. Neighborhoods like Riverchase, Inverness, and others that fall under the umbrella of Hoover offer pleasant wooded communities nestled near major transportation arteries that provide easy access to downtown. But really, these are just some of the more popular locations in the region to purchase a home. Surrounding communities like Gardendale, Irondale, Helena, Hueytown, Trussville, and Alabaster offer pleasant small-town alternatives to living closer to the city center.

Much is made about the relative safety of the suburbs versus the crime rate in the city. When one compares data on safety, Birmingham seems less safe than it actually

is. Ask a resident of the Birmingham-Hoover Metropolitan Area and chances are they don't have too many worries about crime. The *Birmingham News'* Joey Kennedy put it well in a piece on how the statistics often cited about Birmingham's crime rate are not a fair indicator of the city's safety. "Birmingham, unlike many municipal areas that have merged with surrounding suburbs, still goes it alone," he writes. "Look at the Birmingham-Hoover metro area. If we were one big city (as we should be), our violent crime rate would be 87th in the nation. And remember, these statistics rank Birmingham among cities with a population above 100,000. We're smallish in that range. When all cities are included, regardless of population, Birmingham ranks 200th in murder." Crime is an issue anywhere, but when looking at statistics, Kennedy's observations are something to keep in mind.

Urban Living

In just a few short years, the options for living downtown have dramatically grown. CiTYViLLE Block 121, for instance, a $35-million, 255-unit apartment community located at 20th Street South between 1st and 2nd Avenue South in the heart of UAB is just the latest new property to be developed. Renovation of the Burger-Phillips Department Store for 35 apartment units, the 24-unit Blach's Lofts, and the 40-unit Terrace Court building in Five Points South are other recent historical structures renovated to suit the needs of urban dwellers.

i Among the nation's 340 metropolitan areas, Birmingham-Hoover ranks among the top 35 in the attraction of young, single college-educated professionals according to the US Census Bureau.

REALTORS

There are thousands of realtors and hundreds of real-estate firms serving the Birmingham region. Here's a list of some of the bigger, better-known firms found in the area. For more, try the **Birmingham Association of Realtors,** (205) 871-1911; www .barbham.com.

BAYER PROPERTIES
2222 Arlington Ave., South, Birmingham
(205) 939-3111
www.bayerproperties.com

BOSTANY REALTY
2900 Central Ave., Suite 140, Homewood
(205) 870-7637

CENTURY21 ADVANTAGE
2200 Valleydale Rd., Suite 100, Birmingham
(205) 823-6677
www.myc21advantage.com

DANIEL REALTY SERVICES
2204 Lakeshore Dr., Suite 219, Homewood
(205) 871-8006
www.danielcorp.com

EDDLEMAN PROPERTIES
2700 Hwy. 280, Suite 425, Birmingham
(205) 871-9755
www.eddleman.com

ERA OXFORD REALTY
612 Montgomery Hwy., Suite 100, Vestavia Hills
(205) 979-2335
www.eraoxford.com

INGRAM & ASSOCIATES
1906 Cahaba Rd., Mountain Brook
(205) 871-5360
www.ingramnewhomes.com

J.H BERRY & GILBERT
3125 Independence Dr., Suite 100, Homewood
(205) 252-6999
www.jhberry.com

KELLER WILLIAMS REALTY
3535 Grandview Pkwy., Suite 350, Birmingham
(205) 397-6500
www.kw.com

LAH REAL ESTATE
2850 Cahaba Rd., Suite 200, Mountain Brook
(205) 870-8580
www.lahrealestate.com

REAL LIVING ADVANCED REALTY
3659 Lorna Rd., Suite 101, Hoover
(205) 824-9490
www.realliving.com

REALTY SOUTH
2807 Cahaba Rd., Mountain Brook
(205) 870-5420
www.realtysouth.com

RE/MAX PREFERRED
2 Office Park Circle, Suite 5, Birmingham
(205) 879-7665
www.bpreferred.com

REAL ESTATE GUIDES

APARTMENT FINDER
www.apartmentfinder.com/Alabama

APARTMENTS.COM
www.apartments.com/Alabama

BIRMINGHAM FOR RENT
www.birmingham.forrent.com

HOME GALLERY
www.realtysouth.com

MEDIA

Newspapers

BLACK & WHITE
2210 2nd Ave. North
(205) 933-0460
www.bwcitypaper.com
Around since 1992 *Black & White* is the most established "alternative" publication. In its distinctive 11-by-17-inch format, the newspaper is known for the colorful original artwork features on the cover each issue. A good source for city politics coverage, arts and entertainment, and extensive local listings of live music, dining, local news, and more, the free bi-weekly can be found at area restaurants, bookstores, libraries, and other public locations throughout the city. Expect direct and often confrontational editorials and one of the city's more entertaining and provocative editor's letters in the form of publisher Chuck Geiss' "Naked Birmingham."

THE BIRMINGHAM NEWS
2201 4th Ave. North
(205) 325-4444
www.bhamnews.com

Birmingham's principal news daily, *The Birmingham News* is the largest newspaper in Alabama. It was founded in 1888. In 2006 the *News* moved into a new $25-million building across the street from the historic building that had been their home since 1917. Until just recently the Hanson family ran the *News*. It is owned by Advance Publications. For daily updates, www.al.com is an aggregate site that displays content from *The Birmingham News, The Huntsville Times* and *Mobile Press-Register* newspapers.

BIRMINGHAM WEEKLY
2014 6th Ave. North
(205) 939-4030
www.bhamweekly.com
Another strong alternative publication the weekly magazine covers arts and culture, local news and politics, music, opinion, food and drink, and a wide assortment of items that often slip through the crack of more traditional news outlets. *Birmingham Weekly* enjoys strong support locally and is available in numerous free locations around the city.

THE NORTH JEFFERSON NEWS
1110 Main St., Gardendale
(205) 631-8716
www.njeffersonnews.com
A semi-weekly newspaper that publishes on Wed and Sat, *The North Jefferson News* covers the northern part of Jefferson County as well as western Blunt County, including the communities of Fultondale, Gardendale, Morris, Warrior, Kimberly, and Hayden. It was established in 1970, and covers news, sports, lifestyle, and other local concerns. The online version updates daily.

OVER THE MOUNTAIN JOURNAL
2016 Columbiana Rd.
(205) 823-9646
www.otmj.com

A suburban bi-weekly newspaper geared toward readers in Mountain Brook, Homewood, Vestavia Hills, Hoover, and North Shelby counties, the *Over the Mountain Journal* is delivered free to homes in its coverage area. The focus is on social events, people, charity events, and local school and sporting events coverage. It is enjoyed for the many pictures and snapshots of people featured in its pages.

SHELBY COUNTY REPORTER
115 North Main St., Columbiana
(205) 669-3131
www.shelbycountyreporter.com

Based in Columbiana in Shelby County, the *Shelby County Reporter* covers news, sports, schools, business, and the general culture of Shelby County. The paper publishes every Wed, though the online site updates several times daily.

i Bhamwiki.com, founded in 2006 by John Morse, contains over 7,400 articles about local topics large and small. Maintained by Morse and a small group of loyal contributors, the site is a living, growing encyclopedia about Birmingham and the surrounding region. It's also a good source of Birmingham-related news.

Magazines

ALABAMA MAGAZINE
1740 Oxmoor Rd., Suite 210, Homewood
(205) 870-8177
www.alabama-magazine.com

A statewide lifestyle title based in Birmingham, *Alabama Magazine* is a bimonthly showcase of the state's culture, people, heritage, and business. The first issue came out in January 2011.

ALABAMA BABY AND CHILD
130 Wildwood Blvd.
(205) 924-3636
www.albabymag.com

Available by subscription or complimentary copies at baby and maternity retailers in and around Birmingham, *Alabama Baby and Child* covers issues near and dear to expectant mothers and parents. It is also a resource for parents with products and services, shopping guides, calendars of events, and more. It publishes quarterly.

BIRMINGHAM HOME & GARDEN
2204 Lakeshore Dr., Suite 120
(205) 802-6363
www.pmtpublishing.com

Covering fashions and trends in home and garden topics primarily in the Over the Mountain communities, *Birmingham Home & Garden* tends toward the affluent audience. The magazine publishes 6 bi-monthly issues along with 3 special issues: *Decorators' Show-House, Second Homes,* and *Historic Homes.*

BIRMINGHAM MAGAZINE
505 20th St. North, Suite 200
Financial Center
(205) 241-8180
www.bhammag.com

The oldest and most pedigreed magazine serving the Birmingham area, *Birmingham Magazine* reaches nearly 150,000 readers. Areas of coverage include food and drink, art openings, concerts, home and garden, fashion, restaurants, business profiles, and more.

It has a strong online offering as well, with a number of relevant blogs and calendars. *Birmingham Magazine*'s City Guide iPhone app is a continually updated, searchable database listing accommodations, attractions, dining, events, nightlife, and shopping options in the city.

B METRO
2805 2nd Ave., Suite 200
(205) 202-4182
www.b-metro.com
B Metro is a lifestyle monthly magazine focusing on fashion, people, food and drink, and photography, as well as the social scene of metro Birmingham. The online version hosts a number of blogs by local writers covering a range of offerings.

Television

WBRC 6 (Fox)
WBIQ 10 (PBS)
WVTM 13 (NBC)
WTTO 21 (CW)
WBMA 33/40 (ABC)
WIAT 42 (CBS)
WPXH 44 (ION)
WABM 68 (MyNetworkTV)

Radio

Adult Contemporary
WMJJ 96.5 FM

Christian Contemporary
WDJC 93.7 FM

College
WJSR 91.1 FM

Contemporary
WQEN 103.7 FM

Country
WNCB 97.3 FM
WZZK-FM 104.7 FM
WNCB 97.3 FM
WDXB 102.5 FM

Gospel
WAGG 610 AM
WXJC 850 AM
WAYE 1220 AM

Jazz
WVSU-FM 91.1 FM

News/Talk
WAPI 100.5 FM
WJOX 94.5 FM
WERC 105.5 FM
WERC 960 AM
WAPI 1070 AM
WYDE 1260 AM

NPR Affiliate
WBHM 90.3 FM

Religious
WLJR 88.5 FM
WBFR 89.5 FM
WGIB 91.9 FM
WQOH 1480 AM

Rock
WZRR 99.5 FM
WBPT 106.9 FM
www.bhammountainradio.com

Spanish
WZGX 1450 AM

Sports
WJOX 94.5 FM
WJOX 690 AM

R & B

WUHT 107.7 FM
WBHK 98.7 FM
WBHJ 95.7 FM
WENN 102.1 FM

ℹ️ According to the author of *Rise of the Creative Class,* Richard Florida, Birmingham has an overall ranking of 9th among its 32 peer communities (mid-size metropolitan areas) in lifestyle amenities that attract the "creative class." Birmingham ranks 6th for creative workforce, 7th in high-tech, 26th in innovation, and 10th in diversity.

Blogs

They may come and go. They may not be "published" in the traditional sense, but there's no denying bloggers and other online sources deliver good inside information on the Magic City. Here are a few of the city's blogs that enjoy a local following. There are certainly more. Enjoy:

ACTIVECULTURE.INFO

A great starting point for all the events, attractions, and happenings in Birmingham, activeculture or Birmingham 365 is a program of the Cultural Alliance of Greater Birmingham which seeks to fund, support, nurture, and promote arts and cultural organizations and working artists in central Alabama. If you are looking for something to do in Birmingham, activeculture is your first stop.

BIRMINGHAMMOMMY.COM

Perhaps the premier parenthood blog, BirminghamMommy.com is all about talking honestly to moms (and some dads) about the experience—good and bad—of being a mom. There's parenting information, articles, resources, ideas, and more geared to making life a little better and easier for moms and the kids they love.

BIRMINGHAMREWOUND.COM

A fun, quirky, even slightly awkward site dedicated to memories of the Magic City, this blog is a treasure of old photos and relics of Birmingham's past. Run by Russell Wells and chockfull of local pop culture guru Tim Hollis, it is nostalgic and a wonderful place to spend time looking back and remembering.

BHAMTERMINAL.COM

More than just a blog, The Terminal is a repository of opinion, arts and culture, news, and happenings with a strong focus on downtown politics and goings on. Publisher and frequent contributor André Natta created the site in 2007, and it updates several times a day.

BHAMWIKI.COM

A resource without peer the site documents the Birmingham area, serving as an encyclopedia-like compendium of more than 7,200 individual entries in the wiki format about the city. Enjoy news articles, factoids, and nostalgic images as well as current events all about Birmingham.

FOODIMENTARY.COM

Calling itself a "Food Lover's Notebook," the popular online blog is all about the enjoyment of food. With more than 270,000 Twitter followers, the site has developed quite a following. Look for food facts, tips, recipes, quotes, history, and more.

LEGALSCHNAUZER.BLOGSPOT.COM

Run by Roger Shuler, a journalist and editor, Legal Schnauzer is a political blog with a sense of humor that covers all facets of Alabama politics. In particular the site is a fantastic resource for those looking for other Alabama and national political blogs, as well as blogs that emphasize citizen justice. The tag line says it all: "One couple's encounter with corrupt judges, slimy lawyers, and incompetent prosecutors in Alabama . . . and how you can avoid being cheated by the vermin who make a mockery of our justice system."

WELDBHAM.COM/SECONDFRONT

Local journalist Kyle Whitmire is the principal contributor to the Second Front, a blog about news, public affairs, and politics in Birmingham. It's a good source for original reporting that goes deeper than the typical local news coverage available in more traditional local media.

EDUCATION & CHILD CARE

Home to 14 institutions of higher education, Birmingham's colleges and universities offer opportunities for career advancement that rival those available in much larger cities. In Birmingham one can attend one of the nation's top medical schools at the University of Alabama at Birmingham, one of the top liberal arts colleges at Birmingham-Southern College, or one of the most highly respected law schools at Samford University's Cumberland School of Law. Additionally, Birmingham contains a variety of technical schools and community colleges to suit the needs of all aspiring students and professionals.

Birmingham's elementary and high school students are predominantly served by two school systems: the Jefferson County School System and the Birmingham City School System. Like many cities education and school-zoning play a major role in home-buying decisions. As the Birmingham metropolitan area has expanded, so too have the number of suburban school systems within Jefferson County and the surrounding areas. In addition to the many public schools that the county and city has to offer, Birmingham features some of the most prestigious private schools in the region—even the nation.

PUBLIC SCHOOLS

Like many southern cities Birmingham and Jefferson county's various school systems are very much a reflection of their segregated past. As the civil-rights movement progressed and Birmingham became an increasingly integrated city, the phenomenon known as "white flight" led to suburban sprawl and prompted many municipalities to establish their own school systems. As a result the Jefferson County and Birmingham City School Systems, although the second and fourth largest school systems in the state, respectively, have a much smaller enrollment than one might expect.

With 57 schools serving 27,000 elementary, middle, and high school students, the **Birmingham City School System,** (205)

231-4600, www.bhm.k12.al.us, is the fourth largest in the state and has a budget of over $200 million. Some of the system's underperforming schools are located in areas of high poverty and crime, further complicating efforts to enhance education. Nevertheless, many brilliant young people have come out of Birmingham's schools and a few of the city's systems score consistently high marks on achievement tests.

Birmingham features three magnet schools, **Huffman, Woodlawn,** and **Ramsay.** These schools attract the city's brightest students and generally outperform other city schools. Unfortunately, they often lag behind many suburban and private schools that are able to operate on larger budgets.

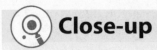

Close-up

ASFA's New Performing Arts Theater & New School Additions

The **Alabama School of Fine Arts (ASFA)** began construction on their new $7.6-million, 500-seat **Performance Network Theater** in late 2010. The 19,212-square-foot, professional theater will be used for students and the community and will be completed by early 2012. In addition to initiatives like ASFA, a number of other Birmingham schools have undergone vast improvements in recent years thanks to a capital improvement plan funded by a one-cent Jefferson County sales tax.

Located below Vulcan Park on the side of Red Mountain, **Ramsay High School** is in many ways the jewel of Birmingham's public schools. In 2008 Ramsay began a $21-million renovation that will allow the school to accommodate a larger base of students with all the amenities a 21st-century education requires. In 2002, through the generosity of local patrons and with the help of city funds, the new state-of-the-art **George Washington Carver High School** was built. Designed by the prominent Birmingham architecture firm Giattina Fisher Aycock (now Giattina Aycock), Carver High School offers its students the facilities necessary to foster the skills needed to compete in the global marketplace.

The **Jefferson County School System,** (205) 379-2000, www.jeffcoed.com, serves county residents outside of the Birmingham city limits and includes such municipalities as Bessemer, Gardendale, Hueytown, Irondale, McCalla, Oak Grove, and Pinson. As the second-largest school system in the state, Jefferson County is responsible for over 35,000 students at 52 schools and has a budget of over $100 million. Included among the county schools is the **Jefferson County International Baccalaureate School (JCIB),** ranked number two among the country's public high schools in 2010 by *Newsweek* magazine. Located in Irondale on the campus of Shades Valley High School, the JCIB seeks to challenge the county's most gifted students by placing them among their gifted peers in a stimulating environment that nurtures and cultivates their innate abilities.

While the city's schools and even these magnet schools have suffered the pangs of integration in the years following the civil-rights movement, a number of efforts to enhance the system's programs have been made by forward-thinking members of the community both inside and outside of Birmingham. For example, the **Alabama School of Fine Arts (ASFA),** located downtown near the Birmingham Museum of Art in the heart of Birmingham's Cultural District, opened at its current location in 1992. This publicly funded school serves students in grades 7 through 12 and is dedicated to fostering its students' artistic talents. ASFA is free to any resident of the state of Alabama that is able to meet its strict admission and audition requirements.

PRIVATE & PAROCHIAL SCHOOLS

Birmingham and its surrounding areas have over 100 private elementary, middle, and secondary schools. Although many of these are religiously affiliated and predominantly Christian, there are some secular private schools in the area. Tuition and fees vary from school to school and can range anywhere from $1,000 to $16,000. Many schools offer financial aid packages and scholarships to students that qualify, alleviating much of the burden of already stressed parents. The **Catholic Diocese of Birmingham** in Alabama is the single largest private school system in Birmingham with 27 schools, including 5 high schools, serving over 6,000 children in the Birmingham area. The Diocese operates a "Beacon of Hope" program that allows children to receive a private-school education entirely through private donations and at no cost to the child's family. Unless otherwise mentioned in an individual listing, all Catholic schools enforce a uniform policy for all students and usually require the student body to attend weekly Mass.

i In recent *Newsweek* magazine rankings of the nation's top 1,000 high schools, Jefferson County International Baccalaureate School was named the top public high school in the country. Additionally, 2 other public high schools have excelled: Alabama School of the Fine Arts has ranked as high as 4th in the nation and Mountain Brook ranked 248th.

Elementary & Middle Schools

ADVENT EPISCOPAL DAY SCHOOL
2019 6th Ave. North, Birmingham
(205) 252-2535
www.adventepiscopalschool.org
Housed within Birmingham's famed Cathedral Church of the Advent, the mother church for Birmingham's Episcopal diocese, Advent Day School has been providing quality education for children in grades kindergarten through 8th grade for nearly 60 years. Throughout its history Advent Day School has been at the forefront of elementary and middle school education and was, in 1969, the first independent school in Jefferson County to integrate. Serving 340 students, admission to Advent is very competitive.

CREATIVE MONTESSORI SCHOOLS
1650 28th Court South, Homewood
(205) 879-3278
www.creative-montessori.org
Located in suburban Homewood, Creative Montessori School opened in 1968 and is Birmingham's oldest Montessori school. Offering classes to children in pre-kindergarten to 6th grade, Creative Montessori seeks to create an environment that puts the power of choice in the hands of the student and to promote abstract thinking through environmental cues. Creative Montessori School also offers a number of programs that you'll be hard-pressed to find at any other school. Programs specifically geared towards young people include yoga, Young Rembrandts, and Kindermusik. Such programs broaden the horizons of Creative students and enhance the child's education beyond that of the average school.

HILLTOP MONTESSORI SCHOOL
6 Abbot Sq., Town of Mt. Laurel
(205) 437-9343
www.hilltopmontessori.com
With the mantra "Where learning comes naturally," Hilltop seeks to provide its students with both the necessary skills needed to excel in the world and a respect for that very world in which they work, live, and play. In a society that demands immediate results at all costs,

these two ideals of the Montessori education may seem unrealistic, but Hilltop proves year in and year out that it can be done, and with fantastic results. Hilltop serves students from pre-kindergarten to 8th grade. To fill in any perceived gap between a traditional education and a Montessori education, and to allay the fears of some parents, Hilltop's middle-school curriculum aligns very closely with that of the state of Alabama, all the while maintaining the unique distinctions that make a Montessori education so appealing.

Hilltop's location in Shelby County near the Shoal Creek Community allows the students ample opportunity to explore the scenery. The Hilltop school building is itself a structure to be admired. Housed in the first US Green Building Council LEED-certified building in the state of Alabama, Hilltop not only teaches its students respect for the natural environment, it practices it, too.

ISLAMIC ACADEMY OF ALABAMA
1810 25th Court South, Homewood
(205) 870-0422
www.iaaschool.com
Birmingham's newest parochial school is a Muslim preschool and K-8 with plans to develop into a K-12. The Islamic Academy offers a well-rounded educational experience that also incorporates Islamic studies as well as Arabic instruction. Truly a multicultural establishment the Islamic Academy has students from 14 different countries and teachers from 5 different countries. With the addition of the Hoover Crescent Islamic Center in Hoover and the continued worship at the next door Homewood masjid, the Islamic Academy of Alabama fulfills a needed role in the lives of Birmingham's Muslims.

JOSEPH S. BRUNO MONTESSORI ACADEMY
5509 Timber Hill Rd.,
Indian Springs Village, Shelby County
(205) 995-8709
www.jsbacademy.org
Founded in 1982 through the generosity of the Joseph S. Bruno Charitable Foundation, Bruno Montessori serves the educational needs of over 200 students from pre-kindergarten to 8th grade. With an emphasis on creative learning and natural discovery, the method of Montessori education has attracted many followers over the years. The school's rural Shelby County surroundings

The Montessori Method

In the world of childhood education, alternative approaches that don't work usually fade away rather quickly. The **Montessori Method** was established almost 100 years ago as an alternative to traditional education. That Birmingham has three such schools speaks to their effectiveness. Montessori schools focus on creativity and individualized, self-directed education. While this may seem like scholarly talk for a school with no teachers, studies of children educated under the Montessori Method reveal that Montessori students consistently score at or above the average for their age group on standardized tests and above average on tests that determine social development. For more information on Montessori education, visit www.montessori.edu.

provide the perfect backdrop for a Montessori education. Teachers and staff strive to create a learning environment that keeps the student in touch with his or her natural surroundings. And with 25 acres of trees, ponds, gardens, and wildlife, they achieve this with brilliant results. But for Bruno students nature doesn't just end with what's immediately around them. Bruno Montessori is home to the second-largest observatory telescope in the state of Alabama, allowing young learners to experience the universe around them.

N.E. MILES JEWISH DAY SCHOOL
4000 Montclair Rd., Birmingham
(205) 879-1068
www.nemjds.org

Founded in 1973 the N.E. Miles Jewish Day School is located on the Levite Jewish Community Center campus on Montclair Road and serves 81 children in kindergarten through 8th grade. The current building in which the school is housed was completed in 1993 and includes a library with over 10,000 English and Hebrew texts. Additionally, the school is close to the Levite Jewish Community Center, which provides children with access to a number of activities including tennis, swimming, and various other exercise programs offered through the LJCC. Students at NE Miles Jewish Day School not only receive an exceptional education in language, math, and the sciences, but also receive proper instruction in Judaic studies and learn to read, write, and speak Hebrew.

OUR LADY OF SORROWS CATHOLIC SCHOOL
1720 Oxmoor Rd., Homewood
(205) 879-3237
www.olsschool.com

Located on the grounds of Our Lady of Sorrows Catholic Church on Oxmoor Road in Homewood, Our Lady of Sorrows Catholic School, or simply OLS, is the largest Catholic elementary and middle school in the Birmingham Diocese, serving over 400 students from pre-kindergarten to 8th grade. With the Homewood Public Library conveniently located directly across the street from the school's entrance and Homewood Central Park to the rear of the school, OLS's location has something that can make both parents and kids happy. Additionally, the OLS Church has its own Family Life Center with a library of theological texts, gymnasium, and recreation room. The school itself has 2 classrooms and 2 teachers for each grade from kindergarten through 8th grade. OLS features a standard curriculum for all students with advanced classes available to higher-achieving students.

i As the city's largest private school system, the Catholic Diocese of Birmingham operates 27 various elementary, middle, and high schools. Many of the schools under the Diocese enjoy a reputation for academic excellence and discipline that attracts Catholics and non-Catholics alike. For more information on all of the area Catholic schools, visit www.bhmdiocese.org.

PRINCE OF PEACE CATHOLIC SCHOOL
4650 Preserve Pkwy., Hoover
(205) 824-7886
www.popcatholic.org

Opened in 2000 to serve the ever-expanding Hoover community, Prince of Peace has quickly earned a reputation as one of the top private schools in the area. In a decade's time Prince of Peace has grown to serve over 200 students from pre-kindergarten to 8th grade. Through the generosity of its parishioners, Prince of Peace has a number of facilities including 6 pre-school classrooms, an elementary school, middle school, 2 state-of-the-art technology labs, and a gymnasium.

THE REDMONT SCHOOL
1220 50th St. South, Birmingham
(205) 592-0541
www.theredmontschool.org
Also known as the Alabama Waldorf School, The Redmont School serves students from their first steps through 8th grade. Known for its emphasis on creativity and the importance of diversity, the Waldorf Education has gained international notoriety in the past three decades with new schools popping up all over the world. The Redmont School was established by Sheila Rubin in 1987 as Alabama's first, and currently only, Waldorf school.

The Redmont School features a number of unique educational opportunities. For example, students continue from kindergarten through 8th grade with the same teacher, which, according to the Waldorf method, fosters a sense of confidence and self-assuredness that allows students to fully harness their creative potential without inhibition. While The Redmont School may take a somewhat unorthodox approach to the overall educational experience, it still adheres to a traditional curriculum of math, science, and language courses that provides students with the education to excel at the high school and university levels. For more information on the Waldorf method, visit www.whywaldorfworks.org.

ST. FRANCIS XAVIER CATHOLIC SCHOOL
2 Xavier Circle, Birmingham
(205) 871-1687
www.stfrancisxavierschool.com
Located just outside Mountain Brook off Montclair Road and located on the grounds of St. Francis Xavier Catholic Church, St. Francis Xavier Catholic School, or SFX, serves over 100 students from kindergarten through the 8th grade. Although many of the students' families are members of the SFX Parish, a number of non-Catholics also attend SFX. As the Hispanic population in the Birmingham area has grown in recent years, St. Francis Xavier has become a flag-bearer in promoting cultural diversity throughout the community and in its schools. SFX offers a challenging curriculum taught by lay teachers that is grounded in the Catholic faith.

ST. ROSE OF LIMA ACADEMY
1401 22nd St. South, Birmingham
(205) 933-0549
www.saintroseacademy.com
Located on Red Mountain since its founding in 1956, St. Rose has built a reputation for rigorous academic standards in a Catholic environment. With the general decline in vocations, many Catholic schools have seen the gradual disappearance of nuns in schools. Not at St. Rose, where the Dominican Sisters operate the school and live on the grounds. Although it is one of the smallest of the Diocesan schools, St. Rose is one of the most prestigious, serving students from kindergarten through 8th grade.

National Excellence in Pre-kindergarten

For four consecutive years, Alabama and North Carolina tied for the top spot nationwide for all quality standards in pre-kindergarten. A national education report rated Alabama's First Class Pre-kindergarten program as being one of the nation's best. The downside? The nationally recognized program reaches only a fraction of the state's 60,000 eligible 4-year olds. Much like Alabama's acclaimed—and emulated—Alabama Reading Initiative, which allowed 4th-graders a few years ago to make historic gains in reading on the National Assessment of Educational Progress test, First Class is underfunded. Alabama spends $18.3 million annually on pre-kindergarten programs while Arkansas ($111 million), North Carolina ($170 million), and Georgia ($332 million) radically outspend the state. If the proven success of the First Class program was matched by the funding to spread this program to every child in Alabama, the results could be phenomenal.

total enrollment of just over 300 students. The Altamont School, or simply Altamont, was established in 1975 with the merger of the Birmingham University School and the all-girls Brooke Hill School. Today, Altamont is one of the most highly respected schools in the southeast. Just 5 minutes from Downtown Birmingham near the Highland area, many families living within the Birmingham City limits have found Altamont to be a convenient alternative to the public schools system.

Altamont's low student-teacher ratio (7 to 1) gives teachers the opportunity to engage their students more directly and explore subjects in greater depth. Graduates of Altamont generally score very high on standardized testing and go on to attend some of the country's finest colleges. But while Altamont values the classroom experience, special emphasis is also placed on extracurricular activities. Whether it's sports, music, painting, or acting, Altamont encourages its students to explore their interests outside of the classroom. Student art lines the halls and the school plays always sell out. With 2 campuses positioned on 28 acres of land, Altamont has the space and resources to support a multitude of extracurricular clubs and organizations that offer something to stimulate virtually every student's interest. A number of notable graduates began their budding artistic careers at Altamont, including award-winning authors Walker Percy, Diane McWhorter, and Daniel Wallace.

Secondary Schools

THE ALTAMONT SCHOOL
4801 Altamont Rd. South, Birmingham
(205) 879-2006
www.altamontschool.org
Hidden away atop Red Mountain, The Altamont School is a secular, independent school serving grades 5 through 12 with a

THE ARLINGTON SCHOOL
1312 22nd St. South, Birmingham
(205) 939-3665
www.arlingtonschool.net
After having experienced the pitfalls of large schools as a teacher for 25 years, Debbie Petitto finally decided to make a change.

In 1999 Petitto established The Arlington School with the idea that, "a small school can make a big difference." With an enrollment that is capped at 30 students in grades 6 through 12, Arlington teachers can focus on addressing the needs of each student. Unlike larger schools where teachers may be overwhelmed by large classes, students' strengths and weaknesses are recognized and attended to at The Arlington School without hindering the progress of other students. While Arlington may not be able to offer Friday night football games and homecoming dances, it does offer a unique educational experience.

BRIARWOOD CHRISTIAN SCHOOL
6255 Cahaba Valley Rd., Shelby County
(205) 776-5900
www.briarwoodchristianschool.com
Briarwood Christian School, affiliated with Briarwood Presbyterian Church, operates 2 campuses in the Birmingham area. The elementary school is located just off I-459 near Altadena Road in Jefferson County and the middle and high schools are located in Shelby County along Highway 119 near Oak Mountain State Park. With over 175,000 square feet making up the academic and fine-arts buildings, Briarwood students have plenty of space to expand their minds and talents. The latest addition to the Briarwood campus is the new 44,000-square-foot gymnasium for basketball, volleyball, and various other events and activities.

Briarwood is unabashedly Evangelical Christian and appeals to many people in the Birmingham area. As a result admission to Briarwood is highly competitive and in order to ensure a reasonable student-teacher ratio, there is usually a waiting list. With its Evangelical Christian roots, Briarwood's students participate in various service activities. A great number of students travel abroad on mission trips and gain a new perspective on their place in the ever-shrinking modern world. In addition to these trips abroad, many Briarwood students participate in service activities right here in Birmingham, recognizing the importance of ministering to those in need right in their own backyard.

INDIAN SPRINGS SCHOOL
190 Woodward Dr., Shelby County
(205) 988-3350
www.indiansprings.org
Founded by Birmingham businessman Harvey Woodward in 1952, Indian Springs has since grown to become the premiere boarding school in the Birmingham area, serving students from grades 8 to 12. Located on 350 acres of land in Shelby County, the Indian Springs campus is a world unto itself. Complete with hiking, running, and biking trails, a garden that provides fruits and vegetables for the cafeteria, and a 12-acre lake that students can swim and canoe in, there is little reason to leave the campus. Twenty-five percent of Indian Springs' 269 students are boarded, representing 9 states and 7 countries. Whether day students or boarding students, all of Indian Springs' graduates will leave Birmingham with a broader, more refined outlook on the world.

Indian Springs is known for its high academic standards and has worked hard to maintain a reputation for high achievement. A low teacher-student ratio of 1 to 8 plays a big role in achieving this goal and the results speak for themselves. In 2010, 100 percent of the graduating class was accepted into college and 13 percent of the class were National Merit Recipients. Education at Indian Springs does not end at the school doors. Many students participate in various clubs and activities. In fact, Indian Springs pioneered the sport of soccer in Alabama in the 1960s with the first high school soccer program. For many years the team was forced to look out of state for opponents. Now the Indian Springs men's soccer program is one of the top teams in their classification, competing for state championships on a consistent basis.

JOHN CARROLL CATHOLIC HIGH SCHOOL
300 Lakeshore Pkwy., Birmingham
(205) 940-2400
www.jcchs.org
Since 1947 John Carroll Catholic has served as the Diocese of Birmingham's largest high school and has produced many distinctive and varied alumni such as Heisman Trophy–winning quarterback Pat Sullivan, Nobel Prize–winning biologist Eric Wieschaus, and Apostolic Nuncio Joseph Marino, among others. Located just inside the Birmingham city limits near the Wildwood area of Homewood, John Carroll is noted for its richly diverse student body, perhaps the most diverse in the area. With over 650 students from various religious, ethnic, cultural, and socioeconomic backgrounds, John Carroll fosters an environment of understanding and acceptance grounded in the Catholic faith.

John Carroll offers its students a challenging curriculum aimed at building strong foundations in math and science, language and reading, and the social sciences. Honors classes operating at an accelerated pace are available to high-achieving students, while a teacher-student ratio of roughly 1 to 13 enables teachers to actively engage the class without ignoring the needs of individual students. All students are required to take four years of theology classes that explores not only Catholic theology, but also the various issues facing the world and the role of the Church and religion in addressing those issues. In keeping with the Catholic tradition of service, all students are required to complete at least 50 hours of community service between the end of their freshman year and the beginning of their senior year; however, many students often find their service so gratifying that it is not uncommon for students to do more. John Carroll students are also encouraged to explore extracurricular activities and a great many of them are involved in the school's many programs and clubs. John Carroll boasts a rich athletic tradition that has included a number of former and current NBA, NFL, and Olympic athletes. Their soccer program has won a record nine men's' soccer state championships, including the last three in a row, and consistently finishes among the top teams in the nation.

SHADES MOUNTAIN CHRISTIAN SCHOOL
2290 Old Tyler Rd., Hoover
(205) 978-6001
www.smcs.org
Founded by Pastor Dick Vigneulle in 1974, Shades Mountain Christian School serves nearly 400 students in pre-kindergarten through 12th grade and is affiliated with Shades Mountain Independent Church. Offering an education that is grounded in Evangelical Christian principles, Shades Mountain attracts many area families looking for such attributes in their child's educational experience. Shades Mountain seeks to integrate the lessons of the Bible in each class. Whether it is math, science, or English, Shades Mountain believes that the Bible is relevant to any and every subject. Shades

Mountain also emphasizes extracurricular involvement and many of its students participate in many of the school's sports and clubs.

HOMESCHOOLING

Regional traditions, customs, and tendencies have made homeschooling an increasingly popular option for Birmingham area parents. If there is any one aspect of homeschooling that might make parents reluctant to pull their kids out of public or private school systems and educate them at home, it is the lack of clubs, organizations, and athletic teams that homeschooling can't provide.

A number of organizations exist to ease the homeschooling process for parents and to provide some of the amenities that are enjoyed by children educated in traditional school systems such as field trips, organizations, and college advising. These groups also make parents aware of the Alabama state law regarding homeschool education and the necessary requirements under the law. Religious beliefs often play a major factor in the decision to homeschool and two local organizations are particularly popular among Christian homeschooling parents. Both the **Christian Home Education Fellowship,** (334) 288-7229, www.chefofalabama.org, and the **Alabama Homeschool Academy,** (205) 525-KIDS, www.alabamahomeschoolacademy.com, provide resources and advice to parents to get the most of their child's home education. A number of advocacy groups also exist to keep homeschooling parents abreast of the law and any changes to it as it pertains to homeschool education. Visit www.homeschoolinginalabama.com or the **Alabama State Department of Education,** (334) 242-9700, www.alsde.edu, for more information.

HIGHER EDUCATION

Birmingham is home to a number of institutions of higher education. From private to public, universities to community colleges, Birmingham has plenty to offer those in search of higher learning. Interestingly, Birmingham's transition from a capitol of industry to a center of health and medicine was driven by higher education. On the Southside of the city sits the University of Alabama at Birmingham, or UAB, medical center. Driving around Southside, it is not uncommon to see medical students in scrubs walking to and from class. Less than 15 minutes away in suburban Homewood, sits the picturesque campus of Samford University. A short trip down I-59 will take you to Birmingham-Southern College and Miles College. In addition to these larger colleges and universities, there are also a number of community colleges and technical schools that offer courses to suit the various needs of those hoping to further their education. In fact, many of these schools offer degrees online that can be earned without ever having to leave your personal computer.

Community Colleges & Technical Schools

JEFFERSON STATE COMMUNITY COLLEGE
2601 Carson Rd., Birmingham (Jefferson County campus)
(205) 853-1200

4600 Valleydale Rd., Pelham (Shelby County Campus)
(205) 983-5911
www.jeffstateonline.com
Jefferson State, known simply as "Jeff State," is part of the Alabama Community College System and has 4 campuses in Jefferson and

Shelby counties and 2 campuses in St. Clair County. With an enrollment of over 7,000 students, Jeff State is one of the most popular and convenient two-year colleges in the area. Since the advent of online classes, Jeff State's popularity has only risen.

Jeff State offers over 120 university transfer programs and 40 career programs. With nearly 100 percent of its students hailing from the state of Alabama, Jeff State has served the Birmingham area and Alabama well since its inception in 1965. Jeff State works hard to accommodate the various needs of its students. With programs for college students of all ages, Jeff State strives to defy the community-college stereotype by offering a wide variety of night and weekend classes for many working men and women seeking advancement. Over 20 percent of Jeff State students are over 30 years of age. The college also features a number of associate degrees available completely online (most online classes do have two or three mandatory on-campus meetings). In addition to online associate degrees, Jeff State allows students to complete the entire core curriculum for most Alabama state schools online. For those looking to continue their education beyond a two-year degree, though, Jeff State has partnerships with many state and private four-year colleges to enable Jeff State grads to transition smoothly to a larger university. In addition to university partnerships, Jeff State also maintains partnerships with area businesses and companies to provide students with the work experience to supplement their classroom education. For example, one of Jeff State's most popular programs, nursing, is involved with Birmingham's St. Vincent's Health System, giving students real hospital experience to prepare them for life after college.

LAWSON STATE COMMUNITY COLLEGE
3060 Wilson Rd., Southwest, Birmingham
(Birmingham Campus)
(205) 925-2515

1100 9th Ave., Southwest, Bessemer
(Bessemer Campus)
(205) 925-2515
www.ls.cc.al.us

Recently named by *Washington Monthly* as one of America's "Top 50 Community Colleges," Lawson State has served the Birmingham area for over 60 years. At times, "community college" can have a negative connotation, associated with lax academic standards and inadequate facilities. Lawson State, however, turns this stereotype on its head. In many ways Lawson functions as a four-year school with its residence halls and athletic programs. Most importantly, though, Lawson students are, for the most part, serious about their education.

With the influx of automotive corporations in Alabama like Mercedes, Honda, and Hyundai, the curriculum at Lawson State has kept up with the need for highly skilled technicians. Located at Lawson State's Bessemer campus, the Alabama Center for Automotive Excellence (ACAE) is one of the top automotive-technician-training facilities in the nation. What sets the ACAE, and Lawson State, apart from other such facilities is their ability to look forward. As the dangers of fossil fuels become increasingly evident, forward-thinking minds are of utmost importance for the survival of the auto industry. As the host of the Alabama Clean Fuels Coalition's Odyssey Day, Lawson State showcased its efforts at uncovering new and reusable energy sources and the effort to make what we use now cleaner and safer. While many of Lawson's students are young people, a number of older men and women also come to Lawson to stay abreast of developments in their field or train in a new occupation.

THE CULINARY INSTITUTE OF
VIRGINIA COLLEGE
436 Palisades Blvd., Birmingham
(205) 802-1200
www.culinard.com
With experienced chefs from all over the world, The Culinary Institute has quickly become the place to go for those seeking culinary careers. In just 36 weeks students will learn the necessary skills and techniques to become great chefs. It's not just cookery at The Culinard, however; world-class equipment and facilities make The Culinard a truly educational experience. And at The Culinard Cafe at Innovation Depot, the school's new downtown teaching lab, budding chefs of the Culinary Institute are able to test their skills for willing patrons. In fact, many of the school's graduates have gone on to work in some of Birmingham's best restaurants including Satterfield's Restaurant, Hot and Hot Fish Club, and Chez Fon Fon.

Colleges & Universities

BIRMINGHAM-SOUTHERN COLLEGE
900 Arkadelphia Rd., Birmingham
(205) 226-4600
www.bsc.edu
Under the patronage of the United Methodist Church, Birmingham-Southern has cultivated many brilliant minds in its nearly 100 years. Located on 192 acres of land in western Birmingham, complete with a lake, walking trails, and an ecoscape, Birmingham-Southern is a world unto itself and was included in *The Princeton Review*'s "Guide to 286 Green Colleges." Birmingham-Southern has over 1,500 students representing more than 30 states and 15 foreign countries.

Birmingham-Southern's professors are some of the best around with over 95 percent of full-time faculty holding either a doctoral degree or the highest degree available in their respective fields. Students choose from over 50 majors in 5 programs of study including the arts, science, fine arts, music, and music education. It must be mentioned that Birmingham-Southern recently underwent a number of funding cuts as a result of a few major accounting errors. Unfortunately, this led to the elimination of a number of popular fields of study. Birmingham-Southern lives on and it is the hope of many that these programs will return soon.

Birmingham-Southern maintains athletic programs in a variety of sports competing at the NCAA Division III level. After a brief flirtation with Division I in the early 2000s, Birmingham-Southern, unlike many of today's colleges and universities, chose academics over athletics and dropped down to Division III. For this they received considerable praise from a number of sports writers, most notably Frank DeFord, former *Sports Illustrated* editor and current NPR contributor. The Panthers have since added a football team to their list of varsity sports, adding yet another interesting dimension to this already fascinating school. Despite recent financial hardships, Birmingham-Southern remains one of the most highly respected liberal arts colleges in the United States.

i Birmingham-Southern College is home to the Southern Environmental Center, an organization dedicated to fostering sustainable energy practices that are both environmentally responsible and cost-cutting. For more on the SEC, see Attractions.

MILES COLLEGE
5500 Myron Massey Blvd., Fairfield
(205) 929-1000
www.miles.edu

Miles College was founded in 1898 by the Colored Methodist Episcopal Church (now the Christian Methodist Episcopal Church), with the goal of educating young African Americans who were otherwise denied education at state schools and many private institutions. Today, Miles College is the only Historically Black College in the Birmingham area and serves a student body of over 1,500. Although not all students that attend Miles are African American, a great majority of them are and the schools remains committed to promoting its African-American heritage but with the greater goal of fostering peace and understanding. Miles is located in predominantly African-American Fairfield, a town established to house the often mistreated workers of the Birmingham steel industry, and has served as a beacon of hope for many young African-Americans for over a century.

Miles offers bachelor's degrees in the arts, sciences, social work, and music education with over 25 majors for students to choose from. As a Historically Black College, Miles is a member of the United Negro College Fund, a program which seeks to alleviate the burden the tuition costs can bring to bear on young people and their families. Miles features a variety of athletic teams that compete at the Division II level of the NCAA. Until his abrupt retirement for health reasons, legendary coach Billy Joe led the Miles football team. Perhaps more popular than the Golden Bears sports teams, however, is the marching band, known as the Miles Purple Marching Machine. Locals treasure the Purple Marching Machine and know that when the band lines up to perform, spectators are in for one of the most exciting musical performances around.

SAMFORD UNIVERSITY
800 Lakeshore Dr., Homewood
(205) 726-2011
www.samford.edu

Originally founded in Marion, Alabama, in 1841, Samford University, then known as Howard College, moved to the suburb of Homewood in 1957. Samford is a private university affiliated with the Alabama Baptist State Convention. With an undergraduate enrollment of over 4,500, it is Alabama's largest private university. In addition, *US News & World Report* ranks Samford in the top tier of national doctoral research universities. To this day Samford values its heritage, but keeps a keen eye on the future.

Samford is home to 8 different schools, each offering a number of majors. From the School of the Arts, to the prestigious Brock School of Business, Samford has something for everyone. Samford is home to one of only three accredited law schools in the state of Alabama, the Cumberland School of Law, and is one of only two colleges with an accredited pharmacy school. The highly respected Beeson School of Divinity is the only divinity school in the state and the first such school on the campus of a Southern Baptist–affiliated institution. Due to one of the nation's largest university endowments, Samford remains relatively affordable for a private university and was named among *The Princeton Review*'s "100 Best College Values" in 2010.

The campus of Samford University adheres to a strict architectural code and every building is designed in the Georgian tradition, creating a uniform aesthetic that is rare on many modern campuses. Despite the best efforts of the university to diversify its student population, around 90 percent of students are white and many of these are members of various Protestant Christian denominations, most notably the Southern Baptist Convention. The campus, however, remains very open to members of all ethnic backgrounds and religious creeds and the university has made great efforts to encourage diversity on its campus. The University requires that all students under the age of 21 live on campus. As a result Samford has a large and active on-campus student population and hosts a considerable amount of events both by and for students.

The Samford Bulldogs athletic teams participate in the Southern Conference at the Division I level of the NCAA. Since the introduction of former Heisman Trophy–winner Pat Sullivan to the Samford family in 2006, a number of new facilities have been built to improve the state of the Bulldogs sports programs.

UNIVERSITY OF ALABAMA AT BIRMINGHAM
University Boulevard and 20th Street, Birmingham
(205) 934-4011
www.uab.edu

In many ways the University of Alabama at Birmingham, or simply UAB, has become the face of the city of Birmingham. Since its establishment as an autonomous branch of the University of Alabama system in 1969, UAB has grown to become the state's third-largest university and its largest employer. Whereas only 30 years ago it was impossible to drive into Birmingham and not notice the smoggy haze rising out of the steel mills,

today, it is impossible to enter downtown Birmingham and not notice UAB. With its seemingly ever expanding Medical Center, ranked by *US News* as one of America's "Best Hospitals" for 19 consecutive years, and its growing student body, UAB has in some ways turned Birmingham into a college town. In a good way, of course.

UAB's evolution is an interesting one that is distinctly Birmingham. It began less than a hundred years ago when the University of Alabama recognized the need to open a satellite extension in Birmingham to meet the needs of the city's rapidly growing population. In 1945 Alabama opened its Medical College of Alabama in Birmingham to take advantage of the city's growth and wealth. As the city underwent the tumultuous period of the civil-rights movement, its problems were made worse by the steady decline of the steel industry. Aid, however, would come in the form of federal dollars for medical research and hospital expansion. In his efforts to lobby southern lawmakers to support his landmark civil-rights legislation and later Medicare and Medicaid, President Lyndon B. Johnson offered Birmingham federal money to support its budding health-care industry in exchange for southern votes on these pieces of legislation. The bills passed, federal dollars came in, and Birmingham was set on its path as a center of medical progress. Soon, however, UAB grew so large that it demanded its own autonomy from the University of Alabama in Tuscaloosa and in 1969, the University System was established and UAB became a full university. Since that time, UAB has grown to offer nearly 140 degrees from 12 schools and the UAB graduate program. While the School of Medicine might be what put UAB on the map, its other schools, from public health to business, are highly respected as well. The Schools of Medicine, Public Health, Optometry, Nursing, and Health Professions are consistently ranked among the top in the nation. The UAB School of Medicine trails only Duke University and the University of North Carolina–Chapel Hill in federal research funding.

The relationship between UAB and Birmingham has been a truly symbiotic one. UAB's athletic programs compete in Conference USA of the NCAA's Division I. Its football program suffers from recruiting competition from Auburn and Tuscaloosa, but they do enjoy hometown support at their games in the city's only large stadium, Legion Field. The popular men's basketball program, led by former Alabama star and Indiana head coach Mike Davis, attracts thousands to Bartow Arena, otherwise known as the Gene Dome, on winter nights. The basketball rivalry between UAB and the University of Memphis, dubbed the "Battle of the Bones" for the two cities' affinity for good barbecue, is always a high-stakes affair with the regular season conference title usually on the line.

i UAB's student body is extremely diverse. Over 100 different nations are represented on UAB's campus, making for an enhanced learning environment that opens students to the world. The *Princeton Review* has ranked UAB third in the nation in campus diversity.

UNIVERSITY OF MONTEVALLO
Highland Avenue Sta. 6100
(205) 665-6000
www.montevallo.edu
A four-year public university founded in 1896, the University of Montevallo is the state's only public liberal arts college. It opened as the Alabama Girls' Industrial School, and then later became Alabama College, State College for Women in 1923, becoming a pioneer in offering teacher education in art, music, physical education, and commercial subjects, as well as in home economics. After becoming coeducational in 1956, it was renamed the University of Montevallo in 1969.

One of the school's biggest attractions is the idyllic small-town setting of Montevallo itself, located some 30 miles south of downtown Birmingham. Set near the geographical center of Alabama, Montevallo's campus holds 28 buildings on the National Register of Historic Places and the entire campus is classified as a National Historic District. It is a calm, secluded academic environment that many find a perfect setting for a collegiate experience. Nearly everything on campus is a short walking distance apart, and the town itself lies just beyond the college gates. For a quick orientation be sure to stop by the Welcome Center located in the historic Will Lyman House at Oak and Middle streets, just beyond the campus gates.

Today, more than 30 degree programs are offered with more than 70 academic majors. The programs are contained within four colleges: College of Arts & Sciences, Michael E. Stephens College of Business, College of Education, and the College of Fine Arts. Enrollment is just over 3,000, making the student/faculty ratio 16–1. Nearly 90 percent of the faculty holds terminal degrees in their respective fields. *US News & World Report* has ranked the University as a Tier One master's-level institution, giving UM the distinction of being the highest ranked public master's-level university in Alabama.

CHILD CARE

The state of Alabama ranks among the top in the nation in pre-kindergarten education. Sadly, due to lack of funding, only a small percentage of children receive quality pre-kindergarten care. Nevertheless, a good number of established child-care centers are located in and around Birmingham and depending on your economic status, financial aid may be available. There are over 300 child-care facilities in the Birmingham area. Some of these are licensed while many others remain unlicensed. Just because a child-care center is unlicensed doesn't mean that they don't provide good care, but it's always a good idea to check out the people and facilities for yourself before entrusting them with the welfare of your child.

The **Alabama Department of Human Resources,** (334) 242-1425, www.dhr.state .al.us, has a complete listing of every licensed child-care facility in the state and many unlicensed ones as well. On the site you can sort by zip code and county to find a child-care facility near you. The Alabama DHR also provides a thorough parents' guide to choosing a day-care facility with questions to ask prospective facilities. While the Alabama Department of Human Resources is a great starting place, your best bet may be to just ask friends and neighbors who are more familiar with the local child-care facilities and can guide you to a center that suits your needs and the needs of your child. Also, many places of worship also offer quality pre-kindergarten education.

For children with special needs, **Hand in Hand,** under the provision of **United Cerebral Palsy of Greater Birmingham,** (205) 944-3900, www.ucpbham.com, operates a state-of-the-art facility on Lakeshore Drive that serves hundreds of children with disabilities from the Birmingham area. Hand in Hand's Early Intervention program, has been recognized nationally for their work in the Birmingham area, receiving the National Program of the Year award from United Cerebral Palsy Associations. Additionally, Hand in Hand features a "mainstreaming program" in which typical children, meaning children with no significant disabilities, attend pre-kindergarten with their disabled peers. In such a program the children with disabilities, in merely being kids, imitate their typical classmates in such ordinary functions as holding a cup or sipping a straw while their typical peers develop compassion and understanding for those with disabilities.

HEALTH CARE & WELLNESS

Starting in the 1960s Birmingham began transforming into the world-class health-care hub it is today. Many of the nation's—even the world's—best doctors call Birmingham home, and many of them are products of the University of Alabama at Birmingham (UAB) School of Medicine. The school offers medical education in one of the most technologically advanced medical facilities in the country—the vast medical complex extends to more than 80 city blocks in downtown Birmingham. In 2010 11 UAB medical specialties were listed among the nation's top 50 evaluated at 4,852 US hospitals by *US News & World Report.* Nearby downtown, the Sports Medicine and Orthopedic Center at St. Vincent's Hospital is recognized around the country for its treatment of sports-related injuries. Athletes such as Jack Nicklaus, Troy Aikman, Charles Barkley, Roger Clemens, Allen Iverson, Bo Jackson, Michael Jordan, John Smoltz, and Doug Williams—as well as your average high school football star—receive treatment at St. Vincent's. Birmingham is also known for its cardiovascular specialists. Pioneers in the field of cardiovascular medicine established UAB's prestigious Cardio-vascular Center. Additionally, UAB's trauma center is the only Level I Trauma Center in the state of Alabama and is equipped to handle any emergency.

As the two largest healthcare systems in the area, UAB and St. Vincent's may have their own rivalry issues, but the two receive considerable additional competition from Brookwood Medical Center in Homewood as well as the Baptist Health System, which operates a number of hospitals and clinics in the area. Each of these systems has specialties in which it excels. They all provide quality care and adhere to high standards of service. Competition among these four healthcare systems has, in fact, resulted in better quality of care for all of Birmingham's residents and the thousands of patients from around the world that come to these hospitals each year in seeking the best possible care and treatment. In addition, HealthSouth, the nation's largest provider of inpatient rehabilitative healthcare services, is headquartered in Birmingham. Through its rehabilitation hospitals, long-term acute care hospitals, and outpatient rehabilitation clinics, HealthSouth improves the level of rehabilitation for those recovering from strokes, brain and spinal cord injuries, cardiac conditions, orthopedic problems, and amputations. Between UAB and Samford University, Birmingham has major colleges of medicine, dentistry, optometry, pharmacy, law, and nursing.

OVERVIEW

Staying well, however, is not just about hospitals: It is often about avoiding a hospital in the first place. Accordingly, Birmingham contains a number of clinics and wellness centers, many of which are operated by one of the larger hospital systems. In addition to clinics that offer traditional medicine, there are also quite a few clinics that take a holistic approach. Though many of these serve their patients very well, it is always best to consider a licensed physician or nurse and to inquire about the certifications of the individuals operating holistic clinics before entrusting them with your health.

BAPTIST HEALTH SYSTEM
www.bhsala.com

PRINCETON BAPTIST MEDICAL CENTER
701 Princeton Ave. Southwest, Birmingham
(205) 783-8100

SHELBY BAPTIST MEDICAL CENTER
1000 1st St. North, Alabaster
(205) 620-8100

WALKER BAPTIST MEDICAL CENTER
3400 Hwy. 78 East, Jasper
(205) 837-4000

Since 1922 the hospitals of the Baptist Health System have been providing quality care to citizens in Birmingham and elsewhere across the state. Today, Baptist operates 4 hospitals—3 of which are in the Birmingham area—and a number of clinics throughout the area. The largest of the 3 hospitals in the Birmingham area is Princeton Baptist, located in downtown Birmingham. With just under 500 beds and over 400 physicians, Princeton is larger than the Walker and Shelby locations combined. The Walker and Shelby locations have 267 and 192 beds, respectively. The Princeton location is also better equipped to handle a wide variety of medical issues whereas the Walker

and Shelby locations serve the primary care needs of a number of patients and the needs of the elderly as well. In addition to these hospitals, the Baptist Health System is also seeking to build a medical center in Hoover off Highway 280. There are a number of hurdles to be cleared before this can happen, but there is no doubt that the residents of the Hoover/Shelby County area are in need of a hospital with an emergency room. Currently, Hoover has the highest population of any city in Alabama without a hospital.

i *Ladies Home Journal* rated Birmingham #1 in the nation in Health in its issue of "The Best Cities."

BROOKWOOD MEDICAL CENTER
2010 Brookwood Medical Center Dr., Homewood
(205) 877-8800
www.bwmc.com

Located in suburban Homewood, Brookwood provides care for many of Birmingham's Over the Mountain residents. As Birmingham's suburban population grew in the late 1960s and 1970s, the need for a hospital in the area became more and more evident. As a result Brookwood Medical Center was founded in 1973 with the goal of building a hospital with all the facilities and amenities of a big-city hospital, but with the feel of a community clinic. Despite its growth—the complex seems to take up nearly the entire side of Shades Mountain overlooking Highway 31—Brookwood maintains a community atmosphere while providing quality care to thousands of patients yearly. Brookwood is owned by Dallas-based Tenet Healthcare and is the largest of Tenet's 49 hospitals. The hospital itself has 602 beds and 200 doctors, while more than 900 physicians in private practice refer their patients to Brookwood for hospital-related services. Additionally, many area physicians are affiliated with Brookwood and use its surgery center for operations, such as notable orthopedist Dr. Joseph Sherrill.

i The health department is an extremely useful resource for all of your health and wellness needs. From restaurant health ratings to immunizations, the health department offers numerous vital services. Jefferson County Department of Health, 1400 6th Ave. South, Birmingham, (205) 933-9110, www.jcdh.org.

HEALTHSOUTH LAKESHORE REHABILITATION HOSPITAL
3800 Ridgeway Dr., Homewood
(205) 868-2000
www.healthsouthlakeshorerehab.com
The nation's largest rehabilitation services provider, HealthSouth is headquartered right here in Birmingham. Following a lengthy battle between its former CEO Richard Scrushy and shareholders over fraudulent accounting that was played out on national news and radio stations, HealthSouth is working diligently to regain its image. HealthSouth continues to operate their Lakeshore Rehabilitation Hospital in Homewood and the facility is one of the top rehabilitation centers in the nation. The site, home to the Lakeshore Foundation, specializes in comprehensive long-term rehabilitative care with a focus on improving the quality of life for patients facing serious injuries and disabilities.

ST. VINCENT'S HEALTH SYSTEM
www.stvhs.com

ST. VINCENT'S BIRMINGHAM
810 St. Vincent's Dr., Birmingham
(205) 939-7000

ST. VINCENT'S BLOUNT
150 Gilbreath Dr., Oneonta
(205) 274-3000

ST. VINCENT'S EAST
50 Medical Park East Dr., Birmingham
(205) 838-3000

ST. VINCENT'S ONE-NINETEEN HEALTH AND WELLNESS
7191 Cahaba Valley Rd., Hoover
(205) 408-6600

St. Vincent's St. Clair
2805 Dr. John Haynes Dr., Pell City
(205) 338-3301
As Birmingham's oldest hospital St. Vincent's has seen Birmingham go from a one-horse steel town to medical hub in just over a century's time. Founded in 1898 by the Catholic Daughters of Charity holy order, the hospital was named for 17-century Catholic priest St. Vincent de Paul, founder of the order. Today, it is not uncommon to see Sisters in habit walking alongside surgeons in scrubs, an appropriate image for the extent and range of care that St. Vincent's provides its patients. St. Vincent's combines the traditional Catholic ideals of its founders the Daughters of Charity with 21-century medical technology. In fact St. Vincent's recently became Birmingham's first "iHospital," with a new iPhone app that allows users to consult with registered nurses with a touch of their fingertips. St. Vincent's continues its Catholic tradition of care: A chapel located inside the main hospital is open 24 hours for prayer and contemplation and no birth control procedures are performed in the hospital. St. Vincent's has 776 beds at its 4 full-service hospitals to serve

Close-up

Lakeshore Foundation

That the **Lakeshore Foundation** is special surprises no one in town. Decades ago they formed a wheelchair basketball team giving people with physical disabilities the basic opportunities to enjoy an active and independent lifestyle that most of us take for granted. Their wheelchair rugby competitions were made famous in the 2005 documentary, *Murderball*. Since then the foundation has shone as one of the premier facilities in the world for people with physical disabilities ranging from stroke to spinal cord injuries, from arthritis to progressive disorders such as multiple sclerosis and Parkinson's disease.

Birmingham also ranks among the elite American cities that are home to the Olympic Rings. In 2003 the United States Olympic Committee approved Lakeshore Foundation as an official Olympic and Paralympic Training Site. It is the first time such an important designation specifically provided for the Olympic athlete and the Paralympic athlete to train together, side by side. In addition to this unique status, this also means Homewood is one of only a handful of Olympic-training facilities in the country and the first city in the southeast. Chances are if an athlete—Paralympic or Olympic—headed to Athens, Greece, in 2004 or Beijing, China, in 2008, their journey passed through Homewood.

Lakeshore Foundation's multi-million-dollar 128,000-square-foot facility is impressive. The field house can accommodate a variety of sports such as wrestling, Judo, and Tae Kwon Do. The field house's maple flooring is for wheelchair basketball and rugby. The Boccia courts and 200-meter track are made of Mondo Super X Classic Surface, the surface of choice for the Olympics. A 6,000-square-foot Fitness and Aerobics Center holds all the latest cardiovascular stations as well as weight- and strength-training machines. Yet the significance is in the details: Braille on the treadmills, removable benches for wheelchair access, and assisted dressing rooms nearby. The Aquatic Center's 2 pools, an air rifle marksmanship range, an archery range, and a sports-science lab with classrooms round out the facilities.

But that's not all. Lakeshore Foundation's Lima Foxtrot programs include a number of weekend-long camps that bring injured military personnel and their families from across the country to Alabama. Each camp is offered at no charge for the participants. Other services include the Family Health & Fitness membership for local residents; recreational trips to nearby outdoor destinations; competitive athletics like wheelchair basketball, tennis, track and field, and rugby; and a series of land- and aquatic-based classes, youth athletics, and recreation programs. While the average resident may think Lakeshore is just a rehabilitation hospital, that merely scratches the surface.

the needs of its patients. Its One-Nineteen location serves as one of the 280 Corridor's finest health and wellness centers and also houses the offices of a number of primary-care physicians.

While other healthcare systems have first-class women's centers, St. Vincent's is still known to locals as the place "where babies come from." A great many of Birmingham's residents were delivered at St.

Vincent's and many more of its future residents surely will, too.

Among St. Vincent's most notable physicians is world-renowned orthopedic surgeon Dr. James Andrews. The well-respected surgeon has contributed to Birmingham's success as a center of medicine. There's a good chance that Dr. Andrews or a member of his prestigious team of surgeons has operated on your favorite sports star. St. Vincent's is a not-for-profit healthcare system operated by Ascension Health, the largest Catholic and largest non-profit health system in the United States. According to the tenets of the Daughters of Charity and the Catholic Church, St. Vincent's has a policy of providing care to anyone who ever enters its doors. Such mercy and charity have endeared the hospital to the city of Birmingham in its more than 100 years in the Magic City.

TRINITY MEDICAL CENTER
800 Montclair Rd., Birmingham
(205) 592-1000
www.trinitymedicalonline.com
Purchased from the Baptist Health System in 2005, Trinity Hospital has 560 beds and 239 active physicians serving a number of Birmingham's residents from its location on Montclair Road near Mountain Brook. While Trinity specializes in a number of medical fields, it is known around the area for its cardiology services in particular. Trinity's Heart Center is ranked among the top 10 percent in the nation for cardiology services and received the 2010 Coronary Intervention Excellence Award from HealthGrades. Hospital administrators received permission from the state of Alabama to relocate Trinity Medical Center to the former HealthSouth Medical Center on Highway 280.

i What has been called "the world's most technologically advanced hospital" sits empty. HealthSouth halted construction on the building on Highway 280 in 2005 after its $2.6-billion accounting scandal rocked the company.

UNIVERSITY OF ALABAMA AT BIRMINGHAM HEALTH SYSTEM
www.health.uab.edu

UAB HOSPITAL
1802 6th Ave. South, Birmingham
(205) 934-4011

UAB WOMEN AND INFANTS CENTER
1700 6th Ave. South, Birmingham
(205) 934-4011

THE KIRKLIN CLINIC
2000 6th Ave. South, Birmingham
(205) 934-4011

CALLAHAN EYE FOUNDATION HOSPITAL
1720 University Blvd., Birmingham
(205) 325-8100

UAB MEDICAL WEST
Highway 11 South, Bessemer
(205) 481-7000

UAB HIGHLANDS
1201 11th Ave. South, Birmingham
(205) 933-7000

HAZELRIG-SALTER RADIATION ONCOLOGY CENTER
1700 6th Ave. South, Birmingham
(205) 934-9999

THE KIRKLIN CLINIC AT ACTON ROAD (UAB HEART HEALTH CENTER)
2145 Bonner Way, Vestavia
(205) 978-4300

As a direct result of the growth and prestige of the UAB School of Medicine, the UAB Health System and Birmingham itself are increasingly seen as an international healthcare destination. As Alabama's largest academic medical center, some of the world's most-respected doctors are graduates of the UAB School of Medicine and many more great doctors practice medicine and conduct research at one of UAB's many hospitals and clinics. In fact an astounding 297 of UAB's physicians were included in *The Best Doctors in America* publication. Imminent physicians such as Dr. John W. Kirklin have opened facilities under the auspices of the UAB Health System. Today, the Kirklin Clinic serves as one of the country's premiere cardiovascular centers. In addition to cardiology UAB is counted among the world's leaders in a number of other medical fields, notably oncology and neurology. UAB Hospital is also Alabama's only Level I Trauma Center, capable of handling any emergency, no matter how severe. In all, UAB's various hospitals house over 1,500 beds and provide quality care to thousands of patients from Birmingham and around the world each year.

Some would argue, though, it is in the fields of medical research that UAB truly shines: Their research foundation has generated more than 40 startup companies based on UAB technologies and completed over 400 option and licensing agreements, generating approximately $46 million in revenues for the university. UAB researchers were pioneers in HIV and AIDS research and the first to discover the origin of HIV, the virus that causes AIDS. Because of the work of its researchers, the university's cancer center was one of the first to be designated as "comprehensive" by the National Institutes of Health. UAB research discovered the protein that led to the development of the little blue pill, Viagra.

In addition to the various hospitals and clinics within the UAB Health System, UAB is also affiliated with the Children's Hospital, housed in the UAB School of Medicine's Department of Pediatrics. UAB has helped to make Children's Hospital the state's single largest provider of care for all forms of pediatric cancer. Many families with children who are suffering from cancer cross state lines to come to Birmingham to receive top-quality care at Children's Hospital. UAB also features the newly built Women and Infants Center, a modern OB/GYN clinic with plush rooms and hotel-like amenities. In association with the Children's Hospital, UAB's new Women and Infants Center houses Alabama's only Level IIIC Regional Neonatal Intensive Care Unit, offering incredible care for premature babies unavailable anywhere in the region. All of UAB's state-of–the-art facilities and world-class doctors are irrelevant if patients are unhappy, which is why UAB's greatest honor is being awarded the "Consumer's Choice Award" from the National Research Corporation. UAB's reach is felt not only in the region, but also all throughout the state. With clinics and facilities in a number of neighboring counties and cities, UAB is working diligently to combat illness and disease all over the state of Alabama.

i *The Best in Medicine* ranked the University of Alabama at Birmingham (UAB) medical center 3rd in the nation (behind Mayo Clinic and Massachusetts General Hospital) in overall quality of healthcare.

GOVERNMENT-SUPPORTED HOSPITALS

COOPER-GREEN MERCY HOSPITAL
1515 6th Ave. South, Birmingham
(205) 930-3200
www.coopergreenmercyhospital.org
As the only county hospital in the Birmingham metro area, Cooper Green fills a vital role for inpatient and outpatient services. Cooper Green Cooper Hospital has been nationally recognized for three Centers of Excellence: The Balm of Gilead (palliative care), St. George's Clinic (HIV/AIDS care), and the Women's Health Link (women's services). Owned by Jefferson County the 319-bed general-care hospital provides care for Birmingham's indigent population. In 2008 the hospital underwent a $28-million renovation program and modernization of systems.

VETERANS AFFAIRS MEDICAL CENTER
700 19th St. South, Birmingham
(205) 933-1801
www.birmingham.va.org
A 313-bed acute tertiary care facility located in the city's Southside district, the Veterans Affairs Medical Center offers medical care for veterans in and around the city. It has 136 operating beds. Most staff physicians have joint appointments with the VA's primary affiliation, University of Alabama at Birmingham. The center offers support in 8 community-based outpatient clinics in surrounding communities

WALK-IN CLINICS

There are a number of walk-in clinics to accommodate those who are unable to make it to a hospital or don't have the time to wait in an emergency room. Many of these clinics are operated under the auspices

of one of the major healthcare systems in the area—clinic locations are detailed on each health system's website. There are also a number of independently operated walk-in clinics. **American Family Care,** www.americanfamilycare.com, also runs a number of walk-in clinics in the Birmingham area.

AMERICAN FAMILY CARE LOCATIONS
5410 Hwy. 280, Birmingham
(205) 201-7290
www.americanfamilycare.com
With more than a dozen urgent-care centers in the Birmingham area, American Family Care has been in the local market since the early 1980s. The clinics are on a walk-in basis with no appointment needed for medical services for those needing attention for non-life-threatening illness and injuries when an emergency room visit is not necessary or the patient's primary-care physician is not available. American Family Care is open 7 days a week from 8 a.m. to 6 p.m. See their website for additional locations.

IN-HOME & HOSPICE CARE

Many illnesses require round-the-clock care, but do not necessarily call for the individual to be hospitalized. Comfort plays an important role in improving patient health and for many people nothing beats the comforts of home. For this, there is hospice care. There are a number of organizations that provide in-home hospice care to the elderly and disabled as well as to those who are receiving cancer treatment. Many of the area hospitals and major health systems provide hospice services as well.

In addition to the major health systems, there are a number of private organizations that specialize in hospice care.

Emergency and Information Telephone Numbers

Emergencies: fire, police, ambulance, dial 911

Alcoholics Anonymous: (205) 290-0060

American Cancer Society: (205) 558-7860

American Diabetes Association: (205) 870-5172

American Heart Association: (205) 510-1500

American Lung Association of the Central States: (205) 987-7433

American Red Cross: (205) 458-8282

Crisis Center: (205) 323-7777

Jefferson-Blount-St. Clair Mental Health Authority: (205) 595-4555

Jefferson County Department of Health: (205) 933-9110

Jefferson County Emergency Management Agency: (205) 254-2039

Lifesouth Community Blood Center: (205) 943-6000

Narcotics Anonymous: (205) 941-2655

Overeaters Anonymous: (205) 823-7226

Poison Control Center: (205) 939-9201

Social Security Administration: (205) 731-1950

Two prominent organizations include **Alacare Home Health & Hospice** and **Hospice Services of Alabama,** both based in Birmingham.

ALACARE HOME HEALTH & HOSPICE
2400 John Hawkins Pkwy., Birmingham
(205) 981-8000
www.alacare.com

HOSPICE SERVICE OF ALABAMA
2367 Lakeside Dr., Birmingham
(205) 682-9996
www.hsofal.com

ALTERNATIVE MEDICINE

Although Birmingham is one of the most advanced cities in terms of medical technology, not everyone sees the need for such technology to deal with all illnesses. Many would rather receive holistic care. There are a number of area clinics offering alternative and holistic care ranging from acupuncture to hypnotherapy. For more information on alternative medicine options in town, visit the **Golden Temple Health Foods and Cafe,** (205) 933-8933, www.goldentemple healthfoods.com, in Five Points South. A

Birmingham staple since 1973, Golden Temple is a hub of the holistic medicine community in Birmingham.

ALABAMA HYPNOTHERAPY CENTER
2007 Lancaster Rd., The Synergy Center, Homewood
(205) 837-2133
www.alabamahypnotherapycenter.com
Melissa Roth, CHt, PhD, is CEO and founder of Alabama Hypnotherapy Center and Hypnosis Associates and is the only licensed practitioner in Alabama. Her center specializes in medical applications of hypnotherapy to provide care and treatment for complaints that do not respond to conventional treatment. The programs are provided in one-on-one, small group, or telephone consultations, as well as custom CDs.

ALABAMA ORIENTAL MEDICAL ARTS
607 37th St. South, Birmingham
(205) 324-6003
www.acudok.com
As a practitioner of traditional Chinese medicine, Alabama Oriental Medical Arts offers Chinese herbs, acupuncture, massage acupressure, and qigong in order to treat a variety of symptoms and disorders. Consultations are by appointment only. Martha Ivey, OMD, Lac offers infertility therapy. The standard traditional Chinese medicine evaluation of face, tongue, and pulse exam is given.

ALABAMA MIDWIVES
www.alabamamidwives.net
An online resource for a healthcare service not readily available in most of Alabama, Alabama Midwives helps people find a midwife in Birmingham and the state in general for a home, birth center, or hospital birth

with Direct Entry Midwives, Certified Nurse Midwives, Certified Midwives, Certified Professional Midwives, Licensed Midwives, Registered Midwives, and Lay Midwives.

Banning Midwifery

Although Alabama has not established an outright ban on midwives, state regulations on their practices have made things very complicated. While pregnant women and progressives would certainly enjoy having more childbirth options (especially considering that many counties in Alabama have no providers of obstetrical care and no hospital where a woman can deliver her baby), that's probably not going to happen any time soon. In Alabama it is not illegal to birth at home; it is, however, illegal for a midwife to attend that birth. See **www.alabamamidwivesalliance.org** and **www.alabamabirthcoalition.org** for more information on this contentious issue. Try **www.alabamamidwives.net** for a listing of midwifery services in the Birmingham area. For help locating doulas in the Birmingham area, see **DONA International,** www.dona.org, (888) 788-3662.

CHINESE HERBS AND ACUPUNCTURE CENTER
1564 Montgomery Hwy., Hoover
(205) 822-5552
www.chineseherbsacupuncture.com
Acupuncture provided by Stephen Zhao OMD provides patients relief from a

variety of symptoms such as drug addiction, asthma, carpal tunnel syndrome, fibromyalgia, migraine headache, insomnia, and more. The practice also offers a host of herbal Chinese medicinal products.

McMINN CLINIC
3125 Independence Dr., Homewood
(205) 868-1313
www.mcminnclinic.com
Rather than follow the traditional "disease-oriented" approach of most modern medicine, Dr. McMinn pursues what he calls a "Health Care System," looking at total wellness instead of the treatment of sickness. Called "Birmingham's Wellness Doctor," Dr. McMinn has served on the faculty of Harvard Medical School, and currently is a clinical instructor of medicine at UAB School of Medicine downtown. Traditional medicine is practiced but alternative holistic treatments are also pursued when deemed necessary by both the patient and Dr. McMinn.

RETIREMENT COMMUNITIES

DANBERRY AT INVERNESS
235 Inverness Center Dr., Hoover
(205) 981-6679
www.danberryatinverness.com
Danberry at Inverness is not your ordinary senior-living community. To begin it seems more inspired by European resorts than retirement homes. Found on Lake Heather the resort-style community offers cottage homes and luxury senior apartments for rent. Assisted-living rental apartments are also available. Cottage homes start at $290,000. Active adults will find country-club-like amenities such as post fitness centers, cafes, and a pool.

GALLERIA WOODS
3850 Galleria Woods Dr.
(205) 985-7537
www.brookdaleliving.com/galleria woods.aspx
Found near Highway 150, a commercial stretch near the Riverchase Galleria Mall that is full of restaurants, shopping, and amenities, Galleria Woods offers independent living, personalized assisted living, and skilled nursing care options. The accommodations are varied and offer a number of options tailored to each resident's needs. It is a Brookdale Senior Living community.

GREENBRIAR AT THE ALTAMONT
2831 Highland Ave. South
(205) 323-2724
www.greenbriaratthealtamont.com
Found along Highland Avenue, one of Birmingham's grand old drives, Greenbriar at the Altamont's location in Southside makes it convenient to a number of downtown attractions and services, including most of the city's hospitals, which are only a short walk or drive away.

Private accommodations include studio, one-bedroom, and two-bedroom apartments. Each includes a kitchenette, basic utilities, a monitored emergency response system, and more. Assisted-living accommodations are offered, as are skilled nursing services around-the-clock.

KIRKWOOD BY THE RIVER
3605 Ratliff Rd.
(205) 956-2184
www.kirkwoodbytheriver.com
Located near the junction of I-20 and I-459 close to the Cahaba River, Kirkwood by the River is on 120 wooded acres. Independent Presbyterian Church sponsors the

not-for-profit continuing care retirement
community—though it is open to all regardless of religious affiliation. It contains 72
independent-living apartments, 24 assisted-
living units, 20 specialty-care assisted living
units, and a 60-bed skilled nursing facility.
Residents can enter any of the four types
of care.

**SOMERBY AT ST. VINCENT'S ONE
    NINETEEN**
200 One Nineteen Blvd., Hoover
(800) 401-6335
www.somerbyatstvincents.com
In partnership with the St. Vincent's Health
System and their new One Nineteen Health
& Wellness center (where the facility shares
a campus and complimentary membership),
Somerby offers retiring seniors one-, two-,
and three-bedroom apartment homes in a
superb new facility just off Highway 280
near Greystone. It is maintenance-free living
with white-linen dining, champagne Sunday
brunches, an O'Henry's Coffee House on campus, and other luxury perks and amenities.

**ST. MARTIN'S IN THE PINES OF
    BIRMINGHAM**
4941 Montevallo Rd., Irondale
(205) 956-9381
www.stmartins.ws
St. Martin's in the Pines of Birmingham offers
comprehensive retirement options, including an assisted-living facility, a skilled nursing
center, an Alzheimer's community, Evergreen
at St. Martin's, and a 4-story retirement apartment building. St. Martin's is Episcopalian in
its orientation, but those of all religious persuasions are welcome. It is located near East-
wood Shopping Plaza off Montclair Road.

INDEX

INDEX